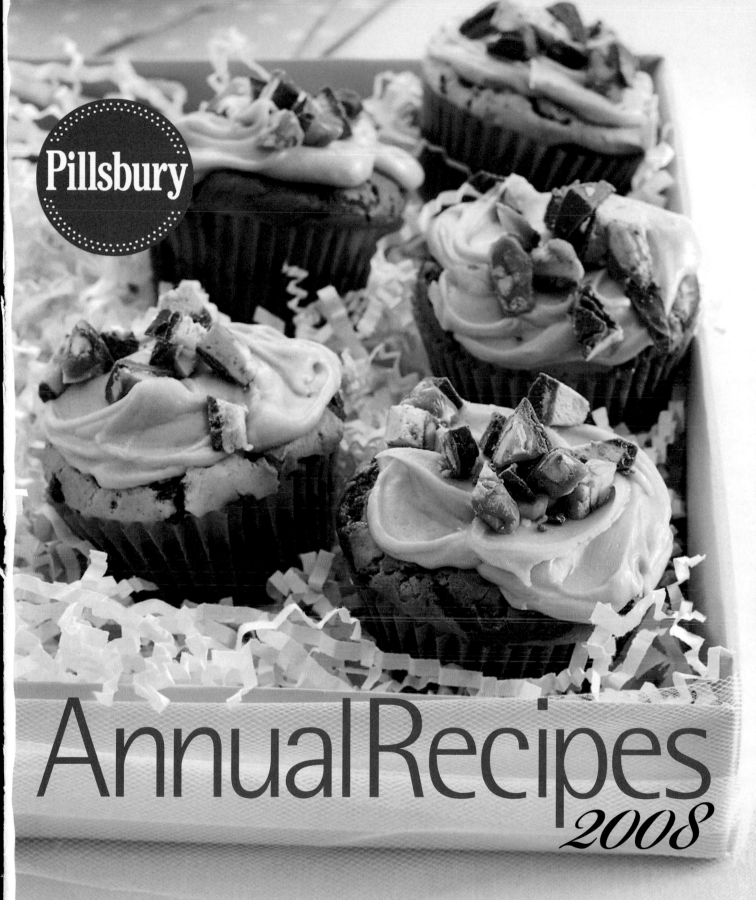

Pillsbury

AnnualRecipes
2008

INCLUDING PILLSBURY BAKE-OFF® CONTEST WINNERS

Pillsbury Annual Recipes 2008

Our recipes have been tested in the Pillsbury Kitchens and meet our standards of easy preparation, reliability and great taste.

For more great recipes, visit pillsbury.com

Copyright © 2008 General Mills, Inc.
Minneapolis, Minnesota

PUBLISHED BY
Taste of Home Books
Reiman Media Group, Inc.
5400 S. 60th St., Greendale, WI 53129
www.reimanpub.com

This edition published by arrangement with Wiley Publishing, Inc.

Printed in U.S.A.
Second Printing, March 2008

International Standard Book Number (10):
0-89821-652-4
International Standard Book Number (13):
978-0-89821-652-3
International Standard Serial Number:
1930-7349

CREDITS
General Mills, Inc.
PUBLISHER, COOKBOOKS: MAGGIE GILBERT/
LYNN VETTEL
EDITOR: LOIS TLUSTY
RECIPE DEVELOPMENT AND TESTING: PILLSBURY TEST KITCHENS
PHOTOGRAPHY: GENERAL MILLS PHOTO STUDIOS

Reiman Media Group, Inc.
PRESIDENT AND CHIEF EXECUTIVE OFFICER:
MARY G. BERNER
PRESIDENT, FOOD & ENTERTAINING:
SUZANNE M. GRIMES
EDITOR IN CHIEF: CATHERINE CASSIDY
VICE PRESIDENT, EXECUTIVE EDITOR/BOOKS:
HEIDI REUTER LLOYD
CREATIVE DIRECTOR: ARDYTH COPE
SENIOR EDITOR/BOOKS: MARK HAGEN
ART DIRECTOR: GRETCHEN TRAUTMAN
CONTENT PRODUCTION SUPERVISOR: JULIE WAGNER
LAYOUT DESIGNERS: CATHERINE FLETCHER,
KATHY CRAWFORD
PROOFREADER: LINNE BRUSKEWITZ
INDEXER: JEAN STEINER

COVER PHOTOGRAPHY: REIMAN PUBLICATIONS PHOTO STUDIO
PHOTOGRAPHER: DAN ROBERTS
FOOD STYLIST: SARA THOMPSON
SET STYLIST: JENNY VENT

FRONT COVER PHOTOGRAPHS:
Prosciutto- and Spinach-Stuffed Shells, Pg. 178; Turtle Brownie Ice Cream Dessert, Pg. 318; Chicken and Broccoli Casserole, Pg. 181; Pear and Cranberry Pie, Pg. 322; and Vermicelli with Fresh Herb-Tomato Sauce, Pg. 131.

PAGE 5 PHOTOGRAPHS:
Ranch Medley Casserole, Pg. 172; Fudgy-Caramel Cashew Brownies, Pg. 297; Rib-Eye Steaks with Avocado Salsa, Pg. 201; and Caramel Apple and Pear Crisp, Pg. 337.

BACK COVER PHOTOGRAPHS:
Layered Beef and Potato Casserole, Pg. 151; Chocolate Cranberry Bread Pudding, Pg. 340; Orange Zested Chicken Breasts, Pg. 160; and Country Blueberry Coffee Cake, Pg. 21.

contents

"Starting Today, Serving A Home-Cooked Meal Is Easier Than Ever!"

introduction

It's true! Creating memories at the supper table doesn't take much planning, effort or time in the kitchen. In fact, with *Pillsbury Annual Recipes 2008*, the solution to a hearty meal is always at your fingertips.

Featuring 404 incredible dishes, this third edition in our popular line of cookbooks offers the comforting tastes your family is sure to treasure. Regardless of how busy your weeknight schedule is, no matter what holiday is approaching and despite last-minute requests for classroom treats, *Pillsbury Annual Recipes 2008* has you covered!

Want to whip up a meal before driving the kids to soccer practice? Choose from more than 50 ideas in the Main Dishes chapter (p. 140). You can even mix up your supper standbys with entrees from the sections titled Grilled Greats (p. 184) and A Taste of the Southwest (p. 206).

A casual dinner or filling lunch is always within reach when you turn to the Soups, Sandwiches & Breads chapter (p. 102). And you can round out any of your menus with lip-smacking recipes from Refreshing Salads (p. 84) and No-Fuss Sides (p. 122).

When holidays, special occasions and family celebrations approach, you're bound to grab *Pillsbury Annual Recipes 2008*. It offers dozens of seasonal favorites that keep guests asking for seconds. Just consider Holiday Appetizer Pizza (p. 83), Dad's Day Burgers (p. 202) or Easter Bird's Nest Cupcakes (p. 273).

Mix up some family magic by bringing little chefs into the kitchen. See the Kid-Friendly Fare chapter (p. 238) for simple bites such as Granola Fruit Kabobs (p. 240) and Piglets in Blankets (p. 243).

You'll also enjoy hundreds of full-color photos, step-by-step instructions and tips that will help you set satisfying meals on the table...often in less than 30 minutes.

Best of all, every single recipe has been tested and approved by the experts at the Pillsbury Test Kitchens, so you know that all of the dishes will receive a thumbs-up approval from your gang.

Take a look inside and you'll see that many of the recipes rely on brand-name products you trust. These ingredients give you tasty results without all the effort of "from scratch" cooking. That's important to us, because we want you to serve your family the best without asking you to spend hours in the kitchen.

After all, with *Pillsbury Annual Recipes 2008* at your side, you're only moments away from creating comforting, homemade meals...as well as all of the heartfelt memories that are sure to follow.

HANDY ICONS

Everyone is short on time nowadays, and family cooks are certainly no exception. That's why we've highlighted the easy recipes in this book with an icon that looks like the one at left...now you can find these dishes at a glance. These recipes call for 6 ingredients or less OR are ready to cook in 20 minutes or less OR are ready to eat in 30 minutes or less.

At the top of each recipe, we've also included "Prep" and "Ready in..." times. That way, you'll know exactly how long it takes to prepare each dish.

In addition, we've added a low-fat icon to recipes that contain 10 grams of fat or less (main dishes) or 3 grams of fat or less (all other recipes). We know that it's important to you to understand exactly what you're feeding your family, so we've also included Nutrition Facts with the majority of this book's recipes.

Finally, we've included a number of Pillsbury Bake-Off® Contest Winners. Submitted by family cooks from coast to coast, these sensational dishes were judged the best of the best at a Pillsbury Bake-Off® Contest, so they're sure to be tops at your home. As you flip through the book, simply look for the Bake-Off® symbol to locate these popular recipes.

FINDING A RECIPE

This cookbook is indexed in two helpful ways. Look up any major ingredient, and you'll find a list of the recipes in which it is included.

For example, if you'd like to make a main dish with ground beef, turn to "ground beef" in the general index for 45 delicious options.

The alphabetical index starts on page 345. Once you have found a few favorite recipes for your family, you can easily locate them by title the next time you want to make them.

Or perhaps you just want to page through this book and look at all the eye-catching photos until you find one that looks like a winner for today's supper, tomorrow's breakfast or this weekend's get-together.

Whichever Pillsbury dish you decide to toss together, we're willing to bet that it will become a welcomed staple in your home for years to come.

Breakfast & Brunch

Stir sleepyheads with a selection of these delightful rise-and-shine specialties.

BREAKFAST HASH BROWNS, BACON AND EGG BAKE
PG. 36

CREAM CHEESE FRENCH TOAST BAKE WITH STRAWBERRY TOPPING
PG. 30

COUNTRY BLUEBERRY COFFEE CAKE
PG. 21

CHOCOLATE CHIP-CINNAMON
BREAKFAST RING
PG. 19

Microwave Caramel-Pecan Rolls

PREP TIME: 15 MINUTES (READY IN 15 MINUTES)
SERVINGS: 5

EASY

TOPPING

¼ cup butter

½ cup packed brown sugar

2 tablespoons light corn syrup

2 tablespoons whipping cream

½ cup chopped pecans

ROLLS

2 tablespoons butter

⅓ cup packed brown sugar

½ teaspoon ground cinnamon

1 can (10.2 oz) Pillsbury® Grands!® refrigerated buttermilk biscuits (5 biscuits)

1) In 9-inch microwavable pie plate, place ¼ cup butter. Microwave uncovered on High 40 to 60 seconds or until melted. Stir in remaining topping ingredients except pecans. Microwave uncovered on High 1 minute. Stir; sprinkle evenly with pecans.

2) In shallow microwavable dish, microwave 2 tablespoons of the butter on High 20 to 30 seconds until melted. In another shallow dish, mix ⅓ cup brown sugar and the cinnamon.

3) Separate dough into 5 biscuits. Dip biscuits into melted butter to coat all sides, then into brown sugar mixture to coat well. Arrange biscuits in circle over topping in pie plate, leaving center open.

4) Microwave uncovered on High 4 to 6 minutes or until centers of biscuits are no longer doughy. Cool in pan 30 seconds. Place heatproof serving plate upside down over pan; turn plate and pan over. Remove pan. Serve the rolls warm.

HIGH ALTITUDE (3500-6500 FT.): No change.

Nutrition Information Per Serving:	
Calories: 600	From Fat: 295
Total Fat	33g
Saturated Fat	13g
Cholesterol	45mg
Sodium	810mg
Total Carbohydrate	71g
Dietary Fiber	2g
Sugars	48g
Protein	5g

tip

The butter in these rolls delivers great homemade flavor. This recipe is best if you don't substitute margarine for the butter.

Mini Cinnamon Crescents

PREP TIME: 20 MINUTES (READY IN 45 MINUTES)
SERVINGS: 20 CRESCENTS

ⓔ EASY

1 can (8 oz) Pillsbury® refrigerated crescent dinner rolls

¼ cup butter or margarine, softened

4 teaspoons granulated sugar

2 teaspoons ground cinnamon

½ cup raisins

½ cup powdered sugar

1 tablespoon apple juice or milk

1) Heat oven to 375°F. Separate dough into 4 rectangles; firmly press perforations to seal. Spread 1 tablespoon butter evenly over each dough rectangle. In small bowl, mix granulated sugar and cinnamon. Sprinkle evenly over rectangles. Sprinkle each with raisins.

2) Starting with short side of each rectangle, roll up; pinch edges to seal. With serrated knife, cut each roll into 5 slices. Place slices, cut side down, in ungreased 8 or 9-inch square pan.

3) Bake 17 to 23 minutes or until golden brown. Cool 5 minutes.

4) Meanwhile, in small bowl, mix powdered sugar and apple juice until smooth. Drizzle icing over rolls. Serve warm.

HIGH ALTITUDE (3500-6500 FT.): No change.

Nutrition Information Per Serving:	
Calories: 90	From Fat: 45
Total Fat	4.5g
Saturated Fat	2.5g
Trans Fat	0.5g
Cholesterol	5mg
Sodium	105mg
Total Carbohydrate	11g
Dietary Fiber	0g
Sugars	7g
Protein	0g

tip

Serve these warm tender rolls with scrambled eggs and orange juice for a tasty start to a new day.

Cream Cheese-Raspberry Coffee Cake

PREP TIME: 30 MINUTES (READY IN 1 HOUR)
SERVINGS: 12

COFFEE CAKE

- 2 cans (8 oz each) Pillsbury® refrigerated crescent dinner rolls
- 1 package (8 oz) cream cheese, softened
- ¼ cup granulated sugar
- 2 teaspoons grated orange peel
- 1 teaspoon vanilla
- 1 egg
- 1 pint (2 cups) fresh raspberries
- 1 teaspoon granulated sugar

GLAZE

- ½ cup powdered sugar
- 1 tablespoon butter, softened
- 2 teaspoons orange juice

1) Heat oven to 350°F. Spray large cookie sheet or 14-inch pizza pan with cooking spray. Unroll both cans of dough; separate into 16 triangles. Reserve 4 triangles for topping.

2) On cookie sheet, arrange 12 triangles in circle with points toward center, leaving 3-inch hole in center. Press dough to form 14-inch ring; press seams together to seal. Fold outer and center edges up ¼ inch.

3) In medium bowl, mix cream cheese, ¼ cup granulated sugar, the orange peel, vanilla and egg until well blended. Gently stir in raspberries. (Mixture will be thin.)

4) Spoon raspberry mixture evenly over dough. With scissors or pizza cutter, cut each reserved dough triangle lengthwise into thirds. Place 1 teaspoon granulated sugar on work surface. Press each dough strip into sugar. Arrange sugared dough strips, sugar side up, evenly in spoke-fashion over filling. Press ends to seal at center and outer edges.

5) Bake 25 to 30 minutes or until golden brown. Cool 10 minutes.

6) In small bowl, mix powdered sugar, butter and orange juice until smooth. Drizzle over coffee cake. Serve warm.

HIGH ALTITUDE (3500-6500 FT.): No change.

Nutrition Information Per Serving:		
Calories: 280	From Fat:	150
Total Fat		16g
Saturated Fat		8g
Trans Fat		2.5g
Cholesterol		40mg
Sodium		360mg
Total Carbohydrate		27g
Dietary Fiber		2g
Sugars		13g
Protein		5g

Vegetable-Cheddar Quiche

PREP TIME: 25 MINUTES (READY IN 1 HOUR 15 MINUTES)
SERVINGS: 6

1 Pillsbury® refrigerated pie crust (from 15-oz box), softened as directed on box

1½ cups shredded Cheddar cheese (6 oz)

2 tablespoons all-purpose flour

2 cups frozen bell pepper and onion stir-fry (from 1-lb bag), thawed, drained and patted dry

1 can (4 oz) Green Giant® mushroom pieces and stems, drained

4 eggs

1 cup milk

¼ teaspoon salt

⅛ teaspoon pepper

1) Heat oven to 425°F. Place pie crust in 9-inch glass pie plate as directed on box for One-Crust Filled Pie. Bake 5 to 7 minutes or just until edge begins to brown. If crust puffs up in center, gently push down with back of wooden spoon.

2) Meanwhile, in large bowl, toss cheese and flour to coat. Add stir-fry vegetables and mushrooms; toss to mix.

3) Remove partially baked crust from oven; reduce oven temperature to 375°F. Spoon cheese mixture into partially baked crust. In same bowl, beat remaining ingredients with wire whisk until well blended. Pour over cheese mixture.

4) Bake at 375°F for 35 to 45 minutes longer or until filling is puffed and knife inserted in center comes out clean. If necessary, cover edge of crust with strips of foil during last 15 to 20 minutes of baking to prevent excessive browning. Let stand 5 to 10 minutes before serving.

HIGH ALTITUDE (3500-6500 FT.): No change

Nutrition Information Per Serving:	
Calories: 375	From Fat: 205
Total Fat	23g
Saturated Fat	12g
Cholesterol	180mg
Sodium	560mg
Total Carbohydrate	27g
Dietary Fiber	1g
Sugars	5g
Protein	15g

tip

Prebaking the refrigerated pie crust for just a few minutes helps to eliminate the soggy texture often found in the crusts of custard-type pies.

Smoky Brunch Pizza

PREP TIME:	30 MINUTES (READY IN 30 MINUTES)	
SERVINGS:	8	EASY

1 can (13.8 oz) Pillsbury® refrigerated pizza crust

2 tablespoons butter or margarine

¼ cup chopped red bell pepper

4 green onions, sliced (¼ cup)

8 eggs

¼ cup milk

⅛ teaspoon pepper

1 package (4 oz) smoked salmon, flaked

½ cup chives-and-onion cream cheese (from 8-oz container)

1) Heat oven to 425°F. Grease 12-inch pizza pan or 13x9-inch pan. Unroll dough; place in pan. Starting at center, press out dough with hands. Bake 6 to 7 minutes or until crust begins to brown.

2) Meanwhile, in 10-inch skillet, melt butter over medium heat. Add bell pepper and onions; cook and stir 3 to 4 minutes or until tender.

3) In medium bowl, beat eggs, milk and pepper. Add egg mixture to skillet. Cook 4 to 5 minutes, stirring occasionally, until thoroughly cooked but still moist. Fold in salmon. Remove from heat.

4) Spread cream cheese evenly over crust. Spoon cooked egg mixture over cream cheese.

5) Bake 9 to 12 minutes longer or until toppings are hot and crust is deep golden brown. If desired, garnish with additional green onions.

HIGH ALTITUDE (3500-6500 FT.): In Step 1, bake 8 to 10 minutes. In Step 5, bake 10 to 14 minutes.

Nutrition Information Per Serving:	
Calories: 290	From Fat: 130
Total Fat	15g
Saturated Fat	7g
Trans Fat	0g
Cholesterol	235mg
Sodium	650mg
Total Carbohydrate	25g
Dietary Fiber	0g
Sugars	5g
Protein	14g

Lemon Pull-Apart Coffee Cake

PREP TIME: 10 MINUTES (READY IN 35 MINUTES)
SERVINGS: 6

 EASY

- ¼ cup sugar
- ¼ cup golden or dark raisins
- ¼ cup chopped walnuts, almonds or pine nuts
- 2 teaspoons grated lemon peel
- 2 tablespoons butter or margarine, melted
- 1 can (12 oz) Pillsbury® Golden Layers® refrigerated buttermilk or original flaky biscuits

Nutrition Information Per Serving:		
Calories: 320	From Fat: 135	
Total Fat		15g
Saturated Fat		5g
Cholesterol		10mg
Sodium		710mg
Total Carbohydrate		41g
Dietary Fiber		1g
Sugars		21g
Protein		5g

1) Heat oven to 375°F. Line bottom of 8- or 9-inch round cake pan with waxed paper. In large bowl, mix all ingredients except biscuits.

2) Separate dough into 10 biscuits. Cut each into quarters. Place biscuit pieces in sugar mixture; toss to coat. Arrange in single layer in waxed paper-lined pan. Sprinkle top with any remaining sugar mixture.

3) Bake 20 to 25 minutes or until deep golden brown. Run knife around side of pan to loosen. Place heatproof serving plate upside down over pan; turn plate and pan over. Remove pan and waxed paper. Cut coffee cake into wedges or pull apart. Serve warm.

HIGH ALTITUDE (3500-6500 FT.): No change.

For a festive weekend breakfast, serve this pretty coffee cake with slices of honeydew melon or cantaloupe and fluffy scrambled eggs.

Poinsettia Coffee Cake

PREP TIME: 15 MINUTES (READY IN 30 MINUTES)
SERVINGS: 8

 EASY

- 1 can (13.9 oz) Pillsbury® refrigerated orange sweet rolls
- ¼ cup sweetened dried cranberries

Nutrition Information Per Serving:		
Calories: 180	From Fat: 60	
Total Fat		7g
Saturated Fat		1.5g
Trans Fat		2g
Cholesterol		0mg
Sodium		340mg
Total Carbohydrate		28g
Dietary Fiber		0g
Sugars		13g
Protein		2g

1) Heat oven to 400°F. Grease cookie sheet. Remove dough and icing from can. Place 1 sweet roll in center of cookie sheet; press to 2½ inches in diameter. Place remaining rolls around center roll, seams toward center; press each to 2½ inches.

2) Pinch outside edge of each roll into a point. (Exaggerate the points, as they tend to shrink into original shape during baking.)

3) Bake 11 to 14 minutes or until golden brown. Carefully spread with icing; sprinkle with cranberries except on center roll. Cool 1 minute. With broad metal spatula, carefully loosen coffee cake from cookie sheet and slide onto serving plate.

HIGH ALTITUDE (3500-6500 FT.): No change.

Egg, Broccoli and Ham Ring-Around

PREP TIME: 30 MINUTES (READY IN 1 HOUR)
SERVINGS: 8

1 tablespoon butter or margarine

1½ cups Green Giant® frozen chopped broccoli (from 1-lb bag), thawed

¼ cup chopped onion (½ medium)

1 package (3 oz) cream cheese, softened

6 eggs

¼ cup milk

¼ teaspoon salt

⅛ teaspoon pepper

¾ cup cubed (¼-inch) cooked ham (4 oz)

½ cup shredded Cheddar cheese (2 oz)

2 cans (8 oz each) Pillsbury® refrigerated crescent dinner rolls

1) Heat oven to 375°F. Spray large cookie sheet or 14-inch pizza pan with cooking spray. In 10-inch nonstick skillet, melt butter over medium heat. Cook broccoli and onion in butter 2 to 3 minutes, stirring frequently, until tender.

2) In medium bowl, beat cream cheese with electric mixer until smooth. Beat in eggs, milk, salt and pepper until well combined. Add egg mixture to vegetables in skillet; cook over medium heat, stirring occasionally from outside edge to center, until eggs are set but still moist. Stir in ham and Cheddar cheese.

3) Unroll both cans of the dough; separate into 16 triangles. Arrange triangles on cookie sheet with short sides of triangles toward center, overlapping into wreath shape and leaving 4-inch hole in center. Lightly press short sides of dough to flatten slightly.

4) Spoon egg mixture onto widest part of dough. Pull end points of triangles over filling and tuck under dough in center to form ring (filling will be visible).

5) Bake 25 to 30 minutes or until deep golden brown. Immediately remove from cookie sheet. Cut into crosswise slices. Serve warm.

HIGH ALTITUDE (3500-6500 FT.): Bake 20 to 25 minutes.

Nutrition Information Per Serving:	
Calories: 390	From Fat: 220
Total Fat	25g
Saturated Fat	11g
Trans Fat	3.5g
Cholesterol	190mg
Sodium	860mg
Total Carbohydrate	25g
Dietary Fiber	1g
Sugars	6g
Protein	16g

Get Up 'n Go Breakfast Sandwiches

PREP TIME: 15 MINUTES (READY IN 45 MINUTES)
SERVINGS: 8

ⓔ EASY

1 can (16.3 oz) Pillsbury® Grands!® refrigerated buttermilk or southern style biscuits

8 thin slices Canadian bacon (about 4$\frac{1}{2}$ oz)

8 slices (1 oz each) American cheese

8 thin slices tomato, if desired

1) Bake biscuits as directed on can. Cool completely, about 20 minutes.

2) Split warm biscuits. Fill each with 1 slice Canadian bacon and 1 slice cheese cut to fit. Wrap sandwiches individually in microwavable plastic wrap. Place in large resealable freezer plastic bag; seal bag and freeze. For best quality, use within 3 months.

3) To heat 1 frozen sandwich, loosen wrapping. Microwave on High 45 to 60 seconds or until thoroughly heated and cheese is melted. Let stand 30 to 60 seconds to cool slightly before serving. Add tomato slice to each sandwich.

HIGH ALTITUDE (3500-6500 FT.): No change.

Nutrition Information Per Serving:

Calories: 320	From Fat: 160
Total Fat	18g
Saturated Fat	9g
Trans Fat	3g
Cholesterol	35mg
Sodium	1270mg
Total Carbohydrate	25g
Dietary Fiber	0g
Sugars	5g
Protein	14g

tip

It works best to microwave the breakfast sandwiches one by one. Start with the minimum time and check the middle of the biscuit before adding more time.

Chocolate Hazelnut Twists

PREP TIME: 15 MINUTES (READY IN 45 MINUTES)
SERVINGS: 8

🅔 EASY

2 cans (8 oz each) Pillsbury® refrigerated crescent dinner rolls

½ cup hazelnut spread with skim milk and cocoa (from 13-oz jar)

½ cup finely chopped hazelnuts (filberts)

3 tablespoon powdered sugar

Nutrition Information Per Serving:

Calories:	370	From Fat:	200
Total Fat			22g
Saturated Fat			5g
Trans Fat			3g
Cholesterol			0mg
Sodium			450mg
Total Carbohydrate			38g
Dietary Fiber			2g
Sugars			17g
Protein			6g

1) Heat oven to 375°F. Grease 8 regular-size muffin cups. Unroll 1 can of dough on work surface; firmly press perforations to seal. Press into 13x7-inch rectangle. Spread hazelnut spread evenly over dough to within ¼ inch of sides; sprinkle with hazelnuts.

2) Unroll remaining can of dough on work surface; firmly press perforations to seal. Press into 13x7-inch rectangle. Place over filling; press firmly and seal edges. Cut into 8 (13-inch) strips. Twist each strip 5 to 6 times; shape into tight coil. Place 1 coil in each muffin cup. (Muffin cups will be very full.)

3) Bake 20 minutes or until golden brown. Immediately remove from muffin cups to cooling rack. Cool 5 minutes. Sprinkle with powdered sugar. Serve warm.

HIGH ALTITUDE (3500-6500 FT.): No change.

Cinnamon-Pecan Pull Apart

PREP TIME: 20 MINUTES (READY IN 1 HOUR)
SERVINGS: 12

🅔 EASY

¾ cup chopped pecans

⅔ cup packed brown sugar

½ cup butter or margarine, melted

½ cup sour cream

1 teaspoon maple flavor or vanilla

2 cans (12.4 oz each) Pillsbury® refrigerated cinnamon rolls with icing

Nutrition Information Per Serving:

Calories:	380	From Fat:	190
Total Fat			21g
Saturated Fat			8g
Trans Fat			3g
Cholesterol			25mg
Sodium			520mg
Total Carbohydrate			44g
Dietary Fiber			0g
Sugars			26g
Protein			4g

1) Heat oven to 350°F. Grease 12-cup fluted tube cake pan or 10-inch angel food (tube cake) pan (pan must not have a removable bottom). In large bowl, mix all ingredients except cinnamon rolls.

2) Separate both cans of dough into 16 rolls; cut each into quarters. Add dough pieces to pecan mixture; toss gently to coat. Spoon mixture into the pan.

3) Bake 30 to 40 minutes or until deep golden brown. Cool 10 minutes. Turn upside down onto serving plate. Spread with icing. Serve warm.

HIGH ALTITUDE (3500-6500 FT.): Bake 40 to 50 minutes.

Cherry Cream Cheese Coffee Cake

PREP TIME: 20 MINUTES (READY IN 1 HOUR 15 MINUTES)
SERVINGS: 12

EASY

- 1 package (3 oz) cream cheese, softened
- 2 tablespoons granulated sugar
- 1 teaspoon almond extract
- 1/4 cup sliced almonds
- 1/4 cup chopped maraschino cherries, well drained
- 1 can (8 oz) Pillsbury® refrigerated crescent dinner rolls
- 1/2 cup powdered sugar
- 2 teaspoons milk

1) Heat oven to 375°F. Grease cookie sheet with shortening. In small bowl, beat cream cheese and granulated sugar until light and fluffy. Stir in almond extract, almonds and cherries; set aside.

2) Unroll dough onto cookie sheet; press into 13x7-inch rectangle, firmly pressing perforations to seal. Spoon cream cheese mixture lengthwise down center 1/3 of rectangle.

3) On each long side of dough rectangle, make cuts 1 inch apart to edge of filling. Fold opposite strips of dough over filling and cross in center to form a braided appearance; seal ends.

4) Bake 18 to 22 minutes or until golden brown. Remove from cookie sheet to cooling rack. Cool completely, about 30 minutes.

5) In small bowl, mix powdered sugar and milk until smooth; drizzle over coffee cake. If desired, garnish with additional sliced almonds and cherries. Store in refrigerator.

HIGH ALTITUDE (3500-6500 FT.): No change.

Nutrition Information Per Serving:

Calories:	140	From Fat:	70
Total Fat			7g
Saturated Fat			3g
Trans Fat			1g
Cholesterol			10mg
Sodium			170mg
Total Carbohydrate			16g
Dietary Fiber			0g
Sugars			10g
Protein			2g

Apple-Cranberry-Pistachio Bread

PREP TIME: 20 MINUTES (READY IN 3 HOURS)
SERVINGS: 1 LOAF (16 SLICES)

e EASY

BREAD

1 1/2 cups all-purpose flour

3/4 cup granulated sugar

2 teaspoons baking powder

1/2 teaspoon salt

1/4 cup vegetable oil

1/3 cup apple cider or apple juice

2 eggs, beaten

1 cup shredded peeled apple (1 medium)

1/2 cup sweetened dried cranberries

1/3 cup chopped pistachios

TOPPING

1/2 cup powdered sugar

2 to 3 teaspoons apple cider or apple juice

2 tablespoons finely chopped pistachios

1) Heat oven to 350°F. Grease and flour bottom only of 8x4-inch loaf pan. In large bowl with wooden spoon, mix flour, granulated sugar, baking powder and salt. Beat in oil, 1/3 cup cider and eggs until smooth. Stir in apple, cranberries and 1/3 cup pistachios. Spoon and spread evenly in pan.

2) Bake 50 to 60 minutes or until toothpick inserted in center comes out clean. Cool in pan 10 minutes. Remove from pan. Cool completely, about 1 hour 30 minutes.

3) In small bowl, mix powdered sugar and enough of the 2 to 3 teaspoons cider for desired glaze consistency. Spread over top of bread. Sprinkle with 2 tablespoons pistachios.

HIGH ALTITUDE (3500-6500 FT.): Decrease baking powder to 1-1/2 teaspoons.

Nutrition Information Per Serving:		
Calories: 180	From Fat:	50
Total Fat	6g	
Saturated Fat	1g	
Trans Fat	0g	
Cholesterol	25mg	
Sodium	140mg	
Total Carbohydrate	28g	
Dietary Fiber	1g	
Sugars	17g	
Protein	3g	

Chocolate Chip–Cinnamon Breakfast Ring

PREP TIME: 10 MINUTES (READY IN 55 MINUTES)
SERVINGS: 16

ⓔ EASY

½ cup butter, softened

2 cans (12.4 oz each) Pillsbury® refrigerated cinnamon rolls with icing

1 box (4-serving size) vanilla pudding and pie filling mix (not instant)

½ cup packed brown sugar

¼ cup miniature semisweet chocolate chips

Nutrition Information Per Serving:

Calories: 260	From Fat: 100
Total Fat	12g
Saturated Fat	6g
Trans Fat	2.5g
Cholesterol	15mg
Sodium	420mg
Total Carbohydrate	36g
Dietary Fiber	0g
Sugars	22g
Protein	2g

1) Heat oven to 375°F. Using 1 tablespoon of the butter, generously butter 12-cup fluted tube cake pan. In small microwavable bowl, microwave remaining butter on High 1 minute or until melted when stirred.

2) Separate dough into 16 rolls. Cut each roll in half crosswise; place half of roll pieces in pan. Sprinkle with half of the pudding mix and half of the brown sugar. Drizzle with half of the melted butter. Repeat with remaining roll pieces, pudding mix, brown sugar and melted butter. Sprinkle with chocolate chips.

3) Bake 24 to 28 minutes or until rolls are deep golden brown and dough appears done when slightly pulled apart. Cool in pan 2 minutes. Place heatproof serving platter upside down over pan; turn platter and pan over. Remove pan; cool 15 minutes.

4) Microwave icing on High 10 seconds to soften. Drizzle icing over ring. Cut into wedges; serve warm.

HIGH ALTITUDE (3500-6500 FT.): No change.

Maple Pecan Crescent Twists

PREP TIME: 40 MINUTES (READY IN 40 MINUTES)
SERVINGS: 8

TWISTS

- ½ cup finely chopped pecans
- 3 tablespoons granulated sugar
- 1 teaspoon cinnamon
- ⅛ teaspoon nutmeg
- 2 cans (8 oz) Pillsbury® refrigerated crescent dinner rolls
- 2 tablespoons margarine or butter, melted

GLAZE

- ½ cup powdered sugar
- ¼ teaspoon maple extract
- 2 to 3 teaspoons milk

1) Heat oven to 375°F. Spray 1 large or 2 small cookie sheets with cooking spray or lightly grease. In small bowl, combine pecans, granulated sugar, cinnamon and nutmeg; mix well.

2) Unroll both cans of dough; separate into 8 rectangles. Firmly press perforations to seal. Brush each rectangle with margarine. Sprinkle 1 tablespoon pecan-sugar mixture evenly over each rectangle; press in lightly. Starting at longer side, roll up each rectangle; pinch edges to seal.

3) With sharp knife, cut one roll in half lengthwise, forming 2 strips. With cut side up, carefully overlap strips 2 times to form twist. Press ends together to seal. Place on sprayed cookie sheet. Repeat with remaining dough. Sprinkle with any remaining pecan-sugar mixture.

4) Bake at 375°F for 10 to 15 minutes or until golden brown.

5) In small bowl, blend all glaze ingredients, adding enough milk for desired drizzling consistency. Drizzle over warm rolls. Serve warm.

HIGH ALTITUDE (3500-6500 FT.): No change.

Nutrition Information Per Serving:		
Calories: 340	From Fat:	180
Total Fat		20g
Saturated Fat		5g
Trans Fat		4g
Cholesterol		0mg
Sodium		470mg
Total Carbohydrate		35g
Dietary Fiber		1g
Sugars		16g
Protein		5g

Country Blueberry Coffee Cake

WENDY L. HART | RAY CITY, GEORGIA

Bake-Off® CONTEST 38, 1998

PREP TIME: 15 MINUTES (READY IN 1 HOUR 10 MINUTES)
SERVINGS: 9

EASY

½ cup packed brown sugar

½ teaspoon ground cinnamon

1 can (12 oz) Pillsbury® Golden Homestyle® refrigerated buttermilk biscuits

¼ cup butter or margarine, melted

1 cup quick-cooking oats

1½ cups fresh or frozen blueberries

¼ cup sugar

2 tablespoons butter or margarine, cut into small pieces

1) Heat oven to 375°F. Generously grease 8- or 9-inch square (2-quart) glass baking dish. In small bowl, mix brown sugar and cinnamon with fork.

2) Separate dough into 10 biscuits. Cut each biscuit into quarters. Dip each piece in melted butter; coat with brown sugar mixture. Arrange in single layer in baking dish. Sprinkle with ½ cup of the oats.

3) In medium bowl, toss blueberries and sugar until coated. Spoon over oats and biscuits; sprinkle with remaining ½ cup oats. Top with butter pieces.

4) Bake 30 to 35 minutes or until golden brown and center is done. Cool 20 minutes. Serve warm.

HIGH ALTITUDE (3500-6500 FT.). Heat oven to 350°F. Bake 50 to 55 minutes.

Nutrition Information Per Serving:		
Calories: 300	From Fat:	110
Total Fat		13g
Saturated Fat		6g
Trans Fat		2g
Cholesterol		20mg
Sodium		460mg
Total Carbohydrate		43g
Dietary Fiber		2g
Sugars		22g
Protein		4g

Saving time is a snap. There's no need to thaw frozen blueberries before assembling this yummy coffee cake.

Pumpkin and Maple Turnover

PREP TIME: 10 MINUTES (READY IN 1 HOUR)
SERVINGS: 8

e EASY

TURNOVER

- 1 Pillsbury® refrigerated pie crust (from 15-oz box), softened as directed on box
- ½ cup canned pumpkin (not pumpkin pie mix)
- ⅓ cup packed brown sugar
- ½ teaspoon maple flavor
- ¼ teaspoon pumpkin pie spice
- Dash salt

GLAZE

- ½ cup powdered sugar
- ¼ teaspoon maple flavor
- 1 tablespoon milk
- ¼ cup chopped walnuts, toasted

1) Heat oven to 375°F. Remove crust from pouch; place on ungreased large cookie sheet. In medium bowl, mix pumpkin, brown sugar, ½ teaspoon maple flavor, the pumpkin pie spice and dash of salt until smooth.

2) Spread pumpkin mixture over half of pie crust to within ¾ inch of edge. Brush edge with water; fold crust over filling. Carefully move turnover to center of cookie sheet. With fork, press edge to seal and prick top several times.

3) Bake 23 to 30 minutes or until golden brown. Cool 5 minutes. Remove from cookie sheet to cooling rack.

4) In small bowl, mix powdered sugar, ¼ teaspoon maple flavor and the milk until smooth and desired drizzling consistency. Drizzle over warm turnover. Sprinkle with chopped walnuts. Let stand 10 minutes. Serve warm or cool.

HIGH ALTITUDE (3500-6500 FT.): No change.

Nutrition Information Per Serving:		
Calories: 210	From Fat:	90
Total Fat		9g
Saturated Fat		3g
Trans Fat		0g
Cholesterol		0mg
Sodium		135mg
Total Carbohydrate		31g
Dietary Fiber		0g
Sugars		17g
Protein		0g

Sour Cream Chocolate Swirl Coffee Cake

PREP TIME: 25 MINUTES (READY IN 1 HOUR 25 MINUTES)
SERVINGS: 16

COFFEE CAKE

- ¼ cup finely chopped pecans
- 3 oz semisweet chocolate, chopped
- 1 cup sugar
- ½ cup butter or margarine, softened
- 1 container (8 oz) sour cream
- 2 teaspoons vanilla
- 3 eggs
- 2 cups all-purpose flour
- 1½ teaspoons baking powder
- ¼ teaspoon salt

GLAZE

- 1 oz semisweet chocolate, chopped
- ½ teaspoon oil

1) Heat oven to 350°F. Generously grease 12-cup fluted tube pan. Sprinkle with pecans, tilting pan to coat sides with some of the nuts. Set pan aside. In 1-quart microwavable bowl, place 3 ounces chocolate. Microwave on High 30 seconds; stir. If necessary, microwave in 10-second increments, stirring each time, until melted. Set aside to cool.

2) In large bowl beat sugar and butter with electric mixer on medium speed 1 to 2 minutes or until light and fluffy. Beat in ½ cup of the sour cream, the vanilla and eggs until smooth. On low speed, beat in 1 cup of the flour, the baking powder and salt until dry ingredients are moistened. Beat in remaining sour cream and flour just until blended.

3) Spoon 2 cups of the batter into cooled chocolate; stir until mixed. Spoon half of the remaining batter into pan. Drop half of the chocolate batter over the vanilla batter. With table knife, gently swirl. Spoon remaining vanilla batter into pan. Top with remaining chocolate batter. Gently swirl; smooth top.

4) Bake 38 to 45 minutes or until toothpick inserted in center comes out clean. Cool in pan 15 minutes. Invert onto serving platter.

5) Place 1 ounce chocolate and the oil in small microwavable bowl. Microwave on High 20 seconds; stir until smooth. Drizzle over coffee cake. Serve warm or cool.

HIGH ALTITUDE (3500-6500 FT.): Decrease baking powder to 1-¼ teaspoons. In Step 2, add ¼ cup water with the sour cream, vanilla and eggs. Bake 45 to 52 minutes.

Nutrition Information Per Serving:		
Calories: 250	From Fat: 120	
Total Fat		13g
Saturated Fat		7g
Trans Fat		0g
Cholesterol		65mg
Sodium		140mg
Total Carbohydrate		30g
Dietary Fiber		1g
Sugars		17g
Protein		4g

Cranberry-Pecan Scones

PREP TIME: 20 MINUTES (READY IN 35 MINUTES)
SERVINGS: 12

e EASY

2 cups all-purpose flour

3 tablespoons granulated sugar

3 teaspoons baking powder

2 teaspoons grated orange peel

½ teaspoon salt

½ cup chopped dried sweetened cranberries

½ cup chopped pecans

½ cup white vanilla baking chips

1⅓ cups whipping cream

1 cup powdered sugar

2 to 3 tablespoons orange juice

1) Heat oven to 400°F. Lightly grease cookie sheet. In large bowl, mix flour, granulated sugar, baking powder, orange peel and salt until well blended. Stir in cranberries, pecans and baking chips. Add whipping cream all at once; stir just until dry ingredients are moistened.

2) On lightly floured surface, knead dough 6 or 7 times until smooth. Divide dough in half. Pat each half into 6-inch round; cut each into 6 wedges. Place 2 inches apart on cookie sheet.

3) Bake 10 to 13 minutes or until light golden brown. Cool 5 minutes. Meanwhile, in small bowl, mix powdered sugar and enough orange juice for desired drizzling consistency. Drizzle icing over warm scones. Serve warm.

HIGH ALTITUDE (3500-6500 FT.): Increase flour to 2-1/4 cups; decrease whipping cream to 1 cup and add 1/3 cup water.

Nutrition Information Per Serving:		
Calories: 270	From Fat: 100	
Total Fat		11g
Saturated Fat		7g
Trans Fat		0g
Cholesterol		30mg
Sodium		250mg
Total Carbohydrate		40g
Dietary Fiber		1g
Sugars		23g
Protein		4g

Double Chocolate-Almond Scones

PREP TIME: 20 MINUTES (READY IN 35 MINUTES)
SERVINGS: 12

 EASY

2 cups all-purpose flour

3 tablespoons granulated sugar

3 teaspoons baking powder

1/2 teaspoon salt

1/2 cup semisweet chocolate chips

1/2 cup white vanilla baking chips

1 1/3 cups whipping cream

1/4 teaspoon almond extract

1 cup powdered sugar

1/4 teaspoon almond extract

2 to 3 tablespoons water

2 tablespoons sliced almonds

1) Heat oven to 400°F. Lightly grease cookie sheet. In large bowl, mix flour, granulated sugar, baking powder and salt until well blended. Stir in chocolate chips and white baking chips. Add whipping cream all at once and 1/4 teaspoon almond extract; stir just until the dry ingredients are moistened.

2) On lightly floured surface, knead dough 6 or 7 times until smooth. Divide dough in half. Pat each half into 6-inch round; cut each into 6 wedges. Place 2 inches apart on cookie sheet.

3) Bake 10 to 13 minutes or until light golden brown. Cool 5 minutes. Meanwhile, in small bowl, mix powdered sugar, remaining extract and enough water for desired drizzling consistency. Drizzle icing over warm scones. Sprinkle tops of scones with almonds. Serve warm.

HIGH ALTITUDE (3500-6500 FT.): Increase flour to 2-1/4 cups; decrease whipping cream to 1 cup and add 1/3 cup water.

tip For the lightest, most tender scones, quickly mix and shape the dough, handling it as little as possible. Use only a sprinkle of flour on the work surface.

Apricot-Orange Cream Scones

PREP TIME: 20 MINUTES (READY IN 35 MINUTES)
SERVINGS: 12

 EASY

2 cups all-purpose flour

3 tablespoons granulated sugar

3 teaspoons baking powder

2 teaspoons grated orange peel

1/2 teaspoon salt

1/2 cup chopped dried apricots

1/2 cup white vanilla baking chips

1 1/3 cups whipping cream

1 cup powdered sugar

2 to 3 tablespoons orange juice

1) Heat oven to 400°F. Lightly grease cookie sheet. In large bowl, mix flour, granulated sugar, baking powder, orange peel and salt until well blended. Stir in apricots and baking chips. Add whipping cream all at once; stir just until dry ingredients are moistened.

2) On lightly floured surface, knead dough 6 or 7 times until smooth. Divide dough in half. Pat each half into 6-inch round; cut each into 6 wedges. Place 2 inches apart on cookie sheet.

3) Bake 10 to 13 minutes or until light golden brown. Cool 5 minutes. Meanwhile, in small bowl, mix powdered sugar and enough orange juice for desired drizzling consistency. Drizzle icing over warm scones. Serve warm.

HIGH ALTITUDE (3500-6500 FT.): Increase flour to 2-1/4 cups; decrease whipping cream to 1 cup and add 1/3 cup water.

Blueberry Pudding Pie

PREP TIME: 15 MINUTES (READY IN 1 HOUR 30 MINUTES)
SERVINGS: 8

e EASY

1 Pillsbury® refrigerated pie crust (from 15-oz box), softened as directed on box

1½ cups fresh or frozen blueberries, thawed, well drained

3 eggs

1 cup sour cream

¾ cup half-and-half

⅓ cup sugar

1½ teaspoons vanilla

¼ teaspoon ground nutmeg

¼ teaspoon ground cinnamon

¼ teaspoon salt

1) Heat oven to 425°F. Make pie crust as directed on box for One-Crust Filled Pie using 9-inch glass pie plate. Bake 7 minutes.

2) Remove crust from oven; sprinkle blueberries over bottom of crust.

3) In large bowl, beat all remaining ingredients with electric mixer on medium speed 1 to 2 minutes or until smooth. Pour over blueberries.

4) Return to oven; bake 10 minutes. Reduce oven temperature to 350°F; cover edges of crust with foil. Bake 30 to 32 minutes or until knife inserted in center comes out clean. Let stand 20 minutes. Serve warm or cool. Store in refrigerator.

HIGH ALTITUDE (3500-6500 FT.): In Step 1, bake 10 minutes.

Nutrition Information Per Serving:

Calories:	280	From Fat:	160
Total Fat			17g
Saturated Fat			8g
Trans Fat			0g
Cholesterol			110mg
Sodium			230mg
Total Carbohydrate			28g
Dietary Fiber			0g
Sugars			13g
Protein			4g

Crescent Cranberry Wreaths

PREP TIME: 20 MINUTES (READY IN 35 MINUTES)
SERVINGS: 6

 EASY

- ¹/₃ cup finely chopped sweetened dried cranberries
- 2 tablespoons cherry or strawberry preserves
- 1 can (8 oz) Pillsbury® refrigerated crescent dinner rolls
- 1 oz white chocolate baking bar, chopped
- ¹/₂ teaspoon oil

1) Heat oven to 375°F. Lightly spray cookie sheet with cooking spray. In small bowl, mix cranberries and preserves.

2) Unroll dough into 2 rectangles. Press each to form 8x6-inch rectangle; press perforations to seal. Spread cranberry mixture over 1 rectangle to edges. Place second rectangle on top; press lightly. With sharp knife or pizza cutter, cut lengthwise into six 8-inch-long strips. Twist each strip 3 times and shape into ring on cookie sheet; pinch ends to seal.

3) Bake 9 to 12 minutes or until golden brown. Cool on cookie sheet 2 minutes.

4) In small microwavable bowl, place baking bar and oil. Microwave on High 30 seconds; stir until melted and smooth. If necessary, microwave 10 to 20 seconds longer. Drizzle over warm rolls. Serve warm.

HIGH ALTITUDE (3500-6500 FT.): No change.

Nutrition Information Per Serving:	
Calories: 210	From Fat: 90
Total Fat	10g
Saturated Fat	3.5g
Trans Fat	2g
Cholesterol	0mg
Sodium	300mg
Total Carbohydrate	28g
Dietary Fiber	0g
Sugars	14g
Protein	3g

Cranberry Fizz

PREP TIME: 10 MINUTES (READY IN 10 MINUTES)
SERVINGS: 16 (1/2 CUP EACH)

e EASY   **f** LOW FAT

1 quart (4 cups) cranberry juice cocktail, chilled

1 cup grapefruit juice, chilled

1 cup orange juice, chilled

½ cup sugar

2 cups ginger ale, chilled

1) In large nonmetal pitcher or punch bowl, mix cranberry juice cocktail, grapefruit juice, orange juice and the sugar until well blended.

2) Just before serving, stir in ginger ale.

HIGH ALTITUDE (3500-6500 FT.): No change.

Nutrition Information Per Serving:

Calories: 90	From Fat: 0
Total Fat	0g
Saturated Fat	0g
Trans Fat	0g
Cholesterol	0mg
Sodium	5mg
Total Carbohydrate	22g
Dietary Fiber	0g
Sugars	21g
Protein	0g

Petite Caramel-Pecan Rolls

PREP TIME: 15 MINUTES (READY IN 45 MINUTES)
SERVINGS: 16

e EASY

¼ cup packed brown sugar

¼ cup butter or margarine, softened

2 tablespoons light corn syrup

1 can (8 oz) Pillsbury® refrigerated crescent dinner rolls

2 tablespoons granulated sugar

½ teaspoon ground cinnamon

¼ cup finely chopped pecans

Nutrition Information Per Serving:

Calories: 120	From Fat: 60
Total Fat	7g
Saturated Fat	3g
Trans Fat	1g
Cholesterol	10mg
Sodium	135mg
Total Carbohydrate	13g
Dietary Fiber	0g
Sugars	7g
Protein	1g

1) Heat oven to 375°F. In small bowl, mix brown sugar, butter and corn syrup. Spread in bottom of ungreased 8- or 9-inch round cake pan.

2) Separate dough into 4 rectangles; firmly press perforations to seal. In small bowl, mix granulated sugar and cinnamon; sprinkle evenly over rectangles. Sprinkle 1 tablespoon of the pecans over each rectangle.

3) Starting at shorter side, roll up each rectangle; pinch edges to seal. Cut each roll into 4 slices. Place cut side down over brown sugar mixture in pan.

4) Bake 20 to 27 minutes or until golden brown. Cool in pan 1 minute; invert onto serving platter or foil. Serve warm or cool.

HIGH ALTITUDE (3500-6500 FT.): No change.

tip Drop the nuts from this recipe, or substitute walnuts for the pecans. Shape, cover and refrigerate the rolls up to 2 hours ahead of time. Bake as directed, allowing a few extra minutes for baking time.

Scrambled Egg-Parmesan Soft Crust Pizza

PREP TIME: 25 MINUTES (READY IN 35 MINUTES)
SERVINGS: 6

4 slices bacon

1 box (10.6 oz) Pillsbury® refrigerated Parmesan with garlic breadsticks

8 eggs

¼ cup milk

½ teaspoon salt

Dash pepper

2 cups shredded pizza cheese blend (8 oz)

1 small tomato, very thinly sliced

Salsa, if desired

Nutrition Information Per Serving:

Calories:	380	From Fat:	200
Total Fat			22g
Saturated Fat			9g
Cholesterol			310mg
Sodium			1130mg
Total Carbohydrate			22g
Dietary Fiber			0g
Sugars			5g
Protein			24g

1) In 10-inch skillet, cook bacon until crisp. Remove bacon from skillet; drain on paper towels. Crumble bacon; set aside. Drain all but 2 teaspoons drippings from skillet. Set skillet aside.

2) Heat oven to 400°F. Unroll dough; separate into 10 breadsticks. Starting in center of ungreased 12-inch pizza pan or large cookie sheet, shape 1 breadstick into a coil. Add breadsticks, pinching ends firmly to seal until all are used. Press dough to form 12-inch round. Stir Parmesan topping; spread evenly over dough.

3) Bake 10 to 12 minutes or until light golden brown. Meanwhile, in large bowl, beat eggs, milk, salt and pepper with wire whisk until well blended. Add to drippings in skillet; cook over medium heat about 5 minutes, stirring occasionally, until set but still moist. Stir in 1 cup of the cheese. Remove from heat. Let stand 1 to 2 minutes or until cheese is melted.

4) Remove partially baked crust from oven. Sprinkle ½ cup cheese evenly over crust. Top evenly with eggs, crumbled bacon and remaining ½ cup cheese. Arrange tomato slices over top.

5) Bake 5 to 7 minutes longer or until pizza is thoroughly heated and cheese is melted. Serve with salsa.

HIGH ALTITUDE (3500-6500 FT.): Bake dough round topped with Parmesan topping 7 to 9 minutes.

Cream Cheese French Toast Bake with Strawberry Topping

PREP TIME: 30 MINUTES (READY IN 9 HOURS)
SERVINGS: 6

FRENCH TOAST BAKE

1 container (8 oz) pineapple cream cheese spread

1 loaf (1 lb) French bread (about 18 inches long), cut into 24 ($\frac{3}{4}$-inch-thick) slices

4 eggs

1 cup milk

$\frac{1}{4}$ cup sugar

$\frac{1}{4}$ teaspoon salt

$\frac{1}{4}$ teaspoon ground cinnamon

2 tablespoons butter or margarine, melted

TOPPING

3 cups fresh strawberries

$\frac{1}{4}$ cup sugar

2 tablespoons amaretto, if desired

1 cup fresh blueberries

1) Spray 13x9-inch (3-quart) glass baking dish with cooking spray. Spread about 1 tablespoon cream cheese on each of 12 bread slices. Top with remaining bread slices to make 12 sandwiches. Place sandwiches in baking dish to cover bottom of pan.

2) In medium bowl, beat eggs. Add milk, $\frac{1}{4}$ cup sugar, the salt and cinnamon; beat well. Pour over sandwiches in baking dish. Let stand at room temperature 5 minutes. Turn sandwiches over. Cover; refrigerate about 8 hours or overnight.

3) Chop 1 cup of the strawberries. (Refrigerate remaining berries.) In nonmetal bowl, gently stir together chopped strawberries, $\frac{1}{4}$ cup sugar and the amaretto. Cover; refrigerate about 8 hours or overnight.

4) Heat oven to 400°F. Uncover baking dish; drizzle sandwiches with melted butter. Bake 25 to 30 minutes or until golden brown.

5) Meanwhile, slice remaining strawberries and add with blueberries to chilled strawberry mixture; mix lightly. Serve French toast with berry topping.

HIGH ALTITUDE (3500-6500 FT.): Heat oven to 425°F.

Nutrition Information Per Serving:		
Calories: 530	From Fat: 200	
Total Fat		22g
Saturated Fat		12g
Trans Fat		1g
Cholesterol		190mg
Sodium		880mg
Total Carbohydrate		68g
Dietary Fiber		4g
Sugars		27g
Protein		16g

Light Italian Zucchini Crescent Pie

PREP TIME: 30 MINUTES (READY IN 1 HOUR 10 MINUTES)
SERVINGS: 6

(lf) LOW FAT

4 cups thinly sliced zucchini (about 4 medium)

2 medium onions, chopped (1 cup)

2 tablespoons parsley flakes

1/4 teaspoon salt

1/8 teaspoon garlic powder

1/8 teaspoon dried basil leaves

1/8 teaspoon dried oregano leaves

1/8 teaspoon pepper

1/2 cup fat-free egg product

1 1/2 cups shredded fat-free mozzarella cheese (6 oz)

1 can (8 oz) Pillsbury® refrigerated reduced-fat crescent dinner rolls

2 teaspoons yellow mustard

1) Heat oven to 375°F. Spray 12-inch skillet with cooking spray; heat over medium-high heat until hot. Add zucchini and onions; cook 7 to 9 minutes, stirring frequently, until tender. Stir in parsley flakes, salt, garlic powder, basil, oregano and pepper.

2) In large bowl, mix egg product and cheese. Stir in cooked vegetable mixture.

3) Separate dough into 8 triangles. In ungreased 10-inch glass pie plate, press dough triangles in bottom and up side of plate to form crust; firmly press perforations to seal. Spread mustard over bottom of crust. Pour egg mixture evenly into crust-lined plate.

4) Bake 25 to 30 minutes or until knife inserted near center comes out clean. If necessary, cover edge of crust with strips of foil after first 15 minutes of baking to prevent excessive browning. Let pie stand for at least 10 minutes before serving.

HIGH ALTITUDE (3500-6500 FT.): Bake 30 to 35 minutes, covering edge of crust with foil after first 15 minutes of baking.

Nutrition Information Per Serving:

Calories: 225	From Fat: 65
Total Fat	7g
Saturated Fat	2g
Cholesterol	5mg
Sodium	810mg
Total Carbohydrate	26g
Dietary Fiber	1g
Sugars	9g
Protein	14g

Fanciful Fruit Pizza

PREP TIME: 20 MINUTES (READY IN 2 HOURS 10 MINUTES)
SERVINGS: 12

e EASY

1 roll (16.5 oz) Pillsbury® refrigerated sugar cookies

1 package (8 oz) cream cheese, softened

1/3 cup sugar

1/2 teaspoon vanilla

2 kiwifruit, peeled, halved lengthwise and sliced

1 cup halved or quartered fresh strawberries

1 cup fresh or frozen blueberries

1/2 cup apple jelly

1) Heat oven to 350°F. Grease 12-inch pizza pan or spray with cooking spray. In pan, break up cookie dough; press dough evenly in bottom of pan to form crust. Bake 16 to 20 minutes or until golden brown. Cool completely, about 30 minutes.

2) In small bowl, beat cream cheese, sugar and vanilla with electric mixer on medium speed until fluffy. Spread mixture over cooled crust. Arrange fruit over cream cheese. Stir jelly until smooth; spoon or brush over fruit. Refrigerate until chilled, at least 1 hour. To serve, cut into wedges or squares. Cover and refrigerate any remaining pizza.

HIGH ALTITUDE (3500-6500 FT.): Bake crust 18 to 21 minutes.

Nutrition Information Per Serving:

Calories:	320	From Fat:	130
Total Fat			15g
Saturated Fat			6g
Trans Fat			2g
Cholesterol			35mg
Sodium			170mg
Total Carbohydrate			43g
Dietary Fiber			1g
Sugars			28g
Protein			3g

Raspberry-Almond Fanciful Fruit Pizza

PREP TIME: 20 MINUTES (READY IN 2 HOURS 10 MINUTES)
SERVINGS: 12

e EASY

1 roll (16.5 oz) Pillsbury® refrigerated sugar cookies

1 package (8 oz) cream cheese, softened

1/3 cup sugar

1/2 teaspoon vanilla

2 cups fresh raspberries

1/2 cup apple jelly

Toasted sliced almonds

1) Heat oven to 350°F. Grease 12-inch pizza pan or spray with cooking spray. In pan, break up cookie dough; press dough evenly in bottom of pan to form crust. Bake 16 to 20 minutes or until golden brown. Cool completely, about 30 minutes.

2) In small bowl, beat cream cheese, sugar and vanilla with electric mixer on medium speed until fluffy. Spread mixture over cooled crust. Arrange berries over cream cheese. Stir jelly until smooth; spoon or brush over fruit. Refrigerate until chilled, at least 1 hour. Top with almonds just before serving. To serve, cut into wedges or squares. Cover and refrigerate any remaining pizza.

HIGH ALTITUDE (3500-6500 FT.): Bake crust 18 to 21 minutes.

For best results, always keep the cookie dough very cold until you are ready to use it. And to decrease the fat in these pizzas, use light cream cheese.

Lemon Fanciful Fruit Pizza

PREP TIME: 20 MINUTES (READY IN 2 HOURS 10 MINUTES)
SERVINGS: 12

e EASY

1 roll (16.5 oz) Pillsbury® refrigerated sugar cookies

4 oz cream cheese, softened

1/4 cup powdered sugar

1/3 cup lemon curd

1 cup fresh raspberries

1 cup fresh or frozen blueberries

1 cup green grape halves

1/2 cup apple jelly

1) Heat oven to 350°F. Grease 12-inch pizza pan or spray with cooking spray. In pan, break up cookie dough; press dough evenly in bottom of pan to form crust. Bake 16 to 20 minutes or until golden brown. Cool completely, about 30 minutes.

2) In small bowl, beat cream cheese, powdered sugar and lemon curd with electric mixer on medium speed until fluffy. Spread mixture over cooled crust. Arrange berries and fruit over cream cheese. Stir jelly until smooth; spoon or brush over fruit. Refrigerate until chilled, at least 1 hour. To serve, cut into wedges or squares. Cover and refrigerate any remaining pizza.

HIGH ALTITUDE (3500-6500 FT.): Bake crust 18 to 21 minutes.

Provolone and Pesto Quiche

PREP TIME:	15 MINUTES (READY IN 1 HOUR 10 MINUTES)
SERVINGS:	8

🅔 EASY

1 Pillsbury® refrigerated pie crust (from 15-oz box), softened as directed on box

2 cups shredded Provolone cheese (8 oz)

3 tablespoons refrigerated pesto

¼ cup grated Parmesan cheese

½ cup chopped red bell pepper

5 eggs

1½ cups milk

¼ teaspoon salt

1) Heat oven to 425°F. Make pie crust as directed on box for One-Crust Filled Pie using 9-inch glass pie plate. Bake 7 minutes.

2) Remove crust from oven; sprinkle 1 cup of the Provolone cheese over bottom of the crust.

3) In small bowl, mix pesto and Parmesan cheese until smooth. Carefully spread over Provolone cheese. Sprinkle with bell pepper and the remaining Provolone cheese.

4) In large bowl, with wire whisk, beat eggs, milk and salt until well blended. Pour over cheese.

5) Bake 7 minutes. Reduce oven temperature to 325°F; bake 15 minutes. Cover edge of crust with foil. Bake 23 to 28 minutes longer or until set and knife inserted in center comes out clean. Let stand for 5 minutes before serving.

HIGH ALTITUDE (3500-6500 FT.): No change.

Nutrition Information Per Serving:		
Calories: 330	From Fat: 210	
Total Fat		23g
Saturated Fat		10g
Trans Fat		0g
Cholesterol		165mg
Sodium		590mg
Total Carbohydrate		17g
Dietary Fiber		0g
Sugars		4g
Protein		15g

Sugarplum Brunch Ring

PREP TIME: 20 MINUTES (READY IN 2 HOURS)
SERVINGS: 16

 EASY

¾ cup sugar

1 teaspoon ground cinnamon

18 frozen bread dough rolls, thawed (½ of 48-oz package)

4 tablespoons butter or margarine, melted

½ cup chopped pecans

½ cup maraschino cherries, chopped

⅓ cup dark corn syrup

Nutrition Information Per Serving:		
Calories: 240	From Fat:	70
Total Fat		8g
Saturated Fat		3g
Trans Fat		0g
Cholesterol		10mg
Sodium		240mg
Total Carbohydrate		38g
Dietary Fiber		2g
Sugars		17g
Protein		4g

1) Grease 12-cup fluted tube pan. In small bowl, mix sugar and cinnamon. Cut each roll in half. Dip in butter; roll in sugar mixture. Place half of rolls in pan. Sprinkle with half of pecans and half of cherries. Drizzle with half of corn syrup. Repeat with remaining half of ingredients.

2) Drizzle any remaining butter over top; sprinkle with any remaining sugar mixture. Cover with greased plastic wrap and cloth towel. Let rise in warm place (80 to 85°F) until light and doubled in size, about 1 hour.

3) Heat oven to 350°F. Uncover dough. Bake 30 to 35 minutes or until top is deep golden brown. Cool in pan 5 minutes. Invert onto serving plate; remove pan. Serve warm to pull apart, or cool completely and slice.

HIGH ALTITUDE (3500-6500 FT.): Bake 35 to 40 minutes.

Pat the maraschino cherries dry with a paper towel to prevent the juice from bleeding.

Upside-Down Apple Coffee Cake

PREP TIME: 20 MINUTES (READY IN 1 HOUR)
SERVINGS: 8

 EASY

1½ cups chopped peeled apples

1 can (12.4 oz) Pillsbury® refrigerated cinnamon rolls with icing

½ cup pecan halves or pieces

2 tablespoons butter or margarine, melted

⅓ cup packed brown sugar

2 tablespoons corn syrup

Nutrition Information Per Serving:		
Calories: 280	From Fat:	110
Total Fat		12g
Saturated Fat		3.5
Trans Fat		2g
Cholesterol		10mg
Sodium		370mg
Total Carbohydrate		40g
Dietary Fiber		2g
Sugars		24g
Protein		3g

1) Heat oven to 350°F. Spray 9-inch glass pie plate with cooking spray. Spread 1 cup of the apples in pan. Separate dough into 8 rolls. Cut each roll into quarters; place in large bowl. Add remaining ½ cup apples and pecans.

2) In small bowl, stir together butter, brown sugar and corn syrup. Add brown sugar mixture to dough mixture; toss gently. Spoon mixture over apples in pie plate.

3) Bake 28 to 38 minutes or until deep golden brown. Cool 5 minutes. Turn upside down onto serving platter. Remove lid from icing. Microwave icing on High 10 to 15 seconds or until thin enough to drizzle. Drizzle over warm coffee cake. Serve warm.

HIGH ALTITUDE (3500-6500 FT.): Bake 33 to 38 minutes.

Breakfast Hash Browns, Bacon and Egg Bake

PREP TIME: 25 MINUTES (READY IN 9 HOURS 25 MINUTES)
SERVINGS: 6

4 cups frozen O'Brien potatoes with onions and peppers (from 24-oz bag)

1½ cups shredded Colby-Monterey Jack cheese blend (6 oz)

6 eggs

½ cup milk

1 teaspoon salt-free garlic-herb blend

½ teaspoon salt

½ teaspoon red pepper sauce

5 slices precooked bacon, cut into ½-inch pieces (about ¼ cup)

1 can (8 oz) Pillsbury® refrigerated crescent dinner rolls

1) Spray 11x7-inch (2-quart) glass baking dish with cooking spray. Spread potatoes evenly in baking dish. Add cheese; stir gently to mix.

2) In medium bowl, beat eggs thoroughly with wire whisk. Add milk, garlic-herb blend, salt and pepper sauce; beat until well blended. Pour over potato-cheese mixture. Top with bacon. Cover; refrigerate at least 8 hours or overnight.

3) When ready to serve, heat oven to 350°F. Uncover baking dish; bake 30 minutes.

4) Remove baking dish from oven. Separate dough into 4 rectangles. If desired, with small canapé cutters, cut out a few shapes from each rectangle. Carefully place rectangles over hot potato mixture so corners of rectangles meet in center; do not seal seams. Carefully press edges to sides of baking dish. Place cutout shapes on top of rectangles.

5) Bake 15 to 20 minutes longer or until potatoes are tender and crust is deep golden brown. Let stand 10 minutes before serving.

HIGH ALTITUDE (3500-6500 FT.): When ready to serve, bake uncovered 35 minutes. After topping with dough, bake 18 to 23 minutes longer.

Nutrition Information Per Serving:	
Calories: 475	From Fat: 205
Total Fat	23g
Saturated Fat	10g
Cholesterol	245mg
Sodium	1010mg
Total Carbohydrate	47g
Dietary Fiber	3g
Sugars	9g
Protein	20g

Baked Caramel French Toast

PREP TIME:	20 MINUTES (READY IN 8 HOURS 45 MINUTES)	
SERVINGS:	4 (2 SLICES EACH)	**e** EASY

TOPPING

1 cup packed brown sugar

6 tablespoons butter or margarine

$^1/_3$ cup whipping (heavy) cream

1 tablespoon light corn syrup

FRENCH TOAST

3 eggs

$^1/_2$ cup milk

1 teaspoon vanilla

$^1/_4$ teaspoon salt

8 ($^3/_4$-inch-thick) diagonal cut slices French bread

1) Spray 13x9-inch (3-quart) glass baking dish with cooking spray. In 2-quart saucepan, mix topping ingredients. Cook over medium heat, stirring constantly, until smooth. Do not boil. Spread topping in baking dish.

2) In shallow bowl, beat eggs with fork. Beat in milk, vanilla and salt. Dip bread slices into egg mixture, making sure all egg mixture is absorbed; arrange over topping in dish. Cover; refrigerate at least 8 hours or overnight.

3) When ready to bake, heat oven to 400°F. Uncover baking dish; bake 20 to 25 minutes or until bubbly and toast is golden brown. Remove from oven; let stand 3 minutes.

4) Place large heatproof serving platter upside down over baking dish; turn platter and baking dish over. Remove baking dish, scraping any extra caramel topping onto toast. Serve immediately.

HIGH ALTITUDE (3500-6500 FT.): No change.

Nutrition Information Per Serving:	
Calories: 660	From Fat: 270
Total Fat	30g
Saturated Fat	15g
Trans Fat	1.5g
Cholesterol	230mg
Sodium	680mg
Total Carbohydrate	87g
Dietary Fiber	1g
Sugars	58g
Protein	11g

FROSTY MOCHA
PG. 49

Dippers, Sippers & Munchies

Snack time is full of flavor and fun with these recipes for dipping, sipping and more!

CHIVE 'N ONION DEVILED EGGS
PG. 43

ROASTED BELL PEPPER DIP
PG. 53

CRISPY DELI WRAPS
PG. 40

Crispy Deli Wraps

BOBBIE KEEFER | BYERS, COLORADO

Pillsbury Bake-Off

BAKE-OFF® CONTEST 42, 2006

PREP TIME: 15 MINUTES (READY IN 45 MINUTES)
SERVINGS: 4 WRAPS

⊖ EASY

---

1 box (9 oz) Green Giant® frozen spinach

2 cups Bugles® original corn snacks

1/4 cup butter, melted

16 thin slices cooked ham or turkey (about 1/2 lb)

4 sticks (1 oz each) mozzarella string cheese

1 can (8 oz) Pillsbury® refrigerated crescent dinner rolls

DIPPING SAUCE, IF DESIRED

1/3 cup mayonnaise or salad dressing

1/3 cup Dijon mustard

1/3 cup honey

1) Heat oven to 375°F. Line large cookie sheet with cooking parchment paper. Remove frozen spinach from pouch; place in colander. Rinse with warm water until thawed; drain well. Squeeze spinach dry with paper towel; divide evenly into 4 portions. Set aside.

2) Meanwhile, place corn snacks in resealable food-storage plastic bag; seal bag. With rolling pin, finely crush snacks; pour into shallow dish or pie plate. In another shallow dish or pie plate, place melted butter; set aside. Unroll dough; separate into 4 rectangles. Press each into 6x4-inch rectangle, firmly pressing perforations to seal.

3) Arrange ham in 4 stacks with 4 slices each. Top each stack with 1 portion of spinach, spreading spinach evenly over ham. Place 1 stick of cheese on one short side of spinach-topped ham. Roll up each stack.

4) Place 1 filled ham roll on one long side of each dough rectangle. Fold sides of dough up over ham roll and roll to opposite long side; press edge and ends to seal and completely cover ham roll. Roll each in butter, then in crushed corn snacks to coat; place seam side down on cookie sheet.

5) Bake 20 to 28 minutes or until deep golden brown. Meanwhile, in small bowl, mix all sauce ingredients with wire whisk. Serve warm wraps with sauce for dipping.

HIGH ALTITUDE (3500-6500 FT.): Bake 24 to 28 minutes.

Nutrition Information Per Serving:

Calories:	560	From Fat:	330
Total Fat			36g
Saturated Fat			19g
Trans Fat			4g
Cholesterol			75mg
Sodium			1520mg
Total Carbohydrate			32g
Dietary Fiber			2g
Sugars			5g
Protein			26g

Caramel-Chocolate Apple Fondue

PREP TIME: 10 MINUTES (READY IN 10 MINUTES)
SERVINGS: 4

ⓔ EASY

- ½ cup caramel topping, room temperature
- ¼ cup chocolate-flavored syrup, room temperature
- ¼ cup finely chopped salted peanuts
- 2 medium apples or pears, cut into 1-inch chunks

  Toothpicks

1) Place caramel topping, chocolate syrup and peanuts in individual small bowls; place bowls in center of large platter. Surround bowls with apple chunks. Spear apple chunks with toothpicks.

2) To eat, dip apple chunks in caramel, then in chocolate and peanuts.

HIGH ALTITUDE (3500-6500 FT.): No change.

Nutrition Information Per Serving:

Calories:	260	From Fat:	45
Total Fat		5g	
Saturated Fat		1g	
Trans Fat		0g	
Cholesterol		0mg	
Sodium		230mg	
Total Carbohydrate		51g	
Dietary Fiber		3g	
Sugars		37g	
Protein		3g	

Be sure to cut the apples just before serving so they don't start to turn brown. You can add cashews, pear chunks or butterscotch topping to the dipping assortment.

Orange Cream Floats

PREP TIME: 10 MINUTES (READY IN 10 MINUTES)
SERVINGS: 8 (1-1/2 CUPS EACH)

e EASY

2   pints (4 cups) vanilla ice cream, softened

1   can (6 oz) frozen orange juice concentrate, thawed

¾   cup water

½   teaspoon vanilla

    Red and yellow food color, if desired

1   bottle (2 liters) ginger ale

Nutrition Information Per Serving:

Calories:	300	From Fat:	80
Total Fat			9g
Saturated Fat			5g
Trans Fat			0g
Cholesterol			35mg
Sodium			90mg
Total Carbohydrate			53g
Dietary Fiber			0g
Sugars			48g
Protein			3g

1) In large bowl, mix ice cream, orange juice concentrate, water, vanilla and food color until almost smooth.

2) For each serving, scoop heaping ½ cup ice cream mixture into 16-ounce glass. Pour about 1 cup ginger ale over top of each.

HIGH ALTITUDE (3500-6500 FT.): No change.

tip You can make the ice cream mixture up to 6 hours before serving and store it in the freezer. Let the mixture soften slightly at room temperature before scooping it into the glasses. Just before serving, top with the ginger ale.

Cheese and Corn Dip Olé

PREP TIME: 10 MINUTES (READY IN 35 MINUTES)
SERVINGS: 2 CUPS

e) EASY

1 can (11 oz) Green Giant® Niblets® golden sweet corn, drained

1 can (4.5 oz) Old El Paso® chopped green chiles, drained

1/2 cup cubed American cheese (2 oz)

1 tablespoon all-purpose flour

1 tablespoon chopped pimientoes

Torilla chips

1) Heat oven to 350°F. In 1-quart casserole, mix all ingredients except tortilla chips; cover.

2) Bake for 20 to 25 minutes or until bubbly. Serve with tortilla chips.

tip

Feel free to use whatever cheese you have on hand, or try combining different cheeses for a fun, truly unique flavor.

Chive 'n Onion Deviled Eggs

PREP TIME: 35 MINUTES (READY IN 50 MINUTES)
SERVINGS: 12

6 eggs

1/4 cup chives-and-onion cream cheese spread (from 8-oz container)

1/8 teaspoon salt

1 teaspoon milk

1 teaspoon yellow mustard

1/8 teaspoon paprika

2 teaspoons chopped fresh chives

Nutrition Information Per Serving:		
Calories: 50	From Fat.	35
Total Fat		4g
Saturated Fat		1.5g
Trans Fat		0g
Cholesterol		110mg
Sodium		95mg
Total Carbohydrate		0g
Dietary Fiber		0g
Sugars		0g
Protein		4g

1) In 2-quart saucepan, place eggs in single layer; add enough cold water to cover eggs by 1 inch. Cover saucepan; heat to boiling. Remove from heat; let stand covered 15 minutes. Drain. Immediately place eggs in cold water with ice cubes or run cold water over eggs until completely cooled.

2) Peel eggs; cut in half lengthwise. Carefully remove yolks; place in small bowl. Add cream cheese spread, salt, milk and mustard; mash with fork until well blended and smooth. Spoon or pipe yolk mixture into egg whites. Sprinkle with paprika and chives.

HIGH ALTITUDE (3500-6500 FT.): In Step 1, cover saucepan; heat to boiling and boil 5 minutes.

Pastry-Wrapped Cranberry Brie

PREP TIME: 20 MINUTES (READY IN 1 HOUR)
SERVINGS: 12

⊖ EASY

1 can (8 oz) Pillsbury® refrigerated crescent dinner rolls

1 round (8 oz) Brie cheese (Do not use triple creme Brie)

3 tablespoons whole berry cranberry sauce

1 tablespoon apricot preserves

1/2 teaspoon dried rosemary leaves, crushed

2 medium pears, unpeeled, thinly sliced

Nutrition Information Per Serving:

Calories:	160	From Fat:	80
Total Fat			9g
Saturated Fat			4.5g
Trans Fat			1g
Cholesterol			20mg
Sodium			270mg
Total Carbohydrate			15g
Dietary Fiber			1g
Sugars			7g
Protein			5g

1) Heat oven to 350°F. Unroll dough and separate crosswise into 2 sections; press dough into 2 (7-inch) squares, firmly pressing perforations to seal.

2) Cut cheese round horizontally to make 2 rounds. Place 1 cheese round, rind side down, on center of 1 dough square. (Do not remove rind from cheese.) In small bowl, mix cranberry sauce and preserves. Spread over top of cheese; sprinkle with rosemary. Top with remaining cheese round, rind side up.

3) With small cookie or canapé cutter, or sharp knife, make 1/2- to 1-inch cutouts to resemble poinsettia leaves from each corner of remaining dough square. Roll 3 small pieces of dough into 3 small balls; set cutouts and dough balls aside. Place remaining dough on top of cheese round. Press dough evenly around cheese, folding top edges over bottom edges; press to seal completely. Place on ungreased cookie sheet.

4) On 7x7-inch foil square, arrange dough leaves with balls in center on top of dough. Lift foil square with poinsettia and place on cookie sheet next to wrapped Brie.

5) Bake poinsettia petals 8 to 11 minutes or until light golden brown around edges. Lift from cookie sheet with foil; cool. Bake wrapped cheese 25 to 30 minutes or until golden brown. Remove from cookie sheet; place on serving plate. Place poinsettia on top of wrapped cheese. Let stand 15 minutes before serving. Serve warm with pears.

HIGH ALTITUDE (3500-6500 FT.): No change.

Onion-Cheese Custard Tartlets

PREP TIME: 20 MINUTES (READY IN 45 MINUTES)
SERVINGS: 12

ⓔ EASY

1 can (8 oz) Pillsbury® refrigerated crescent dinner rolls

1/3 cup shredded Gruyère cheese (about 1 1/2 oz)

4 green onions, sliced (1/4 cup)

1 tablespoon diced pimientos

1 egg

3 tablespoons whipping cream

1) Heat oven to 375°F. Unroll dough into 1 large rectangle; press into 12x9-inch rectangle, firmly pressing perforations to seal. Cut dough into 12 squares. Gently press squares into 12 ungreased mini muffin cups, shaping edges to form rims 1/4 inch high.

2) Spoon cheese evenly into dough-lined cups. Top each with onions and pimientos. In small bowl, beat egg and whipping cream with wire whisk until blended. Spoon scant 1 tablespoon mixture into each cup.

3) Bake 15 to 20 minutes or until edges are golden brown and filling is set. Cool 5 minutes. Remove from muffin cups.

HIGH ALTITUDE (3500-6500 FT.): No change.

Nutrition Information Per Serving:	
Calories: 100	From Fat: 60
Total Fat	7g
Saturated Fat	3g
Trans Fat	1g
Cholesterol	25mg
Sodium	170mg
Total Carbohydrate	8g
Dietary Fiber	0g
Sugars	2g
Protein	3g

Cheesy Pinwheels with Italian Dip

PREP TIME: 15 MINUTES (READY IN 35 MINUTES)
SERVINGS: 16

e EASY

1 can (8 oz) Pillsbury® refrigerated crescent dinner rolls

½ teaspoon garlic powder

¾ cup shredded mozzarella cheese (3 oz)

1 egg, beaten

½ teaspoon Italian seasoning

½ cup tomato pasta sauce

1) Heat oven to 350°F. Unroll dough and separate into 2 long rectangles; press each into 12x4-inch rectangle. Firmly press perforations to seal. Sprinkle garlic powder and cheese over rectangles; gently press into dough.

2) Starting with one short side, roll up each rectangle; press edges to seal. With serrated knife, cut each roll into 8 slices; place cut side down on ungreased cookie sheet. Brush tops with beaten egg; sprinkle with Italian seasoning.

3) Bake 15 to 18 minutes or until edges are golden brown. Immediately remove from cookie sheet. In small saucepan, heat pasta sauce over medium heat until hot, stirring occasionally. Serve warm pinwheels with pasta sauce.

HIGH ALTITUDE (3500-6500 FT.): No change.

Nutrition Information Per Serving:		
Calories: 80	From Fat:	40
Total Fat		4.5g
Saturated Fat		2g
Trans Fat		1g
Cholesterol		15mg
Sodium		180mg
Total Carbohydrate		7g
Dietary Fiber		0g
Sugars		2g
Protein		3g

tip

Make the pinwheels and cover with plastic wrap. Refrigerate up to 2 hours before baking.

Layered Ranch Taco Dip

PREP TIME:	20 MINUTES (READY IN 20 MINUTES)
SERVINGS:	16 (1/4 CUP DIP AND 1 OZ CHIPS EACH)

EASY

1 can (16 oz) Old El Paso® traditional refried beans

1 container (8 oz) sour cream

1 package (0.4 oz) ranch dressing mix (buttermilk recipe)

2 small tomatoes, seeded, finely chopped

1/2 cup sliced ripe olives, drained

6 medium green onions, sliced (6 tablespoons)

1/2 medium red bell pepper, chopped

1 cup shredded Cheddar cheese (4 oz)

16 oz tortilla chips

1) On flat 10- to 12-inch plate, spread refried beans. In small bowl, mix sour cream and dressing mix; spread over beans.

2) Top with tomatoes, olives, onions and bell pepper; sprinkle with cheese. Serve with tortilla chips.

HIGH ALTITUDE (3500-6500 FT.): No change.

Nutrition Information Per Serving:	
Calories: 240	From Fat: 120
Total Fat	13g
Saturated Fat	4g
Trans Fat	0g
Cholesterol	20mg
Sodium	400mg
Total Carbohydrate	25g
Dietary Fiber	3g
Sugars	2g
Protein	6g

tip Monterey Jack or Colby-Monterey Jack cheese can be used instead of the Cheddar cheese in this tasty dip.

Scoop Tacos™

PREP TIME: 20 MINUTES (READY IN 20 MINUTES)
SERVINGS: 12

e EASY

1 box (4.6 oz) Old El Paso® taco shells (12 shells)

1 lb lean (at least 80%) ground beef

1 package (1.25 oz) Old El Paso® taco seasoning mix

3 cups shredded lettuce

1 cup shredded Cheddar cheese (4 oz)

1 medium tomato, diced

1 cup Old El Paso® Thick 'n Chunky salsa

Nutrition Information Per Serving:		
Calories: 170	From Fat:	90
Total Fat		10g
Saturated Fat		4g
Trans Fat		1g
Cholesterol		35mg
Sodium		560mg
Total Carbohydrate		11g
Dietary Fiber		0g
Sugars		1g
Protein		10g

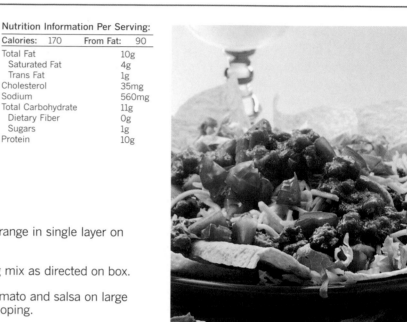

1) Heat oven to 375°F. Break taco shells in half; arrange in single layer on ungreased cookie sheet. Bake 5 to 7 minutes.

2) Meanwhile, prepare ground beef with seasoning mix as directed on box.

3) Layer lettuce, seasoned ground beef, cheese, tomato and salsa on large plate. Serve with warm taco shell halves for scooping.

HIGH ALTITUDE (3500-6500 FT.): No change.

Crescent-Wrapped Brie

PREP TIME: 10 MINUTES (READY IN 50 MINUTES)
SERVINGS: 12

e EASY

1 can (8 oz) Pillsbury® refrigerated crescent dinner rolls

1 round (8 oz) natural Brie cheese

1 egg, beaten

48 water crackers or baguette French bread slices

Nutrition Information Per Serving:		
Calories: 190	From Fat:	80
Total Fat		9g
Saturated Fat		4g
Cholesterol		35mg
Sodium		440mg
Total Carbohydrate		19g
Dietary Fiber		0g
Sugars		3g
Protein		8g

1) Heat oven to 350°F. Unroll dough and separate crosswise into 2 sections; press dough into 2 squares, firmly pressing perforations to seal. Place cheese round on the center of the 1 dough square.

2) With small cookie cutter, cut 1 shape from each corner of remaining dough square; set cutouts aside. Place dough square on top of cheese round. Press dough evenly around cheese, folding bottom edge over top edges; press to seal completely. Place on ungreased cookie sheet.

3) Brush dough with egg. Arrange dough cutouts on top; brush with egg.

4) Bake 20 to 24 minutes or until golden brown. Remove from cookie sheet; place on serving plate. Cool 15 minutes. Serve warm with crackers.

HIGH ALTITUDE (3500-6500 FT.): No change.

Frosty Mocha

PREP TIME: 10 MINUTES (READY IN 10 MINUTES)
SERVINGS: 4 (1 CUP EACH)

e EASY   **f** LOW FAT

1½ cups milk

⅓ cup chocolate-flavored syrup

2 tablespoons instant malted milk powder, if desired

2 tablespoons instant coffee (dry)

3½ cups small ice cubes

1) In blender container, place all ingredients except ice; blend until well mixed.

2) Add ice cubes a few at a time, blending well after each addition until mixture is smooth.

HIGH ALTITUDE (3500-6500 FT.): No change.

Nutrition Information Per Serving:

Calories:	120	From Fat:	20
Total Fat		2g	
Saturated Fat		1.5g	
Trans Fat		0g	
Cholesterol		5mg	
Sodium		55mg	
Total Carbohydrate		22g	
Dietary Fiber		0g	
Sugars		17g	
Protein		4g	

Taco Snack Mix

PREP TIME:	15 MINUTES (READY IN 1 HOUR 40 MINUTES)
SERVINGS:	10 (3/4 CUP EACH)

ⓔ EASY

3 cups Corn Chex® cereal

2 cups mini cheese-filled buttery cracker sandwiches (from 9¹/₂-oz box)

1³/₄ cups fish-shaped pretzels (from 8.7-oz package)

1 cup salted peanuts

2 tablespoons vegetable oil

2 tablespoons Old El Paso® taco seasoning mix (from 1.25-oz package)

1) Heat oven to 250°F. In 4-quart bowl, mix cereal, cracker sandwiches, pretzels and peanuts.

2) In small bowl, mix oil and taco seasoning mix. Pour over cereal mixture; toss to coat. Pour into ungreased 13x9-inch pan.

3) Bake 1 hour, stirring every 15 minutes. Cool completely, about 25 minutes.

HIGH ALTITUDE (3500-6500 FT.): No change.

Nutrition Information Per Serving:		
Calories:	260	From Fat: 140
Total Fat		16g
Saturated Fat		3g
Trans Fat		1.5g
Cholesterol		0mg
Sodium		580mg
Total Carbohydrate		25g
Dietary Fiber		2g
Sugars		7g
Protein		7g

tip

Kids love the fun flavors and shapes of this not-too-spicy snack mix. Stored in snack-size resealable plastic food-storage bags, it's perfect to take along for car trips, hikes, picnics or bicycle rides.

Tiny Ham and Pineapple Pot Pies

PREP TIME: 40 MINUTES (READY IN 1 HOUR)
SERVINGS: 16

½ cup finely chopped cooked ham

½ cup finely shredded Swiss cheese (2 oz)

½ cup canned crushed pineapple, well drained

1 tablespoon finely chopped green onions

½ teaspoon ground mustard

1 box (15 oz) Pillsbury® refrigerated pie crusts, softened as directed on box

1 egg, beaten

1 teaspoon sesame seed, if desired

1) Heat oven to 450°F (425°F for dark or nonstick pans). In small bowl, mix ham, cheese, pineapple, onions and mustard.

2) Remove pie crusts from pouches; unroll crusts on work surface. From each crust, cut 8 (3-inch) rounds and 8 (2-inch) rounds, rerolling crusts if necessary. In 16 ungreased mini muffin cups, press 3-inch rounds in bottoms and up sides so edges of crusts extend slightly over the sides of the cups.

3) Spoon about 1 rounded tablespoon ham mixture into each crust-lined cup. Brush crust edges lightly with beaten egg.

4) Cut small vent in each 2-inch pie-crust round. Place 1 round over filling in each cup; press edges together, pushing toward cup so crust does not extend over sides. Brush top crusts with beaten egg. Sprinkle with sesame seed.

5) Bake 10 to 14 minutes or until crust is deep golden brown. Remove from muffin cups. Let stand 5 minutes before serving.

HIGH ALTITUDE (3500-6500 FT.): No change.

Nutrition Information Per Serving:		
Calories: 120	From Fat: 65	
Total Fat		7g
Saturated Fat		3g
Cholesterol		25mg
Sodium		160mg
Total Carbohydrate		11g
Dietary Fiber		0g
Sugars		2g
Protein		3g

Pastry-Wrapped Jalapeño Brie with Fruit

PREP TIME: 15 MINUTES (READY IN 1 HOUR)
SERVINGS: 12

e EASY

1 can (8 oz) Pillsbury® refrigerated crescent dinner rolls

1 round (8 oz) Brie cheese, about 4 inches in diameter

2 tablespoons green or red jalapeño jelly or hot pepper jelly

2 tablespoons chopped fresh cilantro

1 egg, beaten

8 small clusters seedless red or green grapes

1 kiwifruit, unpeeled, sliced

½ cup fresh strawberry halves

½ orange, cut into wedges

1) Heat oven to 350°F. Spray cookie sheet with cooking spray. Unroll dough onto cookie sheet; pat dough and firmly press perforations to seal.

2) Cut cheese horizontally into 2 equal layers. Place bottom half of cheese on center of dough on cookie sheet. Spread jelly over cheese. Sprinkle with chopped cilantro. Top with remaining cheese half.

3) Lift and gently press dough evenly around cheese. Gather dough together over top of cheese; twist to form bow. Brush dough with beaten egg.

4) Bake 20 to 25 minutes or until dough is golden brown. Cool 15 minutes before serving.

5) To serve, place warm pastry-wrapped Brie on platter. Arrange fruit around Brie. Cover and refrigerate any remaining Brie.

HIGH ALTITUDE (3500-6500 FT.): Heat oven to 375°F. Unroll dough and separate crosswise into 2 sections; press dough into 2 squares, firmly pressing perforations to seal. Place 1 square on ungreased cookie sheet and cut off corners with a sharp knife. (Cutouts will have a leaf appearance.) Set cutouts aside. Continue with Step 2. With sharp knife, cut off corners of remaining dough square. Set cutouts aside. Place remaining dough on top of cheese round. Press around cheese, folding bottom edges over top edges. Press to seal completely. Brush dough with egg. Arrange cutouts over top and edges; brush with egg. Bake 25 to 30 minutes.

Nutrition Information Per Serving:

Calories:	170	From Fat:	90
Total Fat			10g
Saturated Fat			5g
Trans Fat			1g
Cholesterol			35mg
Sodium			270mg
Total Carbohydrate			15g
Dietary Fiber			0g
Sugars			7g
Protein			6g

Roasted Bell Pepper Dip

PREP TIME: 20 MINUTES (READY IN 20 MINUTES)
SERVINGS: 12 (2 TABLESPOONS DIP EACH)

🄴 EASY

- 1 package (8 oz) cream cheese, softened
- ¼ cup sour cream
- ½ cup finely chopped roasted red bell peppers (from a jar)
- 3 tablespoons chopped fresh cilantro
- ¼ teaspoon red pepper sauce
- 1 clove garlic, finely chopped
- 2 fresh cilantro sprigs
  Assorted crackers

1) In medium bowl, mix all ingredients except cilantro sprigs and crackers. Spoon into serving bowl. Garnish with cilantro sprigs.

2) Serve immediately with crackers, or cover and refrigerate until serving time. If refrigerated, let stand 10 to 15 minutes before serving.

HIGH ALTITUDE (3500-6500 FT.): No change.

Nutrition Information Per Serving:

Calories:	80	From Fat:	70
Total Fat			8g
Saturated Fat			4.5g
Trans Fat			0g
Cholesterol			25mg
Sodium			60mg
Total Carbohydrate			1g
Dietary Fiber			0g
Sugars			1g
Protein			2g

Baby carrots, celery or cauliflower also make great dippers for this delicious dip. And if your guests aren't cilantro fans, simply leave it out.

Mini Monte Cristos

COLLEEN VROOMAN | WAUKESHA, WISCONSIN

Pillsbury Bake-Off®

BAKE-OFF® CONTEST 41, 2004

PREP TIME: 20 MINUTES (READY IN 40 MINUTES)
SERVINGS: 16

EASY

1 egg

2 tablespoons milk

1 can (8 oz) Pillsbury® Refrigerated Crescent Dinner Rolls

16 very thin slices (about 4x4 inches) smoked turkey (5½ oz)

16 cubes (2½ oz) Colby-Monterey Jack cheese blend (from 8-oz package)

Powdered sugar

Maple syrup or Dijon mustard, if desired

1) Heat oven to 375°F. Grease cookie sheet with shortening or spray with nonstick cooking spray. In small bowl, beat egg and milk with fork until well blended; set aside.

2) Unroll dough; separate crosswise into 2 (6x8-inch) rectangles, firmly pressing perforations to seal. With knife or pizza cutter, cut each rectangle into 8 (3x2-inch) rectangles.

3) Fold each slice of turkey in half; place on dough rectangles. Place 1 cheese cube in center of each; fold turkey around cheese cube. Wrap dough up around turkey and cheese, shaping into a ball; pinch tightly to seal. Brush top and sides of each ball with egg mixture; place on greased cookie sheet.

4) Bake for 10 to 14 minutes or until golden brown. Sprinkle with powdered sugar. Cool 2 minutes; remove from cookie sheet. Serve warm with maple syrup or Dijon mustard for dipping.

HIGH ALTITUDE (3500-6500 FT.): No change.

Nutrition Information Per Serving:

Calories:	80	From Fat:	35
Total Fat			4g
Saturated Fat			2g
Cholesterol			20mg
Sodium			320mg
Total Carbohydrate			7g
Dietary Fiber			0g
Sugars			3g
Protein			4g

Orange-Mint Slush

PREP TIME: 15 MINUTES (READY IN 5 HOURS 15 MINUTES)
SERVINGS: 15 (1 CUP EACH)

e EASY   **f** LOW FAT

2 cups sugar

7 cups water

3/4 cup fresh mint leaves

1 can (12 oz) frozen orange juice concentrate, thawed

1 can (6 oz) frozen lemonade concentrate, thawed

4 bottles (10 oz each) club soda (5 cups), chilled

Additional fresh mint leaves, if desired

1) In 4-quart saucepan, heat sugar, 3 cups of the water and 3/4 cup mint leaves to boiling. Reduce heat; simmer 2 minutes. Cool 1 hour to blend flavors.

2) Strain and reserve liquid. In nonmetal freezer container, mix reserved liquid, remaining water, orange juice concentrate and lemonade concentrate; freeze until slush consistency.

3) To serve, spoon about 2/3 cup slush mixture into each serving glass; pour 1/3 cup club soda over each. Garnish with mint leaves.

HIGH ALTITUDE (3500-6500 FT.): No change.

Nutrition Information Per Serving:	
Calories: 180	From Fat: 0
Total Fat	0g
Saturated Fat	0g
Trans Fat	0g
Cholesterol	0mg
Sodium	20mg
Total Carbohydrate	45g
Dietary Fiber	0g
Sugars	43g
Protein	0g

tip

Make slush mixture ahead and freeze. Thaw 30 minutes before serving. A 5-quart ice cream pail is perfect for storing the slush.

Cilantro-Marinated Shrimp with Fruit

PREP TIME: 25 MINUTES (READY IN 1 HOUR 25 MINUTES)
SERVINGS: 12

¼ cup balsamic vinegar

2 tablespoons olive oil

2 tablespoons honey

2 tablespoons lemon juice

¼ teaspoon salt

¼ cup chopped fresh cilantro

2 lb cooked deveined peeled large shrimp (with tails left on)

1 medium avocado, cut into ¾-inch cubes

1 medium mango, cut into ¾-inch cubes

1 cup small fresh strawberries, halved

Fresh cilantro sprigs

Nutrition Information Per Serving:		
Calories: 140	From Fat:	45
Total Fat		5g
Saturated Fat		1g
Trans Fat		0g
Cholesterol		145mg
Sodium		210mg
Total Carbohydrate		8g
Dietary Fiber		1g
Sugars		5g
Protein		16g

Try cubed papaya, cantaloupe or honeydew in place of the mango. The shrimp can be marinated up to 8 hours ahead.

1) In large nonmetal bowl, mix vinegar, oil, honey, lemon juice and salt. Stir in chopped cilantro. Add shrimp; toss to coat. Cover; refrigerate at least 1 hour to marinate.

2) To serve, remove shrimp from marinade; reserve marinade. Arrange shrimp on large platter. Add avocado, mango and strawberries to marinade; toss to coat. Surround shrimp with avocado, mango and strawberries. Drizzle some of the reserved marinade over top; discard remaining marinade. Garnish with cilantro sprigs. Serve with decorative toothpicks or cocktail forks.

HIGH ALTITUDE (3500-6500 FT.): No change.

Mud Sodas

PREP TIME: 10 MINUTES (READY IN 10 MINUTES)
SERVINGS: 8 (1 CUP EACH)

 EASY

4 cups chocolate milk, chilled

4 cups root beer, chilled

1 pint (2 cups) chocolate ice cream

Nutrition Information Per Serving:		
Calories: 220	From Fat:	60
Total Fat		6g
Saturated Fat		4g
Trans Fat		0g
Cholesterol		20mg
Sodium		120mg
Total Carbohydrate		36g
Dietary Fiber		1g
Sugars		36g
Protein		5g

1) In each of 8 tall glasses, place ½ cup milk and ½ cup root beer; stir to mix.

2) Top each serving with ¼ cup ice cream.

HIGH ALTITUDE (3500-6500 FT.): No change.

Mexican Chicken Dip with Lime

PREP TIME: 20 MINUTES (READY IN 3 HOURS 20 MINUTES)
SERVINGS: 18 (1/4 CUP DIP AND 1 OZ TORTILLA CHIPS EACH)

e EASY

1 package (3 oz) cream cheese, softened

¹/₃ cup sour cream

³/₄ teaspoon grated lime peel

1 package (9 oz) frozen cooked southwestern-seasoned chicken strips, thawed, finely chopped (2 cups)

1 can (3.8 oz) sliced ripe olives, drained

1 can (16 oz) Old El Paso® refried beans

¹/₃ cup Old El Paso® Thick 'n Chunky salsa

1 medium Italian plum tomato, chopped

¹/₂ cup shredded Cheddar cheese (2 oz)

2 tablespoons chopped fresh cilantro, if desired

1 bag (18 oz) tortilla chips

1) Line 9-inch pie pan with plastic wrap, allowing wrap to extend over edge of pan. In small bowl, mix cream cheese and sour cream until well blended. Stir in lime peel. Spread mixture in pie pan.

2) Sprinkle chicken and olives over cream cheese mixture. In small bowl, stir refried beans to soften. Spread beans over chicken mixture. Cover with plastic wrap; refrigerate at least 3 hours but no longer than 6 hours.

3) To serve, unmold dip onto 10-inch flat serving platter; remove plastic wrap. Top dip with salsa, tomato, cheese and cilantro. Serve with tortilla chips.

HIGH ALTITUDE (3500-6500 FT.): No change.

Nutrition Information Per Serving:		
Calories: 240	From Fat:	110
Total Fat		12g
Saturated Fat		3.5g
Trans Fat		0g
Cholesterol		25mg
Sodium		440mg
Total Carbohydrate		23g
Dietary Fiber		3g
Sugars		1g
Protein		8g

Crusty Bread Boat with Crab and Artichoke Spread

PREP TIME: 20 MINUTES (READY IN 1 HOUR 20 MINUTES)
SERVINGS: 6

EASY

1 can (11 oz) Pillsbury® refrigerated crusty French loaf

1 package (3 oz) cream cheese, softened

2 tablespoons mayonnaise or salad dressing

1 tablespoon white wine Worcestershire sauce

¼ teaspoon crushed red pepper flakes

1 small garlic clove, finely chopped

1 cup shredded Asiago cheese (4 oz)

1 can (14 oz) artichoke hearts, drained, chopped

1 can (6 oz) crabmeat, well drained

1 jar (2 oz) diced pimientos, drained

1 tablespoon chopped fresh parsley

1) Heat oven to 350°F. Bake French loaf as directed on can. Cool 30 minutes.

2) In medium microwavable bowl, mix remaining ingredients except the parsley. Set aside.

3) Cut 1 inch from top of cooled loaf. Cut top into 1-inch pieces; place in serving basket. With sharp knife, cut around inside of loaf, leaving ½-inch-thick sides. Remove bread, leaving inside of loaf hollow. Cut removed bread into 1-inch pieces; place in serving basket.

4) Microwave cream cheese mixture on Medium 3 to 4 minutes, stirring twice, until hot. Spoon hot mixture into hollowed out loaf. Sprinkle with parsley. Serve spread with bread pieces and/or crackers.

HIGH ALTITUDE (3500-6500 FT.): No change.

Nutrition Information Per Serving:	
Calories: 350	From Fat: 145
Total Fat	16g
Saturated Fat	7g
Cholesterol	55mg
Sodium	990mg
Total Carbohydrate	32g
Dietary Fiber	4g
Sugars	5g
Protein	20g

Italian Spinach Dip

PREP TIME: 10 MINUTES (READY IN 2 HOURS 10 MINUTES)
SERVINGS: 8 (2 TABLESPOONS DIP AND 4 CRACKERS EACH)

EASY

1 cup Green Giant® frozen cut leaf spinach

1 package (3 oz) cream cheese, cut into 1-inch cubes

½ cup sour cream

1 tablespoon zesty Italian dressing mix (from 0.6-oz packet)

Assorted vegetables, bread or crackers

1) Place spinach in microwavable bowl; cover with microwavable plastic wrap, venting one corner. Microwave on High 3 to 4 minutes or until hot. Drain well. Chop spinach with kitchen scissors or knife.

2) Add cream cheese to spinach in bowl; stir until cream cheese is softened. Mix in the sour cream and the dressing mix until well blended. Cover and refrigerate at least 2 hours or until chilled. Serve with vegetables, bread or crackers.

HIGH ALTITUDE (3500-6500 FT.): No change.

Nutrition Information Per Serving:

Calories:	110	From Fat:	70
Total Fat			8g
Saturated Fat			4.5g
Trans Fat			0.5g
Cholesterol			20mg
Sodium			250mg
Total Carbohydrate			7g
Dietary Fiber			0g
Sugars			3g
Protein			2g

tip

The flavors of this savory dip improve when the dip is made early. Make it at least 2 hours ahead, keeping it in the refrigerator until serving time.

Appetizer Party Buffet

Planning a get-together is a breeze with this assortment of party starters!

TURKEY CLUB TORTILLA ROLL-UPS
PG. 73

FOCACCIA DIPPING STICKS
PG. 67

EASY VEGETABLE PIZZA
PG. 72

FLAKY SAUSAGE FOLDOVERS
PG. 65

Pastry Tart with Havarti and Peppers

PREP TIME: 20 MINUTES (READY IN 40 MINUTES)
SERVINGS: 16

⊖ EASY

2 tablespoons butter or margarine

1 small onion, thinly sliced

½ cup thinly sliced red bell pepper

½ cup thinly sliced green bell pepper

1 can (8 oz) Pillsbury® refrigerated crescent dinner rolls

¼ teaspoon Italian seasoning

⅛ teaspoon garlic powder

5 slices (1 oz each) Havarti cheese

1) Heat oven to 425°F. In 10 inch skillet, melt butter over medium-low heat. Cook onion in butter 10 minutes, stirring frequently, or until light golden brown and caramelized. Add bell peppers; cook 5 to 6 minutes, stirring frequently, until peppers are tender.

2) On ungreased cookie sheet, unroll dough into 1 large rectangle; firmly press perforations to seal. Press into 12x7-inch rectangle, forming ¼-inch rim around edge of dough. Sprinkle with Italian seasoning and garlic powder; top with half of cheese, pepper mixture and remaining cheese.

3) Bake 10 to 14 minutes or until edges are golden brown and cheese is melted. Let stand 5 minutes. To serve, cut in half lengthwise, then crosswise into strips. Serve warm.

HIGH ALTITUDE (3500-6500 FT.): No change.

Nutrition Information Per Serving:		
Calories: 110	From Fat:	70
Total Fat		8g
Saturated Fat		4g
Trans Fat		1g
Cholesterol		15mg
Sodium		190mg
Total Carbohydrate		6g
Dietary Fiber		0g
Sugars		1g
Protein		3g

Ranch Deviled Eggs

PREP TIME: 30 MINUTES (READY IN 1 HOUR)
SERVINGS: 24 APPETIZERS

€ EASY

12 eggs

3 teaspoons dry ranch dressing mix
(from 1-oz envelope)

1/3 cup mayonnaise or salad dressing

1 teaspoon Dijon mustard

1 tablespoon chopped chives

Nutrition Information Per Serving:		
Calories: 60	From Fat:	45
Total Fat		5g
Saturated Fat		1g
Trans Fat		0g
Cholesterol		105mg
Sodium		105mg
Total Carbohydrate		0g
Dietary Fiber		0g
Sugars		0g
Protein		3g

1) In 4-quart saucepan or Dutch oven, place eggs in single layer. Add enough water to cover eggs by 1 inch. Heat to boiling. Immediately remove from heat; cover and let stand 15 minutes. Drain; rinse with cold water. Place eggs in bowl of ice water; let stand 10 minutes.

2) To remove shell, crack it by tapping gently all over; roll between hands to loosen. Peel, starting at large end.

3) Cut eggs lengthwise in half. Into medium bowl, slip out yolks; mash with fork. Stir dressing mix, mayonnaise and mustard into yolks.

4) Spoon or pipe yolk mixture into egg white halves. Sprinkle with chives. Refrigerate at least 30 minutes before serving.

HIGH ALTITUDE (3500-6500 FT.): In Step 1, heat eggs to boiling and boil 5 minutes; remove from heat. Cover and let stand 15 minutes.

Pizza Crisps

PREP TIME: 20 MINUTES (READY IN 40 MINUTES)
SERVINGS: 36 APPETIZERS

€ EASY

1 1/4 lb lean (at least 80%) ground beef

1/2 cup diced pepperoni
(from 6-oz package)

1 can (8 oz) pizza sauce

1 cup shredded 6 cheese Italian cheese blend (4 oz)

2 cups shredded Cheddar-American cheese blend (8 oz)

36 slices sourdough cocktail bread

Nutrition Information Per Serving:		
Calories: 80	From Fat:	45
Total Fat		5g
Saturated Fat		2.5g
Trans Fat		0g
Cholesterol		20mg
Sodium		230mg
Total Carbohydrate		3g
Dietary Fiber		0g
Sugars		0g
Protein		6g

1) Heat oven to 350°F. In 10-inch skillet, cook ground beef over medium-high heat 5 to 7 minutes, stirring occasionally, until thoroughly cooked; drain. Stir in pepperoni and pizza sauce. Cook 2 to 3 minutes over medium heat until hot. Stir in Italian cheese blend and 1 cup of the Cheddar-American cheese blend until melted.

2) Arrange bread slices on 2 ungreased cookie sheets. Spread generous tablespoon of beef mixture on each slice. Top each with about 1 teaspoon of the remaining cheese.

3) Bake 15 to 20 minutes or until thoroughly heated and crisp. Serve warm.

HIGH ALTITUDE (3500-6500 FT.): No change.

Thai Chicken Salad Appetizers

PREP TIME: 20 MINUTES (READY IN 1 HOUR 30 MINUTES)
SERVINGS: 36 APPETIZERS

e EASY

1 tablespoon butter, melted

1 teaspoon hot pepper sauce

1 box (15 oz) Pillsbury® refrigerated
pie crusts, softened as directed
on box

2½ cups finely chopped cooked chicken

⅓ cup Thai peanut sauce
(from 11.5-oz bottle)

⅓ cup mayonnaise

⅓ cup finely chopped green onions

⅓ cup finely chopped red bell pepper

Fresh thyme leaves, if desired

1) Heat oven to 450°F. In small bowl, mix
butter and hot pepper sauce. Remove
crusts from pouches; place on work
surface. Cut crusts into 2-inch squares;
place on ungreased cookie sheet.

2) Bake 5 to 7 minutes or until golden
brown. Brush with butter mixture.
Cool completely, about 30 minutes.

3) In large bowl, mix chicken, peanut
sauce, mayonnaise, onions and bell
pepper. Top each pastry square with
about 1 tablespoon chicken mixture;
garnish with thyme. Refrigerate 30
minutes or until cold.

HIGH ALTITUDE (3500-6500 FT.): No change.

Nutrition Information Per Serving:

Calories:	90	From Fat:	60
Total Fat			6g
Saturated Fat			2g
Trans Fat			0g
Cholesterol			10mg
Sodium			75mg
Total Carbohydrate			6g
Dietary Fiber			0g
Sugars			0g
Protein			3g

Flaky Sausage Foldovers

| PREP TIME: | 25 MINUTES (READY IN 40 MINUTES) |
| SERVINGS: | 22 APPETIZERS |

ⓔ EASY

6 oz bulk hot pork sausage

¼ teaspoon garlic powder

1 can (15 oz) pizza sauce

1 box (15 oz) Pillsbury® refrigerated pie crusts, softened as directed on box

1 egg, beaten

Nutrition Information Per Serving:

Calories: 80	From Fat: 40
Total Fat	4.5g
Saturated Fat	1.5g
Trans Fat	0g
Cholesterol	15mg
Sodium	170mg
Total Carbohydrate	8g
Dietary Fiber	0g
Sugars	0g
Protein	1g

1) Heat oven to 425°F. In 8-inch skillet, cook sausage over medium-high heat 6 to 8 minutes, stirring occasionally until thoroughly cooked; drain well. Stir in garlic powder and 1/4 cup of the pizza sauce.

2) Remove 1 crust from pouch. On work surface, roll into 13-inch round. With 3-inch round cutter, cut 11 rounds. Repeat with second crust.

3) Spoon about 1 teaspoon sausage mixture onto each round. Fold each in half; seal edges with fork. Cut small slit in top of each with sharp knife. Place on ungreased large cookie sheet. Brush each foldover with beaten egg. If desired, cut decorative shapes from remaining dough and attach with beaten egg.

4) Bake 9 to 11 minutes or until golden brown. Meanwhile, in 1-quart saucepan, heat remaining pizza sauce until hot. Serve warm appetizers with warm pizza sauce for dipping.

HIGH ALTITUDE (3500-6500 FT.): No change.

Feta Crescent Triangles

PREP TIME: 20 MINUTES (READY IN 35 MINUTES)
SERVINGS: 24 APPETIZERS

e EASY   **f** LOW FAT

1 cup tomato-basil feta cheese, finely crumbled (4 oz)

2 tablespoons finely chopped green onions

1 egg, well beaten

1 can (8 oz) Pillsbury® refrigerated crescent dinner rolls

1 tablespoon grated Parmesan cheese

1) Heat oven to 375°F. In small bowl, mix feta cheese, green onions and 3 tablespoons of the beaten egg.

2) Do not unroll dough; separate long roll into 2 shorter rolls at center perforations. Unroll 1 roll until 1 rectangle can be separated from roll. Refrigerate remaining dough. Press dough into 7½x5-inch rectangle, pressing diagonal perforations to seal. Cut the rectangle into 6 (2½-inch) squares.

3) Top each dough square with slightly rounded measuring teaspoon feta cheese mixture. Fold dough over filling, forming triangle; press edges to seal. On ungreased cookie sheets, place triangles 2 inches apart. Repeat with remaining 3 dough rectangles and feta cheese mixture.

4) Brush tops with remaining beaten egg. Sprinkle lightly with the Parmesan cheese.

5) Bake 9 to 11 minutes or until golden brown. Serve warm.

HIGH ALTITUDE (3500-6500 FT.): No change.

Nutrition Information Per Serving:		
Calories: 55	From Fat:	25
Total Fat		3g
Saturated Fat		1g
Cholesterol		15mg
Sodium		170mg
Total Carbohydrate		5g
Dietary Fiber		0g
Sugars		2g
Protein		2g

Sausage Snack Wraps

PREP TIME: 15 MINUTES (READY IN 30 MINUTES)
SERVINGS: 48 APPETIZERS

🅔 EASY

2 cans (8 oz each) Pillsbury®
refrigerated crescent dinner rolls

48 fully cooked small smoked sausage
links

Ketchup, if desired

Prepared horseradish, if desired

Yellow mustard, if desired

Nutrition Information Per Serving:		
Calories: 70	From Fat:	45
Total Fat		5g
Saturated Fat		1.5g
Trans Fat		0.5g
Cholesterol		5mg
Sodium		190mg
Total Carbohydrate		4g
Dietary Fiber		0g
Sugars		0g
Protein		2g

1) Heat oven to 375°F.

2) Separate dough into 16 triangles. Cut each triangle into thirds lengthwise. Place sausage on shortest side of each triangle. Roll up, starting at shortest side of triangle and rolling to opposite point. On ungreased cookie sheet, place rolls point side down.

3) Bake 12 to 15 minutes or until golden brown. Serve warm with ketchup, horseradish and mustard.

HIGH ALTITUDE (3500-6500 FT.): No change.

Focaccia Dipping Sticks

PREP TIME: 15 MINUTES (READY IN 35 MINUTES)
SERVINGS: 28 APPETIZERS

🅔 EASY

1 can (13.8 oz) Pillsbury®
refrigerated pizza crust

1 tablespoon extra-virgin olive
oil

1/3 cup red bell pepper strips
(1x1/8 inch)

3 tablespoons thinly slivered
pitted ripe olives

1 tablespoon chopped fresh
rosemary

1/4 teaspoon coarse salt

1 cup tomato pasta sauce, heated

Nutrition Information Per Serving:		
Calories: 80	From Fat:	40
Total Fat		4.5g
Saturated Fat		1.5g
Trans Fat		0g
Cholesterol		15mg
Sodium		170mg
Total Carbohydrate		8g
Dietary Fiber		0g
Sugars		0g
Protein		1g

1) Heat oven to 400°F. Grease cookie sheet with shortening or cooking spray. Unroll dough onto cookie sheet into 14x9-inch rectangle. With fingertips, make indentations over surface of dough.

2) Drizzle oil over dough. Top with remaining ingredients except pasta sauce; press lightly into dough.

3) Bake 13 to 18 minutes or until golden brown. Cut focaccia in half lengthwise; cut each half crosswise into 14 sticks. Serve warm sticks with warm pasta sauce for dipping.

HIGH ALTITUDE (3500-6500 FT.): No change.

Mini Aloha Puff Pizzettes

PREP TIME: 25 MINUTES (READY IN 40 MINUTES)
SERVINGS: 24 APPETIZERS

e EASY

1 can (8 oz) Pillsbury® refrigerated crescent dinner rolls

2 tablespoons thick sweet-and-sour sauce

1 cup finely shredded Swiss cheese (4 oz)

4 oz thinly sliced cooked ham, cut into short thin strips

1 can (8 oz) pineapple tidbits in juice, well drained

1) Heat oven to 375°F. Lightly spray cookie sheet with cooking spray. Unroll dough into 2 long rectangles; press perforations to seal. Cut each rectangle into 12 squares. Place squares on cookie sheet.

2) Top each square with ¼ teaspoon sweet-and-sour sauce. Layer each square with cheese, ham, more cheese and the pineapple.

3) Bake 11 to 12 minutes or until edges are golden brown. Serve warm. Store in refrigerator.

HIGH ALTITUDE (3500-6500 FT.): Bake 12 to 13 minutes.

Nutrition Information Per Serving:

Calories:	70	From Fat:	35
Total Fat			3.5g
Saturated Fat			1.5g
Trans Fat			0.5g
Cholesterol			5mg
Sodium			140mg
Total Carbohydrate			6g
Dietary Fiber			0g
Sugars			2g
Protein			3g

tip You can assemble these tiny pizzas ahead of time. Just cover and refrigerate them for up to 2 hours before baking.

Caesar Chicken and Veggie Appetizer Pizza

PREP TIME: 25 MINUTES (READY IN 1 HOUR 10 MINUTES)
SERVINGS: 32

2   cans (8 oz each) Pillsbury® refrigerated crescent dinner rolls

6   oz cream cheese, softened

½   cup Caesar dressing

1½ cups shredded romaine lettuce

¾   cup coarsely chopped broccoli

½   cup finely chopped cooked chicken

½   cup shredded carrot

2   tablespoons chopped cooked bacon

3   tablespoons shredded Parmesan cheese

1) Heat oven to 375°F. Unroll both cans of the dough; separate into 4 long rectangles. Place rectangles in ungreased 15x10x1-inch pan. Press in bottom and up sides to form crust; firmly press perforations to seal.

2) Bake 13 to 17 minutes or until golden brown. Cool completely, about 30 minutes.

3) In small bowl, mix cream cheese and ¼ cup of the dressing. Spread over cooled crust. Top with lettuce, broccoli, chicken, carrot, bacon and Parmesan cheese. Gently press into cream cheese. Drizzle with remaining ¼ cup dressing.

4) Serve immediately, or cover and refrigerate up to 2 hours before serving. To serve, cut into squares.

HIGH ALTITUDE (3500-6500 FT.): No change.

Nutrition Information Per Serving:

Calories:	100	From Fat:	70
Total Fat			7g
Saturated Fat			2.5g
Trans Fat			1g
Cholesterol			10mg
Sodium			190mg
Total Carbohydrate			6g
Dietary Fiber			0g
Sugars			1g
Protein			3g

Deviled Ham and Eggs

PREP TIME: 15 MINUTES (READY IN 15 MINUTES)
SERVINGS: 12 APPETIZERS

EASY

6 hard-cooked eggs, peeled

1 cup finely chopped cooked ham

¼ cup mayonnaise or salad dressing

2 teaspoons sweet pickle relish

2 teaspoons yellow mustard

1 teaspoon vinegar

1 tablespoon chopped fresh chives

Nutrition Information Per Serving:		
Calories: 90	From Fat:	70
Total Fat		7g
Saturated Fat		1.5g
Trans Fat		0g
Cholesterol		115mg
Sodium		240mg
Total Carbohydrate		0g
Dietary Fiber		0g
Sugars		0g
Protein		6g

1) Cut each egg in half lengthwise. Remove yolks; place in medium bowl. Mash yolks with fork. Stir in remaining ingredients except chives. Spoon yolk mixture into egg-white halves. Sprinkle with chives.

HIGH ALTITUDE (3500-6500 FT.): No change.

Meatball Bubble Biscuits

PREP TIME: 15 MINUTES (READY IN 40 MINUTES)
SERVINGS: 20

EASY

1 can (12 oz) Pillsbury® Golden Layers® refrigerated buttermilk or original flaky biscuits

10 frozen cooked Italian-style meatballs (about 5 oz), thawed, each cut in half

2 sticks (1 oz each) string cheese, each cut into 10 pieces

1 tablespoon grated Parmesan cheese

½ teaspoon Italian seasoning

¼ teaspoon garlic powder

1 cup marinara sauce, heated

Nutrition Information Per Serving:		
Calories: 105	From Fat:	45
Total Fat		5g
Saturated Fat		2g
Cholesterol		10mg
Sodium		330mg
Total Carbohydrate		11g
Dietary Fiber		0g
Sugars		3g
Protein		4g

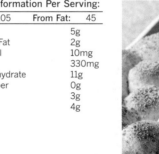

1) Heat oven to 375°F. Separate dough into 10 biscuits. Separate each biscuit into 2 layers. Press each biscuit layer into 3-inch round.

2) Place 1 meatball half, cut side up, and 1 string cheese piece in center of each dough round. Wrap dough around meatball and cheese, pressing edges to seal. In ungreased 8- or 9-inch round cake pan, place seam side down in single layer.

3) Sprinkle evenly with Parmesan cheese, Italian seasoning and garlic powder.

4) Bake 20 to 25 minutes or until golden brown and biscuits are no longer doughy in center. Serve warm biscuits with warm marinara sauce for dipping.

HIGH ALTITUDE (3500-6500 FT.): No change.

tip You can make your own meatballs for this recipe. Use about 1/2 pound of lean ground beef to make the meatballs. Cook and cool them before wrapping them in the dough.

Antipasto Kabobs

PREP TIME: 15 MINUTES (READY IN 2 HOURS 15 MINUTES)
SERVINGS: 20 APPETIZERS

e EASY

½ teaspoon sugar

¼ teaspoon salt

1 clove garlic, chopped

½ cup balsamic vinegar

¼ cup vegetable oil

2 teaspoons Dijon mustard

20 cubes (½ inch each) mozzarella cheese (about 3 oz)

10 cherry or grape tomatoes, each cut in half

20 small pitted ripe olives

Basil leaves, if desired

1) In medium nonmetal bowl or resealable food storage plastic bag, mix sugar, salt, garlic, vinegar, oil and mustard. Add cheese, tomatoes and olives. Cover and refrigerate at least 2 hours to marinate.

2) With slotted spoon or tongs, remove cheese, tomatoes and olives from marinade. On each of 20 decorative toothpicks or bamboo skewers, alternate cheese, tomatoes, olives and basil. Serve immediately or refrigerate until serving time.

HIGH ALTITUDE (3500-6500 FT.): No change.

Nutrition Information Per Serving:

Calories:	45	From Fat:	35
Total Fat		4g	
Saturated Fat		1g	
Trans Fat		0g	
Cholesterol		0mg	
Sodium		100mg	
Total Carbohydrate		1g	
Dietary Fiber		0g	
Sugars		0g	
Protein		1g	

Easy Vegetable Pizza

PREP TIME: 20 MINUTES (READY IN 1 HOUR 10 MINUTES)
SERVINGS: 32

Ⓔ EASY

2 cans (8 oz each) Pillsbury® refrigerated crescent dinner rolls

1 package (8 oz) cream cheese, softened

$\frac{1}{2}$ cup sour cream

1 teaspoon dried dill weed

$\frac{1}{8}$ teaspoon garlic powder

$\frac{1}{2}$ cup small fresh broccoli florets

$\frac{1}{3}$ cup quartered cucumber slices

1 plum (Roma) tomato, seeded, chopped

$\frac{1}{4}$ cup shredded carrot

1) Heat oven to 375°F. Separate cans of dough into 4 long rectangles. In ungreased 15x10x1-inch pan, place dough; press in bottom and up sides to form crust.

2) Bake 13 to 17 minutes or until golden brown. Cool completely, about 30 minutes.

3) In small bowl, mix cream cheese, sour cream, dill and garlic powder until smooth. Spread over crust. Top with vegetables. Serve immediately, or cover and refrigerate 1 to 2 hours before serving. Cut into 16 squares; cut each square in half diagonally.

HIGH ALTITUDE (3500-6500 FT.): No change.

Nutrition Information Per Serving:	
Calories: 90	From Fat: 60
Total Fat	6g
Saturated Fat	3g
Trans Fat	1g
Cholesterol	10mg
Sodium	135mg
Total Carbohydrate	6g
Dietary Fiber	0g
Sugars	1g
Protein	2g

Turkey Club Tortilla Roll-Ups

PREP TIME: 50 MINUTES (READY IN 50 MINUTES)
SERVINGS: 48 APPETIZERS

- ½ cup mayonnaise or salad dressing
- 4 oz cream cheese, softened
- ½ cup chopped drained pepperoncini
- 2 tablespoons chopped fresh cilantro
- 4 slices bacon, crisply cooked, crumbled
- 6 Old El Paso® flour tortillas, 8-inch (from 11.5-oz package)
- ½ cup chopped tomato
- ½ lb thinly sliced cooked turkey
- 6 leaves leaf lettuce

1) In small bowl, mix mayonnaise and cream cheese until smooth. Stir in pepperoncini, cilantro and bacon.

2) Warm tortillas as directed on package.

3) Spread about 2 tablespoons mayonnaise mixture on each tortilla. Top each with 1 rounded tablespoon tomato, 1 slice turkey and 1 lettuce leaf. Roll up each tortilla tightly. Cut each roll into 8 pieces; secure each piece with cocktail toothpick. Serve immediately or cover tightly and refrigerate until serving time.

HIGH ALTITUDE (3500-6500 FT.): No change.

Nutrition Information Per Serving:		
Calories: 50	From Fat:	30
Total Fat		3.5g
Saturated Fat		1g
Trans Fat		0g
Cholesterol		5mg
Sodium		135mg
Total Carbohydrate		3g
Dietary Fiber		0g
Sugars		0g
Protein		2g

Strawberry Spritzer Punch

PREP TIME: 10 MINUTES (READY IN 4 HOURS 10 MINUTES)
SERVINGS: 24 (1/2 CUP EACH)

EASY   LOW FAT

1 bottle (24 oz) white grape juice

2 cans (6 oz each) frozen lemonade concentrate, thawed

2 bags (1 lb each) frozen whole strawberries, partially thawed

2 cans (12 oz each) lemon-lime carbonated beverage (3 cups), chilled

Nutrition Information Per Serving:

Calories: 80	From Fat: 0
Total Fat	0g
Saturated Fat	0g
Trans Fat	0g
Cholesterol	0mg
Sodium	5mg
Total Carbohydrate	20g
Dietary Fiber	0g
Sugars	17g
Protein	0g

1) In blender, place ½ cup of the grape juice, 1 can lemonade and 1 bag strawberries. Cover; blend on high speed until smooth. Pour into 4-quart nonmetal container; repeat. Stir in remaining grape juice.

2) Cover; freeze at least 4 hours, stirring occasionally. Remove container from freezer 30 minutes before serving. Just before serving, stir in carbonated beverage. Garnish as desired.

HIGH ALTITUDE (3500-6500 FT.): No change.

Muffuletta Crescent Pizza

PREP TIME: 20 MINUTES (READY IN 50 MINUTES)
SERVINGS: 24

EASY

1 can (8 oz) Pillsbury® refrigerated crescent dinner rolls

¼ cup chive and onion cream cheese spread

4 oz thinly sliced salami, cut in quarters

⅓ cup thinly sliced red onion

⅓ cup sliced roasted red bell peppers (from a jar)

½ cup chopped ripe olives

1½ cups shredded mozzarella cheese (6 oz)

3 tablespoons Italian dressing

Nutrition Information Per Serving:

Calories: 90	From Fat: 60
Total Fat	6g
Saturated Fat	2.5g
Trans Fat	0.5g
Cholesterol	10mg
Sodium	220mg
Total Carbohydrate	5g
Dietary Fiber	0g
Sugars	1g
Protein	3g

1) Heat oven to 375°F. Unroll dough in ungreased 13x9-inch pan. Press over bottom and ½ inch up sides; firmly press perforations to seal. Bake 10 to 12 minutes or until crust is light golden brown.

2) Remove crust from oven. Spread cream cheese spread over crust; top with remaining ingredients.

3) Return to oven; bake 15 to 18 minutes longer or until edges are golden brown and cheese is melted. To serve, cut into squares.

HIGH ALTITUDE (3500-6500 FT.): No change.

Mushroom-Garlic Cream Tartlets

PREP TIME: 35 MINUTES (READY IN 55 MINUTES)
SERVINGS: 24 APPETIZERS

2 tablespoons butter

1 package (8 oz) fresh whole mushrooms, finely chopped

1 tablespoon finely chopped onion

2 garlic cloves, minced

1 tablespoon all-purpose flour

1/2 cup whipping cream

1/4 cup grated Parmesan cheese

1 can (8 oz) Pillsbury® refrigerated crescent dinner rolls

Fresh thyme sprigs

1) Heat oven to 350°F. In 12-inch skillet, melt butter over medium heat. Cook mushrooms, onion, garlic and flour in butter 5 minutes or until vegetables are tender, stirring frequently. Stir in cream and cheese; cook 2 to 3 minutes or until most of liquid has evaporated, stirring frequently.

2) Unroll dough into 2 long rectangles; firmly press perforations to seal. Cut each rectangle into 12 squares. Place 1 square in each of 24 ungreased miniature muffin cups. Firmly press in bottom and up sides, leaving corners of dough extended over edges of each cup. Spoon 1 heaping teaspoon mushroom mixture into each cup.

3) Bake 9 to 12 minutes or until golden brown. Remove tartlets from oven; sprinkle with thyme. Cool 5 minutes. Remove tartlets from pan. Serve warm. Store in refrigerator.

HIGH ALTITUDE (3500-6500 FT.): Heat oven to 375°F. Bake 12 to 15 minutes.

Nutrition Information Per Serving:

Calories:	70	From Fat:	45
Total Fat		5g	
Saturated Fat		2.5g	
Trans Fat		0.5g	
Cholesterol		10mg	
Sodium		100mg	
Total Carbohydrate		5g	
Dietary Fiber		0g	
Sugars		1g	
Protein		2g	

Asiago Pastry Straws

PREP TIME: 20 MINUTES (READY IN 35 MINUTES)
SERVINGS: 44 APPETIZERS

e EASY   **lf** LOW FAT

- 1 box (15 oz) Pillsbury® refrigerated pie crusts, softened as directed on box
- 2 tablespoons garlic and herb cream cheese (from 8-oz container)
- ¾ teaspoon dried rosemary leaves, crushed
- ¼ cup shredded Asiago cheese

1) Heat oven to 425°F. Remove 1 crust from pouch; place on work surface. Spread crust evenly with cream cheese; sprinkle with rosemary and cheese. Remove remaining crust from pouch; place over filling. Press firmly over entire crust.

2) Cut into 24 (½-inch) strips. Cut middle 20 strips in half; leave 2 uncut strips on each side. Twist each strip 4 to 5 times; place 1 inch apart on ungreased cookie sheets, pressing ends to secure.

3) Bake 9 to 11 minutes or until golden brown. Serve warm or cool.

HIGH ALTITUDE (3500-6500 FT.): No change.

Nutrition Information Per Serving:		
Calories: 45	From Fat:	25
Total Fat		3g
Saturated Fat		1g
Trans Fat		0g
Cholesterol		0mg
Sodium		50mg
Total Carbohydrate		5g
Dietary Fiber		0g
Sugars		0g
Protein		0g

Using fresh chives, tie a few pastry straws into a bundle, and garnish with rosemary sprigs and currants.

Crab Puffs

PREP TIME: 25 MINUTES (READY IN 45 MINUTES)
SERVINGS: 24 APPETIZERS

1 tablespoon butter or margarine, melted

$1/2$ teaspoon garlic powder

1 can (8 oz) Pillsbury® refrigerated crescent dinner rolls

1 egg

$1/2$ cup mayonnaise

1 can (6 oz) crabmeat, drained, flaked

$3/4$ cup shredded sharp Cheddar cheese

$1/3$ cup finely chopped plum (Roma) tomato (1 medium)

3 tablespoons finely chopped green onions (3 medium)

1 teaspoon hot pepper sauce

Nutrition Information Per Serving:		
Calories: 100	From Fat:	70
Total Fat		8g
Saturated Fat		2.5g
Trans Fat		0.5g
Cholesterol		20mg
Sodium		150mg
Total Carbohydrate		4g
Dietary Fiber		0g
Sugars		0g
Protein		3g

1) Heat oven to 375°F. In small bowl, mix butter and garlic powder; set aside. On lightly floured surface, unroll dough; firmly press perforations to seal. Press into 12x8 inch rectangle. Cut into 2-inch squares; place on ungreased cookie sheet. Brush with butter mixture. Bake 4 to 6 minutes or until puffed.

2) Meanwhile, in medium bowl, mix egg and mayonnaise until well blended. Stir in crabmeat, cheese, tomato, onions and hot pepper sauce.

3) Remove baked squares from oven. Spoon generous tablespoon crab mixture on each square. Return to oven; bake 10 to 12 minutes longer or until golden brown and tops are set. Serve warm.

HIGH ALTITUDE (3500-6500 FT.): Heat oven to 350°F. Decrease mayonnaise to 1/3 cup. Bake 11 to 13 minutes.

Pea Pod Wrap-Ups

PREP TIME: 1 HOUR 20 MINUTES (READY IN 1 HOUR 20 MINUTES)
SERVINGS: 35 APPETIZERS

🅔 EASY   🅕 LOW FAT

1 lb cooked deveined peeled large shrimp (about 35)

1 cup (8 oz) Asian ginger dressing

6 oz fresh snow pea pods (about 35)

Toothpicks or appetizer picks

Nutrition Information Per Serving:		
Calories: 35	From Fat:	20
Total Fat		2g
Saturated Fat		0g
Trans Fat		0g
Cholesterol		25mg
Sodium		60mg
Total Carbohydrate		1g
Dietary Fiber		0g
Sugars		1g
Protein		3g

1) In medium bowl, place shrimp. Pour dressing evenly over shrimp; stir to coat. Cover; refrigerate 1 hour. Meanwhile, remove stem and strings from pea pods. To partially cook pea pods, place in boiling water about 1 minute or until pea pods turn bright green. Drain; rinse with cold water and dry with paper towels.

2) Drain dressing from shrimp. Wrap 1 pea pod around each shrimp; secure with toothpick. Cover; refrigerate until serving time.

HIGH ALTITUDE (3500-6500 FT.): No change.

Mini Soft Pretzels and Dip

PREP TIME: 20 MINUTES (READY IN 30 MINUTES)
SERVINGS: 24

e EASY   **f** LOW FAT

1 can (11 oz) Pillsbury® refrigerated
  original breadsticks

1 egg, beaten

  Coarse salt, if desired

1 jar (5 oz) sharp process cheese
  spread with bacon

2 tablespoons milk

Nutrition Information Per Serving:

Calories: 55	From Fat: 20
Total Fat	2g
Saturated Fat	1g
Cholesterol	15mg
Sodium	180mg
Total Carbohydrate	7g
Dietary Fiber	0g
Sugars	1g
Protein	2g

1) Heat oven to 375°F. Unroll
   dough; separate into 12
   breadsticks. Cut each
   in half lengthwise. Roll
   each breadstick lightly to
   form 10-inch-long rope.

2) To shape each pretzel,
   shape rope into a circle,
   overlapping dough about
   2 inches from each end,
   leaving ends free. Take
   1 end in each hand; twist
   once at point where dough overlaps. Lift ends over opposite side of circle.
   On ungreased cookie sheet, place pretzels 1 inch apart. Brush each pretzel
   with beaten egg. Sprinkle with salt.

3) Bake 13 to 15 minutes or until golden brown.

4) Meanwhile, in small microwavable bowl, mix cheese spread and milk.
   Microwave uncovered on High 1 minute, stirring after 30 seconds, until
   melted and hot.

5) Serve warm pretzels with warm cheese dip.

HIGH ALTITUDE (3500-6500 FT.): No change.

Party Snack Mix

PREP TIME: 10 MINUTES (READY IN 1 HOUR 20 MINUTES)
SERVINGS: 24

e EASY

4 cups Corn Chex® cereal

2 cups Wheat Chex® cereal

2 cups small pretzel sticks

2 cups Spanish peanuts or mixed nuts

½ cup butter or margarine, melted

1 tablespoon Worcestershire sauce

⅛ teaspoon hot pepper sauce

1 teaspoon salt

¼ teaspoon garlic powder

Nutrition Information Per Serving:

Calories: 160	From Fat: 90
Total Fat	10g
Saturated Fat	3.5g
Trans Fat	0g
Cholesterol	10mg
Sodium	320mg
Total Carbohydrate	12g
Dietary Fiber	2g
Sugars	2g
Protein	5g

1) Heat oven to 325°F. In large bowl, mix cereals, pretzel sticks and peanuts.

2) In small bowl, mix butter, Worcestershire sauce, hot pepper sauce, salt and
   garlic powder. Pour over cereal mixture; toss to coat. Spread in ungreased
   15x10x1-inch pan.

3) Bake 25 to 30 minutes or until lightly toasted, stirring occasionally. Cool
   30 minutes. Store in tightly covered container.

HIGH ALTITUDE (3500-6500 FT.): Decrease melted butter to 1/3 cup.

Snappy Cheddar Dip

PREP TIME: 10 MINUTES (READY IN 10 MINUTES)
SERVINGS: 21 (1 TABLESPOON DIP AND 2 APPLE SLICES EACH)

ⓔ EASY

1 jar (5 oz) sharp process
   cheese spread

1 cup finely shredded Cheddar
   cheese (4 oz)

¼ cup chive and onion cream cheese
   (from 8-oz container)

2 tablespoons milk

2 teaspoons Worcestershire sauce

1 teaspoon Dijon mustard

   Fresh chives, chopped, if desired

   Apple slices, celery sticks and/or
   assorted crackers

1) In food processor, place all ingredients
   except chives and apples; process 15 to
   20 seconds or until smooth. If desired,
   dip can be refrigerated 1 hour before
   serving. Sprinkle with chives. Serve dip
   with apples, celery and/or crackers.
   Refrigerate any remaining dip.

HIGH ALTITUDE (3500-6500 FT.): No change.

Nutrition Information Per Serving:

Calories:	60	From Fat:	35
Total Fat			4g
Saturated Fat			2.5g
Trans Fat			0g
Cholesterol			15mg
Sodium			180mg
Total Carbohydrate			4g
Dietary Fiber			0g
Sugars			3g
Protein			2g

Mini Tostadas

PREP TIME: 20 MINUTES (READY IN 35 MINUTES)
SERVINGS: 40 APPETIZERS

e EASY **f** LOW FAT

1 package (11.5 oz) Old El Paso® flour tortillas for burritos (8 tortillas)

Cooking spray

1 can (16 oz) Old El Paso® refried beans

8 medium green onions, sliced (1/2 cup)

2 cups finely shredded Mexican cheese blend (8 oz)

2/3 cup sour cream

Nutrition Information Per Serving:

Calories:	50	From Fat:	25
Total Fat			3g
Saturated Fat			1.5g
Trans Fat			0g
Cholesterol			10mg
Sodium			110mg
Total Carbohydrate			4g
Dietary Fiber			0g
Sugars			0g
Protein			2g

1) Place oven rack in lowest rack position; heat oven to 400°F. Spray one side of each tortilla with cooking spray. With 2½-inch round cutter, cut 5 rounds from each tortilla (if desired, stack 2 tortillas to cut).

2) On ungreased large cookie sheets, place tortilla rounds with sprayed sides down. Spread each round with beans. Set aside 1 tablespoon of the onions. Sprinkle rounds with remaining onions and cheese.

3) Bake on lowest oven rack 11 to 13 minutes or until bottoms are crisp and cheese is melted and bubbly. Top each with about 1 teaspoon sour cream and some of the reserved onions.

HIGH ALTITUDE (3500-6500 FT.): Bake on lowest oven rack 9 to 11 minutes.

Buffalo Chicken Pinwheels

PREP TIME: 20 MINUTES (READY IN 35 MINUTES)
SERVINGS: 24 APPETIZERS

e EASY

1 can (8 oz) Pillsbury® refrigerated crescent dinner rolls

1/2 cup finely chopped cooked chicken

3/4 teaspoon hot pepper sauce

2 oz cream cheese, softened

1/4 cup crumbled blue cheese (1 oz)

2 tablespoons chopped fresh chives

Nutrition Information Per Serving:

Calories:	50	From Fat:	30
Total Fat			3.5g
Saturated Fat			1.5g
Trans Fat			0.5g
Cholesterol			5mg
Sodium			100mg
Total Carbohydrate			4g
Dietary Fiber			0g
Sugars			0g
Protein			2g

1) Heat oven to 350°F. Spray cookie sheet with cooking spray. Unroll dough and separate into 4 rectangles; firmly press perforations to seal.

2) In small bowl, mix chicken and hot pepper sauce until well coated. Spread 1 tablespoon cream cheese over each rectangle to within ¼ inch of edges. Sprinkle evenly with chicken, blue cheese and chives.

3) Starting with one short side, roll up each rectangle; press edges to seal. With serrated knife, cut each roll into 6 slices; place cut side down on cookie sheet.

4) Bake 13 to 17 minutes or until edges are golden brown. Serve warm.

HIGH ALTITUDE (3500-6500 FT.): No change.

Baked Artichoke Squares

PREP TIME: 15 MINUTES (READY IN 35 MINUTES)
SERVINGS: 60 APPETIZERS

 EASY

2 cans (8 oz each) Pillsbury® refrigerated crescent dinner rolls

1 can (14 oz) artichoke hearts, drained, chopped

1 box (9 oz) Green Giant® frozen spinach, thawed, squeezed to drain

¾ cup grated Parmesan cheese

⅔ cup mayonnaise

⅔ cup sour cream

⅛ teaspoon garlic powder

1) Heat oven to 375°F. Unroll dough into 4 long rectangles. Place crosswise in ungreased 15x10x1-inch pan; press over bottom and 1 inch up sides to form crust. Press perforations to seal.

2) Bake 10 to 12 minutes or until light golden brown.

3) Meanwhile, in medium bowl, mix all remaining ingredients. Spread evenly over partially baked crust.

4) Bake 8 to 10 minutes longer or until topping is thoroughly heated. Cut into 1½-inch squares. Serve warm.

HIGH ALTITUDE (3500-6500 FT.): Bake 12 to 14 minutes.

Nutrition Information Per Serving:		
Calories: 60	From Fat:	40
Total Fat		4.5g
Saturated Fat		1.5g
Trans Fat		0g
Cholesterol		0mg
Sodium		115mg
Total Carbohydrate		4g
Dietary Fiber		0g
Sugars		0g
Protein		1g

Spicy Mexican Quiche Cups

PREP TIME: 30 MINUTES (READY IN 50 MINUTES)
SERVINGS: 22 APPETIZERS

½ lb bulk hot Italian sausage

6 eggs

6 tablespoons Old El Paso® Thick 'n Chunky salsa

½ cup shredded Cheddar cheese (2 oz)

½ cup shredded mozzarella cheese (2 oz)

½ cup chopped jalapeño chiles, seeds removed

1 box (15 oz) Pillsbury® refrigerated pie crusts, softened as directed on box

1) Heat oven to 425°F. In 8-inch skillet, cook sausage over medium heat, stirring frequently, until no longer pink; drain. Cool 10 minutes.

2) In medium bowl, beat eggs thoroughly. Stir in salsa; set aside. In another medium bowl, mix cheeses and chiles. Stir in cooled cooked sausage; set aside.

3) Remove pie crusts from pouches; unroll crusts on work surface. With rolling pin, roll each crust lightly into 12-inch round. With 3½-inch round cutter, cut 22 rounds from crusts, rerolling scraps as necessary. In 22 ungreased regular-size muffin cups or fluted tartlet pans, press rounds in bottoms and up sides.

4) Spoon 1 heaping tablespoon cheese mixture into each crust-lined cup. Top each with about 1 tablespoon egg mixture; divide any remaining egg mixture among cups.

5) Bake 14 to 18 minutes or until filling is set. Serve warm.

HIGH ALTITUDE (3500-6500 FT.): No change.

Nutrition Information Per Serving:		
Calories: 150	From Fat:	90
Total Fat		10g
Saturated Fat		4g
Cholesterol		70mg
Sodium		220mg
Total Carbohydrate		10g
Dietary Fiber		0g
Sugars		1g
Protein		5g

Holiday Appetizer Pizza

PREP TIME: 25 MINUTES (READY IN 1 HOUR 10 MINUTES)
SERVINGS: 32

1) Heat oven to 375°F. Unroll both cans of the dough; separate into 4 long rectangles. Place rectangles in ungreased 15x10x1-inch pan. Press in bottom and up sides to form crust; firmly press perforations to seal.

2) Bake 13 to 17 minutes or until golden brown. Cool completely, about 30 minutes.

3) In small bowl, mix cream cheese and ¼ cup of the dressing. Spread over cooled crust. Top with spinach, apple, chicken, walnuts, bacon and Parmesan cheese. Gently press into cream cheese. Drizzle with remaining ¼ cup dressing.

4) Serve immediately, or cover and refrigerate up to 2 hours before serving. To serve, cut into squares.

HIGH ALTITUDE (3500-6500 FT.): No change.

2 cans (8 oz each) Pillsbury® refrigerated crescent dinner rolls

6 oz cream cheese, softened

½ cup Caesar dressing

1½ cups shredded spinach

¾ cup chopped, unpeeled red apple

½ cup finely chopped cooked chicken

½ cup chopped walnuts

2 tablespoons chopped cooked bacon

3 tablespoons shredded Parmesan cheese

Served alongside bowls of steaming soup, large slices of either of the two pizzas on this page make great main courses for casual suppers at home.

Ranch Veggie Appetizer Pizza

PREP TIME: 25 MINUTES (READY IN 1 HOUR 10 MINUTES)
SERVINGS: 32

2 cans (8 oz each) Pillsbury® refrigerated crescent dinner rolls

6 oz cream cheese, softened

½ cup ranch dressing

1½ cups shredded romaine lettuce

¾ cup chopped yellow or orange bell pepper

½ cup finely chopped cooked chicken

½ cup chopped plum (Roma) tomatoes

2 tablespoons chopped cooked bacon

3 tablespoons shredded Parmesan cheese

1) Heat oven to 375°F. Unroll both cans of the dough; separate into 4 long rectangles. Place rectangles in ungreased 15x10x1-inch pan. Press in bottom and up sides to form crust; firmly press perforations to seal.

2) Bake 13 to 17 minutes or until golden brown. Cool completely, about 30 minutes.

3) In small bowl, mix cream cheese and ¼ cup of the dressing. Spread over cooled crust. Top with lettuce, bell pepper, chicken, tomatoes, bacon and Parmesan cheese. Gently press into cream cheese. Drizzle with remaining ¼ cup dressing.

4) Serve immediately, or cover and refrigerate up to 2 hours before serving. To serve, cut into squares.

HIGH ALTITUDE (3500-6500 FT.): No change.

LAYERED HAM SALAD
PG. 100

Refreshing Salads

Nothing brightens up mealtime like a colorful salad!
Add any of these fresh favorites to your menu.

MARINATED GARDEN
TORTELLINI SALAD
PG. 97

COBB SALAD WITH
CUCUMBER-RANCH DRESSING
PG. 98

GINGERED FRESH FRUIT SALAD
PG. 101

Fresh Fruit Salad with Poppy Seed Dressing

PREP TIME: 15 MINUTES (READY IN 15 MINUTES)
SERVINGS: 8

 EASY

DRESSING

- ¹/₂ cup honey
- ¹/₄ cup frozen limeade concentrate, thawed
- ¹/₄ cup vegetable oil
- 1 teaspoon grated orange peel
- ¹/₂ teaspoon poppy seed
- ¹/₄ teaspoon ground mustard

SALAD

- 2 cups fresh blueberries
- 4 medium peaches, peeled, sliced
- 4 medium oranges, peeled, sliced
- 4 kiwifruit, peeled, sliced

1) In small bowl, mix dressing ingredients with wire whisk until well blended.

2) Arrange salad ingredients in individual salad bowls. Serve with dressing.

HIGH ALTITUDE (3500-6500 FT.): No change.

Nutrition Information Per Serving:

Calories:	270	From Fat:	70
Total Fat			8g
Saturated Fat			1g
Trans Fat			0g
Cholesterol			0mg
Sodium			0mg
Total Carbohydrate			49g
Dietary Fiber			5g
Sugars			39g
Protein			2g

tip If fresh peaches are not available, use frozen peaches and thaw them. Feel free to add sliced bananas and a sprinkling of slivered almonds as well.

Apple-Cranberry Salad

PREP TIME: 15 MINUTES (READY IN 15 MINUTES)
SERVINGS: 6

 EASY

- 5 cups torn romaine lettuce
- 1 medium unpeeled apple, diced (1 cup)
- 1/2 cup sweetened dried cranberries
- 1/4 cup chopped green onions (4 medium)
- 1/3 cup refrigerated poppy seed dressing

1) In large serving bowl, place lettuce, apple, cranberries and green onions.

2) Pour dressing over salad; toss to coat.

HIGH ALTITUDE (3500-6500 FT.): No change.

Nutrition Information Per Serving:

Calories: 120	From Fat: 50
Total Fat	6g
Saturated Fat	0.5g
Trans Fat	0g
Cholesterol	5mg
Sodium	140mg
Total Carbohydrate	17g
Dietary Fiber	2g
Sugars	15g
Protein	0g

tip Look for refrigerated poppy seed dressing in the produce section of your grocery store.

Layered Mexican Chicken Salad

PREP TIME: 30 MINUTES (READY IN 30 MINUTES)
SERVINGS: 4

 EASY

- 3/4 cup ranch dressing
- 1 teaspoon Old El Paso® 40% less sodium taco seasoning mix
- 4 cups shredded lettuce
- 1 can (15 oz) red kidney beans, drained, rinsed
- 1 1/2 cups shredded deli rotisserie chicken (without skin)
- 1 cup coarsely crushed hint-of-lime white corn tortilla chips (from 13 1/2-oz package)
- 1 cup shredded Mexican-style taco cheese (4 oz)
- 1/2 cup grape or cherry tomatoes, halved

1) In small bowl, mix dressing and taco seasoning mix.

2) On large serving platter or individual serving plates, layer remaining ingredients except tomatoes. Drizzle with dressing. Sprinkle with tomatoes.

HIGH ALTITUDE (3500-6500 FT.): No change.

Nutrition Information Per Serving:

Calories: 660	From Fat: 370
Total Fat	41g
Saturated Fat	11g
Trans Fat	0g
Cholesterol	90mg
Sodium	960mg
Total Carbohydrate	39g
Dietary Fiber	8g
Sugars	4g
Protein	32g

Summer Antipasto Salad with Balsamic Vinaigrette

PREP TIME: 30 MINUTES (READY IN 30 MINUTES)
SERVINGS: 12

📧 EASY

VINAIGRETTE

- ¹/₂ cup balsamic vinegar
- ¹/₂ cup olive oil
- ¹/₄ cup chopped fresh parsley
- 2 teaspoons sugar
- ¹/₂ teaspoon salt

SALAD

- 4 cups shredded romaine lettuce
- 8 oz sliced cooked chicken or turkey, cut into bite-sized strips
- 8 oz sliced salami or summer sausage, cut in half
- 4 oz sliced mozzarella cheese, cut into bite-sized strips
- 4 cups fresh cauliflower florets
- 2 small cucumbers, sliced
- 2 medium tomatoes, each cut in half and sliced, if desired
- 2 medium yellow, red or green bell peppers, coarsely chopped (2 cups)

1) In small bowl, mix all vinaigrette ingredients.

2) Arrange lettuce on large serving platter. Arrange chicken, salami, cheese, cauliflower, cucumbers, tomatoes and bell peppers over lettuce. Drizzle vinaigrette over salad.

HIGH ALTITUDE (3500-6500 FT.): No change.

Nutrition Information Per Serving:

Calories:	230	From Fat:	150
Total Fat			16g
Saturated Fat			4g
Trans Fat			0g
Cholesterol			35mg
Sodium			380mg
Total Carbohydrate			8g
Dietary Fiber			2g
Sugars			5g
Protein			12g

tip If desired, partially cook the cauliflower in boiling water for 2 to 3 minutes. Drain and rinse it under cold water.

Easy Asian Cabbage Salad

PREP TIME: 20 MINUTES (READY IN 20 MINUTES)
SERVINGS: 8

📧 EASY

- 1 package (3 oz) oriental-flavor ramen noodle soup mix
- 4 cups coleslaw mix (from 16 oz bag)
- 1 cup shredded carrots (1¹/₂ medium)
- ¹/₃ cup chopped fresh cilantro
- 5 green onions, sliced (¹/₃ cup)
- ²/₃ cup Asian sesame with ginger dressing
- ¹/₂ cup chopped peanuts

Nutrition Information Per Serving:

Calories:	170	From Fat:	110
Total Fat			12g
Saturated Fat			2g
Trans Fat			0g
Cholesterol			0mg
Sodium			300mg
Total Carbohydrate			11g
Dietary Fiber			2g
Sugars			4g
Protein			4g

1) In large bowl, place noodles from soup mix; break into small pieces. Discard seasoning packet or reserve for another use.

2) Add coleslaw mix, carrots, cilantro, onions and dressing; toss to mix. Sprinkle with peanuts.

HIGH ALTITUDE (3500-6500 FT.): No change.

Garden Vegetable and Ham Salad

PREP TIME: 30 MINUTES (READY IN 30 MINUTES)
SERVINGS: 8

e EASY

SALAD

4 cups uncooked small pasta shells (14 oz)

2 cups chopped cooked ham

2 cups chopped unpeeled cucumbers

1 cup finely chopped carrots

1/2 cup chopped red bell pepper

1/2 cup finely chopped green onions (8 medium)

DRESSING

1 1/2 cups mayonnaise or salad dressing

1/2 cup milk

1/4 cup Dijon mustard

2 tablespoons chopped fresh dill

1/4 to 1/2 teaspoon salt

1) Cook pasta as directed on package. Drain; rinse with cold water to cool. Drain well.

2) Meanwhile, in large bowl, mix remaining salad ingredients. In small bowl, mix all dressing ingredients until well blended.

3) Add cooked pasta to salad. Pour dressing over salad; toss to coat. Serve immediately, or cover and refrigerate until serving time.

HIGH ALTITUDE (3500-6500 FT.): No change.

Nutrition Information Per Serving:	
Calories: 570	From Fat: 320
Total Fat	36g
Saturated Fat	6g
Trans Fat	0g
Cholesterol	35mg
Sodium	1150mg
Total Carbohydrate	46g
Dietary Fiber	4g
Sugars	5g
Protein	16g

tip

The secret to evenly cooked pasta that doesn't stick together is a large pot of continuously boiling water. Use a pot large enough for the pasta to move around freely, and keep the water at a constant boil.

Chicken, Spring Vegetable and Pasta Salad

PREP TIME: 25 MINUTES (READY IN 25 MINUTES)
SERVINGS: 4 (1-1/2 CUPS EACH)

e EASY

SALAD

2 cups uncooked penne or mostaccioli pasta (7 oz)

8 oz fresh asparagus spears, trimmed, cut into 1-inch pieces

1^1/$_3$ cups ready-to-eat baby-cut carrots (about 6 oz), quartered lengthwise

^{1}/$_2$ cup Green Giant Select® LeSueur® frozen baby sweet peas (from 1-lb bag)

2 cups cubed cooked chicken

DRESSING

1 container (6 oz) Yoplait® Original 99% Fat Free lemon burst yogurt

^{1}/$_4$ cup mayonnaise or salad dressing

2 tablespoons chopped fresh chives

^{1}/$_4$ teaspoon salt

^{1}/$_8$ teaspoon pepper

1 clove garlic, minced

1) Cook pasta as directed on package, adding asparagus, carrots and peas during last 5 to 7 minutes of cooking time; cook until asparagus is crisp-tender. Drain; rinse with cold water to cool. Drain well.

2) In large bowl, mix cooked pasta with vegetables and chicken.

3) In small bowl, mix dressing ingredients until well blended. Pour over salad; toss gently to coat. Serve immediately, or cover and refrigerate until serving time. If desired, garnish with additional chives.

HIGH ALTITUDE (3500-6500 FT.): No change.

Nutrition Information Per Serving:		
Calories: 510	From Fat:	160
Total Fat		18g
Saturated Fat		3.5g
Trans Fat		0g
Cholesterol		70mg
Sodium		530mg
Total Carbohydrate		56g
Dietary Fiber		6g
Sugars		12g
Protein		31g

Apple-Almond Tossed Salad

PREP TIME: 10 MINUTES (READY IN 10 MINUTES)
SERVINGS: 12

e EASY   (f) LOW FAT

4 cups torn romaine lettuce

¼ cup diced dried apricots

¼ cup butter toffee-glazed sliced almonds

1 red-skinned apple, unpeeled, cored and cubed

4 green onions, sliced (¼ cup)

¼ cup orange marmalade

2 tablespoons olive oil

1 tablespoon lemon juice

Nutrition Information Per Serving:		
Calories: 80	From Fat:	30
Total Fat		3g
Saturated Fat		0g
Trans Fat		0g
Cholesterol		0mg
Sodium		5mg
Total Carbohydrate		12g
Dietary Fiber		1g
Sugars		9g
Protein		0g

1) In large bowl, mix lettuce, apricots, almonds, apple and onions.

2) In small bowl, mix marmalade, oil and lemon juice until well blended. Drizzle over salad; toss to mix.

HIGH ALTITUDE (3500-6500 FT.): No change.

Lemon Dream Fruit Salad

PREP TIME: 10 MINUTES (READY IN 10 MINUTES)
SERVINGS: 6

e EASY   (f) LOW FAT

1 can (11 oz) mandarin orange segments, drained

1 can (8 oz) pineapple chunks in juice, drained

2 bananas, halved lengthwise, cut into 1-inch chunks

¼ cup halved maraschino cherries, drained

1 container (6 oz) Yoplait® Thick and Creamy Lowfat lemon supreme yogurt

1) In medium bowl, mix all ingredients. Serve immediately or refrigerate until serving time.

HIGH ALTITUDE (3500-6500 FT.): No change.

Nutrition Information Per Serving:		
Calories: 110	From Fat:	5
Total Fat		0.5g
Saturated Fat		0g
Trans Fat		0g
Cholesterol		0mg
Sodium		20mg
Total Carbohydrate		27g
Dietary Fiber		2g
Sugars		20g
Protein		2g

Marinated Bean and Vegetable Salad

PREP TIME: 10 MINUTES (READY IN 2 HOURS 10 MINUTES)
SERVINGS: 6

e EASY   **lf** LOW FAT

2 cups Green Giant Select® frozen broccoli, carrots & cauliflower (from 1-lb bag)

1 can (15 oz) Green Giant® three bean salad, undrained

1 jar (4.5 oz) Green Giant® whole mushrooms, drained

1/2 teaspoon celery seed

Nutrition Information Per Serving:

Calories: 60	From Fat: 0
Total Fat	0g
Saturated Fat	0g
Trans Fat	0g
Cholesterol	0mg
Sodium	360mg
Total Carbohydrate	12g
Dietary Fiber	3g
Sugars	3g
Protein	3g

1) Cook vegetables as directed on bag for 6 minutes or until crisp-tender. Drain; rinse with cold water until cool.

2) In medium bowl, mix cooked vegetables and all remaining ingredients. Cover; refrigerate at least 2 hours to blend flavors.

HIGH ALTITUDE (3500-6500 FT.): No change.

Garden Salad with Herbed Vinaigrette

PREP TIME: 15 MINUTES (READY IN 15 MINUTES)
SERVINGS: 4

e EASY

SALAD

4 cups torn leaf lettuce

1 cup sliced fresh mushrooms

1/2 cup sliced radishes

1 large tomato, chopped

VINAIGRETTE

2 tablespoons chopped fresh basil

1 tablespoon chopped fresh chives

2 teaspoons sugar

1/2 teaspoon dry mustard

1/4 teaspoon salt

1/4 teaspoon pepper

3 tablespoons tarragon or white wine vinegar

2 tablespoons extra-virgin olive oil

Nutrition Information Per Serving:

Calories: 100	From Fat: 60
Total Fat	7g
Saturated Fat	1g
Trans Fat	0g
Cholesterol	0mg
Sodium	170mg
Total Carbohydrate	7g
Dietary Fiber	2g
Sugars	4g
Protein	2g

1) In large bowl, combine all salad ingredients.

2) In small bowl or jar with tight-fitting lid, combine all dressing ingredients; blend or shake until sugar is dissolved. Add dressing to salad; toss gently to coat.

HIGH ALTITUDE (3500-6500 FT.): No change.

tip

For even faster preparation, consider using prepackaged torn lettuce and pre-sliced mushrooms. Both items are available in the produce department.

Lemon-Mint Chicken Salad

PREP TIME: 30 MINUTES (READY IN 3 HOURS 30 MINUTES)
SERVINGS: 24
 LOW FAT

SALAD

1 package (16 oz) uncooked bow-tie (farfalle) pasta

7 cups cubed cooked chicken

5 cups cubed cantaloupe

3 cups thinly sliced celery

2 cups dried cherries

1 cup sliced green onions

DRESSING

2 containers (8 oz each) low-fat lemon yogurt

1/2 cup reduced-calorie mayonnaise or salad dressing

1 to 2 tablespoons chopped fresh mint

1 tablespoon grated lemon peel

1 1/2 teaspoons salt

1/2 teaspoon pepper

GARNISH

1/4 cup sliced almonds, toasted

1) Cook pasta as directed on package to desired doneness. Drain; rinse with cold water. In very large bowl, mix pasta and remaining salad ingredients.

2) In medium bowl, mix dressing ingredients. Add dressing to salad; mix well. Cover; refrigerate 3 hours to blend flavors. Just before serving, sprinkle with almonds.

HIGH ALTITUDE (3500-6500 FT.): No change.

Nutrition Information Per Serving:

Calories: 240	From Fat:	50
Total Fat		6g
Saturated Fat		1.5g
Trans Fat		0g
Cholesterol		40mg
Sodium		320mg
Total Carbohydrate		31g
Dietary Fiber		2g
Sugars		12g
Protein		16g

tip

To toast almonds, heat oven to 350°F. Spread evenly in ungreased shallow pan. Bake uncovered 3 to 5 minutes, stirring occasionally, until light brown.

Chicken Alfredo Pasta Salad

PREP TIME:	30 MINUTES (READY IN 30 MINUTES)	
SERVINGS:	4	EASY

1 box (7.75 oz) classic pasta salad mix

1/2 cup refrigerated Alfredo sauce

1 1/2 cups shredded deli rotisserie chicken (without skin)

1 cup halved grape or cherry tomatoes

1 cup halved sliced cucumber

2 tablespoons sliced fresh basil leaves

1) In 3-quart saucepan, cook pasta as directed on box. Drain; rinse with cold water to cool.

2) In small bowl mix seasoning mix from packet and Alfredo sauce. Place cooked pasta, chicken, tomatoes, cucumber and basil in serving bowl. Add Alfredo mixture; toss to evenly coat. Sprinkle with topping from packet and basil sprig, if desired. Serve immediately or refrigerate until serving time.

HIGH ALTITUDE (3500-6500 FT.): No change.

Nutrition Information Per Serving:

Calories:	390	From Fat:	130
Total Fat			15g
Saturated Fat			7g
Trans Fat			0.5g
Cholesterol			75mg
Sodium			1230mg
Total Carbohydrate			42g
Dietary Fiber			3g
Sugars			7g
Protein			23g

Island Paradise Salad

Pillsbury Bake-Off

JUDITH METTLIN | SNYDER, NEW YORK   BAKE-OFF® CONTEST 39, 2000 | PRIZE WINNER

PREP TIME:	25 MINUTES (READY IN 25 MINUTES)	
SERVINGS:	8 (1-1/4 CUPS EACH)	EASY

DRESSING

1 teaspoon grated lime peel

3 tablespoons honey

2 tablespoons fresh lime juice

1 tablespoon canola or vegetable oil

SALAD

2 cups frozen sugar snap peas (from 1-lb bag)

3 cups torn romaine lettuce

3 cups torn Bibb lettuce

1 avocado, peeled, pitted and cut into 1/2-inch cubes

1 large ripe mango, peeled, seed removed and cut into 1/2-inch cubes

1 small red onion, thinly sliced, separated into rings

1/2 cup shredded coconut

1) In small bowl, mix dressing ingredients.

2) Cook sugar snap peas as directed on bag; drain. Rinse with cold water to cool. Drain well.

3) In large bowl, mix sugar snap peas and remaining salad ingredients except coconut. Add dressing; toss to coat. Sprinkle with coconut.

HIGH ALTITUDE (3500-6500 FT.): No change.

Nutrition Information Per Serving:

Calories:	160	From Fat:	70
Total Fat			7g
Saturated Fat			2.5g
Trans Fat			0g
Cholesterol			0mg
Sodium			25mg
Total Carbohydrate			21g
Dietary Fiber			4g
Sugars			14g
Protein			2g

Creamy Marinated Potato Salad

PREP TIME: 40 MINUTES (READY IN 1 HOUR)
SERVINGS: 12

SALAD

1⅓ lb small red potatoes
    (8 to 12 potatoes)

3 tablespoons cider vinegar

½ teaspoon salt

4 eggs

8 medium green onions,
    sliced (½ cup)

1 medium stalk celery,
    sliced (½ cup)

1 small red bell pepper,
    coarsely chopped

DRESSING

¾ cup mayonnaise or
    salad dressing

¼ cup sour cream

1 teaspoon sugar

2 teaspoons prepared
    horseradish

2 teaspoons yellow mustard

¼ teaspoon coarse ground
    black pepper

1) In 4-quart saucepan or Dutch oven, place potatoes; add enough water to cover. Heat to boiling. Cook about 20 minutes or until tender. Drain; cool slightly. Cut into 1-inch cubes. Place in large nonmetal bowl. Sprinkle with vinegar and salt; toss to coat. Let stand 30 minutes.

2) Meanwhile, in 2-quart saucepan, place eggs in single layer. Add enough water to cover eggs by 1 inch. Heat to boiling. Immediately remove from heat; cover and let stand 15 minutes. Drain; rinse with cold water. Place eggs in bowl of ice water; let stand 10 minutes. Drain.

3) Peel and chop eggs. Add to potatoes with remaining salad ingredients; mix gently.

4) In small bowl, mix dressing ingredients. Pour over salad; mix gently to coat. If desired, garnish with additional sliced green onions.

HIGH ALTITUDE (3500-6500 FT.): In Step 2, heat eggs to boiling and boil 5 minutes; remove from heat. Cover and let stand 15 minutes.

Nutrition Information Per Serving:

Calories:	180	From Fat:	120
Total Fat			14g
Saturated Fat			3g
Trans Fat			0g
Cholesterol			80mg
Sodium			220mg
Total Carbohydrate			11g
Dietary Fiber			1g
Sugars			2g
Protein			3g

Tuna Salad Italiano

PREP TIME: 30 MINUTES (READY IN 2 HOURS)
SERVINGS: 8 (1 CUP EACH)

 LOW FAT

2 cups uncooked small pasta shells (7 oz)

4 small red potatoes, cut in half, sliced

2 cups Green Giant® frozen cut green beans (from 1-lb bag)

1 tablespoon olive or vegetable oil

1 can (6 oz) tuna in water, drained, flaked

1 medium tomato, seeded, chopped (about ³/₄ cup)

¹/₂ cup sliced green onions (8 medium)

¹/₂ cup Italian dressing

2 hard-cooked eggs, sliced

1) In 4-quart saucepan, cook pasta as directed on package, adding potatoes and frozen green beans during last 5 to 7 minutes of cooking time; cook until vegetables and pasta are tender. Drain.

2) In large bowl, gently toss cooked pasta, potatoes and green beans with oil. Refrigerate until chilled, about 1 hour 30 minutes.

3) Stir in tuna, tomato and onions. Pour dressing over salad; stir gently to coat. Top with hard-cooked eggs.

HIGH ALTITUDE (3500-6500 FT.): No change.

Nutrition Information Per Serving:	
Calories: 290	From Fat: 90
Total Fat	10g
Saturated Fat	1g
Trans Fat	0g
Cholesterol	60mg
Sodium	320mg
Total Carbohydrate	38g
Dietary Fiber	5g
Sugars	4g
Protein	12g

Marinated Garden Tortellini Salad

PREP TIME: 20 MINUTES (READY IN 3 HOURS 20 MINUTES)
SERVINGS: 4

e EASY   **lf** LOW FAT

1 package (9 oz) refrigerated cheese-filled tortellini

2 cups Green Giant Select® frozen broccoli florets

1 cup halved cherry tomatoes

4 medium green onions, sliced (¼ cup)

½ medium cucumber, quartered lengthwise, cut into ¼-inch slices

½ cup Italian dressing

1 tablespoon salad supreme seasoning

1) Cook tortellini as directed on package to desired doneness, adding broccoli during last minute of cook time. Drain; rinse with cold water to cool. Drain well.

2) Meanwhile, in large bowl, mix remaining ingredients.

3) Add cooked tortellini and broccoli to salad; toss gently to coat. Cover; refrigerate at least 3 hours to blend flavors. Stir gently before serving.

HIGH ALTITUDE (3500-6500 FT.): No change.

Nutrition Information Per Serving:

Calories:	280	From Fat:	90
Total Fat			9g
Saturated Fat			2.5g
Trans Fat			0g
Cholesterol			25mg
Sodium			700mg
Total Carbohydrate			39g
Dietary Fiber			4g
Sugars			7g
Protein			11g

tip

This pasta salad can be made with any variety of vegetables. Try thinly sliced carrots, sliced zucchini or cooked green beans. Sliced green or ripe olives are also a nice addition.

Cobb Salad with Cucumber-Ranch Dressing

PREP TIME: 20 MINUTES (READY IN 20 MINUTES)
SERVINGS: 6 (2 CUPS SALAD AND 1/4 CUP DRESSING EACH)

e EASY

SALAD

5 cups mixed salad greens

1 large tomato, chopped (1 cup)

1 medium avocado, pitted, peeled, sliced or cubed, and tossed with lemon juice

1 box (9 oz) frozen diced cooked chicken, thawed (1$\frac{1}{2}$ cups)

1 cup crumbled blue cheese (4 oz)

$\frac{1}{4}$ cup sliced green onions (4 medium)

6 slices cooked bacon, chopped

2 hard-cooked eggs, peeled, coarsely chopped

DRESSING

1 cup cucumber ranch dressing

1 small cucumber, seeded and finely chopped ($\frac{3}{4}$ cup)

2 tablespoons chopped fresh dill

1) On large serving platter or in 13x9-inch (3-quart) glass baking dish, arrange salad ingredients in rows or if desired, arrange individual salads on lettuce-lined plates.

2) In medium bowl, mix dressing ingredients. Serve dressing with salad or spoon dressing over individual salads.

HIGH ALTITUDE (3500-6500 FT.): No change.

Nutrition Information Per Serving:	
Calories: 460	From Fat: 340
Total Fat	38g
Saturated Fat	10g
Trans Fat	0g
Cholesterol	135mg
Sodium	990mg
Total Carbohydrate	9g
Dietary Fiber	3g
Sugars	3g
Protein	21g

Pudding Fruit Salad

PREP TIME: 20 MINUTES (READY IN 20 MINUTES)
SERVINGS: 9 (1/2 CUP EACH)

EASY   **LOW FAT**

1 container (4 oz) refrigerated vanilla pudding

½ cup frozen (thawed) whipped topping

1 cup seedless green grapes, halved

1 cup miniature marshmallows

1 can (11 oz) mandarin orange segments, drained

1 can (8 oz) pineapple tidbits in juice, drained

1 cup fresh strawberries, sliced

1) In medium bowl, mix pudding and whipped topping.

2) Gently stir in grapes, marshmallows, oranges and pineapple. Add strawberries; toss gently to coat. Serve immediately or store in refrigerator up to 8 hours.

HIGH ALTITUDE (3500-6500 FT.): No change.

Nutrition Information Per Serving:

Calories:	90	From Fat:	10
Total Fat			1.5g
Saturated Fat			0.5g
Trans Fat			0g
Cholesterol			0mg
Sodium			25mg
Total Carbohydrate			19g
Dietary Fiber			1g
Sugars			15g
Protein			1g

Honey-Lime Berries and Greens

PREP TIME: 25 MINUTES (READY IN 25 MINUTES)
SERVINGS: 6

EASY

SALAD

6 cups mixed salad greens

¾ cup fresh strawberries or raspberries

4 thin red onion slices, separated into rings

2 tablespoons sliced almonds, if desired

DRESSING

¼ cup lime juice

3 tablespoons vegetable oil

3 tablespoons honey

¼ teaspoon poppy seed

¼ teaspoon Dijon mustard

1) In medium bowl, gently toss salad ingredients.

2) In small bowl, mix dressing ingredients. Serve dressing with salad.

HIGH ALTITUDE (3500-6500 FT.): No change.

Nutrition Information Per Serving:

Calories:	120	From Fat:	60
Total Fat			7g
Saturated Fat			1g
Trans Fat			0g
Cholesterol			0mg
Sodium			25mg
Total Carbohydrate			13g
Dietary Fiber			1g
Sugars			11g
Protein			1g

tip

Use your favorite variety of Dijon mustard to make the salad's tangy dressing.

Layered Ham Salad

PREP TIME: 25 MINUTES (READY IN 25 MINUTES)
SERVINGS: 8 (1-3/4 CUPS EACH)

e EASY

SALAD

- 1 bag (10 oz) mixed salad greens
- 6 medium plum (Roma) tomatoes, chopped (2 cups)
- 1 can (11 oz) Green Giant® Mexicorn® whole kernel corn with red and green peppers, drained
- 2 cups cubed (½ inch) cooked ham
- ¼ cup chopped red onion
- 2 cups shredded Mexican cheese blend (8 oz)

DRESSING

- 1 cup mayonnaise or salad dressing
- ¼ cup taco sauce
- 2 tablespoons honey

1) In 5-quart glass salad bowl or 13x9-inch (3-quart) glass baking dish, spread salad greens.

2) Layer remaining salad ingredients except cheese over greens.

3) In small bowl, mix dressing ingredients. Spread dressing evenly over salad. Sprinkle cheese over dressing. Cover; refrigerate up to 3 hours before serving.

HIGH ALTITUDE (3500-6500 FT.): No change.

Nutrition Information Per Serving:

Calories:	450	From Fat:	310
Total Fat			34g
Saturated Fat			10g
Trans Fat			0g
Cholesterol			60mg
Sodium			1050mg
Total Carbohydrate			18g
Dietary Fiber			3g
Sugars			10g
Protein			16g

Gingered Fresh Fruit Salad

PREP TIME: 25 MINUTES (READY IN 25 MINUTES)
SERVINGS: 8 (3/4 CUP EACH)

e EASY   f LOW FAT

DRESSING

2 tablespoons honey

1 teaspoon chopped crystallized ginger

1/4 teaspoon grated lime peel

2 tablespoons fresh lime juice

SALAD

1 cup watermelon cubes

1 cup cantaloupe cubes

2 cups fresh pineapple cubes

1 cup seedless green grapes

1 pint (2 cups) fresh raspberries

1) In 1 cup microwavable measuring cup, mix dressing ingredients. Microwave uncovered on High 20 to 30 seconds or until hot.

2) Cool completely, about 15 minutes.

3) In very large bowl, mix salad ingredients. Pour the dressing over fruit; toss gently to coat.

HIGH ALTITUDE (3500-6500 FT.): No change.

Nutrition Information Per Serving:		
Calories: 90	From Fat:	0
Total Fat		0g
Saturated Fat		0g
Trans Fat		0g
Cholesterol		0mg
Sodium		5mg
Total Carbohydrate		21g
Dietary Fiber		3g
Sugars		15g
Protein		1g

tip

Serve this salad in a hollowed-out watermelon shell. If necessary, trim a thin piece from the bottom of the melon so the shell sits flat.

Soups, Sandwiches & Breads

Thick chowders, piled–high hoagies and freshly baked loaves make for cozy dinners.

CHICKEN-VEGETABLE CHOWDER
PG. 110

CHICKEN SALAD PANINI
PG. 109

APPLE-CREAM CHEESE MUFFINS
PG. 106

CHEESY HOT BEEF SANDWICHES
PG. 107

Cheesy Crescent-Topped Onion-Mushroom Soup

PREP TIME: 50 MINUTES (READY IN 1 HOUR)
SERVINGS: 4 (2 CUPS SOUP AND 2 TOPPERS EACH)

2 tablespoons butter or margarine

1 tablespoon vegetable oil

5 medium onions, thinly sliced (about 5 cups)

1 teaspoon packed brown sugar

2 cups sliced fresh mushrooms

2 teaspoons all-purpose flour

1 teaspoon salt

2 cans (14 oz each) beef broth

2 cups water

1/2 cup dry sherry or water

1 can (8 oz) Pillsbury® refrigerated crescent dinner rolls

2 tablespoons grated Parmesan cheese

1/2 teaspoon dried thyme leaves

1/2 cup finely shredded Swiss cheese (2 oz)

1) In 4-quart Dutch oven or large saucepan, heat butter and oil over medium heat until butter is melted. Add onions; cook about 15 minutes, stirring frequently, until onions are tender and light golden brown.

2) Stir in brown sugar. Cook about 5 minutes, stirring occasionally, until golden brown. Add mushrooms; cook about 5 minutes, stirring occasionally, until tender. Stir in flour and salt. Stir in broth, water and sherry. Heat to boiling. Reduce heat. Cover; simmer 20 minutes.

3) Meanwhile, heat oven to 375°F. On ungreased cookie sheet, unroll dough into 1 large rectangle; press perforations to seal. Sprinkle Parmesan cheese and thyme evenly over dough. Starting with 1 short side, roll up. Cut roll into 8 slices; place cut sides down on cookie sheet. Press slices to form 3-inch rounds.

4) Bake 10 to 14 minutes or until golden brown. Remove baked rounds from oven. Sprinkle each with Swiss cheese. Bake 1 to 2 minutes longer or until cheese is melted and begins to brown.

5) Ladle soup into individual soup bowls. Top each with 1 crescent topper. Serve soup with additional crescent toppers.

HIGH ALTITUDE (3500-6500 FT.): Increase water to 2-1/2 cups.

Nutrition Information Per Serving:		
Calories: 475	From Fat:	205
Total Fat		23g
Saturated Fat		10g
Cholesterol		30mg
Sodium		2320mg
Total Carbohydrate		47g
Dietary Fiber		3g
Sugars		17g
Protein		14g

Cheese Steak Crescent Braids

PREP TIME: 35 MINUTES (READY IN 1 HOUR)
SERVINGS: 6

- 1 tablespoon butter or margarine
- 4 portions thinly sliced frozen sandwich steaks (from 12.25-oz box), cut crosswise into $1/2$-inch strips
- 1 large green bell pepper, cut into thin bite-sized strips ($1^{1}/_{2}$ cups)
- 1 medium onion, chopped ($1/2$ cup)
- 2 cans (8 oz each) Pillsbury® refrigerated crescent dinner rolls
- 1 cup shredded mozzarella cheese (4 oz)
- 1 egg, beaten, if desired

1) Heat oven to 350°F. In 10-inch skillet, melt butter over medium-high heat. Add steak strips; cook 8 to 10 minutes, stirring frequently, until no longer pink. Remove steak from skillet; place on plate. Add bell pepper and onion to skillet; cook about 5 minutes, stirring occasionally, until crisp tender. Return cooked steak to skillet; mix well. If desired, add salt and pepper to taste.

2) Unroll 1 can of dough onto ungreased cookie sheet, firmly press perforations and edges to seal. Press or roll into 13x7-inch rectangle.

3) Spoon heaping cup of steak mixture in 2-inch-wide strip lengthwise down center of dough to within $1/4$ inch of each end. Sprinkle $1/2$ cup of the cheese over steak mixture.

4) Make cuts 1 inch apart on long sides of rectangle just to edge of filling. For braided appearance, fold strips of dough at an angle halfway across filling with ends slightly overlapping, alternating from side to side. Fold ends of braid under to seal. On second ungreased cookie sheet, repeat with remaining can of dough, steak mixture and cheese. Brush braids with beaten egg.

5) Bake 16 to 22 minutes or until golden brown, switching position of cookie sheets in oven halfway through baking. Cool 1 minute; remove braids from cookie sheets. Let stand 5 minutes before serving. Cut into slices.

HIGH ALTITUDE (3500-6500 FT.): No change.

Nutrition Information Per Serving:	
Calories: 410	From Fat: 210
Total Fat	23g
Saturated Fat	9g
Trans Fat	4g
Cholesterol	35mg
Sodium	710mg
Total Carbohydrate	32g
Dietary Fiber	1g
Sugars	7g
Protein	19g

Apple-Cream Cheese Muffins

PREP TIME: 30 MINUTES (READY IN 1 HOUR 10 MINUTES)
SERVINGS: 15 MUFFINS

MUFFINS

- 3/4 cup packed brown sugar
- 1 3/4 cups all-purpose flour
- 1 teaspoon baking powder
- 1/2 teaspoon ground cinnamon
- 1/2 teaspoon salt
- 2 eggs, beaten
- 2/3 cup oil
- 1/4 cup applesauce
- 1 teaspoon vanilla
- 1 large apple, peeled, shredded (about 1 cup)
- 1/3 cup cream cheese (from 8-oz package)

STREUSEL

- 3 tablespoons packed brown sugar
- 2 tablespoons all-purpose flour
- 1 tablespoon butter or margarine, softened

1) Heat oven to 350°F. Line 15 muffin cups with paper baking cups. Reserve 1 tablespoon of the brown sugar in the muffins for filling.

2) In large bowl with electric mixer, mix remaining brown sugar for muffins, 1 3/4 cups flour, baking powder, cinnamon and salt on low speed until mixed. Reserve 1 tablespoon of the beaten egg for filling. Add oil, applesauce, vanilla and remaining egg to flour mixture. Beat on medium speed until mixed. With spoon, stir in apple.

3) In small bowl, mix cream cheese, the reserved 1 tablespoon brown sugar and reserved 1 tablespoon egg. Fill muffin cups slightly less than half full of batter. Top each with 1 teaspoon cream cheese mixture. Top with spoonful of remaining batter to fill cups 2/3 full. In small bowl, mix all streusel ingredients; sprinkle over batter.

4) Bake 22 to 26 minutes or until toothpick inserted in center comes out clean. Remove from pan. Cool slightly, about 10 minutes.

HIGH ALTITUDE (3500-6500 FT.): Decrease baking powder to 3/4 teaspoon. Heat oven to 375°F.

Nutrition Information Per Serving:	
Calories: 240	From Fat: 120
Total Fat	13g
Saturated Fat	3g
Trans Fat	0g
Cholesterol	35mg
Sodium	150mg
Total Carbohydrate	28g
Dietary Fiber	0g
Sugars	15g
Protein	3g

Cheesy Hot Beef Sandwiches

PREP TIME: 20 MINUTES (READY IN 45 MINUTES)
SERVINGS: 8 SANDWICHES

(e) EASY

1½ lb extra-lean (at least 90%) ground beef

1 envelope dry French onion soup mix (from 2.6-oz package)

¼ cup water

½ red bell pepper, chopped (about ½ cup)

2 tablespoons chopped fresh parsley

2 cups shredded Cheddar-Monterey Jack cheese blend (8 oz)

1 loaf (1 lb) French bread, about 24 inches long

tip

Simply use a fork to remove the bread from inside the loaf to form the bread shell.

Nutrition Information Per Serving:	
Calories: 410	From Fat: 160
Total Fat	18g
Saturated Fat	9g
Trans Fat	1g
Cholesterol	80mg
Sodium	940mg
Total Carbohydrate	32g
Dietary Fiber	2g
Sugars	3g
Protein	29g

1) Heat oven to 350°F. Cut 26x18-inch piece of heavy-duty foil. In 12-inch nonstick skillet, cook ground beef over medium-high heat 5 to 7 minutes, stirring occasionally, until thoroughly cooked; drain. Add soup mix, water, bell pepper and parsley. Cook 2 to 3 minutes or until thoroughly heated. Stir in cheese until melted.

2) Cut ½-inch lengthwise slice from top of French bread; set aside. With fork, remove inside of bread, leaving ½ inch around edges. Place loaf on foil. If desired, reserve bread pieces for another use. Fill indentation in bread with ground beef mixture. Place top of bread over ground beef. Wrap loaf in foil. Place on cookie sheet.

3) Bake 20 to 25 minutes or until thoroughly heated. For sandwiches, cut loaf into 8 crosswise sections.

HIGH ALTITUDE (3500-6500 FT.): Bake 30 to 35 minutes.

Family Hamburger Soup

PREP TIME: 45 MINUTES (READY IN 45 MINUTES)
SERVINGS: 6

(lf) LOW FAT

1 lb lean (at least 80%) ground beef

¼ cup chopped onion

2 cups diced peeled potatoes

1 cup sliced celery

1 bag (1 lb) Green Giant® frozen mixed vegetables

3 cups water

2 cans (10½ oz each) condensed beef broth

1 can (14.5 oz) diced tomatoes, undrained

1 tablespoon Worcestershire sauce

Nutrition Information Per Serving:	
Calories: 260	From Fat: 80
Total Fat	9g
Saturated Fat	3.5g
Trans Fat	0.5g
Cholesterol	45mg
Sodium	710mg
Total Carbohydrate	25g
Dietary Fiber	5g
Sugars	6g
Protein	21g

1) In large saucepan or Dutch oven, cook ground beef and onion over medium-high heat 5 to 7 minutes, stirring occasionally, until beef is thoroughly cooked; drain.

2) Stir in all remaining ingredients. Heat to boiling. Reduce heat to low; cover and simmer for 18 to 20 minutes or until the vegetables are tender, stirring occasionally.

HIGH ALTITUDE (3500-6500 FT.): No change.

Quick Quesadilla

PREP TIME: 10 MINUTES (READY IN 10 MINUTES)
SERVINGS: 1

e EASY

2 Old El Paso® flour tortillas for burritos (8 inch; from 11.5-oz package)

¼ cup shredded Cheddar cheese (1 oz)

2 tablespoons real bacon pieces (from 2-oz jar)

1 medium green onion, sliced (1 tablespoon)

¼ cup Old El Paso® Thick 'n Chunky salsa

Nutrition Information Per Serving:		
Calories: 470	From Fat:	180
Total Fat		20g
Saturated Fat		9g
Trans Fat		1g
Cholesterol		40mg
Sodium		1210mg
Total Carbohydrate		55g
Dietary Fiber		2g
Sugars		4g
Protein		18g

1) Heat closed contact grill 5 minutes. When grill is heated, place 1 tortilla on bottom grill surface. Quickly top with cheese, bacon and onion. Place remaining tortilla on top.

2) Close grill; cook 4 to 5 minutes or until tortillas are crisp and cheese is melted. Cut into wedges; serve with salsa.

HIGH ALTITUDE (3500-6500 FT.): No change.

Roast Beef Sandwich Slices

PREP TIME: 15 MINUTES (READY IN 40 MINUTES)
SERVINGS: 8

e EASY

1 Pillsbury® refrigerated pie crust (from 15-oz box), softened as directed on box

4 oz thinly sliced cooked roast beef (from deli), diced

1 small plum (Roma) tomato, chopped

2 thin slices red onion

¾ cup shredded pepper Jack cheese (3 oz)

Nutrition Information Per Serving:		
Calories: 180	From Fat:	100
Total Fat		11g
Saturated Fat		4.5g
Trans Fat		0g
Cholesterol		20mg
Sodium		240mg
Total Carbohydrate		15g
Dietary Fiber		0g
Sugars		1g
Protein		5g

1) Heat oven to 450°F. Remove crust from pouch; place on ungreased large cookie sheet. Place roast beef, tomato, onion and cheese lengthwise down center ⅓ of crust to within 1 inch of top and bottom edge.

2) Brush edge of crust with water. Fold top and bottom edges over filling; fold in sides, overlapping in center and sealing edges. Cut 3 or 4 slits in top crust to allow steam to escape.

3) Bake 17 to 20 minutes or until golden brown. Cool 5 minutes. Cut crosswise into 8 slices. Serve warm.

HIGH ALTITUDE (3500-6500 FT.): Heat oven to 425°F. Bake 20 to 23 minutes.

tip For Turkey Sandwich Slices, use thinly sliced cooked turkey from the deli instead of the beef.

Chicken Salad Panini

PREP TIME: 30 MINUTES (READY IN 30 MINUTES)
SERVINGS: 4

EASY

1 can (13.8 oz) Pillsbury® refrigerated pizza crust

1 teaspoon olive oil

½ teaspoon Italian seasoning

1 package (6 oz) refrigerated cooked Italian-style chicken breast strips, finely chopped

2 tablespoons finely chopped green onions (2 medium)

3 tablespoons mayonnaise or salad dressing

1 large tomato, thinly sliced

4 slices (about 1 oz each) Jarlsberg cheese (from deli)

1) Heat oven to 400°F. Grease large cookie sheet with shortening or cooking spray. Unroll dough onto cookie sheet. Starting at center, press out dough into 15x10-inch rectangle. Brush oil over dough. Sprinkle evenly with Italian seasoning.

2) Bake 10 to 13 minutes or until edges are golden brown. Meanwhile, in medium bowl, mix chicken, onions and mayonnaise.

3) Cut baked crust in half crosswise. Spread chicken mixture on 1 half. Top with tomato and cheese, cutting to fit if necessary. Cover with remaining half of baked crust, seasoning side down. Cut into 4 sandwiches.

4) Heat 12-inch skillet over medium-low heat. Place 2 sandwiches in skillet; cook about 2 minutes, pressing down with pancake turner, until bottom crust is deep golden brown. Turn sandwiches; cook about 2 minutes, pressing again with turner, until cheese is melted. Repeat with remaining 2 sandwiches.

HIGH ALTITUDE (3500-6500 FT.): No change.

Nutrition Information Per Serving:		
Calories: 525	From Fat: 205	
Total Fat		23g
Saturated Fat		7g
Cholesterol		70mg
Sodium		1010mg
Total Carbohydrate		50g
Dietary Fiber		1g
Sugars		9g
Protein		30g

Chicken–Vegetable Chowder

PREP TIME: 10 MINUTES (READY IN 7 HOURS 40 MINUTES)
SERVINGS: 5 (1-3/4 CUPS EACH)

e EASY   **f** LOW FAT

1 lb boneless skinless chicken thighs, cut into 1-inch pieces

1 cup ready-to-eat baby-cut carrots, cut in half lengthwise

1 cup sliced fresh mushrooms

1 medium onion, chopped ($1/2$ cup)

$1/2$ cup water

$1/4$ teaspoon garlic powder

$1/8$ teaspoon dried thyme leaves

1 can (14 oz) chicken broth

1 can ($10^3/4$ oz) condensed 98%-fat-free cream of chicken soup with 30% less sodium

$1/2$ cup milk

3 tablespoons all-purpose flour

1 box (9 oz) Green Giant® frozen broccoli cuts, thawed

1) In 3- to 4-quart slow cooker, mix chicken, carrots, mushrooms, onion, water, garlic powder, thyme and broth.

2) Cover; cook on Low heat setting 7 to 9 hours.

3) About 35 minutes before serving, skim fat from slow cooker. In small bowl, beat soup, milk and flour with wire whisk until smooth. Add soup mixture and broccoli to chicken mixture. Cover; cook on Low heat setting 30 minutes longer or until broccoli is tender.

HIGH ALTITUDE (3500-6500 FT.): No change.

Nutrition Information Per Serving:			
Calories:	260	From Fat:	90
Total Fat		10g	
Saturated Fat		3g	
Trans Fat		0g	
Cholesterol		60mg	
Sodium		660mg	
Total Carbohydrate		17g	
Dietary Fiber		3g	
Sugars		4g	
Protein		26g	

Smoky Barbecue Beef Sandwiches

PREP TIME: 15 MINUTES (READY IN 4 HOURS 15 MINUTES)
SERVINGS: 10

2½ lb lean (at least 80%) ground beef

1½ cups barbecue sauce

⅓ cup teriyaki baste and glaze sauce

1 tablespoon finely chopped chipotle chiles in adobo sauce (from 7-oz can)

1 teaspoon salt

10 soft hoagie buns (6 to 7 inch), split

Nutrition Information Per Serving:	
Calories: 380	From Fat: 130
Total Fat	15g
Saturated Fat	5g
Trans Fat	1g
Cholesterol	70mg
Sodium	1090mg
Total Carbohydrate	38g
Dietary Fiber	1g
Sugars	15g
Protein	24g

1) In 12-inch nonstick skillet or Dutch oven, brown ground beef over medium heat 8 to 10 minutes or until thoroughly cooked, stirring frequently. Drain well.

2) In 3½- to 4-quart slow cooker, mix cooked ground beef and remaining ingredients except buns.

3) Cover; cook on Low heat setting 4 to 6 hours.

4) To serve, stir beef mixture. Spoon ½ cup beef mixture into each bun.

HIGH ALTITUDE (3500-6500 FT.): No change.

Banana Peanut Butter Bread

PREP TIME: 20 MINUTES (READY IN 3 HOURS 40 MINUTES)
SERVINGS: 12

EASY

¾ cup sugar

½ cup butter or margarine, softened

2 eggs

2 tablespoons milk

2 teaspoons vanilla

1 cup mashed ripe bananas (2 large)

2 cups all-purpose flour

1½ teaspoons baking powder

½ teaspoon baking soda

½ teaspoon salt

4 packages (1.5 oz each) chocolate covered peanut butter candy cups, cut into small pieces

1) Heat oven to 350°F (325°F for dark pan). Grease and flour bottom only of 9x5-inch loaf pan. In large bowl with electric mixer, beat sugar and butter on medium speed until creamy.

2) Add eggs, milk, vanilla and bananas. Beat about 30 seconds or until well blended. Add all remaining ingredients except candy. Mix just until moistened. Reserve 2 tablespoons cut up candy. With spoon, fold in remaining candy. Pour into pan.

3) Bake 1 hour to 1 hour 10 minutes or until toothpick inserted near center comes out clean. Cool in pan 10 minutes. Remove from pan to cooling rack. Finely chop the reserved 2 tablespoons candy; sprinkle on warm bread. Cool completely, about 2 hours.

Nutrition Information Per Serving:	
Calories: 300	From Fat: 120
Total Fat	13g
Saturated Fat	7g
Trans Fat	0g
Cholesterol	55mg
Sodium	320mg
Total Carbohydrate	41g
Dietary Fiber	2g
Sugars	22g
Protein	5g

HIGH ALTITUDE (3500-6500 FT.): Decrease baking powder to 1 teaspoon.

Antipasto Focaccia Sandwich Wedges

PREP TIME: 15 MINUTES (READY IN 15 MINUTES)
SERVINGS: 6

EASY

- ½ cup creamy Italian or regular Italian dressing
- 1 focaccia bread (8 to 10 inch), cut in half horizontally
- 4 leaves romaine or iceberg lettuce
- ½ cup roasted red bell peppers (from a jar), cut into 2x¼-inch strips
- 1 package (6 oz) deli sliced provolone cheese
- 6 oz thinly sliced hard salami

Nutrition Information Per Serving:

Calories: 450	From Fat: 270
Total Fat	30g
Saturated Fat	10g
Trans Fat	0g
Cholesterol	45mg
Sodium	1350mg
Total Carbohydrate	27g
Dietary Fiber	1g
Sugars	4g
Protein	18g

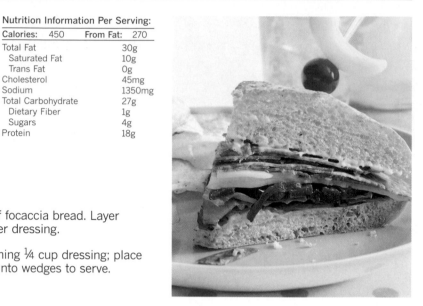

1) Spread ¼ cup of the dressing on bottom half of focaccia bread. Layer lettuce, roasted peppers, cheese and salami over dressing.

2) Spread cut side of top half of bread with remaining ¼ cup dressing; place dressing side down over salami. Cut sandwich into wedges to serve.

HIGH ALTITUDE (3500-6500 FT.): No change.

Louisiana Sloppy Joes

PREP TIME: 35 MINUTES (READY IN 35 MINUTES)
SERVINGS: 12

- 2 lb lean (at least 80%) ground beef
- 1 cup chopped celery
- 1 cup chopped green bell pepper
- ½ cup chopped onion (1 medium)
- 1 can (19 oz) Progresso® Vegetable Classics hearty tomato soup
- 1 can (10¾ oz) condensed chicken gumbo soup
- 2 tablespoons Dijon mustard
- 2 teaspoons dried Cajun seasoning
- 12 burger buns, split

Nutrition Information Per Serving:

Calories: 290	From Fat: 100
Total Fat	11g
Saturated Fat	4g
Trans Fat	1g
Cholesterol	50mg
Sodium	780mg
Total Carbohydrate	30g
Dietary Fiber	2g
Sugars	5g
Protein	19g

1) In 12-inch nonstick skillet, cook ground beef, celery, bell pepper and onion over medium-high heat 5 to 7 minutes, stirring occasionally, until beef is thoroughly cooked; drain.

2) Reduce heat to medium. Stir in all remaining ingredients except buns. Cook 15 to 20 minutes longer or until mixture is bubbly and vegetables are tender, stirring occasionally. Spoon beef mixture into buns.

HIGH ALTITUDE (3500-6500 FT.): No change.

Beefy Nacho Soup

PREP TIME: 20 MINUTES (READY IN 20 MINUTES)
SERVINGS: 4

🄴 **EASY**

1 lb lean (at least 80%) ground beef

1 tablespoon Old El Paso® 40% less-sodium taco seasoning mix (from 1.25-oz package)

1 can (10¾ oz) condensed nacho cheese soup

1 can (10 oz) diced tomatoes and green chiles, undrained

1½ cups milk

¼ cup shredded sharp Cheddar cheese (1 oz)

½ cup crushed corn tortilla chips

1) In 2-quart saucepan, cook ground beef over medium-high heat 5 to 7 minutes, stirring occasionally, until thoroughly cooked; drain.

2) Reduce heat to medium. Stir in remaining ingredients except shredded cheese and tortilla chips. Cook 8 to 12 minutes or until thoroughly heated, stirring frequently. Top individual servings with shredded cheese and tortilla chips.

HIGH ALTITUDE (3500-6500 FT.): No change.

Nutrition Information Per Serving:	
Calories: 430	From Fat: 230
Total Fat	25g
Saturated Fat	11g
Trans Fat	2g
Cholesterol	95mg
Sodium	1210mg
Total Carbohydrate	22g
Dietary Fiber	2g
Sugars	9g
Protein	29g

tip

Offer other favorite nacho toppings for the soup, such as chopped tomatoes, bell peppers, green onions, sour cream, ripe olives and/or guacamole.

Sloppy Joe Confetti Tacos

PREP TIME: 20 MINUTES (READY IN 20 MINUTES)
SERVINGS: 6 (2 TACOS EACH)

EASY

1 lb lean (at least 80%) ground beef

1 box (4.6 oz) Old El Paso® taco shells (12 shells)

1 can (15.5 oz) sloppy joe sauce

1 small red bell pepper, chopped ($^1/_2$ cup)

1 can (11 oz) Green Giant® Niblets® whole kernel sweet corn, drained

1 can (2$^1/_4$ oz) sliced ripe olives, drained

1 cup thinly sliced romaine lettuce

$^1/_2$ cup shredded Colby-Monterey Jack cheese (2 oz)

1) Heat oven to 350°F. In 10-inch skillet, cook ground beef over medium-high heat 5 to 7 minutes, stirring frequently, until thoroughly cooked; drain.

2) Meanwhile, heat taco shells as directed on the box.

3) Stir sloppy joe sauce, bell pepper and corn into ground beef. Cook 2 to 3 minutes longer, stirring occasionally, until mixture is hot and bubbly.

4) Spoon about ¼ cup beef mixture into each warm taco shell; top with olives, lettuce and cheese.

HIGH ALTITUDE (3500-6500 FT.): No change.

Nutrition Information Per Serving:		
Calories: 360	From Fat:	160
Total Fat		18g
Saturated Fat		6g
Trans Fat		2.5g
Cholesterol		55mg
Sodium		800mg
Total Carbohydrate		31g
Dietary Fiber		4g
Sugars		7g
Protein		20g

Teriyaki Beef and Pineapple Lettuce Wraps

PREP TIME: 15 MINUTES (READY IN 15 MINUTES)
SERVINGS: 5

e EASY   **f** LOW FAT

1 lb lean (at least 80%) ground beef

¼ teaspoon salt

⅛ teaspoon pepper

1 can (8 oz) pineapple tidbits in juice, drained, reserving liquid

¼ cup teriyaki baste and glaze sauce

1 tablespoon cornstarch

2 green onions, sliced (2 tablespoons)

¼ cup diced red bell pepper, if desired

5 large Bibb lettuce leaves

Nutrition Information Per Serving:	
Calories: 210	From Fat: 90
Total Fat	10g
Saturated Fat	4g
Trans Fat	0.5g
Cholesterol	55mg
Sodium	490mg
Total Carbohydrate	14g
Dietary Fiber	0g
Sugars	10g
Protein	17g

1) In 10-inch skillet, cook ground beef over medium-high heat 5 to 7 minutes, stirring occasionally, until thoroughly cooked; drain. Stir in salt and pepper.

2) In small bowl, mix reserved pineapple liquid, baste and glaze sauce and cornstarch. Stir mixture into ground beef. Cook and stir until thick and bubbly, stirring frequently. Stir in pineapple, green onions and bell pepper. Cook 1 to 2 minutes, stirring occasionally, until thoroughly heated. Spoon about ½ cup mixture into each lettuce leaf; roll up to serve.

HIGH ALTITUDE (3500-6500 FT.): No change.

Open-Faced Hamburger Phillies

PREP TIME: 20 MINUTES (READY IN 20 MINUTES)
SERVINGS: 4

e EASY

1 lb lean (at least 80%) ground beef

1 medium green bell pepper, cut into ½-inch strips

1 medium red bell pepper, cut into ½-inch strips

1 small onion, cut into thin wedges

½ cup creamy Italian dressing

1 loaf (1 lb) Italian bread (12 inches long), halved lengthwise

4 slices (6 oz) thinly sliced provolone cheese, quartered

1) In 12-inch skillet, cook ground beef, bell peppers and onion over medium-high heat 5 to 7 minutes, stirring occasionally, until beef is thoroughly cooked; drain. Stir in ¼ cup of the dressing.

2) Spread remaining ¼ cup dressing on cut sides of bread. Place both halves, cut sides up, on ungreased large cookie sheet. Broil 4 to 6 inches from heat 3 to 5 minutes or until lightly toasted. Remove bread from broiler. Spread beef mixture on cut halves of bread. Top with cheese.

3) Return to broiler; broil 4 to 6 inches from heat 2 to 3 minutes or until cheese is melted. Cut each half into 2 pieces.

HIGH ALTITUDE (3500-6500 FT.): No change.

Nutrition Information Per Serving:	
Calories: 710	From Fat: 310
Total Fat	34g
Saturated Fat	10g
Trans Fat	2g
Cholesterol	90mg
Sodium	1150mg
Total Carbohydrate	65g
Dietary Fiber	5g
Sugars	7g
Protein	36g

Italian bread has a dense texture, so it works well for these hot broiled sandwiches.

Toasted Turkey and Bacon Sandwiches

PREP TIME: 25 MINUTES (READY IN 25 MINUTES)
SERVINGS: 4

e EASY

2 tablespoons mayonnaise

1 tablespoon ranch dressing

8 slices soft Italian bread
(about ½ inch thick)

4 oz shaved cooked turkey
breast (from deli)

4 slices cooked bacon, halved

4 slices tomato, halved

2 slices (1 oz each) Cheddar
cheese, halved

2 tablespoons butter or margarine,
softened

1) In small bowl, mix
mayonnaise and dressing.
Spread on one side of each
slice of bread. Top each of
4 bread slices with turkey,
bacon, tomato, cheese
and remaining bread
slices, mayonnaise mixture
side down.

2) Spread butter on one side
of each sandwich. In 12-inch
skillet, place sandwiches,
butter side down. Spread butter over
top of each sandwich. Cover; cook
over medium-low heat 6 to 8 minutes
or until bottoms are golden brown.

3) Turn sandwiches; cover and cook 5 to
6 minutes longer or until bottoms are
golden brown and cheese is melted.

HIGH ALTITUDE (3500-6500 FT.): No change.

Nutrition Information Per Serving:		
Calories: 370	From Fat:	210
Total Fat		23g
Saturated Fat		9g
Trans Fat		1g
Cholesterol		65mg
Sodium		630mg
Total Carbohydrate		22g
Dietary Fiber		1g
Sugars		1g
Protein		19g

Cheesy Chicken Quesadillas

PREP TIME: 30 MINUTES (READY IN 30 MINUTES)
SERVINGS: 4

e EASY

1 package (11.5 oz) Old El Paso® flour
tortillas for burritos (8 tortillas)

2 cups shredded deli rotisserie
chicken (without skin)

2 cups shredded Cheddar-Monterey
Jack cheese (8 oz)

¼ cup chopped fresh cilantro

2 teaspoons oil

¼ cup ranch dressing

½ cup Old El Paso® Thick 'n Chunky
salsa

1 tablespoon chopped fresh cilantro

Nutrition Information Per Serving:		
Calories: 710	From Fat:	370
Total Fat		41g
Saturated Fat		16g
Trans Fat		0.5g
Cholesterol		120mg
Sodium		1630mg
Total Carbohydrate		47g
Dietary Fiber		0g
Sugars		2g
Protein		40g

1) On 4 tortillas, layer chicken, cheese and ¼ cup cilantro. Top with remaining
tortillas. Brush top of each quesadilla with about ½ teaspoon oil.

2) Heat 12-inch nonstick skillet over medium heat. Place 1 quesadilla in skillet
oil side down; brush top side with about ½ teaspoon oil. Cook about 1
minute or until light golden brown.

3) Carefully turn quesadilla; cook 1 minute longer or until golden brown.
Repeat with remaining quesadillas. Drizzle quesadillas with dressing and
salsa. Sprinkle with 1 tablespoon cilantro. To serve, cut into wedges.

HIGH ALTITUDE (3500-6500 FT.): No change.

Chicken and Roasted Vegetable Foldover Sandwiches

PREP TIME: 30 MINUTES (READY IN 50 MINUTES)
SERVINGS: 5

1 small or ¹/₂ large red bell pepper, cut into 2x¹/₂-inch strips

1 small onion, cut into ¹/₂-inch wedges

5 slices portabella mushrooms (from 6-oz package)

3 tablespoons olive oil

1 package (6 oz) refrigerated grilled chicken breast strips

1 can (10.2 oz) Pillsbury® Grands!® refrigerated buttermilk biscuits (5 biscuits)

3 tablespoons basil pesto

1 cup shredded Italian cheese blend (4 oz)

1 cup tomato-basil pasta sauce, heated

1) Heat oven to 425°F. In ungreased 15x10-inch pan with sides, place bell pepper, onion and mushrooms. Drizzle with oil. Place chicken strips in same pan.

2) Bake 15 minutes, stirring and turning twice, until vegetables are tender. Remove from oven; set aside. Reduce oven temperature to 375°F.

3) Separate dough into 5 biscuits. On ungreased large cookie sheet, press each biscuit into 6-inch round. Spread pesto evenly over biscuits. Top each with cheese.

4) Bake 12 to 16 minutes or until biscuits are golden brown.

5) Spoon roasted vegetables and chicken evenly onto half of each baked biscuit round; fold biscuit over filling. Serve warm sandwiches with warm pasta sauce for dipping.

HIGH ALTITUDE (3500-6500 FT.): No change.

Nutrition Information Per Serving:	
Calories: 525	From Fat: 280
Total Fat	31g
Saturated Fat	9g
Cholesterol	45mg
Sodium	1360mg
Total Carbohydrate	40g
Dietary Fiber	2g
Sugars	14g
Protein	22g

Pastrami and Swiss Melts

PREP TIME: 10 MINUTES (READY IN 30 MINUTES)
SERVINGS: 4

EASY

1 can (13.8 oz) Pillsbury® refrigerated pizza crust

1 teaspoon grated Parmesan cheese

¼ teaspoon onion powder

¼ teaspoon caraway seed

4 tablespoons Thousand Island dressing

½ lb thinly sliced pastrami (from deli), cut into bite-sized strips

4 thin slices (about 1 oz each) Swiss cheese

1 cup creamy coleslaw (from deli)

1) Heat oven to 400°F. On ungreased cookie sheet, unroll dough into 14x9-inch rectangle. Sprinkle Parmesan cheese, onion powder and caraway seed over dough; press in lightly.

2) Bake 12 to 16 minutes or until golden brown.

3) Cut crust into quarters; separate slightly. Spread each with 1 tablespoon dressing. Top each with pastrami and cheese. Bake 2 to 4 minutes longer or until thoroughly heated and cheese is melted. Top each with coleslaw.

HIGH ALTITUDE (3500-6500 FT.): No change.

Nutrition Information Per Serving:	
Calories: 590	From Fat: 250
Total Fat	28g
Saturated Fat	9g
Cholesterol	65mg
Sodium	1810mg
Total Carbohydrate	55g
Dietary Fiber	2g
Sugars	12g
Protein	29g

Beef and Pork Barbecue Sandwiches

PREP TIME: 30 MINUTES (READY IN 8 HOURS 30 MINUTES)
SERVINGS: 12

1 boneless beef chuck or arm roast (1½ lb), trimmed, cut into 2-inch pieces

1 boneless pork loin or shoulder roast (1½ lb), trimmed, cut into 3-inch pieces

1½ cups chopped onions (3 medium)

1 medium green bell pepper, chopped (1 cup)

½ cup packed brown sugar

3 teaspoons chili powder

1 teaspoon salt

1 teaspoon ground mustard

¼ cup vinegar

2 teaspoons Worcestershire sauce

1 can (6 oz) tomato paste

12 sandwich buns, split

Nutrition Information Per Serving:

Calories: 380	From Fat: 120
Total Fat	13g
Saturated Fat	4.5g
Trans Fat	0.5g
Cholesterol	70mg
Sodium	590mg
Total Carbohydrate	36g
Dietary Fiber	2g
Sugars	15g
Protein	28g

1) In 3½- to 4-quart slow cooker, mix all ingredients except tomato paste and buns.

2) Cover; cook on Low heat setting 8 to 10 hours.

3) With slotted spoon, remove meat from slow cooker. Shred meat with 2 forks; return to slow cooker. Stir in tomato paste. Increase heat setting to High; cover and cook 5 to 10 minutes longer or until thoroughly heated.

4) To serve, spoon about ½ cup mixture into each bun.

HIGH ALTITUDE (3500-6500 FT.): No change.

Grilled Bacon-Cheddar Bread

PREP TIME: 20 MINUTES (READY IN 20 MINUTES)
SERVINGS: 8

🅔 EASY

1 loaf (1 lb) french bread

3 tablespoons butter or margarine, softened

1½ cups shredded sharp Cheddar cheese (6 oz)

4 slices cooked bacon, crumbled

2 tablespoons chopped fresh parsley, if desired

Nutrition Information Per Serving:

Calories: 300	From Fat: 140
Total Fat	15g
Saturated Fat	8g
Trans Fat	1g
Cholesterol	40mg
Sodium	590mg
Total Carbohydrate	29g
Dietary Fiber	2g
Sugars	0g
Protein	12g

1) Heat gas or charcoal grill. Cut loaf of bread into 1-inch-thick slices. Lightly spread one side of each slice of bread with butter. Place slices, butter side down, on ungreased cookie sheet. Sprinkle cheese, bacon and parsley evenly on bread slices.

2) Place bread slices, butter side down, directly on grill. Cover grill; cook over medium-high heat 4 to 6 minutes or until bottom of bread is toasted and cheese is melted.

HIGH ALTITUDE (3500-6500 FT.): Cook over medium heat.

Cheesy Sausage Calzones

PREP TIME: 30 MINUTES (READY IN 45 MINUTES)
SERVINGS: 5

e EASY

½ lb bulk Italian pork sausage

⅓ cup chopped onion

¼ cup chopped red bell pepper

1 can (10.2 oz) Pillsbury® Grands!® refrigerated buttermilk biscuits (5 biscuits)

½ cup shredded mozzarella cheese (2 oz)

1½ cups tomato pasta sauce, heated

Nutrition Information Per Serving:	
Calories: 360	From Fat: 170
Total Fat	19g
Saturated Fat	7g
Trans Fat	3g
Cholesterol	30mg
Sodium	1350mg
Total Carbohydrate	32g
Dietary Fiber	1g
Sugars	8g
Protein	15g

1) Heat oven to 375°F. In 8-inch skillet, cook sausage, onion and bell pepper over medium heat 10 minutes, stirring frequently, until sausage is no longer pink; drain. Cool 10 minutes.

2) Separate dough into 5 biscuits. On ungreased large cookie sheet, press each biscuit into 6-inch round. Top half of each round with sausage mixture and cheese to within ½ inch of edge. Fold dough over filling; press edges firmly with fork to seal.

3) Bake 12 to 15 minutes or until golden brown. Serve warm calzones with warm pasta sauce for dipping.

HIGH ALTITUDE (3500-6500 FT.): No change.

Tangy Barbecued Beef Sandwiches

PREP TIME: 15 MINUTES (READY IN 5 HOURS 15 MINUTES)
SERVINGS: 22 SANDWICHES

e EASY

1 boneless beef chuck roast (3½ to 4 lb), cut crosswise into ¼-inch slices

1 large onion, chopped (1 cup)

4 cloves garlic, finely chopped

½ cup packed brown sugar

2 teaspoons ground mustard

1 teaspoon chili powder

1 teaspoon paprika

⅓ cup vinegar

⅓ cup Worcestershire sauce

3 tablespoons lemon juice

1¾ cups ketchup

22 oval-shaped sandwich buns

1) In 3- to 4-quart slow cooker, mix all ingredients except the buns.

2) Cover; cook on Low heat setting 5 to 6 hours, stirring occasionally. Cut off top of each bun; pull some of bread out of each bun. Fill buns with beef mixture.

HIGH ALTITUDE (3500-6500 FT.): No change.

Nutrition Information Per Serving:	
Calories: 300	From Fat: 100
Total Fat	11g
Saturated Fat	3.5g
Trans Fat	0.5g
Cholesterol	40mg
Sodium	500mg
Total Carbohydrate	33g
Dietary Fiber	1g
Sugars	12g
Protein	18g

Chicken Caesar Sandwich Ring

PREP TIME: 15 MINUTES (READY IN 55 MINUTES)
SERVINGS: 8

e EASY

2 cans (11 oz each) Pillsbury® refrigerated French loaf

1 egg, beaten

1 lb cooked chicken (from deli), cut into 1/8-inch-thick slices

4 tablespoons Caesar dressing

1/4 cup shredded fresh Parmesan cheese (1 oz)

2 cups torn romaine lettuce (about 6 leaves)

1 large tomato, sliced

1) Heat oven to 375°F. Grease large cookie sheet with shortening or nonstick cooking spray. Remove dough from both cans. Place dough seam side down and join ends to form large ring; press ends together firmly to seal.

2) Brush dough ring with beaten egg. With kitchen scissors, cut surface of dough every 2 inches to form V's.

3) Bake 20 to 25 minutes or until deep golden brown. Cool 15 minutes.

4) With serrated knife, cut bread ring in half horizontally. Top bottom half of ring with chicken. Drizzle with 2 tablespoons of the dressing. Sprinkle with Parmesan cheese. Top with lettuce, tomato and remaining 2 tablespoons dressing. Cover with top half of ring. Cut into sandwiches.

HIGH ALTITUDE (3500-6500 FT.): No change.

Nutrition Information Per Serving:	
Calories: 325	From Fat: 110
Total Fat	12g
Saturated Fat	3g
Cholesterol	55mg
Sodium	1310mg
Total Carbohydrate	38g
Dietary Fiber	1g
Sugars	6g
Protein	16g

CREAMY GARDEN COLESLAW
PG. 130

No-Fuss Sides

Round out your suppers with this wide assortment of simply delicious side dishes.

WARM HONEY-MUSTARD
POTATO SALAD
PG. 133

ROASTED VEGETABLES
WITH SPICY AÏOLI DIP
PG. 126

SUMMER SQUASH AU GRATIN
PG. 132

Herb Garden Vegetables

PREP TIME: 20 MINUTES (READY IN 20 MINUTES)
SERVINGS: 6

e EASY

2 tablespoons butter or margarine

1½ cups fresh broccoli florets

1½ cups fresh cauliflower florets

1 cup julienne-cut (2x¼x¼-inch) carrots

½ red bell pepper, chopped

2 garlic cloves, minced

1 tablespoon chopped fresh thyme

1 tablespoon chopped fresh basil

¼ teaspoon salt

1) In large skillet or wok, melt butter over medium heat. Add broccoli, cauliflower and carrots; stir to coat with butter. Cover; cook 4 to 6 minutes or until vegetables are crisp-tender, stirring occasionally.

2) Stir in bell pepper, garlic, thyme, basil and salt. Cook and stir 2 to 3 minutes or until thoroughly heated.

HIGH ALTITUDE (3500-6500 FT.): No change.

Nutrition Information Per Serving:	
Calories: 70	From Fat: 35
Total Fat	4g
Saturated Fat	2.5g
Trans Fat	0g
Cholesterol	10mg
Sodium	150mg
Total Carbohydrate	6g
Dietary Fiber	2g
Sugars	3g
Protein	2g

Cheesy Chicken Oven Fries

PREP TIME:	30 MINUTES (READY IN 30 MINUTES)	⊖ EASY
SERVINGS:	6	

2½ cups frozen cottage fries
(half of 2-lb bag)

1½ cups chopped deli rotisserie chicken
(without skin)

¼ cup mayonnaise

½ teaspoon garlic powder

½ teaspoon chili powder

1½ cups shredded Cheddar cheese
(6 oz)

½ cup chopped precooked bacon
(8 slices from 2.1-oz package)

Sour cream, if desired

Ketchup, if desired

1) Heat oven to 450°F. Line 15x10x1-inch pan with foil. Bake cottage fries as directed on bag.

2) Meanwhile, in small bowl, mix chicken, mayonnaise, garlic powder and chili powder.

3) Sprinkle 1 cup of the cheese evenly over hot cottage fries. Spoon chicken mixture evenly over cheese. Sprinkle with remaining cheese and the bacon.

4) Bake 3 to 5 minutes longer or until cheese is melted. Serve with sour cream and ketchup.

HIGH ALTITUDE (3500-6500 FT.): Bake cottage fries using High Altitude directions on bag.

Nutrition Information Per Serving:

Calories:	330	From Fat:	220
Total Fat			24g
Saturated Fat			9g
Trans Fat			1g
Cholesterol			70mg
Sodium			510mg
Total Carbohydrate			8g
Dietary Fiber			0g
Sugars			0g
Protein			20g

Roasted Vegetables with Spicy Aïoli Dip

PREP TIME: 25 MINUTES (READY IN 50 MINUTES)
SERVINGS: 24

AÏOLI DIP

    1   cup mayonnaise or salad dressing

    1/2 cup sour cream

    1/2 cup garlic ranch dressing

        Fresh chives, if desired

VEGETABLES

    4   medium red bell peppers, cut into
        1 1/2-inch squares

    2   medium red onions, cut into wedges

    4   small yellow summer squash, cut
        into 1-inch-thick slices

    1/2 lb fresh green beans, trimmed

    24 fresh whole mushrooms

    2   tablespoons olive or vegetable oil

    2   teaspoons seasoned salt

1) In medium bowl, mix mayonnaise, sour cream and dressing until smooth. Refrigerate at least 30 minutes to blend flavors. Garnish with chives.

2) Meanwhile, heat oven to 450°F. In large bowl, toss vegetables with oil and seasoned salt to coat evenly. Arrange vegetables in ungreased large shallow roasting pan, at least 16x12 inches.

3) Bake 15 to 20 minutes or until crisp-tender. Refrigerate vegetables at least 8 hours or overnight, and serve cold with dip.

Grilling Directions: Heat gas or charcoal grill. In large bowl, toss vegetables with oil and seasoned salt to coat evenly. Place vegetables, cut side down, on gas grill over medium-low heat or charcoal grill over medium-high coals. Cover grill. Cook 14 to 18 minutes or until crisp-tender, turning once and brushing with additional oil to keep surfaces moist. (Cooking time will vary according to size of vegetables.)

HIGH ALTITUDE (3500-6500 FT.): No change.

Nutrition Information Per Serving:	
Calories: 130	From Fat: 110
Total Fat	12g
Saturated Fat	2.5g
Trans Fat	0g
Cholesterol	10mg
Sodium	210mg
Total Carbohydrate	5g
Dietary Fiber	1g
Sugars	3g
Protein	2g

Orange Caramelized Squash Rings

PREP TIME: 15 MINUTES (READY IN 1 HOUR 15 MINUTES)
SERVINGS: 4

 EASY

2 medium acorn squash

2 tablespoons butter, melted

2 tablespoons orange marmalade

2 tablespoons packed brown sugar

1) Heat oven to 350°F. Wash squash; pierce several times with fork. Place squash on microwavable paper towel in microwave oven. Microwave on High 5 to 6 minutes, turning and rotating twice, until skin starts to soften. Let stand in microwave about 5 minutes to cool slightly.

2) Cut off small portion of each end of each squash. Cut each squash into 4 rings (about 1-inch thick); remove seeds. Place rings in ungreased 15x10x1-inch pan, overlapping slightly if necessary. Brush tops with ½ of the butter. Turn; brush with remaining butter.

3) Bake 30 minutes. In small bowl, mix marmalade and brown sugar. Brush over top of squash. Bake 10 minutes. Turn slices over; brush with remaining mixture. Bake 5 to 10 minutes longer or until squash is tender.

HIGH ALTITUDE (3500-6500 FT.): No change.

Nutrition Information Per Serving:	
Calories: 210	From Fat: 50
Total Fat	6g
Saturated Fat	3.5g
Trans Fat	0g
Cholesterol	15mg
Sodium	55mg
Total Carbohydrate	36g
Dietary Fiber	7g
Sugars	14g
Protein	2g

Baby Peas with Lemon-Pepper and Honey

PREP TIME: 15 MINUTES (READY IN 15 MINUTES)
SERVINGS: 6 (2/3 CUP EACH)

EASY   LOW FAT

1 bag (1-lb) Green Giant Select® LeSueur® frozen baby sweet peas

2 teaspoons honey

1 teaspoon butter

¼ teaspoon lemon-pepper seasoning

¼ teaspoon salt

Nutrition Information Per Serving:	
Calories: 70	From Fat: 10
Total Fat	1g
Saturated Fat	0g
Trans Fat	0g
Cholesterol	0mg
Sodium	170mg
Total Carbohydrate	12g
Dietary Fiber	3g
Sugars	5g
Protein	4g

1) In medium saucepan or microwavable dish, cook peas as directed on bag. Drain; return to saucepan.

2) Add honey, butter, lemon-pepper seasoning and salt; toss to coat. Garnish with lemon peel, if desired.

HIGH ALTITUDE (3500-6500 FT.): No change.

Southwestern Calico Baked Beans

PREP TIME: 15 MINUTES (READY IN 1 HOUR 15 MINUTES)
SERVINGS: 20 (1/2 CUP EACH)

EASY

1 package (12 oz) spicy pork sausage

4 cans (15 oz each) baked beans, drained

1 can (15 or 15.5 oz) dark red kidney beans, drained

1 can (15 oz) black-eyed peas, drained

1 box (9 oz) Green Giant® frozen baby lima beans

1 cup Old El Paso® Thick 'n Chunky salsa

1 package (1.25 oz) Old El Paso® taco seasoning mix

Nutrition Information Per Serving:	
Calories: 180	From Fat: 30
Total Fat	3.5g
Saturated Fat	1g
Trans Fat	0g
Cholesterol	10mg
Sodium	740mg
Total Carbohydrate	27g
Dietary Fiber	7g
Sugars	4g
Protein	9g

1) Heat oven to 350°F. In 10-inch skillet, cook sausage over medium heat, stirring frequently, until no longer pink; drain.

2) In 3-quart casserole, combine sausage and remaining ingredients; stir.

3) Bake uncovered 60 to 70 minutes or until hot and bubbly.

HIGH ALTITUDE (3500-6500 FT.): No change.

Fresh Fruit Orange Fizz

PREP TIME: 10 MINUTES (READY IN 10 MINUTES)
SERVINGS: 12 (1/2 CUP EACH)

EASY   **LOW FAT**

2 cups cubed cantaloupe

2 cups cubed honeydew melon

1 cup halved fresh strawberries

1 large banana, halved lengthwise, sliced

1/2 cup frozen (thawed) orange juice concentrate

3/4 cup orange-flavored carbonated beverage, chilled

Nutrition Information Per Serving:	
Calories: 60	From Fat: 0
Total Fat	0g
Saturated Fat	0g
Trans Fat	0g
Cholesterol	0mg
Sodium	10mg
Total Carbohydrate	15g
Dietary Fiber	1g
Sugars	13g
Protein	0g

1) In large bowl, gently mix all fruit and orange juice concentrate. Stir in carbonated beverage. Serve in small dessert bowls.

HIGH ALTITUDE (3500-6500 FT.): No change.

Asian Noodle Salad

PREP TIME:	20 MINUTES (READY IN 20 MINUTES)
SERVINGS:	12 (1 CUP EACH)

 EASY

SALAD

1 bag (10 oz) Italian blend salad greens

2 cups matchstick-cut carrots (from 10-oz bag)

2 cans (8 oz each) sliced water chestnuts, drained

1 can (11 oz) mandarin orange segments, drained

$1/3$ cup sliced green onions (5 to 6 medium)

1 tablespoon sesame seed, toasted if desired

1 cup chow mein noodles

DRESSING

2 tablespoons sugar

$1/2$ teaspoon ground ginger

$1/4$ teaspoon salt

2 tablespoons vinegar

1 teaspoon red pepper sauce

1 teaspoon soy sauce

$1/4$ cup vegetable oil

1) In 13x9-inch (3-quart) glass baking dish, layer salad greens, carrots, water chestnuts, orange segments and onions. Sprinkle with sesame seed.

2) In small bowl, mix all dressing ingredients except oil with wire whisk. Gradually add oil, beating until well blended. Drizzle dressing evenly over salad. Top with chow mein noodles.

HIGH ALTITUDE (3500-6500 FT.): No change.

Nutrition Information Per Serving:		
Calories: 120	From Fat:	60
Total Fat		6g
Saturated Fat		1g
Trans Fat		0g
Cholesterol		0mg
Sodium		120mg
Total Carbohydrate		14g
Dietary Fiber		2g
Sugars		5g
Protein		2g

tip

For a bit of extra sesame flavor, use 1 teaspoon sesame oil instead of the soy sauce in the dressing.

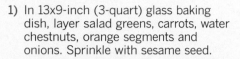

Creamy Garden Coleslaw

PREP TIME: 20 MINUTES (READY IN 40 MINUTES)
SERVINGS: 12 (1/2 CUP EACH)

e EASY

7 cups coleslaw mix

1 small zucchini, shredded
(about 1 cup)

1 cup shredded carrots (1½ medium)

½ cup finely chopped green bell
pepper (½ medium)

¾ cup mayonnaise or salad dressing

2 tablespoons sugar

2 teaspoons lemon juice

1 teaspoon celery seed

½ teaspoon salt

1) In large bowl, gently mix ingredients.
Refrigerate 15 to 20 minutes before
serving.

HIGH ALTITUDE (3500-6500 FT.): No change.

Nutrition Information Per Serving:			
Calories:	130	From Fat:	100
Total Fat			11g
Saturated Fat			1.5g
Trans Fat			0g
Cholesterol			5mg
Sodium			200mg
Total Carbohydrate			8g
Dietary Fiber			2g
Sugars			5g
Protein			1g

Vermicelli with Fresh Herb-Tomato Sauce

PREP TIME: 20 MINUTES (READY IN 20 MINUTES)
SERVINGS: 5 (1-1/4 CUPS EACH)

EASY

7 oz uncooked vermicelli

3 medium tomatoes, seeded, chopped (about 2 cups)

1/2 cup shredded Parmesan cheese (2 oz)

2 tablespoons chopped fresh basil

2 tablespoons chopped fresh chives

2 tablespoons olive oil

1/2 teaspoon salt

1/2 teaspoon finely grated lemon peel

1/8 teaspoon coarse ground black pepper

1 clove garlic, minced

Nutrition Information Per Serving:	
Calories: 260	From Fat: 80
Total Fat	9g
Saturated Fat	2.5g
Trans Fat	0g
Cholesterol	10mg
Sodium	580mg
Total Carbohydrate	35g
Dietary Fiber	3g
Sugars	3g
Protein	10g

1) Cook and drain vermicelli as directed on package.

2) Meanwhile, in large bowl, mix remaining ingredients.

3) Gently stir cooked vermicelli into tomato mixture to coat.

HIGH ALTITUDE (3500-6500 FT.): No change.

Layered Picnic Potato Salad

PREP TIME: 20 MINUTES (READY IN 20 MINUTES)
SERVINGS: 15 (1/2 CUP EACH)

EASY

1 1/2 cups Green Giant Select® LeSueur® frozen baby sweet peas (from 1-lb bag)

1 jar (2 oz) diced pimientos, drained

3 pints deli potato salad (6 cups)

Nutrition Information Per Serving:	
Calories: 150	From Fat: 80
Total Fat	9g
Saturated Fat	1.5g
Trans Fat	0g
Cholesterol	10mg
Sodium	260mg
Total Carbohydrate	15g
Dietary Fiber	2g
Sugars	3g
Protein	2g

1) Cook peas as directed on package. Drain; rinse with cold water until cool.

2) Line 9x5-inch loaf pan with plastic wrap. Stir pimientos into potato salad. Spoon and spread half of potato salad into pan; top with peas. Spoon and carefully spread remaining potato salad evenly over peas; press gently. Serve immediately or refrigerate until serving time.

3) To serve, invert onto serving platter. Peel off plastic wrap.

HIGH ALTITUDE (3500-6500 FT.): No change.

Summer Squash au Gratin

PREP TIME: 20 MINUTES (READY IN 55 MINUTES)
SERVINGS: 8

e EASY

2 medium (about 6 inches long each) zucchini squash

1 medium (about 8 inches long) yellow summer squash

4 green onions, chopped (¼ cup)

½ red bell pepper, chopped (½ cup)

1 packet (1.25 to 1.8 oz) white sauce mix

1½ cups milk

1 cup shredded sharp Cheddar cheese (4 oz)

1 tablespoon butter or margarine, melted

¼ cup Progresso® plain bread crumbs

Nutrition Information Per Serving:		
Calories: 130	From Fat:	70
Total Fat		8g
Saturated Fat		4.5g
Trans Fat		0g
Cholesterol		20mg
Sodium		300mg
Total Carbohydrate		10g
Dietary Fiber		1g
Sugars		4g
Protein		7g

1) Heat oven to 350°F. Cut each squash in half lengthwise; cut into ½-inch-thick slices. Place squash slices, onions and bell pepper in 11x7-inch (2-quart) glass baking dish or 2-quart casserole. Add 1 tablespoon water. Cover with microwavable plastic wrap, venting one corner. Microwave on High 5 to 7 minutes or until crisp-tender; drain well.

2) Meanwhile, in 2-quart saucepan, cook white sauce mix and 1½ cups milk as directed on package. Remove from heat. Stir in cheese. Pour over zucchini mixture in baking dish; stir gently to coat. In small bowl, mix melted butter and bread crumbs. Sprinkle over zucchini mixture.

3) Bake 30 to 35 minutes or until bubbly and golden brown.

HIGH ALTITUDE (3500-6500 FT.): Omit Microwave directions in Step 1. Place squash slices, onions and bell pepper in 11x7-inch (2-quart) glass baking dish.

Speedy Baked Beans

PREP TIME: 10 MINUTES (READY IN 50 MINUTES)
SERVINGS: 6 (1/2 CUP EACH)

e EASY   **lf** LOW FAT

1 can (28 oz) baked beans

⅓ cup packed brown sugar

¼ cup finely chopped onion (½ medium)

¼ cup ketchup

1 teaspoon yellow mustard

Nutrition Information Per Serving:		
Calories: 200	From Fat:	15
Total Fat		1.5g
Saturated Fat		0.5g
Trans Fat		0g
Cholesterol		10mg
Sodium		710mg
Total Carbohydrate		41g
Dietary Fiber		7g
Sugars		21g
Protein		7g

1) Heat oven to 350°F. In 1½-quart casserole, mix ingredients.

2) Bake 30 to 40 minutes or until hot and bubbly.

HIGH ALTITUDE (3500-6500 FT.): Heat oven to 375°F.

Warm Honey-Mustard Potato Salad

PREP TIME: 10 MINUTES (READY IN 10 MINUTES)
SERVINGS: 12 (1/2 CUP EACH)

e EASY   **f** LOW FAT

1 bag (1 lb 4 oz) refrigerated red potato wedges with skins (4 cups)

1/4 cup honey

1/4 cup yellow mustard

1 cup sliced celery (2 stalks)

1/2 cup chopped red bell pepper (1/2 medium)

2 tablespoons chopped green onions (2 medium) or red onion

1/4 teaspoon garlic powder

1/4 teaspoon salt

1/8 teaspoon coarsely ground black pepper

1) In 2-quart microwavable casserole, place potatoes; cover. Microwave on High 3 to 5 minutes or until desired doneness. Cool slightly, about 5 minutes.

2) Meanwhile, in small bowl, mix honey and mustard until well blended.

3) Add remaining ingredients to potatoes in casserole. Pour honey mixture over salad; mix gently to coat.

HIGH ALTITUDE (3500-6500 FT.): No change.

Nutrition Information Per Serving:

Calories: 60	From Fat: 0
Total Fat	0g
Saturated Fat	0g
Trans Fat	0g
Cholesterol	0mg
Sodium	160mg
Total Carbohydrate	13g
Dietary Fiber	2g
Sugars	8g
Protein	2g

Spring Peas and Pasta

PREP TIME: 20 MINUTES (READY IN 2 HOURS 20 MINUTES)
SERVINGS: 14 (1/2 CUP EACH)

e EASY

2 **cups uncooked elbow macaroni (8 oz)**

1 **cup fresh snow pea pods, trimmed**

1 **cup fresh sugar snap peas**

1 **cup Green Giant Select® LeSueur® frozen baby sweet peas (from 1-lb bag)**

½ **cup mayonnaise**

⅓ **cup refrigerated basil pesto**

2 **medium green onions, chopped (2 tablespoons)**

2 **teaspoons lemon juice**

1 **teaspoon salt**

1) Cook macaroni as directed on package, adding pea pods, sugar snap peas and baby sweet peas during last 2 to 3 minutes of cooking time. Drain; rinse with cold water until cool.

2) Meanwhile, in large bowl, mix remaining ingredients.

3) Add cooked macaroni with peas to mayonnaise mixture; toss to coat. Cover; refrigerate at least 2 hours or until chilled before serving.

HIGH ALTITUDE (3500-6500 FT.): No change.

Nutrition Information Per Serving:	
Calories: 160	From Fat: 90
Total Fat	10g
Saturated Fat	1.5g
Trans Fat	0g
Cholesterol	0mg
Sodium	330mg
Total Carbohydrate	15g
Dietary Fiber	2g
Sugars	1g
Protein	4g

Cheese is a great addition to this refreshing salad. Try using cubed mozzarella or even mild Cheddar cheese.

Oven–Steamed Herbed Corn

PREP TIME: 10 MINUTES (READY IN 40 MINUTES)
SERVINGS: 12 (1/2 EAR EACH)

⊖ EASY   ⓕ LOW FAT

6 ears sweet corn, husks removed, cleaned, cut in half

Water

2 tablespoons chopped fresh parsley

2 tablespoons butter, melted

¼ teaspoon seasoned salt

Nutrition Information Per Serving:		
Calories: 80	From Fat:	25
Total Fat		2.5g
Saturated Fat		1.5g
Trans Fat		0g
Cholesterol		5mg
Sodium		70mg
Total Carbohydrate		13g
Dietary Fiber		2g
Sugars		2g
Protein		2g

1) Heat oven to 400°F. Place corn in ungreased 13x9-inch (3-quart) glass baking dish. Add water until ½ inch deep. Cover dish tightly with foil; bake 30 minutes.

2) Meanwhile, in small bowl, mix parsley, butter and seasoned salt.

3) Drain water from corn. Pour butter mixture over corn. Turn corn to coat with butter mixture before serving.

HIGH ALTITUDE (3500-6500 FT.): Bake 30 to 35 minutes.

Cheesy Broccoli and Carrot Casserole

PREP TIME: 25 MINUTES (READY IN 45 MINUTES)
SERVINGS: 6 (1/2 CUP EACH)

⊖ EASY

2 cups small fresh broccoli florets

1 cup sliced (⅛ inch) carrots

½ cup sour cream

¼ cup milk

1½ cups shredded Cheddar-American cheese blend (6 oz)

½ cup French fried onions (from 2.8-oz can)

Nutrition Information Per Serving:		
Calories: 200	From Fat:	140
Total Fat		15g
Saturated Fat		9g
Trans Fat		1g
Cholesterol		40mg
Sodium		500mg
Total Carbohydrate		7g
Dietary Fiber		1g
Sugars		3g
Protein		8g

1) Heat oven to 350°F. In ungreased 1-quart microwavable casserole, mix broccoli, carrots and ½ cup water. Cover with microwavable plastic wrap. Microwave on High 4 to 6 minutes, stirring every 2 minutes, until vegetables are crisp-tender; drain.

2) Stir in sour cream, milk and cheese until well mixed. Sprinkle with onions.

3) Bake uncovered 15 to 20 minutes or until bubbly and vegetables are tender.

HIGH ALTITUDE (3500-6500 FT.): In Step 3, bake 20 to 25 minutes.

Grilled Asparagus and New Potatoes

PREP TIME: 30 MINUTES (READY IN 30 MINUTES)
SERVINGS: 4

e EASY

2 tablespoons olive oil

½ teaspoon salt

½ teaspoon lemon-pepper seasoning

6 small red potatoes (about ¾ lb), unpeeled, quartered

1 lb fresh asparagus spears, trimmed

1) Heat gas or charcoal grill. In large shallow bowl, mix 1 tablespoon of the oil, ¼ teaspoon of the salt and ¼ teaspoon of the lemon-pepper seasoning. Add potatoes; toss to coat. Place in grill basket.

2) Place grill basket on grill over medium heat. Cook 15 minutes, shaking grill basket occasionally to turn and mix potatoes.

3) Meanwhile, place asparagus spears in same shallow bowl. Add remaining tablespoon oil, remaining ¼ teaspoon salt and remaining ¼ teaspoon lemon-pepper seasoning; toss to coat.

4) Add asparagus to potatoes in grill basket. Cook about 10 minutes longer or until potatoes and asparagus are tender, shaking basket occasionally to turn and mix vegetables.

HIGH ALTITUDE (3500-6500 FT.): Grill over medium-low heat.

Nutrition Information Per Serving:		
Calories: 140	From Fat:	60
Total Fat		7g
Saturated Fat		1g
Trans Fat		0g
Cholesterol		0mg
Sodium		350mg
Total Carbohydrate		18g
Dietary Fiber		3g
Sugars		2g
Protein		3g

Grill baskets make it easy to hold and turn vegetables on the grill, but a sheet of foil with a few holes poked through it works just as well.

Mexican Cheesy Potatoes

PREP TIME: 20 MINUTES (READY IN 1 HOUR 30 MINUTES)
SERVINGS: 20 (1/2 CUP EACH)

EASY

1 medium onion, chopped ($\frac{1}{2}$ cup)

1 container (16 oz) sour cream

1 can (10$\frac{3}{4}$ oz) condensed cream of chicken soup

1 can (4.5 oz) Old El Paso® chopped green chiles

1 bag (32 oz) frozen southern-style diced hash-brown potatoes, thawed

2 cups cubed mild Mexican prepared cheese product with jalapeño peppers (12 oz from loaf)

1 cup shredded pepper Jack cheese (4 oz)

1 cup shredded mozzarella cheese (4 oz)

2 cups crushed gold or yellow tortilla chips (about 6 oz)

1) Heat oven to 350°F. Spray 13x9-inch (3-quart) glass baking dish with cooking spray. In large bowl, mix onion, sour cream, soup and green chiles. Stir in hash browns. Fold in cubed and shredded cheeses; pour into baking dish.

2) Bake 1 hour or until potatoes are tender and mixture is hot and bubbly. Sprinkle with crushed chips; bake 5 to 10 minutes longer or until chips are light golden brown.

HIGH ALTITUDE (3500-6500 FT.): Heat oven to 375°F.

Nutrition Information Per Serving:

Calories:	250	From Fat:	120
Total Fat			14g
Saturated Fat			7g
Trans Fat			0g
Cholesterol			40mg
Sodium			600mg
Total Carbohydrate			23g
Dietary Fiber			2g
Sugars			4g
Protein			8g

Dilly Buttered Carrots and Rotini

PREP TIME: 10 MINUTES (READY IN 20 MINUTES)
SERVINGS: 8 (1/2 CUP EACH)

EASY   **LOW FAT**

1 cup uncooked rainbow or plain rotini pasta (3 oz)

2 cups ready-to-eat baby-cut carrots, cut in half lengthwise and crosswise

1 tablespoon butter

1 teaspoon chopped fresh or ¼ teaspoon dried dill weed

¼ teaspoon salt

Dash pepper

Nutrition Information Per Serving:		
Calories: 80	From Fat:	15
Total Fat		2g
Saturated Fat		1g
Trans Fat		0g
Cholesterol		0mg
Sodium		160mg
Total Carbohydrate		14g
Dietary Fiber		2g
Sugars		2g
Protein		2g

1) In 3-quart saucepan, cook pasta as directed on package, adding carrots during last 2 to 3 minutes of cooking time; cook until pasta is tender and carrots are crisp-tender. Drain; return to saucepan.

2) Add butter, dill, salt and pepper; toss gently to coat.

HIGH ALTITUDE (3500-6500 FT.): No change.

Asparagus with Toasted Walnut Butter

PREP TIME: 15 MINUTES (READY IN 15 MINUTES)
SERVINGS: 8

EASY   **LOW FAT**

2 lb fresh asparagus

6 tablespoons butter

3 tablespoons finely chopped walnuts

1 tablespoon walnut oil, if desired

¼ teaspoon salt

Nutrition Information Per Serving:		
Calories: 110	From Fat: 100	
Total Fat		11g
Saturated Fat		6g
Trans Fat		0.5g
Cholesterol		25mg
Sodium		135mg
Total Carbohydrate		1g
Dietary Fiber		1g
Sugars		0g
Protein		2g

1) Wash asparagus; snap off tough stem ends. In large skillet or Dutch oven, bring 1 inch of lightly salted water to a boil. Arrange asparagus spears evenly in skillet. Cover; cook 4 to 5 minutes or until asparagus is crisp-tender. Drain.

2) Meanwhile, in small saucepan, mix butter and walnuts. Cook over low heat until butter browns and walnuts are toasted, watching carefully to prevent butter from burning. Stir in oil and salt.

3) Arrange hot asparagus on large serving platter. Top with walnut butter.

HIGH ALTITUDE (3500-6500 FT.): No change.

Orange-Pecan-Squash Bake

| PREP TIME: | 15 MINUTES (READY IN 30 MINUTES) |
| SERVINGS: | 4 |

e EASY

1 small butternut squash (about 1 lb)

¼ cup packed brown sugar

¼ cup honey

2 tablespoons butter or margarine

2 tablespoons orange juice

2 tablespoons chopped pecans

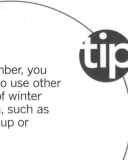

Remember, you can also use other types of winter squash, such as buttercup or acorn.

1) Heat oven to 375°F. Spray 8-inch square (2-quart) glass baking dish with cooking spray. Cut squash into 4 pieces; discard seeds and membranes. Place squash skin side down in baking dish. Cover with microwavable plastic wrap. Microwave on High 5 to 10 minutes or until squash is slightly tender.

2) Meanwhile, in 2-quart saucepan, mix brown sugar, honey, butter and orange juice. Heat to boiling over medium heat, stirring occasionally. Reduce heat to low; simmer uncovered 2 to 3 minutes or until slightly thickened. Remove from heat. Stir in pecans.

3) Spoon brown sugar mixture evenly over squash. Bake 10 minutes or until squash is fork-tender.

HIGH ALTITUDE (3500-6500 FT.): In Step 3, bake 13 minutes.

Nutrition Information Per Serving:		
Calories: 240	From Fat:	70
Total Fat		8g
Saturated Fat		4g
Trans Fat		0g
Cholesterol		15mg
Sodium		50mg
Total Carbohydrate		41g
Dietary Fiber		2g
Sugars		35g
Protein		1g

Main Dishes

Mix up supper-time routines with hearty casseroles, pasta favorites and more.

CHICKEN WAIKIKI
PG. 147

EASY CHICKEN AND DUMPLINGS
PG. 171

RANCH MEDLEY CASSEROLE
PG. 172

LEMONY PORK PRIMAVERA PASTA
PG. 153

Bacon-Cheeseburger Potato Pie

PREP TIME: 45 MINUTES (READY IN 1 HOUR 15 MINUTES)
SERVINGS: 6

1½ lb extra-lean (at least 90%) ground beef

½ cup Progresso® plain bread crumbs

¼ cup finely chopped onion

¼ cup ketchup

2 teaspoons yellow mustard

½ teaspoon salt

1¼ cups water

3 tablespoons butter or margarine

¼ teaspoon garlic salt

¾ cup milk

2 cups mashed potato flakes

1 cup shredded Cheddar cheese (4 oz)

1 medium tomato, chopped

3 slices precooked bacon, crumbled

2 green onions, sliced, if desired

1) Heat oven to 375°F. In medium bowl, mix ground beef, bread crumbs, onion, ketchup, mustard and salt. Press mixture in bottom and up sides of ungreased 9-inch pie plate. Bake 15 minutes.

2) In medium saucepan, place water, butter and garlic salt. Heat to boiling. Remove from heat. Add milk. With fork, stir in potato flakes. Stir in ½ cup of the cheese.

3) Remove partially baked beef crust from oven; pour off any drippings. Spoon potato mixture evenly into crust. Return to oven; bake 10 to 15 minutes longer or until beef is thoroughly cooked and thermometer placed in center of crust reads 160°F, and potatoes are hot.

4) Remove pie from oven. Top with tomato, remaining ½ cup cheese and crumbled bacon; bake 5 minutes longer or until cheese is melted. Remove from oven; top with green onions. Let stand 10 minutes before serving.

HIGH ALTITUDE (3500-6500 FT.): No change.

Nutrition Information Per Serving:		
Calories: 450	From Fat:	220
Total Fat		24g
Saturated Fat		12g
Trans Fat		1g
Cholesterol		110mg
Sodium		770mg
Total Carbohydrate		25g
Dietary Fiber		2g
Sugars		6g
Protein		32g

Cajun Lasagna

PREP TIME: 30 MINUTES (READY IN 1 HOUR 35 MINUTES)
SERVINGS: 8

10 uncooked lasagna noodles

2 cans (14.5 oz each) diced tomatoes with green chiles, drained

1 bag (12 oz) frozen cooked deveined peeled miniature/tiny shrimp (tails off), thawed, rinsed and drained

1/2 lb smoked spicy sausage (andouille or kielbasa), cut into 1/4-inch slices

1 jar (16 oz) Alfredo pasta sauce

2 cups shredded mozzarella cheese (8 oz)

1/2 cup shredded Parmesan cheese (2 oz)

2 tablespoons chopped fresh parsley, if desired

1) Heat oven to 350°F. Cook and drain noodles as directed on package.

2) Spread 1 cup of the tomatoes in ungreased 13x9-inch (3-quart) glass baking dish. Top with 5 noodles, overlapping slightly as needed. Layer with half each of the remaining tomatoes, the shrimp, sausage, Alfredo sauce and mozzarella cheese. Repeat layers. Sprinkle Parmesan cheese over the top.

3) Cover dish with foil. Bake about 30 minutes or until center is hot and bubbly. Uncover; bake 15 to 20 minutes longer or until cheese is melted. Let stand 15 minutes before cutting. Sprinkle with parsley.

HIGH ALTITUDE (3500-6500 FT.): In Step 3, bake covered 40 minutes. Bake uncovered 20 minutes longer.

Nutrition Information Per Serving:		
Calories: 510	From Fat: 260	
Total Fat	29g	
Saturated Fat	17g	
Trans Fat	1g	
Cholesterol	175mg	
Sodium	1370mg	
Total Carbohydrate	31g	
Dietary Fiber	3g	
Sugars	6g	
Protein	32g	

Chicken–Biscuit Bake

PREP TIME: 20 MINUTES (READY IN 1 HOUR)
SERVINGS: 8

 EASY

2 cans (10¾ oz each) condensed cream of chicken soup

1 cup milk

½ teaspoon dried thyme leaves

¼ teaspoon pepper

4 cups cut-up cooked chicken

1 bag (1 lb) Green Giant Select® frozen broccoli, carrots & cauliflower

1 can (16.3 oz) Pillsbury® Grands!® Homestyle refrigerated biscuits

1) Heat oven to 350°F. In 4-quart saucepan, heat soup, milk, thyme, pepper, chicken and vegetables to boiling over medium-high heat, stirring occasionally. Boil and stir 3 to 5 minutes. Spread in ungreased 13x9-inch (3-quart) glass baking dish.

2) Separate dough into 8 biscuits; place evenly over hot chicken mixture.

3) Bake 35 to 40 minutes or until biscuits are golden brown and no longer doughy on bottom. After 20 minutes, cover with foil if necessary to prevent excessive browning.

HIGH ALTITUDE (3500-6500 FT.): Bake 40 to 45 minutes.

Nutrition Information Per Serving:	
Calories: 420	From Fat: 170

Total Fat	19g
Saturated Fat	6g
Trans Fat	3.5g
Cholesterol	70mg
Sodium	1230mg
Total Carbohydrate	35g
Dietary Fiber	2g
Sugars	6g
Protein	28g

Sloppy Joe Squares

PREP TIME: 20 MINUTES (READY IN 55 MINUTES)
SERVINGS: 8

e EASY

1 lb lean (at least 80%) ground beef

1 can (16 oz) sloppy joe sauce

2 cans (10.1 oz each) Pillsbury® refrigerated Big & Buttery crescent dinner rolls

2 cups shredded Cheddar cheese (8 oz)

1 tablespoon sesame seed

Nutrition Information Per Serving:	
Calories: 520	From Fat: 280
Total Fat	31g
Saturated Fat	12g
Trans Fat	4.5g
Cholesterol	65mg
Sodium	1090mg
Total Carbohydrate	36g
Dietary Fiber	1g
Sugars	10g
Protein	23g

1) Heat oven to 350°F. In 10-inch skillet, cook beef over medium heat 8 to 10 minutes, stirring occasionally, until thoroughly cooked; drain. Stir in sauce. Heat to boiling, stirring occasionally.

2) Unroll 1 can of the dough; place in ungreased 13x9-inch (3-quart) glass baking dish. Press in bottom and ½ inch up sides of dish. Spread beef mixture over dough; sprinkle with cheese. Unroll second can of dough; place over cheese. Sprinkle with sesame seed.

3) Bake 30 to 35 minutes or until mixture is bubbly and dough is golden brown. Cut into squares to serve.

HIGH ALTITUDE (3500-6500 FT.): Bake 35 to 40 minutes.

Chicken and Tomato Topped Potatoes

PREP TIME: 30 MINUTES (READY IN 30 MINUTES)
SERVINGS: 4

e EASY

4 medium baking potatoes

2 cups shredded deli rotisserie chicken (without skin)

1 cup shredded mild Cheddar cheese (4 oz)

3 Italian plum (Roma) tomatoes, chopped (1 cup)

½ teaspoon garlic-pepper blend

¾ cup sour cream

¼ cup cooked real bacon pieces (from 2.5-oz package)

Nutrition Information Per Serving:	
Calories: 530	From Fat: 230
Total Fat	25g
Saturated Fat	13g
Trans Fat	0.5g
Cholesterol	125mg
Sodium	670mg
Total Carbohydrate	41g
Dietary Fiber	4g
Sugars	5g
Protein	34g

1) Scrub potatoes; prick several times with fork. Place potatoes on microwavable plate. Microwave on High for 15 to 17 minutes or until fork-tender.

2) Meanwhile, in medium bowl, mix chicken, cheese and tomatoes.

3) Split each potato in half lengthwise; place on microwavable plate. Mash each potato slightly. Sprinkle each with garlic-pepper blend; top with sour cream. Spoon ½ cup chicken mixture on each potato. Sprinkle with bacon pieces. Microwave on High for 2 to 3 minutes or until hot and cheese is melted. Serve warm.

HIGH ALTITUDE (3500-6500 FT.): No change.

Manicotti al Forno

PREP TIME: 35 MINUTES (READY IN 1 HOUR 25 MINUTES)
SERVINGS: 6

12 uncooked manicotti pasta shells

1 lb bulk Italian pork sausage

2 large cloves garlic, finely chopped

1 teaspoon dried oregano leaves

1 jar (26 oz) tomato pasta sauce

1 can (14.5 oz) diced tomatoes with Italian-style herbs, drained

1 egg

1 container (15 oz) part-skim ricotta cheese

3 cups shredded Italian cheese blend or mozzarella cheese (12 oz)

¼ cup fresh basil leaves, cut into strips

1) Heat oven to 350°F. Cook pasta shells as directed on package. Drain; rinse with cold water to cool.

2) Meanwhile, in 12-inch skillet, cook sausage, garlic and oregano over medium heat 8 to 10 minutes, stirring occasionally, until sausage is no longer pink; drain. Stir in pasta sauce and tomatoes. Spread 1 cup of the meat sauce in ungreased 13x9-inch (3-quart) glass baking dish.

3) In medium bowl, beat egg. Stir in ricotta cheese and 2 cups of the Italian cheese blend. Spoon cheese mixture into gallon-size food-storage plastic bag; seal bag. Cut 1-inch hole in one bottom corner of bag. Squeeze bag to pipe about ¼ cup cheese mixture into each pasta shell. Arrange stuffed shells over meat sauce in dish. Pour remaining meat sauce evenly over shells.

4) Cover dish with foil. Bake 35 to 40 minutes or until hot and bubbly. Top with remaining 1 cup Italian cheese blend. Bake uncovered 5 to 10 minutes longer or until cheese is melted. Sprinkle basil over top before serving.

HIGH ALTITUDE (3500-6500 FT.): In Step 4, bake covered 40 to 45 minutes. Top with remaining 1 cup Italian cheese blend. Bake uncovered 20 minutes longer.

Nutrition Information Per Serving:

Calories: 700	From Fat: 320
Total Fat	36g
Saturated Fat	17g
Trans Fat	0.5g
Cholesterol	135mg
Sodium	1970mg
Total Carbohydrate	57g
Dietary Fiber	4g
Sugars	16g
Protein	37g

Chicken Waikiki

PREP TIME: 35 MINUTES (READY IN 1 HOUR 20 MINUTES)
SERVINGS: 6 (1-1/2 CUPS EACH)

LOW FAT

3½ cups chicken broth

1½ cups uncooked regular long-grain white rice

1 can (20 oz) pineapple chunks in juice

1 cup sugar

3 tablespoons cornstarch

1 tablespoon grated gingerroot or ½ teaspoon ground ginger

⅓ cup cider vinegar

2 tablespoons soy sauce

1 medium red bell pepper, cut into 1-inch pieces (1 cup)

1 medium green bell pepper, cut into 1-inch pieces (1 cup)

6 boneless skinless chicken breasts (about 1½ lb)

1) Heat oven to 350°F. Spray 13x9 inch (3-quart) glass baking dish with nonstick cooking spray. In 2-quart saucepan, heat 3 cups of the broth to boiling over high heat. Add rice; reduce heat to medium-low. Cover; simmer about 20 minutes or until liquid is absorbed.

2) Meanwhile, drain pineapple juice into 2-cup measuring cup; add remaining ½ cup broth to make 1¼ cups. In another 2-quart saucepan, mix pineapple liquid, sugar, cornstarch, gingerroot, vinegar and soy sauce. Heat to boiling over high heat. Cook about 2 minutes, stirring constantly. Remove from heat. Stir in bell peppers and pineapple.

3) Cut chicken into 2½x1-inch strips. Spread rice in baking dish; arrange chicken strips over rice. Pour pineapple mixture over chicken and rice.

4) Cover dish with foil. Bake about 45 minutes or until chicken is no longer pink in center and mixture is bubbly.

HIGH ALTITUDE (3500-6500 FT.): No change.

Nutrition Information Per Serving:

Calories:	560	From Fat:	45
Total Fat			5g
Saturated Fat			1.5g
Trans Fat			0g
Cholesterol			70mg
Sodium			960mg
Total Carbohydrate			96g
Dietary Fiber			2g
Sugars			49g
Protein			33g

Pan-Seared Sirloin Steak

PREP TIME:	15 MINUTES (READY IN 15 MINUTES)	
SERVINGS:	4	

e EASY   **lf** LOW FAT

1 lb boneless beef sirloin steak
  (1 inch thick)

¾ teaspoon lemon-pepper seasoning

1 tablespoon grated lemon peel

1 tablespoon soy sauce

2 tablespoons olive oil

Nutrition Information Per Serving:	
Calories: 190 From Fat: 90	
Total Fat	10g
Saturated Fat	2g
Trans Fat	0g
Cholesterol	60mg
Sodium	340mg
Total Carbohydrate	0g
Dietary Fiber	0g
Sugars	0g
Protein	23g

1) Sprinkle beef with lemon-pepper seasoning. In small bowl, mix lemon peel, soy sauce and 1 tablespoon of the oil; brush over both sides of beef.

2) In 10-inch nonstick skillet, heat remaining tablespoon oil over medium heat. Add beef; cook 10 to 12 minutes or until browned on both sides and desired doneness. Cut into 4 serving pieces.

HIGH ALTITUDE (3500-6500 FT.): No change.

Shrimp Primavera Alfredo

PREP TIME:	25 MINUTES (READY IN 25 MINUTES)	
SERVINGS:	4 (1-1/2 CUPS EACH)	

e EASY

6 oz uncooked linguine or spaghetti

8 oz fresh asparagus spears, trimmed, cut into 1½-inch pieces

1 cup ready-to-eat baby-cut carrots (4 oz), quartered lengthwise

1 cup sliced fresh mushrooms

1 box (9 oz) Green Giant® frozen sugar snap peas

1 bag (12 oz) frozen ready-to-cook medium shrimp, thawed, tail shells removed

1 container (10 oz) refrigerated Alfredo sauce

2 tablespoons chopped fresh chives

1 teaspoon grated lemon peel

Nutrition Information Per Serving:	
Calories: 520 From Fat: 220	
Total Fat	24g
Saturated Fat	13g
Trans Fat	1g
Cholesterol	190mg
Sodium	630mg
Total Carbohydrate	48g
Dietary Fiber	6g
Sugars	5g
Protein	28g

tip

If you want to reduce the fat and calories a bit, simply use a reduced-fat Alfredo sauce.

1) Cook and drain linguine as directed on package; cover to keep warm.

2) Meanwhile, in 12-inch skillet, place asparagus, carrots, mushrooms, sugar snap peas and ½ cup water. Heat to boiling. Reduce heat to medium-low; cover and simmer 4 to 6 minutes or until vegetables are crisp-tender.

3) Add shrimp; cook and stir 2 to 3 minutes or until shrimp are pink. Drain; return mixture to skillet.

4) Stir in Alfredo sauce, chives and lemon peel. Simmer uncovered 2 to 4 minutes, stirring occasionally, until mixture is thoroughly heated. Serve over linguine. If desired, garnish with additional chives.

HIGH ALTITUDE (3500-6500 FT.): In Step 3, cook shrimp 3 to 5 minutes.

Chicken and Vegetables with Flaky Pastry

PREP TIME: 35 MINUTES (READY IN 45 MINUTES)
SERVINGS: 6

3 teaspoons olive oil

2 cups sliced baby portabella mushrooms (about 6 oz)

1 tablespoon butter or margarine

2 lb boneless skinless chicken breasts, quartered

1 cup ready-to-eat baby-cut carrots, quartered lengthwise

1 teaspoon salt

¼ teaspoon pepper

1 cup frozen small whole onions (from 1-lb bag)

½ cup white wine

1 Pillsbury® refrigerated pie crust (from 15-oz box), softened as directed on box

1 teaspoon grated Parmesan cheese

½ teaspoon dried thyme leaves

3 tablespoons all-purpose flour

2 tablespoons water

½ cup whipping cream

½ cup Green Giant® frozen sweet peas (from 1-lb bag)

1) In 12-inch skillet, heat 2 teaspoons of the oil over medium-high heat until hot. Add mushrooms; cook 2 to 3 minutes, stirring frequently, until tender. Remove mushrooms from skillet; place in bowl. Set aside.

2) In same skillet, melt butter and remaining 1 teaspoon oil over medium-high heat. Add chicken and carrots; sprinkle with salt and pepper. Cook 5 to 7 minutes, stirring occasionally, until browned. Stir in onions and wine. Heat to boiling. Reduce heat to medium-low. Cover; cook about 20 minutes or until chicken is no longer pink in center.

3) Meanwhile, heat oven to 450°F. Remove pie crust from pouch; unroll crust onto ungreased cookie sheet. Sprinkle evenly with cheese and thyme; roll in lightly with rolling pin. Prick crust generously with fork. With pastry wheel or sharp knife, cut into 12 wedges; separate slightly. Bake 7 to 10 minutes or until light golden brown.

4) In small bowl, mix flour and water until smooth. Add to juices in skillet; cook over medium heat, stirring constantly, until bubbly and thickened. Stir in whipping cream, peas and cooked mushrooms. Cook 3 to 4 minutes, stirring frequently, until thoroughly heated. Serve chicken and vegetables with pastry wedges.

HIGH ALTITUDE (3500-6500 FT.): Add 1/4 cup water with the wine. Thaw peas before using.

Nutrition Information Per Serving:

Calories: 490	From Fat: 220
Total Fat	25g
Saturated Fat	10g
Trans Fat	0g
Cholesterol	125mg
Sodium	670mg
Total Carbohydrate	29g
Dietary Fiber	2g
Sugars	4g
Protein	36g

Beef and Spinach Enchiladas

PREP TIME: 25 MINUTES (READY IN 50 MINUTES)
SERVINGS: 8

1 lb lean (at least 80%) ground beef

2 garlic cloves, minced

1½ cups Green Giant® frozen cut leaf spinach (from 1-lb bag)

4 oz cream cheese, cut into 1-inch cubes

½ teaspoon ground cumin

1 can (4.5 oz) Old El Paso® chopped green chiles

2 cups shredded Monterey Jack cheese (8 oz)

1 package (11.5 oz) Old El Paso® flour tortillas for burritos, 8 inch (8 tortillas)

1 can (8 oz) tomato sauce

1 cup Old El Paso® Thick 'n Chunky salsa

2 tablespoons chopped fresh cilantro, if desired

1) Heat oven to 350°F. Spray 13x9-inch (3-quart) glass baking dish with nonstick cooking spray. In 12-inch skillet, cook ground beef and garlic over medium-high heat 5 to 7 minutes, stirring occasionally, until beef is thoroughly cooked; drain.

2) Add spinach; cook 3 to 5 minutes or until spinach is thawed, stirring frequently. Reduce heat to medium; stir in cream cheese, cumin, chiles and 1½ cups of the cheese until combined. Spoon about ⅓ cup beef mixture down center of each tortilla. Roll up; place seam side down in baking dish.

3) In medium bowl, mix tomato sauce and salsa. Spoon over tortillas; sprinkle with remaining ½ cup cheese.

4) Bake 20 to 25 minutes or until thoroughly heated. Sprinkle with cilantro.

HIGH ALTITUDE (3500-6500 FT.): In Step 4, spray piece of foil with nonstick cooking spray; cover baking dish with foil. Bake 40 to 45 minutes.

Nutrition Information Per Serving:		
Calories: 420	From Fat: 220	
Total Fat		24g
Saturated Fat		12g
Trans Fat		1g
Cholesterol		75mg
Sodium		1160mg
Total Carbohydrate		29g
Dietary Fiber		2g
Sugars		3g
Protein		22g

Layered Beef and Potato Casserole

PREP TIME: 15 MINUTES (READY IN 1 HOUR 20 MINUTES)
SERVINGS: 6

e EASY

1 lb lean (at least 80%) ground beef

2 cups Green Giant® frozen mixed vegetables (from 1-lb bag)

1 jar (12 oz) beef gravy

1/2 teaspoon salt

1 bag (28 oz) frozen potatoes O'Brien with peppers and onions, thawed

2 cups shredded Swiss cheese (8 oz)

1) Heat oven to 350°F. Spray 12x8-inch (2-quart) glass baking dish with nonstick cooking spray. In 10-inch skillet, cook ground beef over medium-high heat 5 to 7 minutes, stirring occasionally, until thoroughly cooked; drain. Stir in mixed vegetables, gravy and salt. Cook 3 to 4 minutes or until vegetables are thawed and mixture is thoroughly heated.

2) In baking dish, layer 3 cups of the potatoes and 1 cup of the cheese. Spoon ground beef mixture over cheese. Top with remaining potatoes. Cover with foil.

3) Bake 55 to 60 minutes or until bubbly. Remove foil. Sprinkle with remaining 1 cup cheese. Bake uncovered 5 minutes longer or until cheese is melted. Sprinkle with paprika before serving.

HIGH ALTITUDE (3500-6500 FT.): No change.

Nutrition Information Per Serving:	
Calories: 450	From Fat: 190
Total Fat	21g
Saturated Fat	11g
Trans Fat	1g
Cholesterol	85mg
Sodium	690mg
Total Carbohydrate	36g
Dietary Fiber	5g
Sugars	3g
Protein	30g

Honey Mustard Pork Tenderloin

PREP TIME: 10 MINUTES (READY IN 45 MINUTES)
SERVINGS: 4

ⓔ EASY　　**ⓕ LOW FAT**

1 pork tenderloin (¾ lb)

1 tablespoon honey

1 tablespoon Dijon mustard

2 teaspoons olive or vegetable oil

1 teaspoon finely chopped garlic (1 to 2 cloves)

½ teaspoon dried oregano leaves

Nutrition Information Per Serving:

Calories: 150	From Fat: 50
Total Fat	6g
Saturated Fat	1.5g
Trans Fat	0g
Cholesterol	55mg
Sodium	130mg
Total Carbohydrate	5g
Dietary Fiber	0g
Sugars	4g
Protein	19g

1) Heat oven to 425°F. Line 15x10x1-inch pan with foil; place pork tenderloin in pan. In small bowl, mix remaining ingredients; brush over pork tenderloin.

2) Bake 25 to 30 minutes or until pork has slight blush of pink in center and meat thermometer inserted in center reads 160°F. Let stand 5 minutes. Cut diagonally into slices.

HIGH ALTITUDE (3500-6500 FT.): No change.

Parmesan Salisbury Steak Skillet

PREP TIME: 35 MINUTES (READY IN 35 MINUTES)
SERVINGS: 4

1 lb extra-lean (at least 90%) ground beef

¼ cup Progresso® Italian style bread crumbs

¼ cup grated Parmesan cheese

¼ cup chopped onion

¼ cup milk

¼ teaspoon salt

¼ teaspoon pepper

2 teaspoons oil

1 bag (19 oz) Green Giant® Chef Inspired™ frozen Vegetables with Parmesan-Asiago Sauce

Nutrition Information Per Serving:

Calories: 340	From Fat: 150
Total Fat	17g
Saturated Fat	7g
Trans Fat	0.5g
Cholesterol	85mg
Sodium	870mg
Total Carbohydrate	17g
Dietary Fiber	3g
Sugars	7g
Protein	30g

1) In medium bowl, mix all ingredients except oil and vegetables. Shape into 4 oval patties, ½-inch thick. In 12-inch nonstick skillet, heat oil over medium heat. Cook patties in oil 3 to 4 minutes or until browned, turning once. Cover; reduce heat to low. Cook 10 minutes; drain.

2) Pour vegetables and sauce chips over patties. Cover; cook 10 minutes or until thermometer inserted in center of patties reads 160°F, and vegetables are crisp-tender, moving patties around and gently stirring vegetables once.

HIGH ALTITUDE (3500-6500 FT.): In Step 1, after cooking patties 3 to 4 minutes, cover, reduce heat to medium-low, then cook 10 minutes. In Step 2, add ¼ cup water with vegetables and sauce chips. Cover and cook over medium heat.

Lemony Pork Primavera Pasta

PREP TIME: 30 MINUTES (READY IN 30 MINUTES)
SERVINGS: 4 (2 CUPS EACH)

€ EASY

6 oz uncooked fettuccine or linguine

1 lb boneless pork loin chops
(¾ inch thick)

1 tablespoon olive or vegetable oil

2 cups fresh broccoli florets
(about 5 oz)

4 oz fresh green beans, trimmed, cut
into 1-inch pieces (about 1 cup)

1 medium red bell pepper, cut into
1½x¼-inch strips

⅓ cup lemon juice

⅓ cup water

2 tablespoons sugar

1 tablespoon cornstarch

½ teaspoon salt

1) Cook and drain fettuccine as directed
on package.

2) Meanwhile, cut pork into 2x¾x¼-inch
strips. In 12-inch nonstick skillet, heat
oil over medium-high heat. Add pork,
broccoli, green beans and bell pepper;
cook 6 to 8 minutes, stirring frequently,
until pork is no longer pink in center
and vegetables are crisp-tender.

3) In small bowl, mix remaining ingredients until smooth. Stir into pork
mixture. Cook 1 to 2 minutes, stirring constantly, until mixture is bubbly
and thickened.

4) Stir cooked fettuccine into sauce mixture; cook, stirring occasionally, until
thoroughly heated.

HIGH ALTITUDE (3500-6500 FT.): Add up to ¼ cup water if sauce gets too thick.

Nutrition Information Per Serving:		
Calories: 420	From Fat: 120	
Total Fat		14g
Saturated Fat		4g
Trans Fat		0g
Cholesterol		105mg
Sodium		540mg
Total Carbohydrate		43g
Dietary Fiber		4g
Sugars		10g
Protein		31g

tip

Prepare all the vegetables and cut the pork up to 4 hours ahead of time. Cover and refrigerate. When you're ready to eat, dinner is just 10 minutes away!

Everyday Lasagna Skillet

PREP TIME: 40 MINUTES (READY IN 55 MINUTES)
SERVINGS: 6

1 lb lean (at least 80%) ground beef

1/2 lb bulk mild Italian sausage

1 jar (26 oz) tomato pasta sauce

1 cup water

5 uncooked lasagna noodles, broken into 2-inch pieces

1 container (12 oz) cottage cheese

1/2 cup grated Parmesan cheese

1 tablespoon dried parsley leaves

1 egg

2 cups shredded Italian cheese blend (8 oz)

1) In 12-inch nonstick skillet, cook the ground beef and sausage over medium-high heat 5 to 7 minutes, stirring occasionally, until thoroughly cooked; drain. Stir in pasta sauce, water and uncooked noodles. Reduce heat to medium-low. Cover; cook 20 to 25 minutes, stirring occasionally, until pasta is almost tender.

2) Meanwhile, in small bowl, mix cottage cheese, Parmesan cheese, parsley and egg. Spread over partially cooked pasta mixture. Sprinkle with shredded cheese. Cover; cook 10 to 15 minutes longer or until cottage cheese mixture is set and pasta is tender.

HIGH ALTITUDE (3500-6500 FT.): In Step 1, cover and cook 35 to 40 minutes.

Nutrition Information Per Serving:		
Calories: 640	From Fat:	300
Total Fat		34g
Saturated Fat		15g
Trans Fat		1g
Cholesterol		150mg
Sodium		1550mg
Total Carbohydrate		40g
Dietary Fiber		3g
Sugars		15g
Protein		43g

Buttermilk Country Fried Chicken

PREP TIME: 30 MINUTES (READY IN 2 HOURS 30 MINUTES)
SERVINGS: 8

 LOW FAT

MARINADE

- 1 cup buttermilk
- 1 teaspoon ground red pepper (cayenne)
- ½ teaspoon salt
- 1 garlic clove, minced

CHICKEN

- 2 lb boneless skinless chicken breasts and/or thighs
- ¾ cup all-purpose flour
- 2 tablespoons cornstarch
- 1 teaspoon dried thyme leaves
- 1 teaspoon paprika

  Oil for frying

1) In large shallow nonmetal dish or large resealable food storage plastic bag, mix all marinade ingredients. Add chicken pieces; turn to coat. Refrigerate at least 2 hours or overnight to marinate.

2) In pie pan, mix flour and all remaining chicken ingredients except oil. Heat about ½ inch oil in 12-inch skillet over medium-high heat.

3) Remove chicken pieces from marinade a few at a time, allowing excess to drip off. Roll chicken in flour mixture until well coated. Add chicken to hot oil in skillet, a few pieces at a time until all pieces are in skillet. Cover; cook over medium-high heat 10 minutes or until deep golden brown. Discard marinade.

4) Uncover skillet. Turn chicken; cook 5 to 8 minutes longer or until juice of chicken is clear when center of thickest part is cut (170°F for breasts; 180°F for thighs). Drain chicken on several layers of paper towels. Serve warm, or refrigerate and serve cold.

HIGH ALTITUDE (3500-6500 FT.): No change.

Nutrition Information Per Serving:		
Calories: 190	From Fat: 50	
Total Fat		6g
Saturated Fat		1.5g
Trans Fat		0g
Cholesterol		70mg
Sodium		330mg
Total Carbohydrate		8g
Dietary Fiber		0g
Sugars		0g
Protein		26g

Salisbury Burger Patties with Caramelized Onions

PREP TIME: 25 MINUTES (READY IN 25 MINUTES)
SERVINGS: 4

EASY

3 tablespoons butter or margarine

1 tablespoon packed brown sugar

2 cups sliced onions (2 medium)

4 ground beef patties (4 to 5 oz each)

1 jar (12 oz) beef gravy

Nutrition Information Per Serving:

Calories: 350	From Fat: 210
Total Fat	24g
Saturated Fat	10g
Trans Fat	1.5g
Cholesterol	90mg
Sodium	600mg
Total Carbohydrate	12g
Dietary Fiber	1g
Sugars	6g
Protein	23g

1) In 12-inch skillet, melt butter over medium-low heat. Stir in brown sugar. Add onions; cook 12 to 16 minutes, stirring occasionally, until onions begin to turn golden brown. Place onions in medium bowl; cover to keep warm.

2) In same skillet, cook beef patties over medium heat 6 to 8 minutes, turning once, until meat thermometer inserted in center of patties reads 160°F.

3) Return onions to skillet; pour gravy over onions and patties. Cook 2 to 3 minutes longer, stirring once or twice, until gravy is thoroughly heated. If desired, sprinkle with chopped fresh parsley.

HIGH ALTITUDE (3500-6500 FT.): No change.

Simple Hamburger Hot Dish

PREP TIME: 25 MINUTES (READY IN 1 HOUR 15 MINUTES)
SERVINGS: 6

3 cups uncooked rotini pasta (8 oz)

1 lb lean (at least 80%) ground beef

1 large onion, chopped (1 cup)

1 teaspoon garlic powder

1/2 teaspoon salt

1 can (14.5 oz) diced tomatoes, undrained

1 can (15 oz) tomato sauce

1 tablespoon sugar

1 cup shredded American-Cheddar cheese blend (4 oz)

Nutrition Information Per Serving:

Calories: 410	From Fat: 140
Total Fat	15g
Saturated Fat	7g
Trans Fat	0.5g
Cholesterol	65mg
Sodium	1120mg
Total Carbohydrate	43g
Dietary Fiber	4g
Sugars	9g
Protein	24g

1) Heat oven to 350°F. Cook and drain pasta as directed on package.

2) Meanwhile, in 10-inch skillet, cook beef, onion, garlic powder and salt over medium heat 8 to 10 minutes, stirring occasionally, until beef is thoroughly cooked; drain.

3) Stir in tomatoes, tomato sauce, sugar and pasta. Pour into ungreased 8-inch square (2-quart) glass baking dish.

4) Cover dish with foil. Bake 30 to 40 minutes or until bubbly around edges. Sprinkle with cheese. Bake uncovered 5 to 10 minutes longer or until cheese is melted.

HIGH ALTITUDE (3500-6500 FT.): No change.

Double Meat Pizzas

PREP TIME: 15 MINUTES (READY IN 30 MINUTES)
SERVINGS: 10

e EASY

- ½ lb lean (at least 80%) ground beef
- 1 can (12 oz) Pillsbury® Golden Layers® refrigerated flaky biscuits
- ⅔ cup pizza sauce
- ¼ to ½ teaspoon dried oregano leaves
- 1 package (3½ oz) sliced pepperoni
- 1 cup shredded mozzarella cheese (4 oz)
- 2 tablespoons grated Parmesan cheese

Nutrition Information Per Serving:

Calories: 230	From Fat: 120
Total Fat	13g
Saturated Fat	5g
Trans Fat	2g
Cholesterol	35mg
Sodium	700mg
Total Carbohydrate	16g
Dietary Fiber	0g
Sugars	3g
Protein	12g

1) Heat oven to 400°F. Lightly grease 2 cookie sheets. In 10-inch skillet, cook ground beef over medium-high heat 5 to 7 minutes, stirring occasionally, until thoroughly cooked; drain.

2) Separate dough into 10 biscuits. On cookie sheets, press or roll each biscuit to 5-inch round, forming ¼-inch rim around outside edge. Spread about 1 tablespoon pizza sauce just to rim of each biscuit; sprinkle with oregano. Top each with pepperoni, cooked ground beef and cheese.

3) Bake 12 to 15 minutes or until crust is golden brown and cheese is melted.

HIGH ALTITUDE (3500-6500 FT.): No change.

tip

You can substitute a different variety for the mozzarella cheese, such as Colby or Cheddar. In fact, feel free to switch any of the pizzas' toppings to fit your family's preferences.

French Onion-Beef-Noodle Bake

PREP TIME: 35 MINUTES (READY IN 1 HOUR 10 MINUTES)
SERVINGS: 8 (1-1/2 CUPS EACH)

Nutrition Information Per Serving:

Calories:	460	From Fat:	160
Total Fat			18g
Saturated Fat			9g
Trans Fat			0.5g
Cholesterol			125mg
Sodium			980mg
Total Carbohydrate			35g
Dietary Fiber			3g
Sugars			4g
Protein			40g

5 cups uncooked wide egg noodles (8 oz)

3 tablespoons butter or margarine

2 lb boneless beef sirloin steak, cut into 1-inch cubes

4 medium onions, thinly sliced (4 cups)

2 cups sliced fresh mushrooms

3 cups beef broth

1/4 cup all-purpose flour

1 teaspoon dried rosemary leaves

1 teaspoon salt

1 teaspoon pepper

2 cups seasoned croutons (4 oz)

2 cups shredded Swiss cheese (8 oz)

1) Heat oven to 350°F. Cook and drain noodles as directed on package.

2) Meanwhile, in 5-quart Dutch oven, melt butter over medium-high heat. Add beef, onions and mushrooms; cook about 20 minutes, stirring frequently, until beef is browned on all sides, onions are soft and mushrooms are browned.

3) Spread noodles in bottom of ungreased 13x9-inch (3-quart) glass baking dish. Spoon beef mixture over noodles.

4) In same Dutch oven, heat 2½ cups of the broth to boiling over medium-high heat. In small bowl, mix remaining ½ cup broth and the flour until smooth. Stir flour mixture into boiling broth. Cook, stirring constantly, until bubbly and thickened. Stir in rosemary, salt and pepper. Pour over beef mixture; stir until well blended. Sprinkle with croutons, and then cheese.

5) Bake 25 to 35 minutes or until bubbly around edges and cheese is melted.

HIGH ALTITUDE (3500-6500 FT.): In Step 4, do not add cheese. In Step 5, bake 20 minutes. Sprinkle with cheese; bake 5 to 15 minutes longer or until bubbly around edges and cheese is melted.

Salmon with Lemon Butter and Pineapple Salsa

PREP TIME: 10 MINUTES (READY IN 20 MINUTES)
SERVINGS: 4

e EASY

1/4 cup butter or margarine, softened

4 teaspoons grated lemon peel

2 teaspoons lemon juice

1 cup chopped fresh pineapple

3 tablespoons chopped fresh cilantro

2 tablespoons finely chopped red onion

1 teaspoon finely chopped jalapeño chile, if desired

4 salmon fillets, about 1 inch thick (1 1/2 lb)

1/4 teaspoon salt

1) Heat oven to 375°F. In small bowl, mix butter, lemon peel and lemon juice; set aside.

2) In medium bowl, mix pineapple, cilantro, onion and chile; refrigerate until serving time.

3) Line 13x9-inch pan with foil. Place salmon, skin side down, in pan; sprinkle with salt.

4) Bake 8 to 10 minutes or until fish flakes easily with a fork. Immediately top salmon with butter mixture. Serve with pineapple salsa.

HIGH ALTITUDE (3500-6500 FT.): No change.

Nutrition Information Per Serving:	
Calories: 360	From Fat: 190
Total Fat	21g
Saturated Fat	9g
Trans Fat	0.5g
Cholesterol	140mg
Sodium	330mg
Total Carbohydrate	6g
Dietary Fiber	0g
Sugars	4g
Protein	37g

tip

This orange chicken is easy to prepare! Serve it with cooked fresh green beans or broccoli, warm breadsticks and a simple fruit salad.

Orange Zested Chicken Breasts

| PREP TIME: | 20 MINUTES (READY IN 20 MINUTES) |
| SERVINGS: | 4 |

e EASY   **lf** LOW FAT

½ teaspoon seasoned salt

¼ teaspoon garlic powder

2 tablespoons butter or margarine

1 teaspoon grated orange peel

4 boneless skinless chicken breasts (1 lb)

1) In small bowl, mix seasoned salt and garlic powder.

2) In 10-inch nonstick skillet, heat butter and orange peel over medium heat until butter is melted. Add chicken; sprinkle with salt mixture. Cook about 15 minutes, turning once, until juice of chicken is clear when center of thickest part is cut (170°F).

HIGH ALTITUDE (3500-6500 FT.): Cook about 18 minutes.

Nutrition Information Per Serving:

Calories:	190	From Fat:	80
Total Fat			9g
Saturated Fat			4.5g
Trans Fat			0g
Cholesterol			85mg
Sodium			270mg
Total Carbohydrate			0g
Dietary Fiber			0g
Sugars			0g
Protein			25g

Rolled Italian Meat Loaf

PREP TIME: 15 MINUTES (READY IN 1 HOUR 40 MINUTES)
SERVINGS: 8

 EASY

1¼ lb extra-lean (at least 90%) ground beef

¾ lb bulk Italian sausage

1 egg

1 can (8 oz) pizza sauce

¼ cup Progresso® Italian style bread crumbs

¼ teaspoon pepper

2 cups shredded 6-cheese Italian cheese blend (8 oz)

2 cups loosely packed fresh spinach leaves

Nutrition Information Per Serving:

Calories: 330	From Fat: 190
Total Fat	22g
Saturated Fat	10g
Trans Fat	0.5g
Cholesterol	120mg
Sodium	900mg
Total Carbohydrate	6g
Dietary Fiber	0g
Sugars	3g
Protein	29g

1) Heat oven to 350°F. In large bowl, mix ground beef, sausage, egg, ½ cup of the pizza sauce, the bread crumbs and pepper.

2) On foil, pat mixture to 12x8-inch rectangle. Sprinkle evenly with cheese; gently press into meat. Top with spinach. Starting at short end, roll up tightly, using foil to start roll and tucking in spinach leaves; seal ends. Place seam side down in ungreased 12x8-inch (2-quart) glass baking dish.

3) Bake 1 hour. Spread remaining pizza sauce over top. Bake 15 minutes longer or until thermometer inserted in meat loaf reads 160°F. Let stand 5 to 10 minutes before serving.

HIGH ALTITUDE (3500-6500 FT.): No change.

Slow Cooker Turkey Breast

PREP TIME: 20 MINUTES (READY IN 7 HOURS 20 MINUTES)
SERVINGS: 8

 EASY   LOW FAT

3 medium red potatoes, cut into 1-inch pieces (about 4 cups)

8 medium carrots, cut into 1-inch pieces (about 2 cups)

1 small onion, cut into wedges (½ cup)

1 bone-in turkey breast with gravy packet (5 to 6 lb)

Nutrition Information Per Serving:

Calories: 340	From Fat: 20
Total Fat	2g
Saturated Fat	0.5g
Trans Fat	0g
Cholesterol	150mg
Sodium	640mg
Total Carbohydrate	23g
Dietary Fiber	3g
Sugars	4g
Protein	56g

1) In 5- to 6-quart slow cooker, mix potatoes, carrots, onion and gravy from turkey breast. Place turkey breast on top.

2) Cover; cook on Low heat setting 7 to 8 hours or until vegetables are tender and thermometer inserted in center of turkey reads 170°F.

HIGH ALTITUDE (3500-6500 FT.): No change.

Zucchini Meat Loaf

PREP TIME: 20 MINUTES (READY IN 1 HOUR 10 MINUTES)
SERVINGS: 8

e EASY

MEAT LOAF

- 2 eggs, slightly beaten
- 2 cups shredded zucchini (1 large or 2 small)
- 1/3 cup Progresso® plain bread crumbs
- 1/3 cup chopped onion
- 1 teaspoon salt
- 1/2 teaspoon dried oregano leaves
- 1/4 teaspoon pepper
- 1 1/2 lb lean (at least 80%) ground beef

TOPPING

- 1 tablespoon packed brown sugar
- 2 tablespoons ketchup
- 1/2 teaspoon yellow mustard

1) Heat oven to 350°F. In large bowl, mix all meat loaf ingredients until well blended. Press mixture into ungreased 9½-inch deep-dish glass pie plate. Bake 35 minutes.

2) Meanwhile, in small bowl, mix all topping ingredients.

3) Remove meat loaf from oven; pour off drippings. Spread topping over loaf. Return to oven; bake 10 to 15 minutes longer or until thoroughly cooked in center and meat thermometer reads 160°F. Let meat loaf stand 5 minutes before serving.

HIGH ALTITUDE (3500-6500 FT.): No change.

Nutrition Information Per Serving:

Calories:	200	From Fat:	100
Total Fat			11g
Saturated Fat			4g
Trans Fat			0.5g
Cholesterol			105mg
Sodium			440mg
Total Carbohydrate			8g
Dietary Fiber			0g
Sugars			4g
Protein			18g

tip

Baking the meat loaf in a shallow pie plate takes less time than baking it in a loaf shape. Dinner can be on the table more quickly.

Fish Fillets with Herbed Tartar Sauce

PREP TIME: 20 MINUTES (READY IN 20 MINUTES)
SERVINGS: 4

e EASY

1 egg

½ cup Progresso® Italian style bread crumbs

3 tablespoons olive oil

1 lb mild-flavored fish fillets (about ½ inch thick), cut into 4 serving pieces

⅓ cup tartar sauce

¼ cup chopped tomato

½ teaspoon dried basil leaves

1) In shallow dish or pie plate, beat egg with wire whisk. In another shallow dish or pie plate, place bread crumbs.

2) In 12-inch skillet, heat oil over medium heat. Dip fish into egg, then coat with bread crumbs; place in skillet. Cook 8 to 10 minutes, turning once, until browned on both sides and fish flakes easily with a fork.

3) In small bowl, mix tartar sauce, tomato and basil; serve with fish.

HIGH ALTITUDE (3500-6500 FT.): No change.

Nutrition Information Per Serving:

Calories:	370	From Fat:	220
Total Fat			24g
Saturated Fat			3.5g
Trans Fat			0g
Cholesterol			120mg
Sodium			440mg
Total Carbohydrate			12g
Dietary Fiber			0g
Sugars			2g
Protein			25g

Honey-Dijon Ham

PREP TIME: 15 MINUTES (READY IN 6 HOURS 15 MINUTES)
SERVINGS: 6

🅔 EASY   🅕 LOW FAT

1 bone-in cooked ham (5 lb)

1/3 cup apple juice

1/4 cup packed brown sugar

1 tablespoon honey

1 tablespoon Dijon mustard

Nutrition Information Per Serving:

Calories:	310	From Fat:	90
Total Fat			10g
Saturated Fat			3.5g
Trans Fat			0g
Cholesterol			95mg
Sodium			2250mg
Total Carbohydrate			17g
Dietary Fiber			0g
Sugars			16g
Protein			38g

1) In 4- to 6-quart slow cooker, place ham. Add apple juice. In small bowl, mix brown sugar, honey and mustard. Spread mixture over ham.

2) Cover; cook on Low heat setting 6 to 8 hours.

3) Remove ham from slow cooker. Cut ham in half; set half aside. Slice remaining ham; place on serving platter.

4) Cut reserved ham into 1/2-inch cubes. Place 1 1/2 cups cubes in each of 2 resealable food-storage plastic bags. Seal and label bags for Ham and Asparagus Chowder (below) and Ham Frittata (at right). Refrigerate for a later use.

HIGH ALTITUDE (3500-6500 FT.): No change.

Ham and Asparagus Chowder

PREP TIME: 20 MINUTES (READY IN 20 MINUTES)
SERVINGS: 4 (1-1/3 CUPS EACH)

🅔 EASY   🅕 LOW FAT

1 1/2 cups cubed unpeeled red potatoes

1/2 cup water

1 1/2 cups (1 1/2-inch pieces) fresh asparagus spears

1 1/2 cups cubed cooked Honey-Dijon Ham (above)

1 can (10 3/4 oz) condensed cream of mushroom soup

1 cup milk

Freshly ground pepper, if desired

Nutrition Information Per Serving:

Calories:	230	From Fat:	80
Total Fat			9g
Saturated Fat			3g
Trans Fat			0g
Cholesterol			30mg
Sodium			1120mg
Total Carbohydrate			23g
Dietary Fiber			2g
Sugars			10g
Protein			15g

1) In 2-quart saucepan, heat potatoes and water to boiling. Reduce heat to medium. Cover; cook about 5 minutes or until potatoes are crisp-tender.

2) Add asparagus and ham. Cover; cook 3 to 5 minutes or until thoroughly heated. Stir in soup and milk. Heat to boiling over high heat, stirring occasionally. Sprinkle with pepper before serving.

HIGH ALTITUDE (3500-6500 FT.): No change.

Ham Frittata

PREP TIME: 20 MINUTES (READY IN 20 MINUTES)
SERVINGS.   4

e EASY

1½ cups frozen southern-style cubed hash brown potatoes (from 32-oz package)

1 medium zucchini, quartered lengthwise, then sliced (1 cup)

1½ cups cubed cooked Honey-Dijon Ham (above left)

4 eggs

¼ cup milk

¼ teaspoon salt

1 cup shredded Cheddar cheese (4 oz)

1) Spray 10-inch skillet with cooking spray; heat over medium-high heat. Add potatoes, zucchini and ham; cook 5 to 8 minutes, stirring frequently, until zucchini is crisp-tender and potatoes are thoroughly cooked.

2) Meanwhile, in medium bowl, beat eggs with wire whisk. Add the milk and salt; beat well.

3) Pour egg mixture over mixture in skillet. Reduce heat to medium-low. Cover; cook 5 to 7 minutes, lifting edges occasionally to allow uncooked egg mixture to flow to bottom of skillet, until center is set.

4) Sprinkle cheese over frittata. Cover; cook 2 to 3 minutes or until cheese is melted. To serve, cut into wedges.

HIGH ALTITUDE (3500-6500 FT.): No change.

Nutrition Information Per Serving:		
Calories: 350	From Fat: 160	
Total Fat		18g
Saturated Fat		9g
Trans Fat		0g
Cholesterol		265mg
Sodium		1170mg
Total Carbohydrate		22g
Dietary Fiber		2g
Sugars		7g
Protein		25g

Thai Peanut Beef and Pea Pods over Noodles

PREP TIME: 25 MINUTES (READY IN 25 MINUTES)
SERVINGS: 4

EASY

- 8 oz uncooked thin spaghetti
- 1 lb lean (at least 80%) ground beef
- 4 green onions, chopped (¼ cup)
- 8 oz fresh pea pods, halved diagonally (about 3 cups)
- 1 red bell pepper, cut into 3x¼x¼-inch thin strips
- 1½ cups chicken broth
- ¼ teaspoon ground red pepper (cayenne)
- ¼ teaspoon salt
- 2 teaspoons cornstarch
- ½ cup peanut butter
- ¼ cup chopped salted peanuts

1) Cook and drain spaghetti as directed on package; cover to keep warm.

2) Meanwhile, in 12-inch skillet, cook ground beef over medium-high heat 5 to 7 minutes, stirring occasionally, until thoroughly cooked; drain. Add onions, pea pods and bell pepper. Cook and stir 3 to 4 minutes or until vegetables are crisp-tender.

3) In small bowl, mix broth, ground red pepper, salt and cornstarch. Stir into beef and vegetables. Add peanut butter. Cook 1 to 2 minutes, stirring frequently, until thick and bubbly. Serve over cooked spaghetti; top with peanuts.

HIGH ALTITUDE (3500-6500 FT.): In Step 3, cook 2 to 3 minutes.

Nutrition Information Per Serving:	
Calories: 730	From Fat: 320
Total Fat	36g
Saturated Fat	9g
Trans Fat	1g
Cholesterol	70mg
Sodium	1000mg
Total Carbohydrate	60g
Dietary Fiber	8g
Sugars	7g
Protein	42g

tip Most purchased peanut sauces are very spicy so we have added a little ground red pepper for a mild heat level in this homemade sauce. If your family likes very hot spicy food, add a little extra red pepper, or a few crushed red pepper flakes.

Herb and Garlic Chicken and Vegetables

PREP TIME: 20 MINUTES (READY IN 1 HOUR 15 MINUTES)
SERVINGS: 4

e EASY

1 cut-up whole chicken (3 to 3½ lb)

2 tablespoons olive or vegetable oil

1 envelope savory herb with garlic soup mix (from 2.4-oz box)

⅓ cup chicken broth

4 medium stalks celery, cut in half lengthwise, then cut into 4-inch pieces

1 large onion, cut into 6 wedges

2 large carrots, cut in half lengthwise, then cut into 4-inch pieces

2 medium unpeeled russet potatoes, each cut into 8 pieces

1) Heat oven to 425°F. Remove skin from chicken if desired. In small bowl, mix oil, soup mix and broth. Brush both sides of chicken pieces with about half of the oil mixture.

2) In large bowl, mix celery, onion, carrots, potatoes and remaining oil mixture. Arrange vegetables in ungreased 15x10x1-inch pan. Bake 15 minutes.

3) Place chicken pieces in pan, overlapping vegetables if necessary. Bake 35 to 40 minutes longer or until vegetables are tender and juice of chicken is clear when thickest piece is cut to bone (170°F for breasts; 180°F for thighs and legs).

HIGH ALTITUDE (3500-6500 FT.): No change.

Nutrition Information Per Serving:	
Calories: 450	From Fat: 150
Total Fat	17g
Saturated Fat	3.5g
Trans Fat	0g
Cholesterol	120mg
Sodium	990mg
Total Carbohydrate	32g
Dietary Fiber	5g
Sugars	6g
Protein	42g

Skillet Chicken Pot Pie

PREP TIME: 45 MINUTES (READY IN 45 MINUTES)
SERVINGS: 6

1 tablespoon vegetable oil

1¼ lb boneless skinless chicken breasts, cut into 1-inch pieces

1 teaspoon salt

1½ teaspoons dried thyme leaves

⅛ teaspoon pepper

2 cups sliced fresh carrots (4 medium)

2 cups frozen southern-style diced hash brown potatoes (from 32-oz bag)

1 jar (12 or 15 oz) chicken gravy

1 cup Green Giant® frozen sweet peas (from 1-lb bag)

1 can (12 oz) Pillsbury® Golden Layers® refrigerated buttermilk or original flaky biscuits

½ teaspoon garlic powder

1) In 12-inch nonstick skillet, heat oil over medium-high heat. Add chicken; sprinkle with salt, ½ teaspoon of the thyme and the pepper. Cook 5 minutes, stirring frequently, until the chicken is browned.

2) Move chicken to 1 side of skillet. Add carrots and potatoes; cook 5 minutes, stirring frequently. Stir gravy into chicken and vegetables. Heat to boiling. Reduce heat to low. Cover; simmer 20 to 25 minutes, stirring occasionally and adding peas during last 5 minutes of cooking time, until chicken is no longer pink in center and vegetables are tender.

3) During last 15 minutes of cooking, heat oven to 400°F. Separate dough into 10 biscuits. Cut each into quarters; place in large bowl. Sprinkle garlic powder and remaining teaspoon thyme over dough; toss to coat. Place on ungreased cookie sheet.

4) Bake 8 to 10 minutes or until biscuit pieces are golden brown. Scatter over top of cooked chicken mixture before serving.

HIGH ALTITUDE (3500-6500 FT.): In Step 1, cook chicken 8 minutes. When adding gravy to chicken and vegetables, also add 1/2 cup water. Heat to boiling. Reduce heat to medium-low. Cover; simmer about 20 minutes, adding peas during last 5 minutes of cooking.

Nutrition Information Per Serving:

Calories:	470	From Fat:	155
Total Fat			17g
Saturated Fat			4g
Cholesterol			60mg
Sodium			1500mg
Total Carbohydrate			51g
Dietary Fiber			4g
Sugars			13g
Protein			28g

Beef Fried Rice

PREP TIME: 30 MINUTES (READY IN 30 MINUTES)
SERVINGS: 6 (1-1/3 CUPS EACH)

e EASY

1 cup uncooked regular long-grain white rice

2 cups water

1 egg, beaten

1 lb lean (at least 80%) ground beef

1 cup sliced fresh mushrooms

1/2 cup sliced celery

1/3 cup soy sauce

1 tablespoon sesame oil

1/2 teaspoon hot pepper sauce

1 1/2 cups fresh snow pea pods, halved diagonally

1/2 cup chopped green onions (8 medium)

1) Cook rice in water as directed on package.

2) Meanwhile, spray 12-inch nonstick skillet with nonstick cooking spray. Heat over medium heat. Add beaten egg to skillet; cook 1 minute or until firm but still moist. Remove from skillet; cut into thin strips. Cover to keep warm.

3) In same skillet, cook ground beef, mushrooms and celery over medium heat 8 to 10 minutes or until beef is thoroughly cooked, stirring frequently.

4) In small bowl, mix soy sauce, sesame oil and hot pepper sauce; stir into beef mixture. Add pea pods, onions, cooked egg and cooked rice; cook 2 to 3 minutes longer or until thoroughly healed, stirring constantly.

HIGH ALTITUDE (3500-6500 FT.): No change.

Nutrition Information Per Serving:		
Calories: 300	From Fat: 110	
Total Fat		12g
Saturated Fat		4g
Trans Fat		0.5g
Cholesterol		80mg
Sodium		1230mg
Total Carbohydrate		30g
Dietary Fiber		1g
Sugars		2g
Protein		19g

tip

Light-colored sesame oil adds a delicate, nutty flavor to salad dressings, sautés or stir-fries. Dark sesame oil has a rich aroma that makes it perfect for flavoring finished recipes. Use either light or dark sesame oil in this fried rice.

Ranch Glazed Chicken Breasts

PREP TIME: 25 MINUTES (READY IN 25 MINUTES)
SERVINGS: 8

e EASY

½ cup grated Parmesan cheese

¼ cup mayonnaise

3 tablespoons ranch dressing

8 frozen chicken breasts
(4½ to 5 oz each)

Nonstick cooking spray or
vegetable oil

Chopped fresh chives, if desired

1) Heat gas or charcoal grill. In small bowl, mix cheese, mayonnaise and dressing; set aside. Spray or brush frozen chicken breasts with nonstick cooking spray or vegetable oil.

2) When grill is heated, place chicken on gas grill over medium heat or on charcoal grill over medium coals. Cover grill; cook 10 to 12 minutes, turning once, until juice of chicken is clear when thickest part is cut (170°F).

3) Spoon and spread 2 tablespoons cheese mixture over entire top of each chicken breast; cook covered 3 minutes longer or until topping is light golden brown and slightly puffy. Sprinkle with chives before serving.

HIGH ALTITUDE (3500-6500 FT.): In Step 2, cook 18 to 20 minutes.

Nutrition Information Per Serving:	
Calories: 280	From Fat: 160
Total Fat	17g
Saturated Fat	4g
Trans Fat	0g
Cholesterol	90mg
Sodium	270mg
Total Carbohydrate	0g
Dietary Fiber	0g
Sugars	0g
Protein	31g

tip

These grilled chicken breasts are wonderful with asparagus and a loaf of crusty bread. For a more casual meal, serve the breasts on toasted sandwich buns, each topped with lettuce and tomato.

Cabbage Rolls in Creamy Bacon Sauce

PREP TIME: 45 MINUTES (READY IN 1 HOUR 15 MINUTES)
SERVINGS: 6 (1 CABBAGE ROLL AND 1/4 CUP SAUCE EACH)

1 large head cabbage, core removed

1 lb extra-lean (at least 90%) ground beef

1/3 cup uncooked instant white rice

1/3 cup milk

1 egg

1 teaspoon Worcestershire sauce

1/2 teaspoon salt

1/4 teaspoon pepper

1 cup beef broth

1/2 teaspoon caraway seed

1/2 cup milk

1/2 cup sour cream

1 tablespoon all-purpose flour

1/4 cup cooked bacon pieces (from 2.1-oz package)

Nutrition Information Per Serving:

Calories: 240	From Fat: 120
Total Fat	13g
Saturated Fat	6g
Trans Fat	0.5g
Cholesterol	100mg
Sodium	530mg
Total Carbohydrate	11g
Dietary Fiber	0g
Sugars	4g
Protein	20g

1) Fill 5- to 6-quart Dutch oven half full of water. Heat to boiling. Place whole cabbage in water, core side down. Cover; cook 2 to 3 minutes, turning over once, or until leaves can be removed from head. With slotted spoon remove cabbage from water. With tongs, carefully remove 6 leaves from head. Save remaining head of cabbage for later use. Shave or trim part of the thick rib from each leaf. Return leaves to water; cook 2 to 3 minutes or until wilted.

2) In medium bowl, mix ground beef, uncooked rice, 1/3 cup milk, the egg, Worcestershire sauce, 1/4 teaspoon of the salt and 1/8 teaspoon of the pepper. Spoon about 1/3 cup of the ground beef mixture on thick end of each cabbage leaf. Roll up, tucking sides in. Place filled cabbage leaves in 12-inch skillet, seam side down. Add broth and caraway seed. Cover; heat to boiling. Reduce heat; simmer 25 to 30 minutes or until thermometer inserted in center of ground beef mixture reads 160°F.

3) With slotted spoon, place cabbage rolls on serving platter; cover to keep warm. In small bowl, mix 1/2 cup milk, the sour cream, flour, remaining 1/4 teaspoon salt and 1/8 teaspoon pepper with wire whisk. Pour into skillet. Cook and stir over medium heat until thick and bubbly. Serve sauce over cabbage rolls; sprinkle with bacon.

HIGH ALTITUDE (3500-6500 FT.): No change.

Easy Chicken and Dumplings

PREP TIME: 5 MINUTES (READY IN 15 MINUTES)
SERVINGS: 2

🅔 EASY

1 can (18.5 oz) Progresso® Carb Monitor™ chicken vegetable soup

2 Pillsbury® Oven Baked frozen buttermilk biscuits (from 25-oz bag)

Nutrition Information Per Serving:

Calories: 265	From Fat: 100
Total Fat	11g
Saturated Fat	3g
Cholesterol	5mg
Sodium	1620mg
Total Carbohydrate	35g
Dietary Fiber	1g
Sugars	4g
Protein	7g

1) In 2-quart saucepan, heat soup just to boiling over medium-high heat.

2) Meanwhile, on microwavable plate, microwave frozen biscuits on High 15 to 30 seconds or just until biscuits begin to thaw. Cut each biscuit into 6 pieces.

3) Place biscuit pieces on top of simmering soup. Reduce heat to low. Cover; simmer 6 to 7 minutes or until dumplings are fluffy and no longer doughy in center.

HIGH ALTITUDE (3500-6500 FT.): Simmer soup with biscuit pieces covered for 8 to 9 minutes.

Ranch Medley Casserole

PREP TIME: 15 MINUTES (READY IN 1 HOUR)
SERVINGS: 6 (1 CUP EACH)

 EASY

1 bag (1 lb) Green Giant Select® frozen broccoli, carrots & cauliflower

2 cups diced (¼ to ½ inch) cooked ham

2 cups refrigerated diced potatoes with onions (from 20-oz bag)

1 container (10 oz) refrigerated Alfredo pasta sauce

½ cup ranch dressing

24 round buttery crackers, crushed (about 1 cup)

2 tablespoons butter or margarine, melted

Nutrition Information Per Serving:

Calories:	490	From Fat:	330
Total Fat			36g
Saturated Fat			16g
Trans Fat			2g
Cholesterol			90mg
Sodium			1240mg
Total Carbohydrate			24g
Dietary Fiber			4g
Sugars			3g
Protein			17g

1) Heat oven to 350°F. In large bowl, mix frozen vegetables, ham, potatoes, Alfredo sauce and ranch dressing. Spread evenly in ungreased 13x9-inch (3-quart) glass baking dish.

2) In small bowl, mix crackers and melted butter. Sprinkle over top of casserole.

3) Bake 40 to 45 minutes or until bubbly and topping is golden brown.

HIGH ALTITUDE (3500-6500 FT.): Heat oven to 375°F. In Step 1, stir ¼ cup water into the vegetable-ham mixture.

Chicken Salad Cups

PREP TIME: 10 MINUTES (READY IN 30 MINUTES)
SERVINGS: 4 SALAD CUPS

 EASY

2 cups chopped cooked chicken

⅓ cup sliced celery

¼ cup mayonnaise or salad dressing

1 tablespoon chopped toasted sliced almonds

1 medium green onion, chopped (1 tablespoon)

⅛ teaspoon freshly ground black pepper

4 Pillsbury® Perfect Portions® refrigerated buttermilk biscuits (twin pack from 15.4-oz package)

¼ cup shredded Cheddar cheese (1 oz)

Nutrition Information Per Serving:

Calories:	350	From Fat:	170
Total Fat			19g
Saturated Fat			6g
Trans Fat			4g
Cholesterol			55mg
Sodium			550mg
Total Carbohydrate			24g
Dietary Fiber			0g
Sugars			4g
Protein			21g

1) Heat oven to 375°F. Lightly grease 4 jumbo muffin cups. In small bowl, mix chicken, celery, mayonnaise, almonds, onion and black pepper until well blended.

2) Press each biscuit to cover bottom and side of muffin cup. Spoon chicken mixture into biscuit cups.

3) Bake 16 to 21 minutes or until edges are deep golden brown. Sprinkle with the cheese.

HIGH ALTITUDE (3500-6500 FT.): No change.

Cheese-Stuffed Pizza

PREP TIME: 15 MINUTES (READY IN 35 MINUTES)
SERVINGS: 8

e EASY

- 1 can (13.8 oz) Pillsbury® refrigerated pizza crust
- 7 sticks (1 oz each) string cheese
- ½ cup pizza sauce
- 24 slices pepperoni (from 3.5-oz package)
- 2 cups shredded Italian cheese blend (8 oz)

1) Heat oven to 425°F. Spray 12-inch pizza pan with nonstick cooking spray. Unroll dough; place in sprayed pan. Starting at center, press out dough to edge of pan, pressing up and extending over edge by at least 1 inch. Place string cheese around inside edge of crust. Fold extended edge of dough over cheese; pinch firmly to seal.

2) Bake 8 to 10 minutes or until crust is set and edges are light golden brown.

3) Remove partially baked crust from oven. Spoon sauce evenly over crust. Top with pepperoni and Italian cheese blend.

4) Bake 12 to 16 minutes longer or until crust is deep golden brown and cheese in center is melted. Cut into wedges.

HIGH ALTITUDE (3500-6500 FT.): No change.

Nutrition Information Per Serving:

Calories:	370	From Fat:	180
Total Fat		20g	
Saturated Fat		11g	
Cholesterol		60mg	
Sodium		1050mg	
Total Carbohydrate		27g	
Dietary Fiber		0g	
Sugars		5g	
Protein		20g	

tip

Kitchen shears or scissors work well for cutting this warm, cheesy pizza into serving portions.

Chili-Cheese Burger Bake

PREP TIME: 30 MINUTES (READY IN 1 HOUR 15 MINUTES)
SERVINGS: 6

1   lb lean (at least 80%) ground beef

2   cups frozen bell pepper and onion stir-fry

1   can (11 oz) Green Giant® Niblets® whole kernel sweet corn, drained

1   package (1.25 oz) Old El Paso® taco seasoning mix

¼   cup water

1   can (16 oz) Old El Paso® refried beans

½   cup Old El Paso® taco sauce

2   cups chili-cheese corn chips

1   cup shredded Cheddar cheese (4 oz)

1) Heat oven to 375°F. Spray 8-inch square (2-quart) glass baking dish with cooking spray. In 12-inch skillet, cook ground beef over medium-high heat 5 to 7 minutes, stirring occasionally, until thoroughly cooked; drain. Stir in bell pepper and onion stir-fry, corn, taco seasoning mix and water. Cook over medium-high heat 5 to 6 minutes or until liquid is absorbed, stirring occasionally.

2) Meanwhile, in small bowl, mix refried beans and taco sauce.

3) Spoon half of beef mixture into baking dish. Top with half of bean mixture and half of corn chips. Top with remaining beef mixture and bean mixture. Cover with foil. Bake 30 minutes.

4) Remove baking dish from oven. Uncover; top with remaining half of chips. Sprinkle with cheese.

5) Return to oven; bake uncovered 10 to 12 minutes longer or until thoroughly heated and cheese is melted. If desired, garnish casserole with chopped fresh cilantro.

HIGH ALTITUDE (3500-6500 FT.): No change.

Nutrition Information Per Serving:	
Calories: 400	From Fat: 170
Total Fat	19g
Saturated Fat	8g
Trans Fat	0.5g
Cholesterol	65mg
Sodium	1340mg
Total Carbohydrate	33g
Dietary Fiber	6g
Sugars	5g
Protein	24g

Greek-Style Beef and Pasta

PREP TIME: 30 MINUTES (READY IN 30 MINUTES)
SERVINGS: 5

ⓔ EASY

2½ cups uncooked penne pasta (8 oz)

2 slices bacon, chopped

1 small onion, chopped

1 lb lean (at least 80%) ground beef

½ cup pitted kalamata olives

1 can (14.5 oz) diced tomatoes with basil, garlic and oregano, undrained

1 can (8 oz) tomato sauce

1 teaspoon dried oregano leaves

½ teaspoon salt

¾ cup crumbled feta cheese (4 oz)

1) Cook and drain pasta as directed on package; cover to keep warm.

2) Meanwhile, in 12-inch skillet, cook bacon and onion over medium heat until bacon is crisp, stirring frequently. Add ground beef. Cook 8 to 10 minutes, stirring occasionally, until beef is thoroughly cooked; drain.

3) Stir in olives, tomatoes, tomato sauce, oregano and salt. Reduce heat to medium-low. Simmer 10 minutes, stirring occasionally, until thoroughly heated. Serve over cooked pasta; sprinkle cheese over top.

HIGH ALTITUDE (3500-6500 FT.): No change.

Nutrition Information Per Serving:

Calories: 460	From Fat: 170
Total Fat	19g
Saturated Fat	8g
Trans Fat	1g
Cholesterol	80mg
Sodium	1250mg
Total Carbohydrate	45g
Dietary Fiber	5g
Sugars	6g
Protein	28g

tip

Feta cheese is typically used in Greek dishes. If your family prefers, you could use Parmesan or mozzarella cheese.

Asparagus, Shrimp and Dill over Fettuccine

PREP TIME: 25 MINUTES (READY IN 25 MINUTES)
SERVINGS: 2

e EASY

6 oz uncooked fettuccine

¾ cup chicken broth

1 tablespoon all-purpose or unbleached flour

1 tablespoon fresh lemon juice

1½ teaspoons finely chopped fresh dill weed

2 teaspoons olive oil

1 cup cut (1-inch) fresh asparagus spears

½ lb uncooked deveined peeled medium shrimp

2 lemon wedges

1) Cook fettuccine as directed on package to desired doneness. Drain; cover to keep warm.

2) Meanwhile, in small bowl, mix broth and flour. Stir in the lemon juice and dill. Set aside.

3) In 10-inch nonstick skillet or Dutch oven, heat olive oil over medium heat until hot. Add asparagus; cook and stir 2 minutes. Add shrimp; cook and stir 3 minutes longer or until shrimp turn pink.

4) Add broth mixture to skillet; cook over medium heat, stirring frequently, until slightly thickened.

5) Add cooked fettuccine to skillet; toss gently to coat. Garnish each serving with lemon wedge.

HIGH ALTITUDE (3500-6500 FT.): No change.

Nutrition Information Per Serving:		
Calories: 470	From Fat: 100	
Total Fat		11g
Saturated Fat		2g
Trans Fat		0g
Cholesterol		225mg
Sodium		950mg
Total Carbohydrate		63g
Dietary Fiber		4g
Sugars		2g
Protein		31g

tip

Fresh, uncooked shrimp can be tightly covered and refrigerated for up to 2 days. Rinse with cold water and pat dry on paper towels before storing.

Wild Rice and Turkey Casserole

PREP TIME: 15 MINUTES (READY IN 1 HOUR 15 MINUTES)
SERVINGS: 6

Ⓔ EASY

1 cup cooked white rice

1 cup cooked wild rice

2 cups diced ($\frac{1}{4}$ to $\frac{1}{2}$ inch) cooked turkey breast

2 cups shredded Monterey Jack or mozzarella cheese (8 oz)

1 can (12 oz) evaporated milk

$\frac{1}{2}$ cup finely chopped red bell pepper

$\frac{1}{2}$ cup finely chopped green bell pepper

2 eggs, slightly beaten

$\frac{1}{2}$ teaspoon salt

$\frac{1}{4}$ teaspoon pepper

1 tablespoon chopped fresh parsley, if desired

Nutrition Information Per Serving:

Calories:	370	From Fat:	160
Total Fat			18g
Saturated Fat			10g
Trans Fat			0g
Cholesterol			155mg
Sodium			730mg
Total Carbohydrate			21g
Dietary Fiber			1g
Sugars			8g
Protein			32g

1) Heat oven to 350°F. Spray 12x8- or 11x7-inch (2-quart) glass baking dish with nonstick cooking spray. In baking dish, mix white rice and wild rice; spread evenly over bottom.

2) In large bowl, mix turkey, cheese, milk, bell peppers, eggs, salt and pepper. Spoon over rice.

3) Bake 45 to 55 minutes or until knife inserted in center comes out clean and top is lightly browned. Sprinkle with parsley. Let casserole stand 5 minutes before serving.

HIGH ALTITUDE (3500-6500 FT.): No change.

Sausage Ravioli Casserole

PREP TIME: 10 MINUTES (READY IN 1 HOUR)
SERVINGS: 6

Ⓔ EASY

1 bag (25 oz) frozen Italian-style sausage-filled ravioli, thawed

1 jar (4.5 oz) Green Giant® sliced mushrooms, drained

1 medium zucchini, cut into $\frac{1}{8}$-inch slices (about 1 cup)

$\frac{1}{2}$ cup pepperoni slices (2$\frac{1}{2}$ oz)

1 jar (26 oz) roasted tomato and garlic pasta sauce

1 cup shredded Swiss cheese (4 oz)

$\frac{1}{8}$ teaspoon Italian seasoning, if desired

Nutrition Information Per Serving:

Calories:	500	From Fat:	200
Total Fat			22g
Saturated Fat			9g
Trans Fat			0g
Cholesterol			1/0mg
Sodium			1840mg
Total Carbohydrate			52g
Dietary Fiber			4g
Sugars			13g
Protein			23g

1) Heat oven to 350°F. In large bowl, mix all ingredients except cheese and Italian seasoning. Spoon into ungreased 8-inch square (2-quart) glass baking dish. Sprinkle with cheese and Italian seasoning.

2) Bake 40 to 50 minutes or until thoroughly heated and bubbly.

HIGH ALTITUDE (3500-6500 FT.): Bake 50 to 55 minutes.

Roasted Salmon and Vegetables

PREP TIME: 10 MINUTES (READY IN 45 MINUTES)
SERVINGS: 4

ⓔ EASY

4 salmon steaks, ½ inch thick
(about 1½ lb)

2 cups refrigerated new potato wedges
with skins (from 20-oz bag)

2 small zucchini, quartered lengthwise,
then cut into 2-inch pieces

1 medium red bell pepper, cut into
2-inch pieces

1 tablespoon lemon juice

1 tablespoon butter or margarine,
melted

½ teaspoon salt

¼ to ½ teaspoon dried tarragon leaves

¼ teaspoon pepper

Nutrition Information Per Serving:		
Calories: 290	From Fat: 100	
Total Fat		11g
Saturated Fat		4g
Trans Fat		0g
Cholesterol		105mg
Sodium		490mg
Total Carbohydrate		14g
Dietary Fiber		3g
Sugars		4g
Protein		34g

1) Heat oven to 425°F. Place salmon steaks in ungreased 15x10x1-inch pan. Arrange potato wedges, zucchini and bell pepper around salmon.

2) Brush salmon with lemon juice. Brush salmon and vegetables with butter; sprinkle with salt, tarragon and pepper.

3) Bake 25 to 35 minutes or until salmon flakes easily with fork and vegetables are tender.

HIGH ALTITUDE (3500-6500 FT.): No change.

Prosciutto- and Spinach-Stuffed Shells

PREP TIME: 35 MINUTES (READY IN 1 HOUR 15 MINUTES)
SERVINGS: 5

24 uncooked jumbo pasta shells
(about 6 oz)

1 jar (26 oz) tomato-basil pasta sauce

3 cups shredded mozzarella cheese
(12 oz)

1 cup cottage cheese

1 cup chopped prosciutto (4½ oz)

1 box (9 oz) Green Giant® frozen
spinach, thawed, squeezed to drain

2 tablespoons chopped fresh basil
leaves, if desired

Nutrition Information Per Serving:		
Calories: 590	From Fat: 200	
Total Fat		22g
Saturated Fat		11g
Trans Fat		0g
Cholesterol		55mg
Sodium		1750mg
Total Carbohydrate		61g
Dietary Fiber		5g
Sugars		17g
Protein		37g

1) Heat oven to 375°F. Cook and drain pasta as directed on package. Spray 13x9-inch (3-quart) glass baking dish with nonstick cooking spray. Spread ⅓ cup of the pasta sauce over bottom of baking dish.

2) In medium bowl, mix 1 cup of the mozzarella cheese, the cottage cheese, prosciutto and spinach. Spoon scant 2 tablespoons mixture into each shell. Arrange filled shells in baking dish. Pour remaining pasta sauce over stuffed shells. Sprinkle remaining 2 cups mozzarella cheese evenly over sauce.

3) Cover dish with foil. Bake 30 to 40 minutes or until thoroughly heated. Sprinkle with basil.

HIGH ALTITUDE (3500-6500 FT.): No change.

Mediterranean Bow-Ties

PREP TIME: 20 MINUTES (READY IN 1 HOUR 10 MINUTES)
SERVINGS: 6 (1 CUP EACH)

⊖ EASY

3 cups uncooked bow-tie (farfalle) pasta (8 oz)

1 envelope (1.8 oz) white sauce mix

2½ cups milk

1 tablespoon butter or margarine

1 box (9 oz) Green Giant® asparagus cuts

½ cup sun-dried tomatoes in oil, drained, chopped

1 cup diced (¼ to ½ inch) cooked ham

1 cup shredded Havarti cheese (4 oz)

2 tablespoons sliced ripe olives, if desired

1) Heat oven to 350°F. Spray 2-quart casserole with cooking spray. Cook and drain pasta as directed on package.

2) Meanwhile, in 3-quart saucepan, mix sauce mix and milk with wire whisk until blended. Add butter. Heat to boiling over medium-high heat, stirring constantly. Reduce heat to low; simmer 1 minute, stirring occasionally.

3) Gently stir pasta, asparagus, tomatoes and ham into sauce. Pour into casserole. Cover; bake 35 to 45 minutes or until bubbly.

4) Remove casserole from oven. Sprinkle with cheese. Bake uncovered about 3 minutes longer or until cheese is melted. Sprinkle with olives.

HIGH ALTITUDE (3500-6500 FT.): No change.

Nutrition Information Per Serving:	
Calories: 410	From Fat: 140
Total Fat	16g
Saturated Fat	9g
Trans Fat	0g
Cholesterol	45mg
Sodium	980mg
Total Carbohydrate	46g
Dietary Fiber	3g
Sugars	9g
Protein	20g

Beef Burgundy

PREP TIME: 20 MINUTES (READY IN 1 HOUR 20 MINUTES)
SERVINGS: 4

e EASY

1 tablespoon olive or vegetable oil

1 lb boneless beef sirloin steak, cut into 1-inch cubes

1 large onion, coarsely chopped (1 cup)

2 teaspoons finely chopped garlic

$\frac{1}{2}$ teaspoon pepper

2 cups ready-to-eat baby-cut carrots

$\frac{1}{4}$ cup red wine or tomato juice

1 can (10$\frac{3}{4}$ oz) condensed golden mushroom soup

5 cups uncooked extra-wide egg noodles (8 oz)

1 tablespoon chopped fresh parsley

1) Heat oven to 350°F. In 10-inch skillet, heat oil over medium-high heat. Add beef, onion and garlic; sprinkle with pepper. Cook 5 to 8 minutes, stirring occasionally, until beef is brown and onion is translucent. Stir in carrots, wine and soup. Spoon mixture into ungreased 1½-quart casserole.

2) Cover; bake about 1 hour or until beef and carrots are tender when pierced with fork. Remove from oven; keep covered.

3) Meanwhile, cook and drain noodles as directed on package. Place noodles on serving platter; ladle beef mixture over top. Sprinkle with parsley.

HIGH ALTITUDE (3500-6500 FT.): No change.

Nutrition Information Per Serving:		
Calories: 550	From Fat: 210	
Total Fat		24g
Saturated Fat		7g
Trans Fat		1g
Cholesterol		115mg
Sodium		880mg
Total Carbohydrate		53g
Dietary Fiber		5g
Sugars		6g
Protein		30g

Chicken and Broccoli Casserole

PREP TIME:	20 MINUTES (READY IN 1 HOUR 5 MINUTES)
SERVINGS:	6 (1-1/2 CUPS EACH)

e EASY

- 1 tablespoon butter or margarine
- 1 package (8 oz) sliced fresh baby portabella mushrooms
- 1 can (10¾ oz) condensed golden mushroom soup
- ½ cup milk
- 1 tablespoon Dijon mustard
- ½ teaspoon salt
- ½ teaspoon dried thyme leaves
- ¼ teaspoon pepper
- 3 cups cut-up cooked chicken
- 1 bag (1 lb) Green Giant® frozen broccoli cuts, thawed
- 1 can (8 oz) sliced water chestnuts, drained
- 1 cup shredded American-Cheddar cheese blend (4 oz)
- 1 can (2.8 oz) French-fried onions

1) Heat oven to 350°F. Spray 13x9-inch (3-quart) glass baking dish with nonstick cooking spray. In 10-inch skillet, melt butter over medium-high heat. Add mushrooms; cook 4 to 6 minutes, stirring frequently, until mushrooms are browned.

2) In large bowl, mix soup, milk, mustard, salt, thyme and pepper. Stir in mushrooms, chicken, broccoli and water chestnuts. Pour into baking dish. Sprinkle with cheese.

3) Cover dish with foil. Bake 30 minutes. Sprinkle French-fried onions over top. Bake uncovered about 15 minutes longer or until mixture is hot and bubbly.

HIGH ALTITUDE (3500-6500 FT.): No change.

Nutrition Information Per Serving:		
Calories: 410	From Fat: 210	
Total Fat		23g
Saturated Fat		9g
Trans Fat		2.5g
Cholesterol		85mg
Sodium		1100mg
Total Carbohydrate		20g
Dietary Fiber		4g
Sugars		4g
Protein		30g

tip

To save time, you can substitute 1 jar (6 oz) Green Giant® sliced mushrooms, drained, for the fresh mushrooms in the casserole. Then you can omit the butter and browning step.

Short Ribs in Red Wine

PREP TIME: 20 MINUTES (READY IN 7 HOURS 35 MINUTES)
SERVINGS: 6

e EASY

2 tablespoons olive or vegetable oil

3 lb bone-in beef short ribs

¼ teaspoon salt

¼ teaspoon pepper

1 can (14.5 oz) stewed tomatoes, undrained

1 medium onion, chopped (½ cup)

2 tablespoons tomato paste

½ cup red wine or beef broth

½ cup beef broth

1 tablespoon Worcestershire sauce

¼ cup water

2 tablespoons cornstarch

1) In 12-inch skillet, heat oil over medium-high heat. Add short ribs; sprinkle with salt and pepper. Cook 4 to 6 minutes, turning occasionally, until browned.

2) In 3- to 4-quart slow cooker, place tomatoes, onion and tomato paste; stir. Add ribs, wine, broth and Worcestershire sauce.

3) Cover; cook on Low heat setting 7 to 9 hours.

4) Remove ribs and bones from cooker; cover ribs to keep warm. Discard bones. Spoon off any fat from mixture in cooker. In small bowl, mix water and cornstarch; stir into mixture in cooker. Increase heat setting to High. Cover; cook 10 to 15 minutes or until sauce is thickened. Serve over ribs.

HIGH ALTITUDE (3500-6500 FT.): No change.

Nutrition Information Per Serving:	
Calories: 270	From Fat: 160
Total Fat	18g
Saturated Fat	6g
Trans Fat	0.5g
Cholesterol	70mg
Sodium	490mg
Total Carbohydrate	10g
Dietary Fiber	1g
Sugars	5g
Protein	18g

tip

If your short ribs don't fit in the slow cooker, you may need to cut them between the bones first. Serve the entree with mashed potatoes and warm rolls for a quick meal.

Pizza Breadstick Casserole

PREP TIME: 15 MINUTES (READY IN 45 MINUTES)
SERVINGS: 6

ⓔ EASY

1 lb lean (at least 80%) ground beef

½ cup diced pepperoni (from 6-oz package)

5 green onions, sliced (5 tablespoons)

1½ cups chunky tomato pasta sauce (from 26-oz jar)

1 box (10.6 oz) Pillsbury® refrigerated Parmesan breadsticks with garlic

1 cup shredded Colby-Monterey Jack cheese blend (4 oz)

Nutrition Information Per Serving:

Calories:	460	From Fat:	230
Total Fat			25g
Saturated Fat			10g
Trans Fat			2g
Cholesterol			75mg
Sodium			1060mg
Total Carbohydrate			33g
Dietary Fiber			1g
Sugars			9g
Protein			25g

1) Heat oven to 375°F. Spray 12x8-inch (2-quart) glass baking dish with nonstick cooking spray. In 10-inch skillet, cook ground beef over medium-high heat 5 to 7 minutes, stirring occasionally, until thoroughly cooked; drain. Stir in pepperoni, onions and pasta sauce. Cook until boiling, stirring frequently.

2) Meanwhile, unroll dough into 1 large rectangle. Spread garlic mixture from box evenly over dough. Separate dough into 10 breadsticks. Cut each breadstick into 3 crosswise pieces.

3) Spoon ground beef mixture into baking dish. Spread dough pieces evenly over hot ground beef mixture.

4) Bake 15 to 18 minutes or until topping is golden brown and no longer doughy. Sprinkle with cheese. Bake 10 minutes longer or until the cheese is melted.

HIGH ALTITUDE (3500-6500 FT.): In Step 4, sprinkle with cheese and bake 5 minutes longer.

Cheesy Kielbasa-Pasta Supper

PREP TIME: 30 MINUTES (READY IN 30 MINUTES)
SERVINGS: 5 (1-1/2 CUPS EACH)

ⓔ EASY

2½ cups uncooked rigatoni pasta (6 oz)

1 bag (1 lb) Green Giant Select® frozen broccoli, carrots & cauliflower

1 can (10¾ oz) condensed Cheddar cheese soup

¾ cup milk

½ lb fully cooked turkey kielbasa, halved lengthwise, sliced

1 jar (2.5 oz) Green Giant® sliced mushrooms, drained

Nutrition Information Per Serving:

Calories:	320	From Fat:	90
Total Fat			11g
Saturated Fat			4g
Trans Fat			1g
Cholesterol			35mg
Sodium			1230mg
Total Carbohydrate			39g
Dietary Fiber			5g
Sugars			5g
Protein			17g

1) In 5-quart Dutch oven or 4-quart saucepan, cook pasta as directed on package, adding broccoli, carrots and cauliflower during last 6 to 7 minutes of cooking time; cook until pasta and vegetables are tender. Drain; return to Dutch oven.

2) Stir in soup, milk, kielbasa and mushrooms. Cook over medium heat 3 to 5 minutes or until thoroughly heated, stirring occasionally.

HIGH ALTITUDE (3500-6500 FT.): No change.

GRILLED SEASONED PORK ROAST
PG. 199

Grilled Greats

Fire up the coals for these made-in-moments specialties ideal for nearly any occasion.

HOEDOWN BBQ CHUCK ROAST
PG. 186

FIESTA GRILLED CHICKEN SANDWICHES
WITH CHIPOTLE MAYONNAISE
PG. 200

CAESAR PITA BURGERS
PG. 203

Hoedown BBQ Chuck Roast

PREP TIME: 15 MINUTES (READY IN 7 HOURS 30 MINUTES)
SERVINGS: 8

ⓔ EASY

1 boneless beef chuck roast (4 lb),
    2 inches thick

¼ cup sugar

½ cup soy sauce

½ cup ketchup

¼ cup red wine vinegar

1 to 2 garlic cloves, minced

⅛ teaspoon pepper

1) Trim fat from beef roast. In 12x8-inch (2-quart) glass baking dish or large resealable food storage plastic bag, mix remaining ingredients. Add roast; turn to coat. Cover dish or seal bag. Refrigerate 6 hours or overnight, turning once or twice, to marinate.

2) Heat gas or charcoal grill. Remove roast from marinade; reserve and refrigerate marinade. Place roast on grill. Cover grill; cook over medium-low heat 50 minutes to 1 hour 15 minutes or until of desired doneness, turning once and basting with reserved marinade during last 15 minutes of cooking time. Discard any remaining marinade.

HIGH ALTITUDE (3500-6500 FT.): Omit sugar from recipe. Spray large sheet of heavy-duty foil with cooking spray. Remove roast from marinade; place on foil and fold foil loosely around roast. Reserve and refrigerate marinade. Place foil-wrapped roast on grill over low heat. Cover grill; cook 40 minutes. Turn roast; brush with reserved marinade. Cook 40 minutes longer or until of desired doneness.

Nutrition Information Per Serving:	
Calories: 460 From Fat: 240	
Total Fat	27g
Saturated Fat	10g
Trans Fat	1g
Cholesterol	130mg
Sodium	1190mg
Total Carbohydrate	12g
Dietary Fiber	0g
Sugars	10g
Protein	43g

Grilled Vegetable Focaccia

PREP TIME: 35 MINUTES (READY IN 35 MINUTES)
SERVINGS: 6

MAYONNAISE SPREAD

$1/3$ cup light mayonnaise

1 tablespoon chopped fresh chives

1 teaspoon chopped fresh thyme leaves

1 teaspoon stone-ground mustard

1 clove garlic, finely chopped

SANDWICH

1 package (6 oz) portabella mushroom caps

1 small red bell pepper, quartered lengthwise

1 small yellow bell pepper, quartered lengthwise

2 slices ($1/2$ inch) red onion

Nonstick cooking spray

1 focaccia bread (10 inch)

1 large tomato, sliced

4 oz Havarti cheese, sliced

1) Heat gas or charcoal grill. In small bowl, mix mayonnaise spread ingredients. Refrigerate. With small metal spoon, scrape underside of mushroom caps to remove dark gills.

2) Spray mushrooms, bell peppers and onion slices with nonstick cooking spray. Place on grill over medium heat. Cover grill; cook 7 to 10 minutes, turning occasionally, until bell peppers and onion are crisp-tender. Remove vegetables from grill; let stand until cool enough to handle.

3) Meanwhile, cut focaccia in half horizontally to form 2 rounds. Spread mayonnaise spread evenly on cut side of bottom half.

4) Slice mushrooms; arrange over mayonnaise spread. Cut bell peppers into thin strips; layer over mushrooms. Separate onion slices into rings; place over peppers. Top with tomato and cheese slices. Cover with the top half of focaccia.

5) If desired, wrap sandwich in foil; place on grill. Cook 1 to 2 minutes or until cheese is melted. To serve, cut into 6 wedges.

HIGH ALTITUDE (3500-6500 FT.): Grill over medium-low heat.

Nutrition Information Per Serving:		
Calories: 360	From Fat: 160	
Total Fat		18g
Saturated Fat		6g
Trans Fat		0g
Cholesterol		25mg
Sodium		800mg
Total Carbohydrate		38g
Dietary Fiber		3g
Sugars		4g
Protein		10g

Grilled Blue Cheese Steak

PREP TIME: 30 MINUTES (READY IN 30 MINUTES)
SERVINGS: 6

e EASY

1 cup blue cheese, crumbled (4 oz)

1 tablespoon mayonnaise or salad dressing

1 teaspoon Worcestershire sauce

2 cloves garlic, minced

1½ lb boneless beef sirloin steak, 1½ inches thick

1) Heat gas or charcoal grill. In small bowl, mix cheese, mayonnaise, Worcestershire sauce and garlic until blended; set aside.

2) Place steak on grill. Cover grill; cook over medium-high heat 15 to 20 minutes, turning once, until desired doneness. Remove steak from grill.

3) Spoon cheese mixture over steak; let stand 1 to 2 minutes or until cheese is slightly melted. Cut steak into pieces to serve.

HIGH ALTITUDE (3500-6500 FT.): No change.

Nutrition Information Per Serving:

Calories: 220	From Fat: 100
Total Fat	11g
Saturated Fat	5g
Trans Fat	0g
Cholesterol	80mg
Sodium	320mg
Total Carbohydrate	1g
Dietary Fiber	0g
Sugars	0g
Protein	30g

tip

You can make the tasty blue cheese mixture several hours ahead of time and store it in the refrigerator until you are ready to use it at dinnertime.

Grilled Bratwurst Reubens

PREP TIME: 10 MINUTES (READY IN 10 MINUTES)
SERVINGS: 8

e EASY

8 cooked bratwurst

1 jar (16 oz) sauerkraut, drained, rinsed

½ cup Thousand Island dressing

8 rye bratwurst buns, split

To reduce the fat in each serving of this recipe by about 13 grams, pick up a package of light bratwurst.

1) Heat gas or charcoal grill. Place bratwurst on grill. Cover grill; cook over medium heat 6 to 8 minutes, turning frequently, until thoroughly heated.

2) Meanwhile, in medium bowl, mix sauerkraut and dressing.

3) To toast buns, place cut side down on grill during last 30 to 60 seconds of cooking time.

4) Place bratwurst in buns. Top each with about ¼ cup sauerkraut mixture.

HIGH ALTITUDE (3500-6500 FT.): No change.

Nutrition Information Per Serving:	
Calories: 420	From Fat: 270
Total Fat	30g
Saturated Fat	10g
Trans Fat	0.5g
Cholesterol	55mg
Sodium	1600mg
Total Carbohydrate	23g
Dietary Fiber	3g
Sugars	4g
Protein	13g

Shrimp Caesar Salad

PREP TIME: 15 MINUTES (READY IN 15 MINUTES)
SERVINGS: 4

e EASY

1 tablespoon lemon juice

1 tablespoon vegetable oil

16 large uncooked fresh shrimp ($^1\!/_2$ lb), peeled, deveined

1 bag (7.5 oz) complete Caesar salad mix

$^1\!/_4$ cup shredded Parmesan cheese (1 oz)

1) Heat gas or charcoal grill. In small bowl, mix lemon juice and oil. Onto 4 (12- to 14-inch) metal skewers, thread shrimp.

2) Carefully oil grill rack. Place kabobs on grill. Cover grill; cook over medium heat 6 to 10 minutes, turning once and brushing frequently with lemon juice mixture, until shrimp are pink.

3) Meanwhile, make salad mix as directed on bag. Add shrimp; toss gently. Sprinkle with Parmesan cheese. Serve immediately.

HIGH ALTITUDE (3500-6500 FT.): Cook over medium-low heat.

Nutrition Information Per Serving:	
Calories: 180	From Fat: 120
Total Fat	14g
Saturated Fat	3g
Trans Fat	0g
Cholesterol	65mg
Sodium	380mg
Total Carbohydrate	4g
Dietary Fiber	1g
Sugars	1g
Protein	9g

tip If you don't have metal skewers, you can use bamboo skewers located near the kitchen utensils at the grocery store. Just be sure to soak the skewers in water for 30 minutes to prevent them from burning during grilling.

Easy Cheesy Topped Burgers

PREP TIME: 30 MINUTES (READY IN 30 MINUTES)
SERVINGS: 12

e EASY

2½ cups shredded Cheddar cheese (10 oz)

½ cup chopped packaged precooked bacon (about 8 slices)

⅓ cup mayonnaise

2 tablespoons ketchup

3 teaspoons red pepper sauce, if desired

12 frozen ground beef patties (3 lb)

Bread or hamburger buns, if desired

Nutrition Information Per Serving:		
Calories: 360	From Fat:	250
Total Fat		28g
Saturated Fat		11g
Trans Fat		1g
Cholesterol		95mg
Sodium		340mg
Total Carbohydrate		1g
Dietary Fiber		0g
Sugars		1g
Protein		26g

1) Heat gas or charcoal grill. In small bowl, mix all ingredients except patties.

2) When grill is heated, place frozen patties on grill. Cover grill; cook over medium heat 4 to 8 minutes, turning once, until meat thermometer inserted in center of patties reads 160°F.

3) Carefully top each patty with about ¼ cup cheese mixture; cook covered 4 minutes longer or until cheese is melted. Serve on bread.

HIGH ALTITUDE (3500-6500 FT.): No change.

Hoagie Sandwiches on the Grill

PREP TIME: 25 MINUTES (READY IN 25 MINUTES)
SERVINGS: 8

e EASY

8 soft hoagie buns (6 to 7 inch), split

¾ cup creamy Dijon mustard-mayonnaise spread

8 slices (1¾ oz each) provolone or mozzarella cheese, each cut into 4 pieces

½ lb thinly sliced salami or summer sausage

1 lb thinly sliced cooked turkey or chicken

1 medium green bell pepper, cut into thin bite-size strips

Nutrition Information Per Serving:		
Calories: 560	From Fat:	230
Total Fat		25g
Saturated Fat		12g
Trans Fat		1g
Cholesterol		105mg
Sodium		1540mg
Total Carbohydrate		43g
Dietary Fiber		2g
Sugars		7g
Protein		39g

1) Heat gas or charcoal grill. Cut 8 (12x12-inch) sheets of heavy-duty foil. Spread cut sides of buns with mustard-mayonnaise spread.

2) On bottom halves of buns, layer cheese, salami, turkey and bell pepper. Cover with top halves of buns. Place sandwiches on foil. Wrap each packet securely using double-fold seals, allowing room for heat expansion.

3) Place packets on grill. Cover grill; cook over medium heat 8 to 10 minutes or until thoroughly heated. Carefully open packets to allow steam to escape.

HIGH ALTITUDE (3500-6500 FT.):
Cook over medium-low heat, rotating and turning every 4 minutes.

Terrific Turkey Burgers

PREP TIME: 25 MINUTES (READY IN 25 MINUTES)
SERVINGS: 8

ⓔ EASY   (f) LOW FAT

2 lb lean ground turkey

1 cup Progresso® plain bread crumbs

2/3 cup finely chopped onion

1/2 cup ketchup or tomato sauce

2 tablespoons lemon juice

4 teaspoons soy sauce

4 teaspoons Worcestershire sauce

1/4 teaspoon pepper

8 burger buns, split

Lettuce, if desired

1) Heat gas or charcoal grill. In large bowl, mix all ingredients except buns and lettuce until well blended. Shape mixture into 8 patties, 1/2 inch thick.

2) Lightly oil grill rack. Place patties on grill. Cover grill; cook over medium heat 10 to 12 minutes, turning once, until meat thermometer inserted in center of patties reads 165°F.

3) Meanwhile, place buns cut sides down on grill. Cook 1 to 2 minutes or until lightly toasted. Place patties in lettuce-lined buns. If desired, serve with ketchup and pickle slices.

HIGH ALTITUDE (3500-6500 FT.): No change.

Nutrition Information Per Serving:	
Calories: 360	From Fat: 80
Total Fat	9g
Saturated Fat	2.5g
Trans Fat	0.5g
Cholesterol	75mg
Sodium	740mg
Total Carbohydrate	37g
Dietary Fiber	2g
Sugars	8g
Protein	31g

tip

To broil patties, place on sprayed broiler pan; broil 4 to 6 inches from heat using times in the recipe as a guide, turning once. Place buns, cut side up, on broiler pan; broil 1 to 2 minutes.

Grilled Dill-Mustard Salmon

PREP TIME: 20 MINUTES (READY IN 20 MINUTES)
SERVINGS: 6

⊖ EASY

1 tablespoon chopped fresh dill

1 tablespoon Dijon mustard

1 tablespoon honey

¼ cup mayonnaise or salad dressing

1½ lb fresh salmon fillet

Nonstick cooking spray

Nutrition Information Per Serving:

Calories:	240	From Fat:	130
Total Fat			14g
Saturated Fat			3g
Trans Fat			0g
Cholesterol			80mg
Sodium			180mg
Total Carbohydrate			3g
Dietary Fiber			0g
Sugars			3g
Protein			24g

1) Heat gas or charcoal grill. In small bowl, mix dill, mustard and honey. In small bowl, place 2 tablespoons mustard mixture; stir in mayonnaise until well blended. Refrigerate sauce until serving time. Reserve remaining mustard mixture for brushing on salmon.

2) Spray skin side of salmon with nonstick cooking spray. Place salmon, skin side down, on grill over medium heat. Spoon reserved mustard mixture onto salmon, spreading evenly. Cover grill; cook 10 to 15 minutes or until fish flakes easily with fork. Serve mayonnaise-mustard sauce mixture with salmon.

Broiling Directions: Place skin side up on broiler pan; do not spread with mustard mixture. Broil with top 4 to 6 inches from heat, using times above as a guide, turning once halfway through broiling and spreading with mustard mixture.

HIGH ALTITUDE (3500-6500 FT.): Grill over medium-low heat.

Taco Burger and Potato Packets

PREP TIME: 40 MINUTES (READY IN 40 MINUTES)
SERVINGS: 4

e EASY

1 lb lean (at least 80%) ground beef

1/2 cup Progresso® plain bread crumbs

2 tablespoons Old El Paso® taco seasoning mix (from 1.25-oz package)

1/4 cup milk

3 cups frozen southern-style diced hash brown potatoes (from 32-oz bag)

1 cup Old El Paso® Cheese 'n Salsa dip

1) Heat gas or charcoal grill. In medium bowl, mix ground beef, bread crumbs, taco seasoning mix and milk until well blended. Shape mixture into 4 (4-inch) patties. In another medium bowl, mix frozen potatoes and dip.

2) Cut 4 (18x12-inch) sheets of heavy-duty foil. Place 1 patty on each; top with 1/4 of potato mixture. Wrap each packet securely using double-fold seals, allowing room for heat expansion.

3) When grill is heated, place packets, seam side up, on grill over medium heat; cover grill. Cook 15 to 25 minutes, rearranging packets several times, until patties are thoroughly cooked.

HIGH ALTITUDE (3500-6500 FT.): Cook over medium-low heat 17 to 22 minutes.

Nutrition Information Per Serving:	
Calories: 470	From Fat: 180
Total Fat	20g
Saturated Fat	7g
Trans Fat	1g
Cholesterol	80mg
Sodium	1620mg
Total Carbohydrate	50g
Dietary Fiber	3g
Sugars	2g
Protein	25g

Seasoned Grilled New Potatoes

PREP TIME: 50 MINUTES (READY IN 50 MINUTES)
SERVINGS: 8 (1/2 CUP EACH)

⊖ EASY

2 lb new red potatoes

¼ cup butter or margarine, melted

2 garlic cloves, minced

1 teaspoon seasoned salt

Nutrition Information Per Serving:

Calories:	140	From Fat:	50
Total Fat			6g
Saturated Fat			3.5g
Trans Fat			0g
Cholesterol			15mg
Sodium			220mg
Total Carbohydrate			20g
Dietary Fiber			3g
Sugars			1g
Protein			2g

1) Heat gas or charcoal grill. If potatoes are large, cut in half or quarter for uniform pieces. Place potatoes in 8-inch square disposable foil pan or in center of large sheet of heavy-duty foil.

2) In small bowl, mix butter, garlic and salt; pour over potatoes. Cover pan with foil or seal foil packet with double-fold seals, allowing room for heat expansion.

3) When grill is heated, place potatoes on gas grill over medium heat or on charcoal grill over medium coals. Cook 35 to 45 minutes or until potatoes are tender, stirring potatoes in foil pan or turning foil packet several times during cooking.

HIGH ALTITUDE (3500-6500 FT.):
Cook over medium-low heat.

tip

You can also add 2 tablespoons of chopped fresh herbs to the seasoning mixture for these grilled potatoes. Try a combination of your favorite herbs, such as rosemary, thyme and/or sage.

Fireside S'Mores

PREP TIME: 10 MINUTES (READY IN 10 MINUTES)
SERVINGS: 4

e EASY

8 graham cracker squares

2 milk chocolate candy bars (1.55 oz each)

4 large marshmallows

4 long-handled forks

1) On each of 4 graham cracker squares, place a candy bar half.

2) Spear each marshmallow on long-handled fork; toast over campfire coals or over grill with low heat.

3) Place 1 toasted marshmallow on top of each chocolate bar. Top each with cracker; press together and hold for a few seconds to melt chocolate.

HIGH ALTITUDE (3500-6500 FT.): No change.

Nutrition Information Per Serving:		
Calories: 200	From Fat:	70
Total Fat		8g
Saturated Fat		3.5g
Trans Fat		0g
Cholesterol		5mg
Sodium		100mg
Total Carbohydrate		29g
Dietary Fiber		0g
Sugars		22g
Protein		2g

Mint S'Mores

PREP TIME: 10 MINUTES (READY IN 10 MINUTES)
SERVINGS: 4

EASY

8 chocolate-covered mint cookies

2 milk chocolate candy bars (1.55-oz each), each halved

4 large marshmallows

4 long-handled forks

1) On each of 4 chocolate-covered mint cookies, place candy bar half.

2) Spear each marshmallow on long-handled fork; toast over campfire coals or over grill with low heat.

3) Place 1 toasted marshmallow on top of each chocolate bar. Top each with a cookie; press together and hold for a few seconds to melt chocolate.

HIGH ALTITUDE (3500-6500 FT.): No change.

Striped S'Mores

PREP TIME: 10 MINUTES (READY IN 10 MINUTES)
SERVINGS: 4

EASY

8 chocolate-striped cookies

2 milk chocolate candy bars (1.55-oz each), each halved

4 large marshmallows

4 long-handled forks

1) On each of 4 chocolate-striped cookies, place candy bar half.

2) Spear each marshmallow on long-handled fork; toast over campfire coals or over grill with low heat.

3) Place 1 toasted marshmallow on top of each chocolate bar. Top each with a chocolate-striped cookie; press together and hold for a few seconds to melt the chocolate.

HIGH ALTITUDE (3500-6500 FT.): No change.

Peanut Butter S'Mores

PREP TIME: 10 MINUTES (READY IN 10 MINUTES)
SERVINGS: 4

EASY

8 graham cracker squares

4 chocolate-covered peanut butter cups

4 large marshmallows

4 long-handled forks

1) On each of 4 graham cracker squares, place a peanut butter cup.

2) Spear each marshmallow on long-handled fork; toast over campfire coals or over grill with low heat.

3) Place 1 toasted marshmallow on top of each peanut butter cup. Top each with cracker; press together and hold for a few seconds to melt chocolate.

HIGH ALTITUDE (3500-6500 FT.): No change.

Hearty Hoedown Burgers

PREP TIME: 25 MINUTES (READY IN 25 MINUTES)
SERVINGS: 6

e EASY

1½ lb lean (at least 80%) ground beef

⅓ cup finely chopped onion (1 small)

⅓ cup finely chopped green bell pepper

2 tablespoons Worcestershire sauce

½ teaspoon seasoned salt

½ teaspoon garlic powder

¼ teaspoon pepper

6 slices (1 oz) American cheese

6 burger buns, split

¼ cup sandwich spread (from 16-oz jar)

Red onion slices, if desired

1) Heat gas or charcoal grill. In medium bowl, mix ground beef, onion, bell pepper, Worcestershire sauce, seasoned salt, garlic powder and pepper until well blended. Shape mixture into 6 patties, ½ inch thick.

2) Place patties on grill. Cover grill; cook over medium heat 13 to 15 minutes, turning once, until meat thermometer inserted in center of patties reads 160°F. To toast buns, place cut sides down on grill during last 1 to 2 minutes of cooking time. Top each patty with cheese slice; cook just until cheese is melted.

3) Spread cut sides of toasted buns with sandwich spread; top with onion slices. Place cheese-topped patties in buns.

HIGH ALTITUDE (3500-6500 FT.): No change.

Nutrition Information Per Serving:	
Calories: 460	From Fat: 230
Total Fat	26g
Saturated Fat	11g
Trans Fat	1.5g
Cholesterol	100mg
Sodium	940mg
Total Carbohydrate	25g
Dietary Fiber	3g
Sugars	8g
Protein	30g

Grilled Seasoned Pork Roast

PREP TIME: 10 MINUTES (READY IN 2 HOURS 40 MINUTES)
SERVINGS: 8

e EASY

- 2 teaspoons garlic powder
- 1½ teaspoons onion powder
- 1 teaspoon salt
- 2 teaspoons poultry seasoning
- 1 teaspoon chili powder
- 1 boneless center-cut pork loin roast (3 lb)

1) Heat gas or charcoal grill for indirect-heat cooking as directed by manufacturer. In small bowl, mix all ingredients except roast. Rub mixture onto all sides of roast. (Do not remove strings until after grilling.)

2) Place roast, fat side up, on grill for indirect cooking. Cover grill; cook 1 hour 30 minutes to 2 hours 15 minutes or until meat thermometer inserted into thickest part of roast reads 160°F. Let roast stand 10 to 15 minutes before slicing.

HIGH ALTITUDE (3500-6500 FT.): No change.

Nutrition Information Per Serving:

Calories:	280	From Fat:	120
Total Fat			13g
Saturated Fat			4.5g
Trans Fat			0g
Cholesterol			110mg
Sodium			360mg
Total Carbohydrate			1g
Dietary Fiber			0g
Sugars			0g
Protein			38g

tip

Some suppliers inject pork roasts with a salt solution to increase shelf life and make the meat moist and flavorful. Read the package label and decrease the amount of salt in the rub if the meat you're using has been injected.

Fiesta Grilled Chicken Sandwiches with Chipotle Mayonnaise

PREP TIME: 30 MINUTES (READY IN 30 MINUTES)
SERVINGS: 4 (2 SANDWICHES EACH)

e EASY

- ¼ cup grated Parmesan cheese
- 2 tablespoons Old El Paso® taco seasoning mix (from 1.25-oz package)
- 4 boneless skinless chicken breasts
- 4 slices (½ oz each) pepper Jack or Monterey Jack cheese
- 8 Pillsbury® Oven Baked frozen crusty French dinner rolls
- ¼ cup chipotle or regular mayonnaise, if desired
- 8 leaves leaf lettuce
- ¼ cup Old El Paso® Thick 'n Chunky salsa

1) Heat gas or charcoal grill. Mix Parmesan cheese and taco seasoning mix. Coat chicken with cheese mixture.

2) Carefully oil grill rack. Place chicken on grill over medium heat. Cover grill; cook 10 to 12 minutes or until juice of chicken is clear when center of thickest part is cut, turning once or twice. Cut each chicken breast in half crosswise; top each with half slice of cheese to melt. To heat dinner rolls, place 4 rolls each in separate foil packets on grill during last 6 to 7 minutes of cook time until hot.

3) Spread mayonnaise on bottom halves of rolls. Top each with lettuce leaf, cheese-topped chicken, salsa and top half of roll.

Broiling Directions: Place chicken on broiler pan; broil 4 to 6 inches from heat, using grilling times above as a guide.

HIGH ALTITUDE (3500-6500 FT.): Flatten chicken breasts to approximately 3⁄4 inch before coating. Grill over medium-low heat 12 to 15 minutes or until juice of chicken is clear, turning once or twice.

Nutrition Information Per Serving:	
Calories: 390	From Fat: 100
Total Fat	11g
Saturated Fat	4.5g
Trans Fat	0g
Cholesterol	90mg
Sodium	1180mg
Total Carbohydrate	35g
Dietary Fiber	0g
Sugars	3g
Protein	38g

Rib-Eye Steaks with Avocado Salsa

PREP TIME: 25 MINUTES (READY IN 25 MINUTES)
SERVINGS: 4

e EASY

1/2 cup Old El Paso® Thick 'n Chunky salsa

1 medium avocado, peeled, pitted and coarsely chopped

2 tablespoons finely chopped red onion

2 tablespoons chopped fresh cilantro

4 boneless beef rib-eye steaks (3/4 inch thick)

1 teaspoon garlic salt

Nutrition Information Per Serving:		
Calories: 350	From Fat:	160
Total Fat		18g
Saturated Fat		5g
Trans Fat		0.5g
Cholesterol		75mg
Sodium		530mg
Total Carbohydrate		7g
Dietary Fiber		3g
Sugars		2g
Protein		40g

1) Heat gas or charcoal grill. In medium bowl, mix the salsa, avocado, onion and cilantro.

2) Sprinkle both sides of each steak with garlic salt. Place steaks on grill. Cover grill, cook over medium heat 8 to 12 minutes or until desired doneness, turning once or twice. Serve steaks with salsa mixture.

HIGH ALTITUDE (3500-6500 FT.): No change.

tip

To broil steaks, place on broiler pan; broil 4 to 6 inches from heat using times in recipe as a guide, turning the steaks once or twice.

Dad's Day Burgers

PREP TIME: 30 MINUTES (READY IN 30 MINUTES)
SERVINGS: 8

e EASY

2 lb lean (at least 80%) ground beef

2 teaspoons Worcestershire sauce

1 teaspoon seasoned salt

1 teaspoon onion powder

¼ teaspoon pepper

8 burger buns, split

8 lettuce leaves

2 medium tomatoes, thinly sliced

Nutrition Information Per Serving:	
Calories: 320	From Fat: 130
Total Fat	15g
Saturated Fat	5g
Trans Fat	1g
Cholesterol	70mg
Sodium	450mg
Total Carbohydrate	23g
Dietary Fiber	1g
Sugars	4g
Protein	24g

1) Heat gas or charcoal grill. In large bowl, mix ground beef, Worcestershire sauce, seasoned salt, onion powder and pepper until well blended. Shape mixture into 8 patties, about ¾ inch thick.

2) Place patties on grill. Cover grill; cook over medium heat 13 to 15 minutes, turning once, until meat thermometer inserted in center of patties reads 160°F.

3) Layer buns with lettuce, tomato slices and burger patties. If desired, serve with ketchup, mustard, pickles and onions.

HIGH ALTITUDE (3500-6500 FT.): No change.

Grilled Whole Turkey

PREP TIME: 20 MINUTES (READY IN 4 HOURS)
SERVINGS: 14

e EASY

1 fresh or frozen whole turkey (10 to 12 lb), thawed

1 teaspoon seasoned salt

¼ teaspoon pepper

3 to 4 tablespoons oil or melted butter

Nutrition Information Per Serving:	
Calories: 400	From Fat: 220
Total Fat	25g
Saturated Fat	7g
Trans Fat	0.5g
Cholesterol	145mg
Sodium	230mg
Total Carbohydrate	0g
Dietary Fiber	0g
Sugars	0g
Protein	44g

1) Heat gas or charcoal grill for indirect grilling as directed in owner's manual. Remove and discard neck and giblets from turkey. Rinse turkey with cold water. Season cavity of turkey with seasoned salt and pepper. Fasten neck skin to back with skewers. Turn wings back and tuck tips under shoulder joints. Refasten drumsticks with metal piece or tuck under band of skin at tail. Rub outside surface of turkey with oil. Insert meat thermometer so tip is in thickest part of thigh and does not touch bone.

2) Place turkey, breast side up, over unheated side of grill directly over drip pan. Cover grill; cook turkey with medium heat 2½ to 3½ hours or until thermometer reads 180°F to 185°F and legs move easily when moved or twisted. Avoid lifting cover until ready to check thermometer. (There is no need to baste or turn turkey.) Let turkey stand 15 to 20 minutes before carving.

HIGH ALTITUDE (3500-6500 FT.): Cook 3 to 4 hours.

Caesar Pita Burgers

PREP TIME: 20 MINUTES (READY IN 20 MINUTES)
SERVINGS: 5

ⓔ EASY

1 lb lean (at least 80%) ground beef

½ cup creamy Caesar dressing

1 egg

½ cup Progresso® plain bread crumbs

5 pita (pocket) bread halves

½ cup shredded Asiago or Parmesan cheese

5 tablespoons diced fresh tomato

5 tablespoons diced fresh cucumber

1) Heat gas or charcoal grill. In medium bowl, mix ground beef, ¼ cup of dressing, egg and bread crumbs. Shape into 5 oval patties, about ½-inch thick.

2) Place patties on grill; cover grill. Cook over medium heat 7 to 10 minutes, turning once, until thermometer inserted in center of patties reads 160°F. During last 1 to 2 minutes of cooking time, top each patty with cheese.

3) If desired, place pita bread halves on grill during last 1 minute of cooking. Fill pita bread halves with remaining ¼ cup dressing, tomato, cucumber and patties.

HIGH ALTITUDE (3500-6500 FT.): No change.

Nutrition Information Per Serving:		
Calories: 510	From Fat: 260	
Total Fat		29g
Saturated Fat		8g
Trans Fat		0.5g
Cholesterol		105mg
Sodium		820mg
Total Carbohydrate		35g
Dietary Fiber		2g
Sugars		3g
Protein		27g

tip

If you are using your own garden cucumbers or English cucumbers, there is no need to peel them. If you are using waxed or oiled cucumbers from the produce department, it's best to peel them.

Santa Fe Grilled Chicken

PREP TIME: 30 MINUTES (READY IN 30 MINUTES)
SERVINGS: 8

e EASY

8 boneless skinless chicken breasts (about 2 lb)

2 tablespoons vegetable oil

2 tablespoons Old El Paso® taco seasoning mix (from 1.25-oz package)

8 slices (¾ oz each) Monterey Jack cheese

1 cup Old El Paso® Thick 'n Chunky salsa

1) Heat gas or charcoal grill. Brush both sides of chicken with oil; sprinkle with taco seasoning mix.

2) Place chicken on grill. Cover grill; cook over medium heat 15 to 20 minutes (turning once and topping each chicken breast with cheese during last minute of cooking time) or until juice of chicken is clear when center of thickest part is cut (170°F). Serve chicken topped with salsa.

HIGH ALTITUDE (3500-6500 FT.): Use medium-low heat.

Nutrition Information Per Serving:

Calories:	260	From Fat:	120
Total Fat			13g
Saturated Fat			6g
Trans Fat			0g
Cholesterol			85mg
Sodium			620mg
Total Carbohydrate			5g
Dietary Fiber			0g
Sugars			1g
Protein			30g

tip Vary the flavor of this easy entree by changing the cheese. Why not try Cheddar or mozzarella instead of the Monterey Jack? Enjoy the chicken with a cool citrus salad of sliced oranges, grapefruit sections and avocado slices.

Frenchy Franks

PREP TIME: 30 MINUTES (READY IN 30 MINUTES)
SERVINGS: 8

EASY

1 cup french fried onions

8 coarse-ground beef franks

8 hot dog or bratwurst buns, split

1/4 cup mustard hot dog relish

1/4 cup French dressing

Nutrition Information Per Serving:	
Calories: 350	From Fat: 190
Total Fat	21g
Saturated Fat	7g
Trans Fat	1.5g
Cholesterol	25mg
Sodium	960mg
Total Carbohydrate	29g
Dietary Fiber	1g
Sugars	8g
Protein	10g

1) Heat gas or charcoal grill. In small skillet, cook onions over medium-high heat 3 to 4 minutes or until slightly browned, stirring occasionally. Set aside.

2) Cut franks in half lengthwise, cutting almost but not completely through. Open franks and place cut sides down on grill. Cover grill; cook over medium heat 5 to 10 minutes or until thoroughly heated, turning once. To toast buns, place cut sides down on grill during last 1 to 2 minutes of cooking time.

3) To serve, spread cut sides of each bun with about 1/2 tablespoon relish. Place frank in each bun. Top with salad dressing and onions.

HIGH ALTITUDE (3500-6500 FT.): No change.

Cheesy Ham Supper Packets

PREP TIME: 30 MINUTES (READY IN 30 MINUTES)
SERVINGS: 4

EASY

1 slice cooked ham, 1/2 inch thick (about 1 lb), cut into 4 equal pieces

2 cups refrigerated new potato wedges (from 1 lb 4-oz package)

2 boxes (10 oz each) Green Giant® frozen broccoli, cauliflower, carrots & cheese flavored sauce, thawed

1 cup shredded Cheddar cheese (4 oz)

Nutrition Information Per Serving:	
Calories: 430	From Fat: 200
Total Fat	23g
Saturated Fat	11g
Trans Fat	1g
Cholesterol	105mg
Sodium	2500mg
Total Carbohydrate	20g
Dietary Fiber	4g
Sugars	6g
Protein	37g

1) Heat gas or charcoal grill. Cut 4 (18x12-inch) sheets of heavy-duty foil. Place ham piece in center of each. Top each evenly with potatoes and vegetable mixture. Bring up foil sides so edges meet. Seal edges, making tight 1/2-inch fold; fold again, allowing space on sides for heat circulation and expansion.

2) Place packets, seam side up, on grill. Cover grill; cook over medium heat 18 to 23 minutes, rearranging packets several times during cooking, until potatoes and vegetables are tender.

3) To serve, carefully open packets to allow steam to escape. Sprinkle each with cheese; close packets and let stand until cheese is melted, 1 to 2 minutes.

HIGH ALTITUDE (3500-6500 FT.): Cook over medium-low heat.

Taste of the Southwest

Shake up meal routines with south-of-the-border entrees, side dishes, desserts and more!

MINI PICADILLO EMPANADAS
PG. 230

DOUBLE CHEESE AND BEAN NACHOS
PG. 224

FAJITAS FOR TWO
PG. 226

CHICKEN-CHILE QUESADILLAS
PG. 209

Skillet Eggs and Rice

PREP TIME: 15 MINUTES (READY IN 45 MINUTES)
SERVINGS: 4

🅔 EASY

½ lb cooked kielbasa or smoked sausage, halved lengthwise, cut into ½-inch pieces

1 box (7.6 oz) Old El Paso® Spanish rice

2½ cups water

½ cup Old El Paso® Thick 'n Chunky salsa

4 eggs

Pepper, if desired

Old El Paso® flour tortillas for soft tacos & fajitas (6 inch; from 10.5-oz package), heated, if desired

1) In 10-inch nonstick skillet, cook sausage over medium heat 2 to 3 minutes, stirring occasionally, until sausage begins to brown. Stir in rice, contents of seasoning packet, water and salsa. Heat to boiling. Reduce heat to low; cover and cook 20 minutes.

2) Break 1 egg onto each quarter of rice mixture (egg will sink into rice). Cover; cook 7 to 9 minutes or until eggs are set and rice is tender. Sprinkle with pepper. Serve with warm tortillas.

HIGH ALTITUDE (3500-6500 FT.): After adding rice, contents of seasoning packet, water and salsa, heat to boiling. Reduce heat to medium-low; cover and cook 25 minutes. After breaking eggs onto rice mixture, cover and cook 9 to 11 minutes.

Nutrition Information Per Serving:	
Calories: 450	From Fat: 200
Total Fat	22g
Saturated Fat	7g
Trans Fat	0g
Cholesterol	245mg
Sodium	1440mg
Total Carbohydrate	47g
Dietary Fiber	2g
Sugars	5g
Protein	16g

Chicken–Chile Quesadillas

PREP TIME: 20 MINUTES (READY IN 20 MINUTES)
SERVINGS: 8 (1 QUESADILLA AND 2 TABLESPOONS SALSA EACH)

e EASY

1 package (11.5 oz) Old El Paso® flour tortillas for burritos (8 tortillas)

2 cups finely shredded Mexican cheese blend (8 oz)

2 cups shredded or finely chopped deli rotisserie chicken (from 2- to 2$\frac{1}{2}$-lb chicken)

1 can (4.5 oz) Old El Paso® chopped green chiles

$\frac{1}{4}$ cup sliced green onions (4 medium)

2 tablespoons butter or margarine, melted

1 cup Old El Paso® Thick 'n Chunky salsa

1) Top one half of each tortilla with cheese, chicken, green chiles and onions. Fold other half of each tortilla over filling; press down with back of pancake turner. Lightly brush melted butter on both sides of each filled tortilla.

2) Heat 12-inch nonstick skillet over medium heat. Cook 2 filled tortillas at a time 3 to 4 minutes, turning once, until golden brown and thoroughly heated. Cut into wedges. Serve with salsa.

HIGH ALTITUDE (3500-6500 FT.): No change.

Nutrition Information Per Serving:

Calories:	340	From Fat:	160
Total Fat			18g
Saturated Fat			9g
Trans Fat			0g
Cholesterol			65mg
Sodium			880mg
Total Carbohydrate			25g
Dietary Fiber			0g
Sugars			2g
Protein			19g

tip

Once you cook a filled quesadilla in the skillet, transfer it to a cookie sheet in a 300°F oven while you cook the remaining quesadillas.

Avocado-Corn Salsa

PREP TIME: 10 MINUTES (READY IN 10 MINUTES)
SERVINGS: 24 (2 TABLESPOONS SALSA AND 6 TORTILLA CHIPS EACH)

e EASY

1 cup Old El Paso® Thick 'n Chunky salsa

1 medium avocado, pitted, peeled and coarsely chopped

1 can (11 oz) Green Giant® Mexicorn® whole kernel corn, red and green peppers, drained

2 tablespoons chopped fresh cilantro

24 oz tortilla chips

Nutrition Information Per Serving:	
Calories: 170	From Fat: 70
Total Fat	8g
Saturated Fat	1g
Trans Fat	0g
Cholesterol	0mg
Sodium	290mg
Total Carbohydrate	22g
Dietary Fiber	2g
Sugars	1g
Protein	2g

1) In medium bowl, mix all ingredients except tortilla chips until well blended.

2) Serve immediately, or cover and refrigerate until serving time.

HIGH ALTITUDE (3500-6500 FT.): No change.

Crescent Burritos

JEANNE HOLT | MENDOTA HEIGHTS, MINNESOTA   **Bake-Off**   BAKE-OFF® CONTEST 31, 1984

PREP TIME: 35 MINUTES (READY IN 1 HOUR)
SERVINGS: 8

½ lb lean (at least 80%) ground beef

2 tablespoons chopped onion

2 tablespoons Old El Paso® taco seasoning mix (from 1.25-oz package)

½ cup water

½ cup Old El Paso® refried beans (from 16-oz can)

2 cans (8 oz each) Pillsbury® refrigerated crescent dinner rolls

½ cup Old El Paso® Thick 'n Chunky salsa

4 slices (¾ oz each) American cheese, cut diagonally in half

1 cup sour cream

¼ cup sliced ripe olives

1) Heat oven to 350°F. Spray cookie sheet with cooking spray. In 10-inch nonstick skillet, cook ground beef and onion over medium-high heat, stirring occasionally, until beef is thoroughly cooked; drain.

2) Stir in taco seasoning mix and water. Reduce heat to medium; cook about 5 minutes, stirring frequently, until water has evaporated. Remove from heat; stir in beans.

3) Separate dough into 8 rectangles; firmly press perforations to seal. Spoon about 2 tablespoons beef mixture and 1 tablespoon of the salsa onto each rectangle; spread to within ½ inch of one short side. Starting with other short side, roll up each rectangle; pinch edges to seal. Place seam side down on cookie sheet.

4) Bake 18 to 23 minutes or until golden brown. Top each burrito with cheese; bake 2 to 3 minutes longer or until cheese is melted. Serve garnished with sour cream and olives.

Nutrition Information Per Serving:	
Calories: 390	From Fat: 220
Total Fat	25g
Saturated Fat	11g
Trans Fat	3.5g
Cholesterol	50mg
Sodium	850mg
Total Carbohydrate	30g
Dietary Fiber	2g
Sugars	7g
Protein	14g

HIGH ALTITUDE (3500-6500 FT.): No change.

Margarita Olé Bars

PREP TIME: 15 MINUTES (READY IN 2 HOURS)
SERVINGS: 36

e EASY

BASE

1¾ cups all-purpose flour

½ cup powdered sugar

1 cup butter, softened

FILLING

4 eggs

1½ cups granulated sugar

¼ cup all-purpose flour

½ teaspoon baking powder

⅓ cup frozen margarita mix concentrate, thawed

2 teaspoons grated lime peel

1 tablespoon powdered sugar

1) Heat oven to 350°F. In large bowl, mix base ingredients with electric mixer on low speed until crumbly. With floured fingers, press mixture firmly in bottom of ungreased 13x9-inch pan. Bake 20 to 25 minutes or until light golden brown.

2) Meanwhile, beat eggs slightly in large bowl. Mix in granulated sugar, ¼ cup flour and the baking powder until well blended. Stir in margarita mix and lime peel.

3) Remove pan from oven. Pour filling over warm base. Bake 18 to 22 minutes longer or until top is golden brown and filling is set. Cool completely, about 1 hour.

4) Just before serving, sprinkle bars with 1 tablespoon powdered sugar. Cut into 6 rows by 6 rows.

HIGH ALTITUDE (3500-6500 FT.): No change.

Nutrition Information Per Serving:		
Calories: 120	From Fat:	50
Total Fat		6g
Saturated Fat		3.5g
Trans Fat		0g
Cholesterol		35mg
Sodium		50mg
Total Carbohydrate		17g
Dietary Fiber		0g
Sugars		11g
Protein		1g

tip

Use a fine-mesh strainer to evenly sprinkle the powdered sugar over the bars. Be sure to sprinkle on just before serving; powdered sugar is readily absorbed into the surface of the bars.

Salsa Fajita Beef

PREP TIME: 20 MINUTES (READY IN 25 MINUTES)
SERVINGS: 4

e EASY

2 to 3 tablespoons vegetable oil

2 Old El Paso® flour tortillas for burritos (8 inch; from 11.5-oz package), cut into $1/2$-inch-wide strips

1 lb boneless beef sirloin steak, cut into bite-size strips

$1^1/2$ cups frozen bell pepper and onion stir-fry (from 1-lb bag)

$1^1/2$ cups Green Giant® Niblets® frozen corn (from 1-lb bag)

$1^1/2$ cups Old El Paso® Thick 'n Chunky salsa

1 tablespoon sugar

1) In 10-inch skillet, heat 2 tablespoons of the oil over medium-high heat. Cook tortilla strips, a few at a time, 1 to 2 minutes, stirring occasionally, until crisp (if necessary, add additional tablespoon oil); drain tortilla strips on paper towels.

2) In same skillet, cook beef over medium-high heat 2 to 4 minutes, stirring occasionally, until browned. Stir in all remaining ingredients. Reduce heat to medium; simmer 5 minutes or until vegetables are crisp-tender. Stir in tortilla strips.

HIGH ALTITUDE (3500-6500 FT.): No change.

Nutrition Information Per Serving:		
Calories: 380	From Fat:	130
Total Fat		14g
Saturated Fat		3g
Trans Fat		0g
Cholesterol		60mg
Sodium		890mg
Total Carbohydrate		39g
Dietary Fiber		2g
Sugars		8g
Protein		26g

Fiesta Enchilada Bake

PREP TIME: 25 MINUTES (READY IN 1 HOUR 10 MINUTES)
SERVINGS: 6

1¼ lb lean ground turkey

1 box (10.35 oz) Old El Paso® taco dinner kit

⅔ cup water

2 cans (10 oz each) Old El Paso® enchilada sauce

½ cup sliced green onions (8 medium)

2 cups shredded Cheddar cheese (8 oz)

3 cups shredded lettuce

½ cup sour cream

1) Heat oven to 325°F. Spray 13x9-inch (3-quart) glass baking dish with cooking spray. In 2-quart saucepan, cook ground turkey over medium-high heat 4 to 6 minutes, stirring occasionally, until no longer pink; drain. Stir in seasoning mix from dinner kit and water. Cook as directed on box.

2) Pour 1 can of the enchilada sauce into baking dish. Break taco shells from kit in half; layer half of the shells over sauce, overlapping if necessary. Top with turkey, onions and 1 cup of the cheese. Layer remaining shells over cheese. Pour remaining can of enchilada sauce over shells, coating well. Cover dish with foil.

3) Bake about 30 minutes or until hot and bubbly. Remove foil; sprinkle remaining 1 cup cheese over top. Bake uncovered about 15 minutes longer or until cheese is melted. Top individual servings with lettuce, sour cream and salsa from kit.

HIGH ALTITUDE (3500-6500 FT.): Heat oven to 350°F. Bake about 40 minutes or until hot and bubbly. Remove foil; sprinkle remaining 1 cup cheese over top. Bake uncovered 5 minutes longer or until cheese is melted.

Nutrition Information Per Serving:

Calories:	480	From Fat:	250
Total Fat			28g
Saturated Fat			13g
Trans Fat			0.5g
Cholesterol			115mg
Sodium			1460mg
Total Carbohydrate			25g
Dietary Fiber			1g
Sugars			5g
Protein			33g

Easy Strawberry Margarita Dessert

PREP TIME: 25 MINUTES (READY IN 3 HOURS 25 MINUTES)
SERVINGS: 10

CRUST

1¼ cups crushed pretzels

¼ cup sugar

½ cup butter or margarine, melted

FILLING

1 package (10 oz) frozen strawberries in syrup, thawed

1 can (14 oz) sweetened condensed milk (not evaporated)

½ cup frozen (thawed) concentrated margarita mix

1 cup whipping cream, whipped

Fresh strawberries, if desired

1) In small bowl, mix all crust ingredients. Press firmly in bottom of ungreased 8- or 9-inch springform pan. Refrigerate while making filling.

2) In large bowl with wire whisk, mix thawed strawberries until broken into small pieces. Beat in condensed milk and margarita mix until well blended. Fold in whipped cream. Pour into crust-lined pan. Freeze at least 3 hours or until firm. Cut into wedges to serve. Garnish with fresh strawberries.

HIGH ALTITUDE (3500-6500 FT.): No change.

Nutrition Information Per Serving:

Calories:	400	From Fat:	200
Total Fat			22g
Saturated Fat			12g
Trans Fat			1g
Cholesterol			70mg
Sodium			250mg
Total Carbohydrate			48g
Dietary Fiber			0g
Sugars			40g
Protein			5g

tip

If this dessert is frozen solid, transfer it to the refrigerator at the start of your meal. By the time you are ready for dessert, it will be easy to cut and serve.

Mexican Margaritas

PREP TIME: 15 MINUTES (READY IN 2 HOURS 45 MINUTES)
SERVINGS: 12

e EASY   **f** LOW FAT

1⅓ cups orange-flavored liqueur

1 cup lime juice

2 to 3 tablespoons powdered sugar, if desired

8 cups ice cubes, crushed

2 limes, cut into wedges, if desired

½ cup coarse salt, if desired

⅔ cup tequila

Nutrition Information Per Serving:	
Calories: 45	From Fat: 0
Total Fat	0g
Saturated Fat	0g
Trans Fat	0g
Cholesterol	0mg
Sodium	10mg
Total Carbohydrate	11g
Dietary Fiber	0g
Sugars	9g
Protein	0g

1) In blender or food processor, place orange liqueur, lime juice, powdered sugar and ice. Cover; blend until smooth. Spoon into nonmetal freezer container. Cover; freeze until almost firm, 2 to 2½ hours.

2) To serve, if mixture freezes completely, let stand at room temperature about 30 minutes. Rub rims of glasses with lime wedges; dip in salt to coat.

3) Into blender or food processor, spoon orange liqueur mixture; blend until slushy. Place ½ cup slush in each salt-rimmed glass; add 1 to 2 tablespoons tequila. Garnish with lime wedges.

HIGH ALTITUDE (3500-6500 FT.): No change.

tip There are several types of orange-flavored liqueurs available, including Triple Sec, Cointreau and curaçao. All will work well in this recipe.

Baked Crescent Churros

PREP TIME: 15 MINUTES (READY IN 30 MINUTES)
SERVINGS: 12

e EASY

2 tablespoons sugar

1 teaspoon ground cinnamon

1 can (8 oz) Pillsbury® refrigerated crescent dinner rolls

2 tablespoons butter or margarine, melted

Nutrition Information Per Serving:	
Calories: 100	From Fat: 50
Total Fat	6g
Saturated Fat	2.5g
Trans Fat	1g
Cholesterol	5mg
Sodium	160mg
Total Carbohydrate	10g
Dietary Fiber	0g
Sugars	3g
Protein	1g

1) Heat oven to 375°F. In small bowl, mix sugar and cinnamon; set aside. Unroll dough; separate into 4 rectangles. Press each to 6x4-inch rectangle, pressing perforations to seal.

2) Brush tops of 2 rectangles with melted butter; sprinkle with about half of the sugar mixture. Top each with remaining rectangle; press edges lightly. Brush tops with melted butter.

3) With sharp knife or pizza cutter, cut each rectangle stack lengthwise into 6 strips. Twist each strip 3 times; place on ungreased cookie sheet.

4) Bake 9 to 11 minutes or until golden brown and crisp. Brush tops with any remaining melted butter; sprinkle with remaining sugar mixture.

HIGH ALTITUDE (3500-6500 FT.): No change.

Cheesy Chicken Enchilada Soup

PREP TIME: 20 MINUTES (READY IN 20 MINUTES)
SERVINGS: 6 (1 CUP EACH)

e EASY

2 cans (10¾ oz each) condensed 98% fat-free cream of chicken soup with 30% less sodium

1 can (10 oz) Old El Paso® enchilada sauce

2 cups milk

1 cup shredded reduced-fat Cheddar cheese (4 oz)

1 package (9 oz) frozen cooked southwestern-flavored chicken strips, thawed, chopped (2 cups)

¾ cup crushed tortilla chips

1) In 3-quart saucepan, mix all ingredients except tortilla chips.

2) Cook over medium heat, stirring occasionally, until thoroughly heated and cheese is melted. Top individual servings with tortilla chips.

HIGH ALTITUDE (3500-6500 FT.): No change.

Nutrition Information Per Serving:		
Calories: 260	From Fat: 100	
Total Fat		11g
Saturated Fat		3g
Trans Fat		0.5g
Cholesterol		45mg
Sodium		1100mg
Total Carbohydrate		22g
Dietary Fiber		0g
Sugars		6g
Protein		19g

Chicken Enchilada Casserole

PREP TIME: 15 MINUTES (READY IN 1 HOUR)
SERVINGS: 4 (1-1/2 CUPS EACH)

e EASY

- 2 cups cut-up cooked chicken
- 1 teaspoon sugar
- ½ cup Old El Paso® Thick 'n Chunky salsa
- 1 can (19 oz) Old El Paso® mild enchilada sauce
- 1 can (11 oz) Green Giant® Niblets® whole kernel corn, drained
- 2 cups coarsely broken tortilla chips
- 4 medium green onions, sliced (¼ cup)
- 1 medium tomato, chopped (¾ cup)
- 1 cup shredded Cheddar-Jack with jalapeño peppers cheese blend (4 oz)

1) Heat oven to 350°F. In medium bowl, mix chicken, sugar, salsa, enchilada sauce and corn.

2) Place tortilla chips in ungreased 8-inch square (2-quart) glass baking dish. Top with chicken mixture. Sprinkle with onions, tomato and cheese.

3) Bake 35 to 45 minutes or until hot and bubbly. If desired, arrange additional tortilla chips around edge of dish.

HIGH ALTITUDE (3500-6500 FT.): No change.

Nutrition Information Per Serving:	
Calories: 550	From Fat: 220
Total Fat	25g
Saturated Fat	7g
Trans Fat	0.5g
Cholesterol	85mg
Sodium	1490mg
Total Carbohydrate	51g
Dietary Fiber	3g
Sugars	9g
Protein	31g

If your family loves beans, try adding 1 can (16 oz) spicy chili beans, undrained, to the chicken mixture for extra flavor and fiber.

Cheeseburger Tacos

PREP TIME: 20 MINUTES (READY IN 20 MINUTES)
SERVINGS: 12

 EASY

1 box (4.6 oz) Old El Paso® taco shells (12 shells)

12 slices ($^2/_3$ oz each) American cheese

1 lb lean (at least 80%) ground beef

1 cup Old El Paso® Cheese 'n Salsa dip

12 lettuce leaves

12 tomato slices

$^3/_4$ cup Old El Paso® Thick 'n Chunky salsa

1) Heat oven to 350°F. Line each taco shell with 1 slice of cheese. Arrange taco shells on ungreased cookie sheet (cheese will fall to one side). Bake 5 to 7 minutes or until cheese is melted.

2) Meanwhile, in 8-inch skillet, cook ground beef over medium-high heat 5 to 7 minutes, stirring frequently, until thoroughly cooked; drain. Stir in dip. Cook until thoroughly heated.

3) To serve, spoon about 2 tablespoons beef mixture into each warm taco shell. Top each with lettuce and tomato. Serve with salsa.

HIGH ALTITUDE (3500-6500 FT.): No change.

Nutrition Information Per Serving:

Calories: 220	From Fat: 130
Total Fat	15g
Saturated Fat	6g
Trans Fat	1g
Cholesterol	45mg
Sodium	650mg
Total Carbohydrate	12g
Dietary Fiber	1g
Sugars	1g
Protein	12g

tip Die-hard cheeseburger fans also can add pickle slices to their tacos.

Taco Potato Rounds

PREP TIME: 5 MINUTES (READY IN 25 MINUTES)
SERVINGS: 6 (1 CUP EACH)

EASY

1 bag (30 oz) frozen crisp shredded potato rounds

Nonstick cooking spray

2 tablespoons Old El Paso® 40% Less-Sodium taco seasoning mix (from 1.25-oz package)

1) Heat oven to 425°F. In 15x10x1-inch pan with sides, place potatoes. Spray potatoes with nonstick cooking spray; toss and spray again. Sprinkle with taco seasoning mix; toss to coat.

2) Bake 18 to 20 minutes until crisp and thoroughly heated.

HIGH ALTITUDE (3500-6500 FT.): Bake 20 to 22 minutes.

Nutrition Information Per Serving:

Calories: 340	From Fat: 140
Total Fat	15g
Saturated Fat	7g
Trans Fat	5g
Cholesterol	0mg
Sodium	1390mg
Total Carbohydrate	47g
Dietary Fiber	5g
Sugars	3g
Protein	5g

Iced Mexican Coffee

PREP TIME: 10 MINUTES (READY IN 10 MINUTES)
SERVINGS: 4

e EASY   **f** LOW FAT

- 1 cup milk
- ¼ cup chocolate-flavored syrup
- ¼ cup tequila, if desired
- 2 tablespoons sugar
- 2 tablespoons instant coffee granules or crystals
- ½ teaspoon ground cinnamon
- 3 cups crushed ice
- Whipped cream, if desired
- Cinnamon sticks, if desired

1) In blender, place all ingredients except ice, whipped cream and cinnamon sticks. Cover; blend on high speed until mixed.

2) Add ice; cover and blend until slushy. Top individual servings with dollop of whipped cream and cinnamon stick.

HIGH ALTITUDE (3500-6500 FT.): No change.

Nutrition Information Per Serving:

Calories:	110	From Fat:	15
Total Fat			1.5g
Saturated Fat			0.5g
Trans Fat			0g
Cholesterol			0mg
Sodium			45mg
Total Carbohydrate			23g
Dietary Fiber			0g
Sugars			18g
Protein			3g

tip

Most home blenders don't handle large ice cubes well. To crush ice cubes, place them in a heavy-duty plastic food-storage bag and seal the bag. Place the bag on a cutting board that's covered with a kitchen towel. Crush the cubes with a hammer or rolling pin.

Chile Chicken Enchiladas

PREP TIME: 30 MINUTES (READY IN 1 HOUR 30 MINUTES)
SERVINGS: 8

2 cups diced cooked chicken

1½ cups shredded Monterey Jack cheese (6 oz)

½ cup sliced roasted red bell peppers (from a jar)

1 can (4.5 oz) Old El Paso® chopped green chiles

1 cup sour cream

1 can (10 oz) Old El Paso® enchilada sauce

1 package (11.5 oz) Old El Paso® flour tortillas for burritos (8 tortillas)

1½ cups shredded Cheddar cheese (6 oz)

1) Heat oven to 350°F. Spray 13x9-inch (3-quart) glass baking dish with nonstick cooking spray. In medium bowl, mix chicken, Monterey Jack cheese, roasted peppers, chiles and sour cream.

2) Spread about 2 teaspoons enchilada sauce on each tortilla. Top each with ½ cup chicken mixture. Roll up tortillas; arrange, seam side down, in baking dish. Top enchiladas with any remaining enchilada sauce. Sprinkle with Cheddar cheese. Spray sheet of foil with cooking spray; cover baking dish with foil, sprayed side down.

3) Bake 45 to 60 minutes or until thoroughly heated. If desired, remove foil during last 5 minutes of baking time. If desired, serve with lettuce, tomato, avocado and additional sour cream.

HIGH ALTITUDE (3500-6500 FT.): Heat oven to 375°F.

Nutrition Information Per Serving:		
Calories: 430	From Fat: 240	
Total Fat		26g
Saturated Fat		14g
Trans Fat		0.5g
Cholesterol		90mg
Sodium		900mg
Total Carbohydrate		25g
Dietary Fiber		0g
Sugars		3g
Protein		24g

Empanada Grande

PREP TIME: 15 MINUTES (READY IN 45 MINUTES)
SERVINGS: 3

e EASY

1 Pillsbury® refrigerated pie crust (from 15-oz box), softened as directed on box

1 egg

4 oz smoked chorizo sausage links or kielbasa, casing removed, coarsely chopped (about 1 cup)

3/4 cup frozen shredded hash brown potatoes (from 30-oz bag), thawed

1/3 cup Green Giant® frozen sweet peas (from 1-lb bag)

1 small onion, chopped (1/4 cup)

1/4 teaspoon salt

Nutrition Information Per Serving:	
Calories: 560	From Fat: 320
Total Fat	35g
Saturated Fat	13g
Trans Fat	0g
Cholesterol	115mg
Sodium	1000mg
Total Carbohydrate	49g
Dietary Fiber	2g
Sugars	2g
Protein	13g

1) Heat oven to 400°F. Remove pie crust from pouch; unroll crust on ungreased large cookie sheet.

2) In large bowl, beat egg thoroughly; reserve 1 tablespoon in small bowl. Into large bowl, stir remaining ingredients.

3) Spoon chorizo mixture evenly onto half of crust to within 1/2 inch of edge. Brush edge of crust with reserved beaten egg. Fold crust over filling; press edges with fork to seal. Cut several slits in top of crust for steam to escape. Brush top with beaten egg

4) Bake 25 to 30 minutes or until golden brown. Cut into wedges.

HIGH ALTITUDE (3500 6500 FT.): Thaw frozen peas before use.

You can thaw the frozen shredded hash browns in a flash by placing them on a microwavable plate. Microwave them uncovered on Medium for 1 minute or so.

Chili Cheese Dip and Potato Wedges

PREP TIME: 25 MINUTES (READY IN 25 MINUTES)
SERVINGS: 24

EASY   **LOW FAT**

1 package (24 oz) frozen potato wedges with skins

$1/2$ lb lean (at least 80%) ground beef

1 small onion, chopped

8 oz prepared cheese product, cut into chunks

1 can (8 oz) tomato sauce

1 can (4.5 oz) Old El Paso® chopped green chiles, drained

1) Heat oven to 450°F. Bake potato wedges as directed on package.

2) Meanwhile, in large saucepan, cook ground beef and onion over medium-high heat 5 to 7 minutes, stirring occasionally, until beef is thoroughly cooked; drain. Stir in cheese, tomato sauce and chiles. Cook over low heat until cheese is melted and mixture is hot, stirring frequently.

3) Serve hot potato wedges with cheese dip.

HIGH ALTITUDE (3500-6500 FT.): No change.

Nutrition Information Per Serving:

Calories:	70	From Fat:	30
Total Fat			3g
Saturated Fat			1.5g
Trans Fat			0g
Cholesterol			15mg
Sodium			300mg
Total Carbohydrate			6g
Dietary Fiber			1g
Sugars			2g
Protein			4g

For a fun presentation, line new, clean clay pots with parchment paper. Serve the potato wedges in the lined clay pots.

Sparkling Sangria

PREP TIME: 20 MINUTES (READY IN 20 MINUTES)
SERVINGS: 20 (1/2 CUP EACH)

e EASY **f** LOW FAT

For a stunning presentation, serve this light and refreshing drink in a clear glass pitcher with lime, lemon and orange slices.

2 limes

2 oranges

1 lemon

$\frac{1}{2}$ cup sugar

$\frac{1}{2}$ cup water

2 bottles (25.4 oz each) white Catawba grape juice

2 tablespoons orange-flavored liqueur or orange juice

2 cups sparkling water, chilled

Nutrition Information Per Serving:	
Calories: 80	From Fat: 0
Total Fat	0g
Saturated Fat	0g
Trans Fat	0g
Cholesterol	0mg
Sodium	0mg
Total Carbohydrate	20g
Dietary Fiber	0g
Sugars	19g
Protein	0g

1) Cut ends off fruit. In 2-quart saucepan, mix sugar and water; add ends of fruit. Heat to boiling; boil 3 minutes. Cool; discard ends. Cut remaining limes, oranges and lemon into thin slices.

2) In 3-quart non-metal container, mix sugar-water mixture, grape juice and liqueur. Add fruit slices; refrigerate. Just before serving, add sparkling water; stir gently.

HIGH ALTITUDE (3500-6500 FT.): No change.

Seven-Layer Taco Salad

PREP TIME: 20 MINUTES (READY IN 1 HOUR 20 MINUTES)
SERVINGS: 6

e EASY

1 bag (12 oz) torn salad greens

3 medium tomatoes, seeded, chopped

8 medium green onions with green tops, sliced ($\frac{1}{2}$ cup)

1$\frac{1}{4}$ cups light mayonnaise

1 package (1.25 oz) Old El Paso® taco seasoning mix

2 packages (9 oz each) frozen cooked fajita-seasoned chicken strips, thawed, coarsely chopped

2 cups shredded sharp Cheddar cheese (8 oz)

6 oz tortilla chips (about 36), broken, if desired

1) In 13x9-inch (3-quart) glass baking dish, layer salad greens, tomatoes and onions. In 1-quart bowl, mix the mayonnaise and taco seasoning mix; spread over onions. Top with chicken and cheese. Cover tightly with plastic wrap.

2) Refrigerate at least 1 hour or until serving time. Top individual servings with tortilla chips.

HIGH ALTITUDE (3500-6500 FT.): No change.

Nutrition Information Per Serving:	
Calories: 560	From Fat: 350
Total Fat	39g
Saturated Fat	12g
Trans Fat	0.5g
Cholesterol	85mg
Sodium	1550mg
Total Carbohydrate	33g
Dietary Fiber	3g
Sugars	6g
Protein	23g

Cinnamon-Honey "Fried" Ice Cream

PREP TIME: 20 MINUTES (READY IN 55 MINUTES)
SERVINGS: 6

🄮 EASY

3 cups chocolate or vanilla ice cream

1½ cups finely crushed Cinnamon Toast Crunch® cereal

4 tablespoons honey

1) Scoop 6 (½-cup) balls of ice cream onto cookie sheet. Freeze 15 minutes.

2) Meanwhile, place cereal in shallow pan. Drizzle 2 tablespoons of the honey evenly over cereal; mix well with fork until crumbly.

3) Quickly roll 1 ball of ice cream at a time in cereal mixture to coat; return to cookie sheet. Freeze ice cream balls until firm, about 20 minutes. (If desired, cover and freeze until serving time.)

4) In small microwavable bowl, microwave remaining 2 tablespoons honey uncovered on High 20 to 30 seconds or until warm. To serve, place ice cream balls in individual dessert dishes; drizzle each with 1 teaspoon of the warm honey.

HIGH ALTITUDE (3500-6500 FT.): No change.

Nutrition Information Per Serving:		
Calories: 260	From Fat:	80
Total Fat		9g
Saturated Fat		5g
Trans Fat		0g
Cholesterol		25mg
Sodium		135mg
Total Carbohydrate		41g
Dietary Fiber		1g
Sugars		31g
Protein		3g

Double Cheese and Bean Nachos

PREP TIME: 10 MINUTES (READY IN 25 MINUTES)
SERVINGS: 8

🄮 EASY

4 cups small round corn tortilla chips

1 cup Old El Paso® refried beans (from 16-oz can)

½ cup Old El Paso® Thick 'n Chunky salsa

2 tablespoons Old El Paso® pickled jalapeño slices, drained, chopped (from 12-oz jar)

½ cup chopped green onions (8 medium)

2 cups shredded Mexican cheese blend (8 oz)

Nutrition Information Per Serving:		
Calories: 210	From Fat:	110
Total Fat		12g
Saturated Fat		6g
Trans Fat		0g
Cholesterol		30mg
Sodium		500mg
Total Carbohydrate		16g
Dietary Fiber		2g
Sugars		1g
Protein		9g

1) Heat oven to 400°F. Line 12-inch pizza pan or 15x10x1-inch pan with foil; spray with nonstick cooking spray. Spread half of the chips evenly on pan.

2) In small bowl, mix refried beans and salsa. Drop about half of mixture by small spoonfuls over chips. Top with half each of jalapeño slices, onions and cheese. Repeat layers ending with cheese.

3) Bake 10 to 12 minutes or until cheese is melted. Serve immediately.

HIGH ALTITUDE (3500-6500 FT.): No change.

tip

Layer the nachos on a microwavable plate; microwave on Medium for 2 to 4 minutes or until cheese is melted. Fresh chopped jalapeño chilies can be used if you like.

Chicken and Cheese Flautas

PREP TIME: 20 MINUTES (READY IN 20 MINUTES)
SERVINGS: 3 (2 FLAUTAS EACH)

e EASY

6 Old El Paso® flour tortillas for soft tacos & fajitas (6 inch; from 10.5-oz package)

1 cup finely shredded pepper Jack cheese (4 oz)

3/4 cup shredded cooked chicken

3/4 teaspoon ground cumin

1/3 cup Old El Paso® Thick 'n Chunky salsa

4 teaspoons vegetable oil

Guacamole, if desired

Sour cream, if desired

1) Heat tortillas as directed on package. Meanwhile, in small bowl, mix cheese, chicken and cumin.

2) Place about 1/4 cup chicken mixture on each warm tortilla. Top each with scant 1 tablespoon salsa. Roll up tightly; secure each with toothpick. Brush filled tortillas with oil.

3) In 10-inch skillet, cook filled tortillas over medium heat 4 to 6 minutes, turning occasionally, until filling is hot and tortillas are toasted. Remove toothpicks. Serve with guacamole and sour cream.

HIGH ALTITUDE (3500-6500 FT.): No change.

Nutrition Information Per Serving:	
Calories: 410	From Fat: 200
Total Fat	22g
Saturated Fat	8g
Trans Fat	0g
Cholesterol	65mg
Sodium	870mg
Total Carbohydrate	30g
Dietary Fiber	0g
Sugars	2g
Protein	21g

Nacho Chicken Casserole

PREP TIME: 15 MINUTES (READY IN 1 HOUR 5 MINUTES)
SERVINGS: 6 (1 CUP EACH)

 EASY

4 cups diced ($\frac{1}{4}$ to $\frac{1}{2}$ inch) cooked chicken

1 can (15 oz) Progresso® pinto beans, drained, rinsed

$\frac{1}{2}$ cup Old El Paso® Thick 'n Chunky salsa

1 can ($10\frac{3}{4}$ oz) condensed nacho cheese soup

$1\frac{1}{2}$ cups shredded Cheddar cheese (6 oz)

1 cup shredded lettuce

1 medium tomato, chopped ($\frac{3}{4}$ cup)

1 can ($2\frac{1}{4}$ oz) sliced ripe olives, drained, if desired

Nutrition Information Per Serving:	
Calories: 440	From Fat: 190
Total Fat	21g
Saturated Fat	10g
Trans Fat	1g
Cholesterol	120mg
Sodium	870mg
Total Carbohydrate	23g
Dietary Fiber	5g
Sugars	3g
Protein	41g

1) Heat oven to 375°F. In large bowl, mix chicken, beans, salsa and soup. Spoon evenly into ungreased 8-inch square (2-quart) glass baking dish. Sprinkle with cheese.

2) Cover dish with foil. Bake 30 to 40 minutes. Uncover dish; bake 5 to 8 minutes longer or until edges are bubbly. Top with lettuce, tomato and olives.

HIGH ALTITUDE (3500-6500 FT.): No change.

tip

Get a head start by making this savory casserole up to 24 hours ahead of time. Cover and refrigerate until you're ready to bake.

Fajitas for Two

PREP TIME: 20 MINUTES (READY IN 20 MINUTES)
SERVINGS: 2 (2 FAJITAS EACH)

 EASY

$\frac{1}{2}$ lb boneless beef sirloin steak ($\frac{1}{2}$ to $\frac{3}{4}$ inch thick)

2 teaspoons vegetable oil

4 teaspoons Old El Paso® taco seasoning mix (from 1.25-oz package)

2 cups frozen bell pepper and onion stir-fry (from 1-lb bag), thawed, well drained

4 Old El Paso® flour tortillas for soft tacos & fajitas (6 inch; from 10.5-oz package), heated

$\frac{1}{2}$ cup Old El Paso® Thick 'n Chunky salsa

1) Heat closed contact grill 5 minutes. Brush both sides of steak with 1 teaspoon of the oil; rub with 2 teaspoons of the taco seasoning mix. In medium bowl, mix oil and vegetables with remaining taco seasoning mix.

2) When grill is heated, place steak and vegetables on bottom grill surface. Close grill; cook 4 to 8 minutes or until desired beef doneness.

3) Slice steak diagonally across grain into thin slices. Wrap steak and vegetables in warm tortillas; top with salsa.

HIGH ALTITUDE (3500-6500 FT.): No change.

Nutrition Information Per Serving:	
Calories: 420	From Fat: 100
Total Fat	11g
Saturated Fat	2.5g
Trans Fat	0g
Cholesterol	60mg
Sodium	1440mg
Total Carbohydrate	54g
Dietary Fiber	3g
Sugars	7g
Protein	28g

Rich Orange Flan

PREP TIME: 30 MINUTES (READY IN 3 HOURS 15 MINUTES)
SERVINGS: 12

¾ cup sugar

3 tablespoons boiling water

6 eggs

¼ cup orange juice

2 tablespoons finely grated orange peel

1 teaspoon vanilla

1 can (14 oz) sweetened condensed milk

1 can (12 oz) evaporated milk

Spun sugar, if desired

1) Heat oven to 325°F. Spread sugar evenly over bottom of heavy skillet. Cook over medium heat, stirring constantly, until sugar melts and turns light caramel color. Add 3 tablespoons boiling water, stirring until sugar is dissolved. Pour into ungreased quiche dish or 10-inch glass deep-dish pie pan or 8-inch (2-quart) square baking dish. Tilt to evenly cover bottom; set aside.

2) In medium bowl, beat remaining ingredients with electric mixer on medium speed 1 to 2 minutes or until thoroughly blended. Pour over caramelized sugar. Place baking dish in large pan (broiler pan). Pour 1 inch hot water into broiler pan.

3) Bake 40 to 45 minutes or until mixture is almost set and knife inserted in center comes out clean. Cool 1 hour; refrigerate 1 hour. Run knife around outside edge to loosen; turn upside down onto 12-inch round serving plate with raised sides to hold liquid. Garnish with spun sugar.

HIGH ALTITUDE (3500-6500 FT.): In Step 1, cook over medium-high heat, stirring constantly, until sugar melts and turns light caramel color. (Do not add water.) Pour into dish and continue as directed.

Nutrition Information Per Serving:		
Calories. 240	From Fat: 70	
Total Fat		8g
Saturated Fat		4g
Trans Fat		0g
Cholesterol		125mg
Sodium		105mg
Total Carbohydrate		34g
Dietary Fiber		0g
Sugars		34g
Protein		8g

Zesty Mexican Soup

PREP TIME:	30 MINUTES (READY IN 30 MINUTES)
SERVINGS:	6 (1 CUP EACH)

 EASY   LOW FAT

2 cups cubed cooked chicken

1 can (14 oz) chicken broth

1 can (11.5 oz) vegetable juice cocktail

1 can (11 oz) Green Giant® Mexicorn® whole kernel corn, red and green peppers, undrained

1 cup Old El Paso® Thick 'n Chunky salsa

1 can (4.5 oz) Old El Paso® chopped green chiles

¼ cup chopped fresh cilantro

1) In large saucepan, mix all ingredients except cilantro. Heat to boiling over medium-high heat.

2) Reduce heat to low; simmer 10 minutes or until thoroughly heated, stirring occasionally. Stir in cilantro.

HIGH ALTITUDE (3500-6500 FT.): No change.

Instead of crackers, serve this spicy soup garnished with a dollop of sour cream and corn tortilla chips. Crunchy breadsticks also make an easy addition.

Nutrition Information Per Serving:

Calories:	170	From Fat:	40
Total Fat			4.5g
Saturated Fat			1g
Trans Fat			0g
Cholesterol			40mg
Sodium			1260mg
Total Carbohydrate			17g
Dietary Fiber			2g
Sugars			7g
Protein			16g

Nacho Skillet Casserole

PREP TIME:	30 MINUTES (READY IN 30 MINUTES)
SERVINGS:	6

EASY

- 1 lb lean (at least 80%) ground beef
- 1 medium onion, chopped
- 1 teaspoon sugar
- 1/2 teaspoon dried oregano leaves
- 1/2 teaspoon chili powder
- 1 can (15.5 oz) kidney beans, drained
- 1 can (15 oz) tomato sauce
- 1 can (11 oz) Green Giant® Mexicorn® whole kernel corn, red and green peppers, undrained
- 2 cups tortilla chips
- 1 cup shredded Cheddar or Monterey Jack cheese (4 oz)

1) In 12-inch skillet, cook ground beef and onion over medium-high heat 5 to 7 minutes, stirring occasionally, until beef is thoroughly cooked; drain. Stir in sugar, oregano, chili powder, kidney beans, tomato sauce and corn. Simmer 10 to 20 minutes, stirring occasionally, until sauce is desired consistency.

2) Sprinkle tortilla chips evenly over meat mixture; top with cheese. Cover; simmer 2 to 3 minutes or until cheese is melted. Serve immediately.

HIGH ALTITUDE (3500-6500 FT.): No change.

Nutrition Information Per Serving:		
Calories: 410	From Fat: 160	
Total Fat		18g
Saturated Fat		8g
Trans Fat		1g
Cholesterol		65mg
Sodium		890mg
Total Carbohydrate		37g
Dietary Fiber		7g
Sugars		8g
Protein		26g

tip

For an extra-pretty presentation, top the skillet meal with the tortilla chips and sprinkle with the cheese. Then, top with some chopped tomatoes.

Mini Picadillo Empanadas

LESLIE PRESS | ROCKVILLE, MARYLAND

BAKE-OFF® CONTEST 39, 2000

PREP TIME: 25 MINUTES (READY IN 50 MINUTES)
SERVINGS: 16 APPETIZERS

½ lb lean ground beef or turkey

1 cup Old El Paso® Thick 'n Chunky salsa

2 tablespoons raisins

½ teaspoon ground cumin

⅛ teaspoon ground cinnamon

20 pimiento-stuffed green olives, sliced (about ⅓ cup)

1 can (16.3 oz) Pillsbury® Grands!® refrigerated buttermilk biscuits

Fresh cilantro, if desired

Additional Old El Paso® Thick 'n Chunky salsa, if desired

1) Heat oven to 350°F. In 10-inch skillet, cook beef over medium-high heat 8 to 10 minutes, stirring frequently, until thoroughly cooked; drain.

2) Add remaining ingredients except biscuits, cilantro and additional salsa. Heat to boiling. Reduce heat to medium; cook 3 to 4 minutes, stirring occasionally, until most of liquid has evaporated. Remove from heat.

3) Separate dough into 8 biscuits. With serrated knife, cut each biscuit in half horizontally to make 16 rounds. Press or roll each to make 4-inch round. Spoon 2 level measuring tablespoons beef mixture in center of each round. Fold dough over filling; press edges with fork to seal. Place on ungreased cookie sheets.

4) Bake 15 to 20 minutes or until golden brown. Cool 5 minutes before serving. Garnish with cilantro. Serve with additional salsa.

HIGH ALTITUDE (3500-6500 FT.): No change.

Nutrition Information Per Serving:

Calories:	130	From Fat:	60
Total Fat			6g
Saturated Fat			2g
Trans Fat			1.5g
Cholesterol			10mg
Sodium			500mg
Total Carbohydrate			15g
Dietary Fiber			0g
Sugars			3g
Protein			5g

Easy Salsa Chicken Burritos

PREP TIME: 20 MINUTES (READY IN 20 MINUTES)
SERVINGS: 8

ⓔ EASY   🕕 LOW FAT

1½ lb chicken breast strips for stir-fry

1 package (1.25 oz) Old El Paso® taco seasoning mix

1 jar (16 oz) Old El Paso® Thick 'n Chunky salsa

1 package (11.5 oz) Old El Paso® flour tortillas for burritos (8 tortillas)

Shredded lettuce, shredded cheese and bell pepper strips, if desired

1) In 10-inch nonstick skillet, cook chicken over medium heat, stirring occasionally, until no longer pink in center.

2) Stir in taco seasoning mix and salsa. Cook until hot.

3) Spoon chicken mixture onto tortillas. Top with lettuce, cheese and bell pepper strips. Roll up tortillas.

HIGH ALTITUDE (3500-6500 FT.): No change.

Nutrition Information Per Serving:	
Calories: 260	From Fat: 60
Total Fat	7g
Saturated Fat	2g
Trans Fat	0g
Cholesterol	50mg
Sodium	1010mg
Total Carbohydrate	27g
Dietary Fiber	0g
Sugars	1g
Protein	22g

Southwestern Chicken Tostada Salad

PREP TIME: 10 MINUTES (READY IN 10 MINUTES)
SERVINGS: 4

ⓔ EASY

1 package (9 oz) frozen cooked fajita-seasoned chicken strips

4 Old El Paso® tostada shells (from 4.5-oz box)

4 cups shredded lettuce

¼ cup quartered pitted ripe olives

1 medium tomato, cut into thin wedges

½ cup ranch dressing

2 tablespoons Old El Paso® taco sauce

½ cup shredded Mexican cheese blend (2 oz)

1) Heat chicken and tostada shells as directed on packages.

2) Meanwhile, in large bowl, gently toss lettuce, olives and tomato. In medium bowl, mix ranch dressing and taco sauce. Pour dressing mixture over salad; toss gently to coat.

3) Place warm tostada shells on individual serving plates. Spoon salad evenly onto shells; top each with warm chicken and sprinkle with cheese.

HIGH ALTITUDE (3500-6500 FT.): No change.

Nutrition Information Per Serving:	
Calories: 360	From Fat: 240
Total Fat	27g
Saturated Fat	7g
Trans Fat	1g
Cholesterol	70mg
Sodium	820mg
Total Carbohydrate	13g
Dietary Fiber	2g
Sugars	3g
Protein	19g

Chicken Enchilada Quiche

JESSICA BARTON | EUGENE, OREGON

Bake-Off
BAKE-OFF® CONTEST 41, 2004

PREP TIME: 15 MINUTES (READY IN 1 HOUR 30 MINUTES)
SERVINGS: 8

e EASY

1 Pillsbury® refrigerated pie crust (from 15-oz box), softened as directed on box

4 eggs

1 cup half-and-half or milk

1 can (12.5 oz) chunk chicken breast in water, drained (1¹⁄₂ cups)

1¹⁄₂ cups broken tortilla chips

2 cups shredded Monterey Jack cheese (8 oz)

1 cup shredded Cheddar cheese (4 oz)

1 cup Old El Paso® Thick 'n Chunky salsa

1 can (4.5 oz) Old El Paso® chopped green chiles

¹⁄₂ teaspoon salt

Pepper to taste, if desired

Sour cream, if desired

Old El Paso® Thick 'n Chunky salsa, if desired

1) Heat oven to 350°F. In 9- or 9¹⁄₂-inch glass deep-dish pie plate, place the pie crust as directed on box for a One-Crust Filled Pie.

2) In medium bowl with wire whisk, beat eggs until blended; beat in half-and-half. Stir in chicken, chips, both cheeses, 1 cup salsa, the green chiles and salt. Pour into pie crust-lined plate. Sprinkle pepper over top of filling.

3) Bake 55 to 65 minutes or until crust is light golden brown and knife inserted in center comes out clean. Let stand 10 minutes before serving. Cut into wedges; serve with sour cream and/or salsa.

HIGH ALTITUDE (3500-6500 FT.): Heat oven to 375°F. Bake 55 to 65 minutes. After 15 minutes of baking, cover edges of crust with strips of foil to prevent excessive browning.

Nutrition Information Per Serving:		
Calories: 480	From Fat: 280	
Total Fat		31g
Saturated Fat		14g
Trans Fat		0.5g
Cholesterol		180mg
Sodium		1260mg
Total Carbohydrate		28g
Dietary Fiber		1g
Sugars		5g
Protein		22g

Speedy Layered Chicken Enchilada Pie

KAREN HALL | MINNEAPOLIS, MINNESOTA

Bake-Off BAKE-OFF® CONTEST 40, 2002

PREP TIME: 25 MINUTES (READY IN 1 HOUR 10 MINUTES)
SERVINGS: 6

e EASY

1 package (11.5 oz) Old El Paso® flour tortillas for burritos (8 tortillas)

2 cups cubed cooked chicken

½ cup uncooked instant rice

2 cups shredded reduced-fat Monterey Jack cheese (8 oz)

1 can (15 oz) black beans, rinsed and drained

1 can (19 oz) Old El Paso® hot enchilada sauce

1 cup Green Giant® frozen shoepeg white corn, thawed

1 cup Old El Paso® Thick 'n Chunky salsa

2 tablespoons thinly sliced green onions (2 medium)

Reduced-fat sour cream, if desired

Chopped green onions, if desired

1) Heat oven to 350°F. Spray 9-inch round (2-quart) glass baking dish or casserole with nonstick cooking spray. Cut 5 of the tortillas in half. Cut remaining tortillas into 2½-inch wide strips.

2) In large bowl, mix chicken, rice, 1 cup of the cheese, the beans and 1 cup of the enchilada sauce.

3) Layer 4 tortilla halves in bottom of baking dish. Top with ¼ cup enchilada sauce and half of the chicken mixture. Top with 2 tortilla halves; fill in empty spaces with 3 tortilla strips. Spoon corn over tortillas. Spread salsa over corn. Layer with 2 tortilla halves and 3 strips. Top with remaining half of chicken mixture. Continue layering with remaining 2 tortilla halves and strips, enchilada sauce, cheese and 2 tablespoons green onions.

4) Bake uncovered 35 to 45 minutes or until mixture is thoroughly heated and cheese is melted. Cool 5 minutes. Top with the sour cream and chopped green onions.

HIGH ALTITUDE (3500-6500 FT.): Heat oven to 375°F. In Step 3, do not add remaining cheese to top of casserole. Bake uncovered 40 to 50 minutes, adding cheese during the last 5 minutes.

Nutrition Information Per Serving:		
Calories: 570	From Fat:	170
Total Fat		19g
Saturated Fat		8g
Trans Fat		0g
Cholesterol		65mg
Sodium		1490mg
Total Carbohydrate		66g
Dietary Fiber		5g
Sugars		6g
Protein		33g

Party Tacos

PREP TIME: 45 MINUTES (READY IN 45 MINUTES)
SERVINGS: 30 (WITHOUT TOPPINGS)

EASY   **LOW FAT**

3 lb lean (at least 80%) ground beef

2 large onions, chopped

2 packages (1.25 oz each) Old El Paso® taco seasoning mix

1½ cups Old El Paso® Thick 'n Chunky salsa

1 cup water

3 boxes (4.7 oz each) Old El Paso® Stand 'N Stuff™ taco shells

1) Cook ground beef in 2 batches. For first batch, spray 12-inch skillet with nonstick cooking spray. Add half of the ground beef and 1 chopped onion. Cook over medium heat 8 to 10 minutes or until beef is thoroughly cooked, stirring frequently. Drain.

2) Stir in 1 package taco seasoning mix, ¾ cup salsa and ½ cup water. Reduce heat to low; simmer 8 to 10 minutes or until most of liquid is absorbed.

3) Cool first batch of beef mixture 15 minutes. Spoon into refrigerator or freezer container; cover tightly. Repeat to make second batch. Serve immediately, or refrigerate up to 24 hours or freeze up to 1 week.

4) To serve immediately, place beef mixture in slow cooker; keep warm on Low setting. If beef mixture is frozen, thaw before heating. Place beef mixture in slow cooker; cover and cook on High setting for 1 hour or until hot. Reduce heat to Low to keep warm. To serve, spoon beef mixture into taco shells. Top with Layered Taco Toppings (at right).

HIGH ALTITUDE (3500-6500 FT.): No change.

Nutrition Information Per Serving:	
Calories: 160	From Fat: 70
Total Fat	8g
Saturated Fat	2.5g
Trans Fat	1.5g
Cholesterol	30mg
Sodium	390mg
Total Carbohydrate	12g
Dietary Fiber	1g
Sugars	0g
Protein	9g

Layered Taco Toppings

PREP TIME: 10 MINUTES (READY IN 2 HOURS 10 MINUTES)
SERVINGS: 30

3 cans (11 oz each) Green Giant® Niblets® whole kernel sweet corn, drained

1 bag (10 oz) shredded lettuce (about 5 1/2 cups)

2 cups chopped red, yellow and/or green bell peppers

1/2 cup sliced green onions

2 cups chopped Italian plum tomatoes

1 medium avocado, pitted, peeled and chopped

1 cup mayonnaise

1/2 cup Old El Paso® Thick 'n Chunky salsa

2 cups finely shredded Mexican cheese blend (8 oz)

1/4 cup chopped fresh cilantro

1) Heat oven to 425°F. Spray 15x10x1-inch pan with cooking spray. Dry corn on paper towels; spread corn in pan. Bake 15 minutes. Stir; bake 10 minutes longer. Cool slightly, about 5 minutes.

2) In ungreased 13x9-inch (3-quart) glass baking dish, layer lettuce, bell peppers, roasted corn, onions, tomatoes and avocado.

3) In small bowl, mix mayonnaise and salsa. Spread over vegetables. Sprinkle with cheese and cilantro. Cover tightly; refrigerate at least 2 hours or overnight. Use toppings for Party Tacos (at left).

HIGH ALTITUDE (3500-6500 FT.): No change.

Nutrition Information Per Serving:

Calories:	130	From Fat:	80
Total Fat			9g
Saturated Fat			2.5g
Trans Fat			0g
Cholesterol			10mg
Sodium			180mg
Total Carbohydrate			8g
Dietary Fiber			1g
Sugars			2g
Protein			3g

Buffalo Chicken Enchiladas with Creamy Ranch Sauce

PREP TIME: 25 MINUTES (READY IN 1 HOUR 15 MINUTES)
SERVINGS: 6 (2 ENCHILADAS EACH)

1 can (10¾ oz) condensed cream of chicken soup

1 cup refrigerated sour cream ranch dip

²/₃ cup chopped green onions (about 10 medium)

3 cups chopped cooked chicken

¾ cup buffalo wing sauce

1 package (10.5 oz) Old El Paso® flour tortillas for soft tacos & fajitas (twelve 6-inch tortillas)

3 cups shredded Cheddar cheese (12 oz)

1) Heat oven to 350°F. Spray 13x9-inch (3-quart) glass baking dish with nonstick cooking spray. In medium bowl, mix soup, dip and ⅓ cup of the onions. In large bowl, mix chicken and buffalo wing sauce until coated.

2) Spoon 2 tablespoons soup mixture down center of each tortilla; set remaining mixture aside. Reserve ½ cup cheese for garnish. Top each tortilla with about ¼ cup chicken mixture and scant ¼ cup cheese. Fold sides of tortillas over filling; place seam side down in baking dish. Spoon remaining soup mixture over filled tortillas.

3) Cover dish tightly with foil. Bake 40 to 45 minutes or until hot and bubbly.

4) Remove from oven. Sprinkle with reserved ½ cup cheese and remaining ⅓ cup onions. Bake uncovered about 5 minutes longer or until cheese is melted.

HIGH ALTITUDE (3500-6500 FT.): In Step 3, bake 45 to 50 minutes.

Nutrition Information Per Serving:	
Calories: 660	From Fat: 360
Total Fat	40g
Saturated Fat	19g
Trans Fat	1g
Cholesterol	135mg
Sodium	2540mg
Total Carbohydrate	35g
Dietary Fiber	0g
Sugars	3g
Protein	40g

Mexican Bean Pizzas

PREP TIME: 15 MINUTES (READY IN 40 MINUTES)
SERVINGS: 4

e EASY

These quick and wholesome meat-free pizzas make a great after-school snack. Best of all, you can bake only as many as you need.

4 Old El Paso® flour tortillas for burritos (8 inch; from 11.5-oz package)

Nonstick cooking spray

1 cup Old El Paso® refried beans (from 16-oz can)

8 medium green onions, sliced (½ cup)

1 medium tomato, seeded, diced

1 cup shredded hot pepper Monterey Jack cheese (4 oz)

Nutrition Information Per Serving:	
Calories: 290	From Fat: 90
Total Fat	10g
Saturated Fat	5g
Trans Fat	0.5g
Cholesterol	25mg
Sodium	700mg
Total Carbohydrate	35g
Dietary Fiber	5g
Sugars	3g
Protein	13g

1) Place oven rack in lowest rack position; heat oven to 400°F. Spray 1 side of each tortilla with nonstick cooking spray. On each of 2 large ungreased cookie sheets, place 2 tortillas sprayed sides down. Spread ¼ cup refried beans on each. Top each with onions, tomato and cheese.

2) Bake 1 cookie sheet at a time on lowest oven rack 10 to 12 minutes or until bottoms are golden brown and cheese is melted and bubbly. Cut into wedges to serve.

HIGH ALTITUDE (3500-6500 FT.): No change.

Quick Salsa Chicken

PREP TIME: 5 MINUTES (READY IN 45 MINUTES)
SERVINGS: 2

e EASY

2 large boneless skinless chicken breasts (about ½ lb)

2 teaspoons Old El Paso® taco seasoning mix (from 1.25-oz package)

½ cup Old El Paso® Thick 'n Chunky salsa

½ cup shredded Cheddar cheese (2 oz)

1 tablespoon sour cream, if desired

Nutrition Information Per Serving:	
Calories: 280	From Fat: 120
Total Fat	13g
Saturated Fat	7g
Trans Fat	0g
Cholesterol	100mg
Sodium	980mg
Total Carbohydrate	8g
Dietary Fiber	0g
Sugars	2g
Protein	32g

1) Heat oven to 375°F. Sprinkle both sides of chicken breasts with taco seasoning mix; place in ungreased 8-inch square (2-quart) glass baking dish. Pour salsa over chicken.

2) Bake 25 to 35 minutes or until chicken is fork-tender and juices run clear. Sprinkle cheese evenly over chicken; bake 3 to 5 minutes longer or until cheese is melted. Serve with sour cream.

HIGH ALTITUDE (3500-6500 FT.): No change.

MEXICAN GRILLED
CHEESE SANDWICHES
PG. 257

Kid-Friendly Fare

Earn raves from your little diners with
these smile-fetching favorites.

SPOOKY SHEPHERD'S PIE
PG. 254

BITE SIZE BOO BUGS WITH
BUG-CATCHING DIP
PG. 258

KID-PLEASING POTATO NUGGET
CASSEROLE
PG. 269

Granola Fruit Kabobs

PREP TIME: 10 MINUTES (READY IN 10 MINUTES)
SERVINGS: 8

e EASY

2 cups granola

2 medium apples, unpeeled, cut into chunks

2 small bananas, peeled, cut into chunks

1 cup fresh pineapple chunks

1 cup Yoplait® Original fruit-flavored yogurt

1) Place granola in shallow bowl. Insert toothpick into each piece of fruit.

2) To serve, dip fruit into yogurt, coating all sides. Roll in granola, coating completely.

HIGH ALTITUDE (3500-6500 FT.): No change.

Nutrition Information Per Serving:		
Calories: 200	From Fat:	45
Total Fat		5g
Saturated Fat		2g
Trans Fat		0g
Cholesterol		0mg
Sodium		30mg
Total Carbohydrate		35g
Dietary Fiber		4g
Sugars		20g
Protein		4g

tip

To prevent cut fruits such as bananas and apples from turning brown, toss the pieces with a small amount of lemon or orange juice.

Garden Garbage Dip

PREP TIME: 15 MINUTES (READY IN 15 MINUTES)
SERVINGS: 20 (2 TABLESPOONS DIP AND 1/2 CUP VEGETABLES EACH)

e EASY

- 1 package (8 oz) cream cheese, softened
- 1 cup sour cream
- ¼ cup finely chopped radishes (about 2 medium)
- ¼ cup finely chopped green onions (4 medium)
- ¼ cup finely chopped cucumber, drained
- ¼ cup finely chopped green bell pepper
- 1 tablespoon sugar
- ½ teaspoon salt
- ¼ teaspoon dried dill weed
- Dash pepper
- 1 medium radish
- 5 ready-to-eat baby-cut carrots
- 1 plastic bat or spider finger ring
- 10 cups assorted cut-up fresh vegetables

1) In large bowl, beat cream cheese, sour cream, chopped radishes, onions, cucumber, bell pepper, sugar, salt, dill weed and pepper with electric mixer on low speed about 1 minute or until well blended. Spoon into 1-quart serving bowl.

2) For garnish, cut 5 small, thin oval slices from radish to resemble red fingernails. Use small amount of dip to attach "fingernails" to small ends of carrots. Arrange carrots in dip to resemble hand emerging from dip. Slip plastic ring onto "ring finger." Serve dip with cut-up vegetables. Store dip in refrigerator.

HIGH ALTITUDE (3500-6500 FT.): No change.

Nutrition Information Per Serving:

Calories: 80	From Fat: 60
Total Fat	6g
Saturated Fat	4g
Trans Fat	0g
Cholesterol	20mg
Sodium	105mg
Total Carbohydrate	4g
Dietary Fiber	0g
Sugars	3g
Protein	2g

Sea Monster Sandwich

PREP TIME: 10 MINUTES (READY IN 55 MINUTES)
SERVINGS: 6

e) EASY   (f) LOW FAT

1 can (11 oz) Pillsbury® refrigerated crusty French loaf

2 tablespoons mayonnaise or salad dressing

1 to 2 leaves leaf lettuce

4 oz thinly sliced cooked ham

3 slices (¾ oz each) mozzarella cheese, each cut in half

2 small pimiento-stuffed olives

Roasted red bell pepper (from 7.25-oz jar)

1) Heat oven to 350°F. Grease large cookie sheet. Place dough seam side down on cookie sheet; form into "S" shape. With kitchen scissors, cut 1-inch deep, v-shaped notches to cover entire top and side surfaces of dough to resemble scales on reptile. Cut 1-inch deep horizontal cut on 1 end of dough to resemble mouth. Crumble small piece of foil to form 1-inch ball. Grease foil and place in mouth opening to hold open during baking.

2) Bake 26 to 30 minutes or until golden brown. Cool at least 15 minutes.

3) Cut bread in half horizontally. Spread cut sides with mayonnaise. Layer lettuce, ham and cheese between halves. Add olives for eyes; secure with toothpicks. Cut 1 roasted pepper piece to resemble flames. Insert into mouth of sea monster. To serve, cut crosswise into 6 pieces.

HIGH ALTITUDE (3500-6500 FT.): No change.

Nutrition Information Per Serving:		
Calories: 220	From Fat:	80
Total Fat		9g
Saturated Fat		2.5g
Trans Fat		0g
Cholesterol		20mg
Sodium		640mg
Total Carbohydrate		24g
Dietary Fiber		0g
Sugars		3g
Protein		11g

Piglets in Blankets

PREP TIME: 15 MINUTES (READY IN 30 MINUTES)
SERVINGS: 8

ⓔ EASY

1 can (8 oz) Pillsbury® refrigerated crescent dinner rolls

24 fully cooked cocktail wieners

Ketchup or sweet-and-sour sauce

Nutrition Information Per Serving:

Calories:	200	From Fat:	130
Total Fat			15g
Saturated Fat			5g
Trans Fat			1.5g
Cholesterol			15mg
Sodium			570mg
Total Carbohydrate			12g
Dietary Fiber			0g
Sugars			3g
Protein			5g

1) Heat oven to 375°F. Grease cookie sheet. Unroll dough; separate into 8 triangles. Cut each triangle into 3 smaller triangles.

2) Place 1 wiener on shortest side of each triangle; roll up to opposite point. Place point side down on cookie sheet.

3) Bake 11 to 15 minutes or until deep golden brown. Immediately remove from cookie sheet. Serve with ketchup.

HIGH ALTITUDE (3500-6500 FT.): No change.

tip You can roll the wieners in crescent dough up to 2 hours in advance. Cover them tightly and refrigerate until it's time to bake them.

Red-Nosed Reindeer Cookies

PREP TIME: 15 MINUTES (READY IN 15 MINUTES)
SERVINGS: 12

ⓔ EASY

12 white fudge coated creme-filled chocolate sandwich cookies

24 miniature pretzel twists

1 can (6.4 oz) white decorating icing

1 tube (.68 oz) black decorating gel

12 small round chewy red candies (from 9.2-oz box)

Nutrition Information Per Serving:

Calories:	160	From Fat:	60
Total Fat			7g
Saturated Fat			5g
Trans Fat			0g
Cholesterol			0mg
Sodium			120mg
Total Carbohydrate			25g
Dietary Fiber			0g
Sugars			19g
Protein			1g

1) Place cookies on tray or flat surface. Break pretzel twists in half to form antlers. Place small amount of white decorating icing on bottom edge of each pretzel; attach 2 pieces at top of each cookie to form reindeer antlers.

2) Using black decorating gel, make 2 small dots to form eyes on each cookie.

3) Cut off top ⅓ of each red candy; attach with small amount of icing to form nose on each cookie.

HIGH ALTITUDE (3500-6500 FT.): No change.

Waffled Pizza Dippers

PATTY KNIGHTON | SAN DIEGO, CALIFORNIA

Pillsbury **Bake-Off®**

BAKE-OFF® CONTEST 41, 2004

PREP TIME: 20 MINUTES (READY IN 20 MINUTES)
SERVINGS: 8 (1 SANDWICH OR 2 SNACKS & 2 TABLESPOONS SAUCE EACH)

e EASY

7 oz (1¾ cups) shredded mozzarella cheese

¼ cup shredded Parmesan cheese (1 oz)

½ teaspoon dried basil leaves

½ teaspoon dried oregano leaves

2 cans (8 oz each) Pillsbury® refrigerated crescent dinner rolls

1 jar (14 oz) pizza sauce

32 small slices pepperoni (about 2½ oz)

1) Heat waffle maker with 8-inch square cooking surface on Medium-High heat setting. In medium bowl, mix both cheeses, basil and oregano; set aside. In 1½-quart saucepan, heat pizza sauce over low heat, stirring occasionally, until hot. Place in small serving bowl.

2) Unroll both cans of dough onto work surface. Separate each crosswise, making 4 (7x6-inch) rectangles; firmly press perforations to seal.

3) Place 1 dough rectangle on bottom surface of heated waffle maker, being careful not to open up perforations. Quickly sprinkle 1 cup cheese mixture evenly on top of dough. Place 16 slices of pepperoni evenly over cheese mixture. Top with another dough rectangle; close waffle maker.

4) Bake 2 to 3 minutes or until sandwich is golden brown. With pancake turner, remove from waffle maker; place on cutting board. Cool 30 seconds before cutting. Cut into 4 square sandwiches or 8 triangular snacks. Repeat with remaining dough, cheese mixture and pepperoni. Serve warm with pizza sauce for dipping.

HIGH ALTITUDE (3500-6500 FT.): No change.

Nutrition Information Per Serving:		
Calories: 350	From Fat:	170
Total Fat		19g
Saturated Fat		7g
Cholesterol		25mg
Sodium		1260mg
Total Carbohydrate		32g
Dietary Fiber		2g
Sugars		10g
Protein		14g

Santa Cookies

PREP TIME: 1 HOUR 45 MINUTES (READY IN 1 HOUR 45 MINUTES)
SERVINGS: 2-1/2 DOZEN COOKIES

½ cup sugar

½ cup butter or margarine, softened

½ teaspoon vanilla

1 egg

1½ cups all-purpose flour

¼ teaspoon baking soda

¼ teaspoon salt

¼ cup semisweet chocolate chips

1 tablespoon red cinnamon candies

½ cup fluffy white whipped ready-to-spread frosting (from 12-oz container)

¼ cup flaked coconut or edible glitter

1 roll (0.75 oz) chewy fruit snack in 3-foot rolls (any red flavor)

1) Heat oven to 350°F. In large bowl, beat sugar and butter with electric mixer on medium speed until blended. Beat in vanilla and egg. On low speed, beat in flour, baking soda and salt.

2) Shape dough into 1-inch balls. For each cookie, flatten ball into about 1½-inch round with fingers; place 2 inches apart on ungreased cookie sheets. Lightly press 2 chocolate chips into upper third of each dough round for eyes.

3) Bake 9 to 11 minutes or until edges are light golden brown. Immediately press 1 cinnamon candy onto each cookie for nose. Remove from cookie sheets to cooling racks. Cool 15 minutes.

4) Place frosting in small resealable food-storage plastic bag. Seal bag; cut off small corner of bag. Squeeze bag to pipe frosting along bottom edge of cookie and above cinnamon candy for beard. Lightly sprinkle coconut over frosting; gently press into frosting.

5) Cut fruit snack into 2-inch-long pieces. Cut each piece diagonally in half to make 2 triangles. With small amount of frosting, attach fruit snack triangle on each cookie for hat. Fold top corner of each triangle over; pipe frosting "tassle" on pointed end of each "hat."

HIGH ALTITUDE (3500-6500 FT.): No change.

Nutrition Information Per Serving:		
Calories: 90	From Fat:	40
Total Fat		4.5g
Saturated Fat		2.5g
Trans Fat		0g
Cholesterol		15mg
Sodium		60mg
Total Carbohydrate		12g
Dietary Fiber		0g
Sugars		7g
Protein		0g

Melting Witch Pudding Cups

PREP TIME: 25 MINUTES (READY IN 25 MINUTES)
SERVINGS: 8

ⓔ EASY

Nutrition Information Per Serving:

Calories:	320	From Fat:	70
Total Fat			8g
Saturated Fat			4g
Trans Fat			1g
Cholesterol			10mg
Sodium			510mg
Total Carbohydrate			55g
Dietary Fiber			2g
Sugars			38g
Protein			6g

1/3 cup semisweet chocolate chips

1 teaspoon shortening

8 Bugles® original snacks

1 box (4-serving size) white chocolate instant pudding and pie filling mix

4 cups cold milk

1 box (4-serving size) chocolate fudge instant pudding and pie filling mix

6 drops green food color

8 creme-filled chocolate sandwich cookies or chocolate-covered mint patties

8 pretzel sticks

1 tablespoon Fiber One® cereal or chow mein noodles, pieces broken in half

16 gummi worm candies

1) Line cookie sheet with waxed paper. In small microwavable bowl, microwave chocolate chips and shortening on High 1½ to 2 minutes or until melted; stir until smooth. To make tops of witch hats, dip snacks, one at a time, into melted coating, letting excess drip off. Place point up on cookie sheet. Let stand until coating is set.

2) Prepare white chocolate pudding with 2 cups of the milk as directed on box. Prepare chocolate fudge pudding with remaining 2 cups milk as directed on box. Stir green food color into white chocolate pudding until well blended.

3) For each pudding cup, spoon 2 tablespoons of the green pudding into bottom of 4-ounce clear plastic cup or serving dish; top with 2 tablespoons of the chocolate fudge pudding. Repeat with each flavor to form four layers. With handle of spoon, gently swirl the two top layers. Insert cookie in pudding; top with chocolate-coated Bugle® to resemble witch hat. Insert tip of pretzel stick into pudding with a few pieces of cereal sprinkled at the base to resemble a broom. Insert ends of 2 gummi worm candies into pudding and hang over edge to resemble the witch's legs.

HIGH ALTITUDE (3500-6500 FT.): No change.

tip

For a fast fix, substitute purchased swirled pudding snacks for the white chocolate and chocolate fudge pudding combination. Assemble the witches directly on top of the pudding cups.

Monster Burgers

PREP TIME: 35 MINUTES (READY IN 35 MINUTES)
SERVINGS: 8

EASY

8 ground beef patties (4 oz each)

8 burger buns, split

8 slices (¾ oz each) American cheese

8 thin slices cooked ham

16 slices dill pickle

Ketchup

Nutrition Information Per Serving:

Calories: 420	From Fat: 200
Total Fat	22g
Saturated Fat	10g
Trans Fat	1.5g
Cholesterol	100mg
Sodium	940mg
Total Carbohydrate	23g
Dietary Fiber	1g
Sugars	4g
Protein	32g

1) Place ground beef patties on broiler pan. Broil 3 to 4 inches from heat for 10 to 12 minutes or until they are thoroughly cooked, turning once.

2) Place bottom halves of buns on serving platter. For each monster burger, place 1 cooked patty on bottom half of bun. Cut cheese slice in half in zigzag pattern to resemble teeth. Place half of cheese slice on burger, with "teeth" hanging off 1 side of patty.

3) Loosely fold ham into tongue shape; place on top of "teeth." Place remaining cheese "teeth" on top of "tongue." Top with top half of bun. Place 2 pickle slices on top for eyes. Dot "eyes" with ketchup for pupils.

HIGH ALTITUDE (3500-6500 FT.): No change.

Chicken Dippers with Sauces

PREP TIME: 15 MINUTES (READY IN 35 MINUTES)
SERVINGS: 8

EASY

2 packages (11 to 12 oz each) breaded chicken nuggets

SWEET AND SOUR SAUCE

¼ cup packed brown sugar

1 tablespoon cornstarch

⅔ cup apple or pineapple juice

¼ cup cider vinegar

2 tablespoons orange juice

TANGY CHILI SAUCE

1 can (8 oz) jellied cranberry sauce

⅔ cup chili sauce

Nutrition Information Per Serving:

Calories: 370	From Fat: 150
Total Fat	16g
Saturated Fat	4g
Trans Fat	2g
Cholesterol	45mg
Sodium	900mg
Total Carbohydrate	38g
Dietary Fiber	2g
Sugars	22g
Protein	17g

1) Bake chicken nuggets as directed on package.

2) Meanwhile, in small saucepan, mix all ingredients for sweet and sour sauce. Cook over medium heat until mixture boils and thickens, stirring constantly.

3) In another small saucepan mix all ingredients for tangy chili sauce. Cook over low heat, stirring mixture until well blended and thoroughly heated. Serve chicken nuggets with warm sauces.

Goblin Good Gorp

PREP TIME: 5 MINUTES (READY IN 5 MINUTES)
SERVINGS: 10

e EASY

2 cups peanuts

1 cup miniature creme-filled chocolate sandwich cookies

1 cup candy corn

$^1/_2$ cup cheese-flavored tiny fish-shaped crackers

$^1/_2$ cup raisins

1) In 1½- to 2-quart container with cover, mix all ingredients. Store tightly covered.

HIGH ALTITUDE (3500-6500 FT.): No change.

Nutrition Information Per Serving:

Calories: 330	From Fat: 150
Total Fat	17g
Saturated Fat	2.5g
Trans Fat	0.5g
Cholesterol	0mg
Sodium	75mg
Total Carbohydrate	36g
Dietary Fiber	3g
Sugars	25g
Protein	9g

Chili Dog Tacos

PREP TIME: 20 MINUTES (READY IN 20 MINUTES)
SERVINGS: 10

e EASY

$^1/_2$ lb lean (at least 80%) ground beef

$^1/_2$ cup Old El Paso® Thick 'n Chunky salsa

1 can (16 oz) pinto beans, drained

10 Old El Paso® taco shells (from 4.6-oz box)

10 hot dogs

$^1/_4$ cup shredded Cheddar cheese (5 oz)

$^1/_4$ cup finely chopped onion

1) Heat oven to 375°F. In 8-inch nonstick skillet, cook ground beef over medium-high heat 5 to 7 minutes. Stir occasionally, until thoroughly cooked; drain. Stir in salsa and beans. Cook until thoroughly heated.

2) Meanwhile, heat taco shells as directed on box.

3) In 10-inch nonstick skillet, cook hot dogs over medium-high heat 2 to 3 minutes, turning frequently, until browned.

4) Place hot dogs in taco shells; top each with ground beef mixture, cheese and onion.

HIGH ALTITUDE (3500-6500 FT.): No change.

Some kids don't like pinto beans. To keep everyone happy, heat the beans separately and let diners add them to their tacos if they wish.

Nutrition Information Per Serving:

Calories: 300	From Fat: 180
Total Fat	20g
Saturated Fat	7g
Trans Fat	1.5g
Cholesterol	40mg
Sodium	770mg
Total Carbohydrate	21g
Dietary Fiber	4g
Sugars	2g
Protein	14g

Carousel Cupcakes

PREP TIME: 30 MINUTES (READY IN 30 MINUTES)
SERVINGS: 6

e EASY

- 6 pretzel sticks
- 1 tablespoons semisweet chocolate chips, melted
- 6 animal crackers
- 1 container (1 lb) strawberry whipped ready-to-spread frosting
- 6 unfrosted cupcakes, paper baking cups removed

  Candy sprinkles
- 6 small paper beverage umbrellas

1) Dip 1 inch of one end of each pretzel into melted chocolate chips; press on back of 1 animal cracker. Place on sheet of waxed paper; let stand until chocolate is set.

2) Meanwhile, spread frosting on sides and bottom of cupcakes. Sprinkle with candy sprinkles. Insert 1 animal cracker on pretzel into each cupcake. Place umbrellas in center of cupcake.

HIGH ALTITUDE (3500-6500 FT.): No change.

Nutrition Information Per Serving:	
Calories: 480	From Fat: 160
Total Fat	17g
Saturated Fat	12g
Trans Fat	0.5g
Cholesterol	20mg
Sodium	170mg
Total Carbohydrate	80g
Dietary Fiber	0g
Sugars	69g
Protein	2g

tip

The melted chocolate chips act as the "glue" to hold the pretzel to the animal cracker. You can refrigerate the pretzels and crackers to "set" the chocolate even quicker.

Chilling Jack-o'-Lantern Smoothies

PREP TIME: 15 MINUTES (READY IN 15 MINUTES)
SERVINGS: 4

🅔 EASY   🅕 LOW FAT

1 tablespoon semisweet chocolate chips

4 plastic cups (8 to 9 oz each)

3 containers (6 oz each) Yoplait® Original 99% Fat Free orange crème or harvest peach yogurt

¼ cup frozen (thawed) orange juice concentrate

1 can (11 oz) mandarin orange segments, chilled, drained

1 banana, sliced

Nutrition Information Per Serving:

Calories:	230	From Fat:	20
Total Fat			2g
Saturated Fat			1.5g
Trans Fat			0g
Cholesterol			10mg
Sodium			65mg
Total Carbohydrate			47g
Dietary Fiber			2g
Sugars			38g
Protein			5g

1) In small microwavable bowl, melt chocolate chips on High for 1 minute or until melted. With tip of knife, spread chocolate on inside of each plastic cup to resemble eyes, nose and mouth of jack-o'-lantern. Repeat with 3 more cups. Refrigerate 5 minutes or until chocolate is set.

2) Meanwhile, in blender container, place all remaining ingredients; cover and blend until smooth. Pour into chocolate painted cups.

HIGH ALTITUDE (3500-6500 FT.): No change.

Serve with a green straw to resemble a pumpkin stem or garnish with a mint leaf.

Goofy Face Topped Soup

PREP TIME: 20 MINUTES (READY IN 20 MINUTES)
SERVINGS: 5

🅔 EASY   🅕 LOW FAT

1 can (10.2 oz) Pillsbury® Grands!® refrigerated biscuits (5 biscuits)

2 cans (18.5 or 19 oz each) any flavor Progresso® soup

Nutrition Information Per Serving:

Calories:	280	From Fat:	90
Total Fat			10g
Saturated Fat			3.5g
Trans Fat			3g
Cholesterol			25mg
Sodium			1460mg
Total Carbohydrate			36g
Dietary Fiber			0g
Sugars			5g
Protein			11g

1) Heat oven to 350°F. Separate dough into 5 biscuits; place on ungreased cookie sheet. Press or roll each biscuit to form 5-inch round. Cut slits on top of one side of each biscuit to resemble hair. With small round cookie cutter, cut holes for mouth and eyes; remove cutout pieces from holes. Use cutout pieces for ears and/or nose.

2) Bake 13 to 17 minutes or until golden brown.

3) Meanwhile, heat soup in medium saucepan as directed on can. Spoon soup into wide shallow bowls. Top each serving with biscuit head.

HIGH ALTITUDE (3500-6500 FT.): No change.

Wart-Topped Quesadilla Wedges

PREP TIME: 10 MINUTES (READY IN 30 MINUTES)
SERVINGS: 8 (2 WEDGES EACH)

EASY

Nonstick cooking spray

4 Old El Paso® flour tortillas for burritos, 8 inch (from 11.5-oz package)

1/2 cup refrigerated original barbeque sauce with shredded pork (from 18-oz container)

2 teaspoons dill pickle relish

1/2 cup shredded Cheddar-American cheese blend (2 oz)

4 teaspoons shredded Cheddar-American cheese blend (1/3 oz)

8 pitted large ripe or green olives, cut in half lengthwise

1) Heat oven to 375°F. Spray cookie sheet with nonstick cooking spray. Place 2 tortillas on cookie sheet. Spread half of barbeque sauce with pork over each tortilla. Sprinkle half of the pickle relish over each. Top each with 1/4 cup cheese and remaining tortillas. Spray top of each with cooking spray.

2) Bake 10 to 12 minutes or until tortillas are lightly browned and filling is hot.

3) Remove partially baked quesadillas from oven. Immediately drop 4 teaspoons cheese by 1/4 teaspoonfuls around edges of quesadillas, spacing evenly and making 8 piles of cheese on each. Top each pile of cheese with 1 olive half to resemble wart.

4) Return to oven; bake about 1 minute longer or until cheese is melted. Let stand 5 minutes before serving. Cut each quesadilla into 8 wedges.

HIGH ALTITUDE (3500-6500 FT.): In Step 2, bake 12 to 14 minutes.

Nutrition Information Per Serving:

Calories:	120	From Fat:	50
Total Fat			5g
Saturated Fat			2g
Trans Fat			0g
Cholesterol			10mg
Sodium			350mg
Total Carbohydrate			14g
Dietary Fiber			0g
Sugars			2g
Protein			5g

Terrifying Twice-Baked Mummies

PREP TIME: 15 MINUTES (READY IN 1 HOUR 15 MINUTES)
SERVINGS: 6

EASY **LOW FAT**

3 baking potatoes (8 to 10 oz each)

12 frozen cooked Italian-style meatballs, about 1-inch each (from 16-oz package)

1 cup tomato pasta sauce (from 14-oz jar)

6 slices ($3/4$ oz each) mozzarella cheese

12 small pimiento-stuffed olives

1 dill pickle, cut into twelve 1x$1/4$-inch pieces

1) Heat oven to 375°F. Wrap each potato in foil. Bake about 1 hour or until fork-tender. Let stand 10 to 15 minutes or until easy to handle.

2) Meanwhile, in medium saucepan, cook meatballs and pasta sauce over medium-high heat 5 to 7 minutes or until meatballs are hot, stirring frequently.

3) Cut each potato in half lengthwise. With spoon, scoop out pulp from each potato, leaving $1/4$-inch shell. Discard pulp or reserve for another use.

4) Place 2 meatballs and about 2 tablespoons sauce in each potato half; place on ungreased 15x10x1-inch pan. Cut cheese into $1/4$-inch wide slices. Arrange cheese slices over meatball filling crossing back and forth to completely cover and resemble "bandages;" tuck ends inside potatoes.

5) Bake about 2 minutes or just until cheese softens; do not melt. Place 2 olives on end of each potato to resemble eyes; place 2 pickle pieces at opposite end to resemble feet.

HIGH ALTITUDE (3500-6500 FT.): No change.

Nutrition Information Per Serving:

Calories:	230	From Fat:	90
Total Fat		10g	
Saturated Fat		4g	
Trans Fat		0g	
Cholesterol		30mg	
Sodium		680mg	
Total Carbohydrate		25g	
Dietary Fiber		2g	
Sugars		5g	
Protein		12g	

Huck Finn Teddy Bear Raft Snacks

PREP TIME: 30 MINUTES (READY IN 30 MINUTES)
SERVINGS: 6

e EASY

6 pieces celery (about 3 inches each)

1/2 cup whipped cream cheese (from 8-oz container)

12 ready-to-eat baby-cut carrots, cut in half lengthwise

6 miniature ranch-flavored tortilla chips (from 2⅝-oz bag)

6 pretzel sticks (about 3x¼-inch each)

12 big square baked cheese snack crackers

6 teddy bear-shaped vanilla or cinnamon graham snacks

1/2 cup small fish-shaped crackers

1) For each snack, fill indentation of celery piece with about 1 tablespoon cream cheese, mounding slightly in center. Place on small plate, cream cheese up. Press 4 carrot halves, flat side up, across celery to make flat surface on celery to resemble raft.

2) Place tiny amount of cream cheese on one edge of 1 tortilla chip; attach to one end of 1 pretzel stick to resemble flag on pole. Push end of pretzel into cream cheese between 2 carrot halves.

3) Place tiny amount of cream cheese on opposite edges of each of 2 cheese snack crackers. Press cream cheese-covered edges of crackers to carrot surface, leaning crackers together to resemble tent. Attach teddy bear to raft near flag with small amount of cream cheese. Scatter fish-shaped crackers on plate around raft.

HIGH ALTITUDE (3500-6500 FT.): No change.

Nutrition Information Per Serving:

Calories:	110	From Fat:	60
Total Fat			7g
Saturated Fat			3.5g
Trans Fat			0.5g
Cholesterol			15mg
Sodium			135mg
Total Carbohydrate			10g
Dietary Fiber			0g
Sugars			2g
Protein			2g

Clown Face Salad

PREP TIME: 10 MINUTES (READY IN 10 MINUTES)
SERVINGS: 1

e EASY

1½ cups torn lettuce

1 oz sliced cooked ham, cut into thin strips

1 hard-cooked egg, shell removed, halved lengthwise

2 slices ripe olive

1 cherry tomato

1 strip red bell pepper

3 ready-to-eat baby-cut carrots, cut into strips

Favorite salad dressing

Nutrition Information Per Serving:

Calories:	230	From Fat:	140
Total Fat			16g
Saturated Fat			4g
Trans Fat			0g
Cholesterol			235mg
Sodium			660mg
Total Carbohydrate			7g
Dietary Fiber			2g
Sugars			4g
Protein			14g

1) Place lettuce on serving plate. Arrange "face" on top of salad using ham strips for hair, egg halves and olive slices for eyes, tomato for nose, bell pepper strip for mouth and carrots for bow tie. Drizzle with dressing.

HIGH ALTITUDE (3500-6500 FT.): No change.

Spooky Shepherd's Pie

PREP TIME: 30 MINUTES (READY IN 55 MINUTES)
SERVINGS: 6

1 lb lean (at least 80%) ground beef

1 medium onion, coarsely chopped (1/2 cup)

2 1/2 cups Green Giant® frozen mixed vegetables (from 1-lb bag)

1 can (14.5 oz) diced tomatoes with Italian herbs, undrained

1 jar (12 oz) beef gravy

1 3/4 cups water

2 tablespoons butter or margarine

1/4 teaspoon garlic powder

1/2 cup milk

2 1/4 cups plain mashed potato mix (dry)

1/4 cup grated Parmesan cheese

1 egg, slightly beaten

1) Heat oven to 375°F. Spray 12-inch skillet with cooking spray. Cook ground beef and onion in skillet over medium-high heat 5 to 7 minutes, stirring occasionally, until beef is thoroughly cooked; drain.

2) Set aside 12 peas for garnish. Add remaining frozen vegetables, tomatoes and gravy to ground beef. Heat to boiling. Reduce heat to medium-low; cover and cook 8 to 10 minutes or until vegetables are crisp-tender, stirring occasionally.

3) Meanwhile, in medium saucepan, bring water, butter and garlic powder to a boil. Remove from heat; stir in milk, dry potato mix and cheese. Stir in egg until well blended.

4) Spoon ground beef mixture into ungreased 8-inch square (2-quart) or oval (2 1/2-quart) glass baking dish. With large spoon, make 6 mounds of potato mixture on top of beef mixture to resemble ghosts. Place 2 reserved peas on each mound to resemble eyes.

5) Bake 20 to 25 minutes or until potatoes are set and mixture is thoroughly heated.

HIGH ALTITUDE (3500-6500 FT.): No change.

Nutrition Information Per Serving:

Calories: 590	From Fat: 150
Total Fat	17g
Saturated Fat	8g
Trans Fat	1g
Cholesterol	100mg
Sodium	630mg
Total Carbohydrate	82g
Dietary Fiber	10g
Sugars	7g
Protein	28g

Wickedly Fun Witches

PREP TIME: 40 MINUTES (READY IN 40 MINUTES)
SERVINGS: 24

- 24 oblong peanut butter-filled sandwich cookies
- ½ cup vanilla creamy ready-to-spread frosting (from 1-lb container)
- 9 drops green food color
- 4 drops yellow food color
- 72 miniature candy-coated chocolate baking bits
- 24 pieces candy corn
- 3 bars (1.55 oz each) milk chocolate candy
- 12 chocolate wafer cookies

1) Line cookie sheet with waxed paper. Place sandwich cookies on cookie sheet. In resealable food storage plastic bag, place frosting and food colors; seal bag. Squeeze bag until frosting is well blended. Cut small opening in bottom corner of bag.

2) Pipe thick line across each sandwich cookie near the top. Pipe 1 large dot of frosting above line on each cookie. Pipe squiggles of frosting to resemble witch's hair below each green line. Pipe 2 dots for eyes, 1 for nose and 1 for mouth on each cookie. Place baking bits on dots for eyes and mouth; place candy corn on dot for nose.

3) Cut candy bars crosswise into quarters. Cut each quarter in half to form 2 triangles. Place 1 candy triangle over large dot of frosting on each cookie to resemble top of witch's hat.

4) With serrated knife and sawing motion, cut each chocolate wafer cookie in half. Place cookie half upright on green line at base of each candy triangle to resemble hat brim.

HIGH ALTITUDE (3500-6500 FT.): No change.

Nutrition Information Per Serving:

Calories:	150	From Fat:	60
Total Fat		7g	
Saturated Fat		2.5g	
Trans Fat		1g	
Cholesterol		0mg	
Sodium		85mg	
Total Carbohydrate		21g	
Dietary Fiber		0g	
Sugars		13g	
Protein		1g	

THE Witchie-Poos

Scary Pancakes

PREP TIME: 30 MINUTES (READY IN 30 MINUTES)
SERVINGS: 8 (1 PANCAKE AND 2 TABLESPOONS TOPPING EACH)

e EASY **f** LOW FAT

1 container (6 oz) Yoplait® Original 99% fat free orange crème yogurt

¼ cup maple-flavored syrup

2 cups all-purpose baking mix

1¼ cups milk

1 egg

1 teaspoon unsweetened baking cocoa

1 teaspoon sugar

Nutrition Information Per Serving:

Calories:	200	From Fat:	50
Total Fat		6g	
Saturated Fat		2g	
Trans Fat		0.5g	
Cholesterol		30mg	
Sodium		470mg	
Total Carbohydrate		33g	
Dietary Fiber		0g	
Sugars		12g	
Protein		5g	

1) In small bowl, mix yogurt and maple syrup until well blended. Set aside.

2) In medium bowl, mix baking mix, milk and egg until well blended. In small bowl, mix 2 tablespoons of the batter, the cocoa and sugar until well blended.

3) Heat large nonstick electric griddle or 12-inch nonstick skillet to 375°F. Oil hot griddle.

4) For each pancake, drop three ¼ to ½-inch drops of dark batter about 1 to 1½ inches apart forming eyes and mouth of ghost. Cook about 30 seconds. Immediately pour ¼ cup regular batter; start the pour to cover the "eyes and mouth" and continue the pour downward to form an irregular ghostly shape. Cook 1 to 2 minutes or until pancake is puffed and dry around edges. Turn pancake; cook about 1 minute longer or until other side is golden brown. Serve with syrup mixture.

HIGH ALTITUDE (3500-6500 FT.): No change.

Marshmallow Mummies

PREP TIME: 30 MINUTES (READY IN 30 MINUTES)
SERVINGS: 6

e EASY **f** LOW FAT

18 large marshmallows

6 thin pretzel sticks (2¾ inch)

1 box (4.5 oz) chewy fruit snack (any flavor)

Black decorating gel (from 0.68-oz tube)

Nutrition Information Per Serving:

Calories:	150	From Fat:	0
Total Fat		0g	
Saturated Fat		0g	
Trans Fat		0g	
Cholesterol		0mg	
Sodium		60mg	
Total Carbohydrate		36g	
Dietary Fiber		0g	
Sugars		22g	
Protein		1g	

1) Thread 3 marshmallows onto each pretzel stick to make 6 "bodies."

2) Unwrap fruit snack rolls (do not unroll). With kitchen scissors or sharp knife, cut rolls into ½-inch strips. Unroll strips; remove plastic.

3) Wrap 2 strips around each "body" to resemble mummy, leaving small amount of 1 marshmallow uncovered for face. With decorating gel, add dots on "face" for eyes.

HIGH ALTITUDE (3500-6500 FT.): No change.

Mexican Grilled Cheese Sandwiches

PREP TIME: 15 MINUTES (READY IN 15 MINUTES)
SERVINGS: 2

EASY

4 slices white bread

4 oz pasteurized prepared cheese product with jalapeño peppers, thinly sliced (from 16-oz box)

2 tablespoons butter or margarine, softened

1 teaspoon Old El Paso® taco seasoning mix (from 1.25-oz package)

½ cup Old El Paso® Thick 'n Chunky salsa

1) Heat griddle to 350°F or heat 12-inch skillet over medium heat. Top 2 slices of the bread with cheese; cover with remaining bread.

2) In small bowl, mix butter and taco seasoning mix. Spread half of mixture on one side of each sandwich.

3) Place sandwiches, buttered sides down, on hot griddle. Spread top sides with remaining butter mixture. Cook 5 to 7 minutes, turning once, until golden brown on both sides and cheese is melted. Serve with salsa as a dip.

HIGH ALTITUDE (3500-6500 FT.): No change.

Nutrition Information Per Serving:	
Calories: 430	From Fat: 230
Total Fat	26g
Saturated Fat	14g
Trans Fat	1.5g
Cholesterol	75mg
Sodium	1800mg
Total Carbohydrate	37g
Dietary Fiber	0g
Sugars	8g
Protein	13g

Bite Size Boo Bugs with Bug-Catching Dip

PREP TIME: 30 MINUTES (READY IN 45 MINUTES)
SERVINGS: 24 SNACKS

EASY

BUGS

1 can (11 oz) Pillsbury® refrigerated breadsticks

24 cocktail-size smoked link sausages (from 14-oz package)

¾ cup shoestring potatoes (from 1¾-oz can) or chow mein noodles

Ketchup, barbecue sauce and/or mustard for decorating

DIP

1 cup ranch dressing (from 16-oz bottle)

1 tablespoon ketchup

1) Heat oven to 375°F. Unroll dough; separate at perforations into 12 breadsticks. With knife or kitchen scissors, cut each breadstick in half crosswise, making 24 pieces.

2) Wrap each piece of dough around center of each sausage, pinching to seal and leaving each end of sausage showing. Place seam side down and ½ inch apart on ungreased large cookie sheet.

3) Bake 11 to 14 minutes or until golden brown. Immediately remove from cookie sheet; place on serving plate or tray. Cool 2 minutes.

4) Insert shoestring potatoes into baked dough to resemble legs and antennae. Decorate "bugs" with dots or stripes of ketchup.

5) Spread dressing in 9-inch glass pie plate or on dinner plate. Spoon ketchup into small resealable food-storage plastic bag. Seal bag and cut tiny hole in bottom corner. Squeeze bag to draw a coil of ketchup over ranch dressing. Drag toothpick through coil from center out, creating a web. Serve dip with "bugs."

HIGH ALTITUDE (3500-6500 FT.): No change.

Nutrition Information Per Serving:

Calories:	130
Total Fat	10g
Saturated Fat	2.5g
Trans Fat	0g
Cholesterol	10mg
Sodium	320mg
Total Carbohydrate	8g
Dietary Fiber	0g
Sugars	1g
Protein	3g

Cheese Pumpkins

PREP TIME: 10 MINUTES (READY IN 25 MINUTES)
SERVINGS: 8 SNACKS

🅔 EASY

8 tablespoons smoked Cheddar cold-pack cheese food (from 8-oz container), well chilled

2 teaspoons finely chopped peanuts

4 butter-flavored pretzel spindles or sticks, broken in half

16 tiny pieces fresh parsley leaves, if desired

1) Line small serving plate with waxed paper. For each pumpkin, roll level tablespoon cold-pack cheese food into a ball; place on plate. Refrigerate 10 to 15 minutes for easier handling.

2) With end of toothpick, draw ridges around balls to resemble pumpkins. Dip bottoms of cheese balls in chopped peanuts.

3) Just before serving, insert pretzel halves into cheese balls for pumpkin stems. Decorate with parsley for leaves. Store pumpkins in refrigerator.

HIGH ALTITUDE (3500-6500 FT.): No change.

Nutrition Information Per Serving:	
Calories: 50	From Fat: 35
Total Fat	4g
Saturated Fat	2.5g
Trans Fat	0g
Cholesterol	10mg
Sodium	115mg
Total Carbohydrate	0g
Dietary Fiber	0g
Sugars	0g
Protein	3g

Cookie Caterpillars

PREP TIME: 25 MINUTES (READY IN 55 MINUTES)
SERVINGS: 18

e EASY

1 roll (16.5 oz) Pillsbury® Create 'n Bake™ refrigerated chocolate chip cookies

¾ cup vanilla creamy ready-to-spread frosting (from 1-lb container)

10 drops green food color

10 pretzel sticks, broken in half

16 miniature candy-coated chocolate baking bits

1) Heat oven to 350°F. Shape teaspoons of dough into 36 (1-inch) balls; place 1 inch apart on ungreased cookie sheets.

2) Bake 9 to 12 minutes or until edges are light golden brown. Cool 1 minute; remove from cookie sheets to cooling racks. Cool completely, about 15 minutes.

3) In small bowl, mix frosting and food color until well blended. Spread about 1 rounded teaspoon frosting between 2 cookies. Add more frosting and cookies, using 18 cookies to make each caterpillar. Repeat with remaining cookies to make 2 caterpillars.

4) Dip pretzel stick halves in frosting. Attach 4 sticks on each side of caterpillar to resemble legs and 2 sticks on top to resemble antennae. Spread frosting on 2 baking bits; attach to resemble eyes. Spread frosting on 6 baking bits; attach to resemble mouth. Add additional baking bits to resemble spots if desired. Repeat for second caterpillar.

HIGH ALTITUDE (3500-6500 FT.): No change.

Nutrition Information Per Serving:

Calories:	160	From Fat:	60
Total Fat			7g
Saturated Fat			2g
Trans Fat			1.5g
Cholesterol			0mg
Sodium			110mg
Total Carbohydrate			24g
Dietary Fiber			0g
Sugars			17g
Protein			0g

Family Tree Cake

PREP TIME: 25 MINUTES (READY IN 1 HOUR 35 MINUTES)
SERVINGS: 20

1 box (1 lb 2.25 oz) yellow cake mix with pudding

1¼ cups water

⅓ cup vegetable oil

3 eggs

1 container (1 lb) vanilla ready-to-spread frosting

½ cup chocolate ready-to-spread frosting (from 1-lb container)

6 spearmint candy leaves, cut in half (from 13-oz package)

8 small red gumdrops, cut in half

Green paper leaves with guest names

1) Heat oven to 350°F. Grease bottom only of 15x10x1-inch pan with shortening. Make cake mix as directed on box using water, oil and eggs. Spread batter in pan.

2) Bake for 20 to 25 minutes or until a toothpick inserted in center comes out clean. Cool completely on cooling rack, about 45 minutes.

3) Spread vanilla frosting on top of cake. With toothpick, draw tree trunk on bottom ⅓ of cake. With chocolate frosting, fill in trunk and branches, using tines of fork to create bark on tree. Place candy leaves over top ⅔ of cake, leaving space between leaves.

4) With sharp knife, cut small slit in side of each gumdrop half. Insert one end of paper leaf in slit; place on cake.

HIGH ALTITUDE (3500-6500 FT.): No change.

Nutrition Information Per Serving:		
Calories: 290	From Fat: 100	
Total Fat		11g
Saturated Fat		6g
Trans Fat		0.5g
Cholesterol		35mg
Sodium		180mg
Total Carbohydrate		45g
Dietary Fiber		0g
Sugars		34g
Protein		2g

Jack-o'-Lantern Sloppy Joe Pie

PREP TIME: 50 MINUTES (READY IN 50 MINUTES)
SERVINGS: 4

1 Pillsbury® refrigerated pie crust (from 15-oz box), softened as directed on box

1 egg yolk, if desired

1 teaspoon water

Red and yellow food color, if desired

1½ lb bulk seasoned turkey sausage

1 medium onion, chopped (½ cup)

1 cup Old El Paso® Thick 'n Chunky salsa

½ cup chili sauce

2 tablespoons packed brown sugar

1 cup Green Giant® Niblets® frozen corn (from 1-lb bag)

1 can (4.5 oz) Old El Paso® chopped green chiles, undrained

2 tablespoons chopped fresh cilantro, if desired

1) Heat oven to 450°F. Remove pie crust from pouch; unroll on ungreased cookie sheet. With sharp knife, cut jack-o'-lantern face from crust. If desired, place cutout pieces on crust to decorate; secure each with small amount of water. In small bowl, mix egg yolk, 1 teaspoon water and food color; brush on crust. Bake 9 to 11 minutes or until crust is light golden brown.

2) Meanwhile, crumble sausage into 12-inch nonstick skillet. Add onion; cook 8 to 10 minutes, stirring occasionally, until sausage is no longer pink. Stir in all remaining ingredients except cilantro. Heat to boiling. Reduce heat to medium-low; simmer 8 to 10 minutes or until corn is cooked and sauce is of desired consistency, stirring occasionally.

3) Stir cilantro into sausage mixture. Carefully place warm baked pie crust over sausage mixture.

HIGH ALTITUDE (3500-6500 FT.): No change.

Nutrition Information Per Serving:

Calories:	690	From Fat:	290
Total Fat			32g
Saturated Fat			9g
Trans Fat			0.5g
Cholesterol			165mg
Sodium			2750mg
Total Carbohydrate			56g
Dietary Fiber			4g
Sugars			15g
Protein			43g

Cornucopia of Snacks

PREP TIME: 5 MINUTES (READY IN 5 MINUTES)
SERVINGS: 12

🅴 EASY

3 cups popped popcorn

½ cup assorted small Halloween candies (such as candy corn)

½ cup salted peanuts

12 waffle cones

1) In medium bowl, mix popcorn, candies and peanuts. Scoop about ⅓ cup mixture into each waffle cone.

HIGH ALTITUDE (3500-6500 FT.): No change.

Nutrition Information Per Serving:	
Calories: 100	From Fat: 40
Total Fat	4.5g
Saturated Fat	0.5g
Trans Fat	0g
Cholesterol	0mg
Sodium	85mg
Total Carbohydrate	14g
Dietary Fiber	0g
Sugars	8g
Protein	2g

Scary-Eyed Owls

PREP TIME: 25 MINUTES (READY IN 25 MINUTES)
SERVINGS: 4

🅴 EASY

4 slices (¾ oz each) American cheese

½ lb lean (at least 80%) ground beef

3 tablespoons Old El Paso® taco seasoning mix (from 1.25-oz package)

⅔ cup water

2 cups frozen O'Brien potatoes with peppers and onions (from 28-oz bag)

2 or 3 pitted small ripe olives, sliced

12 ready-to-eat baby-cut carrots

½ cup chopped leaf lettuce

Nutrition Information Per Serving:	
Calories: 290	From Fat: 120
Total Fat	13g
Saturated Fat	7g
Trans Fat	0.5g
Cholesterol	55mg
Sodium	1040mg
Total Carbohydrate	26g
Dietary Fiber	3g
Sugars	2g
Protein	17g

1) From each cheese slice, cut 2 (1½-inch) rounds; reserve cheese scraps.

2) In 10-inch nonstick skillet, cook ground beef over medium-high heat 5 to 7 minutes, stirring occasionally, until beef is thoroughly cooked; drain. Stir in taco seasoning mix, water and potatoes. Cook 3 to 5 minutes or until thoroughly heated, stirring frequently. Stir in reserved cheese scraps until they are melted.

3) Spoon beef mixture evenly into 4 (10-ounce) ungreased custard cups. Top each with 2 cheese rounds to resemble eyes of owl. Place olive slice on each cheese round to resemble pupils of eyes. Add carrots to resemble beak and ears; sprinkle lettuce to resemble feathers on face.

HIGH ALTITUDE (3500-6500 FT.): No change.

Scary Witch Cake

PREP TIME: 40 MINUTES (READY IN 2 HOURS 15 MINUTES)
SERVINGS: 12

1 box (18.25 oz) yellow cake mix with pudding

1¼ cups water

⅓ cup vegetable oil

3 eggs

⅓ cup Halloween multicolored candy sprinkles

1 container (1 lb) vanilla creamy ready-to-spread frosting

⅛ teaspoon plus 8 drops green food color

1 waffle cone

Black decorating icing (from 6.4-oz can)

Assorted large gumdrops

2 pieces candy corn

1) Heat oven to 350°F. Spray bottom only of 13x9-inch pan with nonstick cooking spray. In large bowl with electric mixer, beat cake mix, water, oil and eggs on low speed 30 seconds. Beat on medium speed 2 minutes, scraping bowl constantly. With rubber spatula, fold in candy sprinkles. Pour batter into pan.

2) Bake 29 to 34 minutes or until toothpick inserted in center comes out clean. Cool completely, about 1 hour.

3) In small bowl, mix frosting and ⅛ teaspoon green food color until well blended. Spread frosting over cake. To form witch's hat, insert waffle cone at an angle into top center of cake until rounded edge is level with surface of cake. Tip of cone should be raised about 2 inches directly above top edge of cake pan.

4) With toothpick make 5-inch-long oval outline of witch's face directly below "hat." Immediately drop 8 drops green food color randomly over surface of frosting, avoiding "witch's face;" swirl with knife.

5) Using ribbon tip, frost "witch's hat" with black icing; add a "brim" around the base of the "hat" and frost small areas below her face to resemble a cape.

6) Cut and shape gumdrops as desired to resemble, eyebrows, eyes, nose, mouth, hat buckle and cape button. Cut candy corn into smaller pieces and add to resemble teeth. Use drawing tip in black icing to draw witch's hair.

HIGH ALTITUDE (3500-6500 FT.): Follow High Altitude directions on cake mix box for 13x9-inch pan.

Nutrition Information Per Serving:		
Calories: 530	From Fat:	200
Total Fat		22g
Saturated Fat		6g
Trans Fat		3.5g
Cholesterol		55mg
Sodium		430mg
Total Carbohydrate		80g
Dietary Fiber		0g
Sugars		63g
Protein		4g

Cinnamon Roll Bats

PREP TIME: 15 MINUTES (READY IN 40 MINUTES)
SERVINGS: 5 ROLLS

e EASY

1 can (1 lb 1.7 oz) Pillsbury® Grands!® cinnamon rolls with cream cheese icing

5 tablespoons chocolate candy sprinkles

5 chocolate wafer cookies

10 gummy ring candies, ³⁄₄ inch

10 miniature candy-coated chocolate baking bits

10 pieces candy corn

5 large or small black gumdrops

1) Heat oven to 350°F. Separate dough into 5 rolls; cut each in half crosswise. For each flying bat, arrange 2 halves, round sides together, on ungreased cookie sheet.

2) Bake 17 to 22 minutes or until golden brown. Reserve 1 tablespoon icing. Frost warm bats with remaining icing. Immediately sprinkle each bat with 1 tablespoon candy sprinkles.

3) With small amount of reserved icing, attach wafer cookie to each bat for head. Use remaining icing and candies to decorate faces as desired.

HIGH ALTITUDE (3500-6500 FT.): Bake 16 to 19 minutes.

Nutrition Information Per Serving:

Calories: 530	From Fat: 120	
Total Fat		13g
Saturated Fat		6g
Trans Fat		2.5g
Cholesterol		0mg
Sodium		710mg
Total Carbohydrate		96g
Dietary Fiber		2g
Sugars		50g
Protein		6g

Creepy Crawler Macaroni and Cheese

PREP TIME: 20 MINUTES (READY IN 20 MINUTES)
SERVINGS: 4

⊖ EASY

6 cups water

1 box (5.5 oz) macaroni and cheese with crazy noodles

1/2 cup chopped carrot

4 hot dogs, each cut lengthwise into 6 strips

3 tablespoons milk

1 1/2 teaspoons butter or margarine

Nutrition Information Per Serving:		
Calories: 290	From Fat:	150
Total Fat		16g
Saturated Fat		7g
Trans Fat		0g
Cholesterol		35mg
Sodium		870mg
Total Carbohydrate		30g
Dietary Fiber		2g
Sugars		7g
Protein		6g

1) In 2-quart saucepan, heat water to boiling. Stir in macaroni from box and carrot; boil over medium heat 10 minutes. Add hot dog strips; continue to boil 2 minutes longer; drain.

2) Stir in cheese sauce mix, milk and butter until well blended.

HIGH ALTITUDE (3500-6500 FT.): Follow High Altitude directions on box for macaroni and cheese.

Crispy Bat Snacks and "Appledy-Goop"

PREP TIME: 15 MINUTES (READY IN 30 MINUTES)
SERVINGS: 4 (1/4 CUP DIP AND 3 BAT SNACKS EACH)

⊖ EASY

6 Old El Paso® flour tortillas for soft tacos & fajitas, 6 inch (from 10.5-oz package)

Nonstick cooking spray

1/2 cup apple butter

1/3 cup crunchy peanut butter

2 teaspoons apple juice or apple cider

1 tablespoon chopped peanuts

Nutrition Information Per Serving:		
Calories: 460	From Fat:	170
Total Fat		19g
Saturated Fat		4g
Trans Fat		0g
Cholesterol		0mg
Sodium		660mg
Total Carbohydrate		62g
Dietary Fiber		3g
Sugars		18g
Protein		11g

1) Heat oven to 350°F. With bat-shaped cookie cutter or kitchen scissors, cut tortillas into bat shapes. Place shapes and large scraps on ungreased cookie sheets. Spray both sides of shapes and scraps with nonstick cooking spray.

2) Bake 8 to 10 minutes or until golden brown and crisp. Cool completely, about 15 minutes.

3) Meanwhile, in small bowl, mix remaining ingredients except peanuts. Sprinkle dip with peanuts. Serve dip with bat snacks.

HIGH ALTITUDE (3500-6500 FT.): No change.

Graveyard Cake

PREP TIME: 55 MINUTES (READY IN 1 HOUR 20 MINUTES)
SERVINGS: 24

1 box (18.25 oz) yellow cake mix with pudding

1¼ cups water

⅓ cup vegetable oil

3 eggs

¼ cup chocolate-flavored candy melts or coating wafers, melted

2 to 3 oval creme-filled or peanut-shaped peanut butter-filled sandwich cookies, each cut in half crosswise

1 container (1 lb) vanilla creamy ready-to-spread frosting

20 drops neon green food color

5 rectangular graham crackers

2 rectangular chocolate graham crackers

Candy-coated peanut butter pieces

Candy corn

Candy pumpkins

1) Heat oven to 350°F. Spray 15x10x1-inch pan with cooking spray. Prepare cake mix as directed on box, using water, oil and eggs. Pour batter into pan; spread evenly. Bake 20 to 25 minutes or until toothpick inserted in center comes out clean. Cool completely in pan, about 30 minutes.

2) Meanwhile, place sheet of foil on cookie sheet. Spoon melted candy melts into small resealable food storage plastic bag; seal bag. Cut small hole in bottom corner of bag. Squeeze melted candy in shape of tree onto foil. Refrigerate tree. Squeeze melted candy on sandwich cookies to resemble tombstones.

3) In small bowl, mix frosting and food color until blended. Reserve ¼ cup frosting for roof and decorations. Frost cake with remaining frosting. With sharp knife, cut peaks in one short side of each of 2 graham crackers. Insert crackers into cake for front and back of haunted house. Break 1 graham cracker in half crosswise; insert into cake for sides of house. Frost 2 graham crackers; place on house for roof.

4) Break up chocolate graham crackers; arrange on cake for walkway and on house for windows and door. Arrange peanut butter pieces along edge of walkway. Pipe line of frosting along top of house; arrange candy corn in frosting.

5) Arrange chocolate tree on cake. Place candy pumpkins near house. Arrange "tombstones" on cake. Crush remaining chocolate graham cracker; mound graham cracker crumbs in front of tombstones for graves.

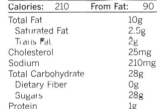

Nutrition Information Per Serving:

Calories:	210	From Fat:	90
Total Fat			10g
Saturated Fat			2.5g
Trans Fat			2g
Cholesterol			25mg
Sodium			210mg
Total Carbohydrate			28g
Dietary Fiber			0g
Sugars			28g
Protein			1g

HIGH ALTITUDE (3500-6500 FT.): No change.

Corny Sloppy Joe Pizzas

PREP TIME: 35 MINUTES (READY IN 35 MINUTES)
SERVINGS: 8

1 can (16.3 oz) Pillsbury® Grands!® Homestyle refrigerated biscuits

1 lb lean (at least 80%) ground beef

1 can (15.5 oz) sloppy Joe sandwich sauce

1 can (11 oz) Green Giant® Niblets® whole kernel sweet corn, drained

8 slices (¾ oz each) American cheese

8 small pieces (1x½ inch each) green bell pepper

1) Heat oven to 375°F. Separate dough into 8 biscuits. Place on ungreased large cookie sheet; press each biscuit to form 4½-inch round. Bake 12 to 15 minutes or until golden brown.

2) Meanwhile, in 12-inch nonstick skillet, cook ground beef over medium heat 8 to 10 minutes, stirring occasionally, until thoroughly cooked; drain. Stir in sloppy Joe sauce and corn. Reduce heat to medium-low; cook 3 to 5 minutes or until thoroughly heated, stirring occasionally.

3) Cut cheese into circles. With knife or canapé cutters, make facial features in the cheese.

4) Remove biscuits from oven. Spoon beef mixture evenly onto biscuit rounds. Arrange cheese pieces over beef mixture to resemble jack-o'-lanterns. Place bell pepper piece on top of each to resemble stem. Return to oven; bake 3 to 5 minutes longer or until cheese is melted.

HIGH ALTITUDE (3500-6500 FT.): No change.

Nutrition Information Per Serving:

Calories:	420	From Fat:	190
Total Fat			21g
Saturated Fat			10g
Trans Fat			3.5g
Cholesterol			55mg
Sodium			1340mg
Total Carbohydrate			36g
Dietary Fiber			2g
Sugars			9g
Protein			20g

Kid-Pleasing Potato Nugget Casserole

PREP TIME: 10 MINUTES (READY IN 1 HOUR 5 MINUTES)
SERVINGS: 4

e EASY

1 can (10$\frac{3}{4}$ oz) condensed cream of chicken soup

1 cup milk

1 tablespoon dried minced onion

2 cups cut-up cooked chicken

2 cups Green Giant® frozen mixed vegetables (from 1-lb bag), thawed

1 bag (16 oz) frozen potato nuggets

$\frac{1}{2}$ cup shredded American-Cheddar cheese blend (2 oz)

1) Heat oven to 375°F. In ungreased 2-quart casserole, mix soup, milk, dried onion, chicken and vegetables. Arrange frozen potato nuggets over top.

2) Bake uncovered 40 to 45 minutes. Sprinkle with cheese. Bake 5 to 10 minutes longer or until bubbly and cheese is melted.

HIGH ALTITUDE (3500-6500 FT.): No change.

Nutrition Information Per Serving:

Calories:	610	From Fat:	250
Total Fat			28g
Saturated Fat			12g
Trans Fat			4.5g
Cholesterol			85mg
Sodium			1720mg
Total Carbohydrate			67g
Dietary Fiber			8g
Sugars			8g
Protein			33g

This casserole also tastes great when prepared with cooked ground beef instead of the chicken.

Chili Mac 'n Cheese

PREP TIME: 30 MINUTES (READY IN 30 MINUTES)
SERVINGS: 6 (1 CUP EACH)

e EASY

1 lb lean (at least 80%) ground beef

2 1/3 cups uncooked rotini pasta (7 oz)

1 teaspoon chili powder

2 1/4 cups hot water

1 can (14 1/2 oz) diced tomatoes with zesty mild green chiles, undrained

2 cups shredded taco-flavored cheese (8 oz)

Chili powder, if desired

1) In 12-inch skillet, cook ground beef over medium-high heat, stirring frequently, until thoroughly cooked; drain.

2) Stir in uncooked pasta, chili powder, water and tomatoes. Heat to boiling, stirring frequently. Reduce heat to medium-low; cover and simmer 10 to 12 minutes, stirring occasionally, until pasta is tender.

3) Remove from heat; let stand uncovered 5 minutes. Stir in cheese until melted. Sprinkle with additional chili powder.

HIGH ALTITUDE (3500-6500 FT.): Increase hot water to 2-3/4 cups. Simmer covered 12 to 14 minutes.

Nutrition Information Per Serving:	
Calories: 430 From Fat: 190	
Total Fat	22g
Saturated Fat	11g
Trans Fat	1g
Cholesterol	85mg
Sodium	480mg
Total Carbohydrate	30g
Dietary Fiber	3g
Sugars	4g
Protein	28g

Breaded Fish Fillets with Nacho Sauce

PREP TIME: 10 MINUTES (READY IN 10 MINUTES)
SERVINGS: 4

● EASY

2 packages (8 oz each) frozen breaded fish fillets (4 fillets)

½ cup Old El Paso® Cheese 'n Salsa dip

1) Heat fish fillets as directed on package. Meanwhile, microwave dip as directed on container.

2) To serve, spoon about 2 tablespoons dip over each fish fillet.

HIGH ALTITUDE (3500-6500 FT.): No change.

Nutrition Information Per Serving:	
Calories: 330	From Fat: 200
Total Fat	22g
Saturated Fat	4g
Trans Fat	2.5g
Cholesterol	30mg
Sodium	740mg
Total Carbohydrate	22g
Dietary Fiber	0g
Sugars	4g
Protein	11g

tip You can use breaded fish sticks instead of fish fillets for this recipe and use the Nacho Sauce as a dip. Kids will love it!

Chili Dog Casserole

PREP TIME: 20 MINUTES (READY IN 45 MINUTES)
SERVINGS: 8

● EASY

2 cans (15 oz each) chili without beans

1 package (16 oz) miniature hot dogs

8 oz prepared cheese product, cut up

1 cup Old El Paso® Thick 'n Chunky salsa

1 can (11.5 oz) Pillsbury® refrigerated cornbread twists

½ teaspoon chili powder

1) Heat oven to 350°F. Spray 13x9-inch (3-quart) glass baking dish with nonstick cooking spray. In Dutch oven or large saucepan, mix chili, hot dogs, cheese product and salsa. Cook over medium heat until cheese is melted and mixture is bubbly, stirring frequently. Spoon into baking dish.

2) Separate dough into 16 strips. Gently twist each strip; arrange over hot chili mixture. Sprinkle twists with chili powder.

3) Bake 20 to 25 minutes or until cornbread twists are deep golden brown.

HIGH ALTITUDE (3500-6500 FT.): No change.

tip Don't have the cornbread twists? You can easily substitute them with an 11-ounce can of Pillsbury® refrigerated breadsticks.

Nutrition Information Per Serving:	
Calories: 510	From Fat: 290
Total Fat	33g
Saturated Fat	13g
Trans Fat	3g
Cholesterol	70mg
Sodium	2100mg
Total Carbohydrate	33g
Dietary Fiber	2g
Sugars	11g
Protein	20g

Scarecrow-d Taco Dip

			EASY
PREP TIME:	15 MINUTES (READY IN 15 MINUTES)		
SERVINGS:	16		

1 package (8 oz) cream cheese, softened

2 teaspoons Old El Paso® taco seasoning mix (from 1.25-oz package)

½ cup Old El Paso® Thick 'n Chunky salsa

¼ cup sliced ripe olives

1 cup shredded Cheddar cheese (4 oz)

1 cup Old El Paso® refried beans (from 16-oz can)

1 cup chopped lettuce

2 cherry tomatoes

Triangular-shaped tortilla chips (about 3 inch)

1) In small bowl, mix cream cheese and taco seasoning mix until smooth. Spread on 10-inch plate. Spoon salsa evenly over cream cheese mixture. Reserve 4 olive slices; sprinkle remaining olives over salsa. Reserve ¼ cup cheese; sprinkle remaining cheese over olives. Spoon beans in center of plate; spread to 6-inch circle to resemble head of scarecrow. Sprinkle lettuce around beans.

2) Cut 1 tomato in half; place each half on scarecrow, cut side up, to resemble eyes. Add remaining tomato to resemble nose. Place 1 reserved olive slice on each "eye" to resemble pupil. Cut the remaining olive slices in half and arrange the pieces to resemble mouth.

3) Arrange tortilla chips to resemble a hat on the scarecrow's head. Arrange the reserved cheese to come out from under the hat and at the bottom of the face to resemble straw. Serve dip with tortilla chips. Store dip in refrigerator.

HIGH ALTITUDE (3500-6500 FT.): No change.

Nutrition Information Per Serving:

Calories:	110	From Fat:	70
Total Fat			8g
Saturated Fat			4.5g
Trans Fat			0g
Cholesterol			25mg
Sodium			280mg
Total Carbohydrate			5g
Dietary Fiber			0g
Sugars			0g
Protein			4g

Easter Bird's Nest Cupcakes

PREP TIME: 30 MINUTES (READY IN 1 HOUR 30 MINUTES)
SERVINGS: 12

24 pastel-colored paper baking cups

1 box (1 lb 2.25 oz) milk chocolate cake mix with pudding

1¼ cups water

⅓ cup vegetable oil

3 eggs

1 cup milk chocolate creamy ready-to-spread frosting (from 1-lb can)

36 pastel-colored candy-coated chocolate pieces

1 bottle (1.75 oz) chocolate decorating decors (⅓ cup)

1) Heat oven to 350°F. Place paper baking cups in each of 24 regular-size muffin cups. Make and bake cake mix as directed on box for cupcakes using water, oil and eggs; cool completely. Freeze 12 of the cupcakes for a later use.

2) With ½ cup of the frosting, frost remaining 12 cupcakes. Place 3 candy-coated chocolate pieces on center of each to resemble eggs.

3) In small resealable food-storage plastic bag, place remaining ½ cup frosting; seal bag. Cut small hole in one bottom corner of bag; pipe frosting around chocolate pieces to create ridge on each cupcake.

4) Carefully spoon chocolate decors onto frosting ridge and around chocolate pieces to resemble nest.

HIGH ALTITUDE (3500-6500 FT.): Make cake mix following high altitude directions on box for cupcakes.

Nutrition Information Per Serving:		
Calories: 290	From Fat:	130
Total Fat		14g
Saturated Fat		8g
Trans Fat		0g
Cholesterol		30mg
Sodium		210mg
Total Carbohydrate		39g
Dietary Fiber		2g
Sugars		31g
Protein		3g

Cookies, Bars & Candies

Turn here the next time you need a treat
sure to satisfy the sweet tooth!

SOFT AND CHEWY
CHOCOLATE CHIP COOKIES
PG. 285

FUDGY-CARAMEL CASHEW BROWNIES
PG. 297

PISTACHIO BRITTLE
PG. 295

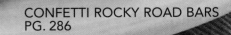

CONFETTI ROCKY ROAD BARS
PG. 286

Blond Brownie Caramel Cups

ALBERTA RICHTER | LOCKPORT, ILLINOIS

BAKE-OFF® CONTEST 34, 1990

PREP TIME: 30 MINUTES (READY IN 50 MINUTES)
SERVINGS: 16 BROWNIES

CUPS

- 1/2 cup butter or margarine
- 1 cup firmly packed brown sugar
- 1 teaspoon vanilla
- 1 egg
- 1 cup all-purpose flour
- 1 teaspoon baking powder
- 1/4 teaspoon salt
- 1/2 cup chopped nuts

TOPPING

- 20 caramels, unwrapped
- 1 tablespoon water
- 1/2 cup semisweet chocolate chips
- 1/4 to 1/2 cup finely chopped nuts

1) Heat oven to 350°F. Line 16 muffin cups with foil or paper baking cups. Melt butter in medium saucepan over low heat. Remove from heat; stir in brown sugar. Add vanilla and egg; mix well. Add flour, baking powder and salt; blend well. Stir in 1/2 cup chopped nuts. Divide batter evenly into lined muffin cups. Bake for 16 to 20 minutes or until golden brown.

2) Meanwhile in a small saucepan over low heat, melt caramels with water; stir constantly until smooth. Immediately after pans are removed from oven, place chocolate chips evenly into middle of each brownie. Spoon 1 scant tablespoon of caramel over chocolate chips in each cup. If necessary, stir additional water into melted caramels to maintain spoonable consistency. Sprinkle 1/4 cup finely chopped nuts evenly over brownies. Cool completely. Store in tightly covered container.

HIGH ALTITUDE (3500-6500 FT.): Increase flour to 1 1/4 cups. Bake as directed above.

Giant Peanut Butter Zebra Cookies

PREP TIME: 35 MINUTES (READY IN 55 MINUTES)
SERVINGS: 1 DOZEN COOKIES

- 1 roll (16.5 oz) Pillsbury® Create 'n Bake® refrigerated peanut butter cookies
- 12 miniature chocolate-covered peanut butter cups, unwrapped
- 1/3 cup semisweet chocolate chips
- 1 teaspoon shortening

Nutrition Information Per Serving:	
Calories: 230	From Fat: 100
Total Fat	11g
Saturated Fat	3.5g
Trans Fat	1.5g
Cholesterol	5mg
Sodium	200mg
Total Carbohydrate	27g
Dietary Fiber	0g
Sugars	17g
Protein	3g

1) Heat oven to 350°F. Divide cookie dough into 12 equal pieces. With floured fingers, wrap 1 piece of dough around each peanut butter cup, shaping into a ball. On ungreased cookie sheet, place 6 balls, arranging evenly apart. Refrigerate remaining 6 balls until ready to bake.

2) Bake 11 to 14 minutes or until golden brown. Cool 1 minute; remove from cookie sheet. Cool completely, about 15 minutes. Bake the remaining balls of dough.

3) In 1-quart saucepan, melt chocolate chips and shortening over low heat, stirring constantly. Drizzle melted chocolate over cooled cookies. Let stand until glaze is set before storing.

HIGH ALTITUDE (3500-6500 FT.): No change.

Chocolate-Filled Russian Tea Cakes

PREP TIME: 2 HOURS (READY IN 2 HOURS 30 MINUTES)
SERVINGS: 4 DOZEN COOKIES

COOKIES

- 1 cup butter or margarine, softened
- 1/2 cup powdered sugar
- 1 teaspoon vanilla
- 2 cups all-purpose flour
- 1/4 teaspoon salt
- 3/4 cup finely chopped walnuts
- 48 milk chocolate stars (from 14-oz bag)

SUGAR COATING

- 1 cup powdered sugar
- 1 tablespoon red sugar
- 1 tablespoon green sugar

1) Heat oven to 400°F. In large bowl, beat butter, 1/2 cup powdered sugar and vanilla with electric mixture on medium speed until well mixed. On low speed, beat in flour, salt and walnuts.

2) For each cookie, shape scant measuring tablespoonfuls dough around chocolate star to make 1-inch ball; place 2 inches apart on ungreased cookie sheets.

3) Bake 12 to 15 minutes or until set and bottoms begin to turn golden brown. Meanwhile, in small bowl, mix sugar coating ingredients.

4) Immediately remove cookies from the cookie sheets; roll in sugar coating. Cool completely on cooling racks, about 30 minutes. Roll in sugar coating again.

HIGH ALTITUDE (3500-6500 FT.): Heat oven to 375°F.

Nutrition Information Per Serving:

Calories: 100	From Fat: 60
Total Fat	6g
Saturated Fat	3g
Trans Fat	0g
Cholesterol	10mg
Sodium	45mg
Total Carbohydrate	11g
Dietary Fiber	0g
Sugars	6g
Protein	1g

tip

For cookies with a little more dazzle, try using coarse red and green sparkling sugar instead of the colored granulated sugar called for.

Merry Berry Wreath Cookies

PREP TIME: 1 HOUR 15 MINUTES (READY IN 1 HOUR 15 MINUTES)
SERVINGS: 2 DOZEN COOKIES

1 roll (16.5 oz) Pillsbury® Create 'n Bake™ refrigerated sugar cookies

1 container (1 lb) vanilla creamy ready-to-spread frosting

4 or 5 drops green food color

2 tubes (0.68 oz each) red decorating gel

About 2 tablespoons holiday red and green candy decors

Nutrition Information Per Serving:

Calories:	200	From Fat:	70
Total Fat		8g	
Saturated Fat		2.5g	
Trans Fat		2.5g	
Cholesterol		5mg	
Sodium		105mg	
Total Carbohydrate		31g	
Dietary Fiber		0g	
Sugars		22g	
Protein		0g	

1) Heat oven to 350°F. Remove half of cookie dough from wrapper; refrigerate remaining dough until needed. Cut dough into 12 slices, ¼ inch thick. On floured work surface, roll each into 6-inch long rope. On ungreased cookie sheet, form into wreath shapes 2 inches apart; pinch ends of each wreath together.

2) Bake 9 to 12 minutes or until edges are light golden brown. Cool 1 minute. Remove from cookie sheet to cooling rack. Cool completely, about 15 minutes. Repeat with remaining half of cookie dough.

3) In medium bowl, mix frosting and food color until well blended. Frost tops of cookies. With decorating gel, form bow at top of each wreath. Sprinkle with candy decors.

HIGH ALTITUDE (3500-6500 FT.): In Step 1, crumble half of dough into medium bowl. Knead 2 tablespoons all-purpose flour into dough and divide into 12 pieces. Repeat with remaining half of cookie dough.

Peanutty Chocolate Candy Cookies

PREP TIME: 30 MINUTES (READY IN 45 MINUTES)
SERVINGS: 3 DOZEN COOKIES

1 box (1 lb 2.25 oz) chocolate fudge cake mix with pudding

1/2 cup butter or margarine, softened

2 eggs

1 bag (14 oz) candy-coated peanut butter pieces

1 cup coarsely chopped salted peanuts

1) Heat oven to 350°F. Grease cookie sheets with shortening or cooking spray. In large bowl, beat cake mix, butter and eggs with electric mixer on low speed just until moistened. With spoon, stir in peanut butter pieces and peanuts.

2) Drop dough by rounded tablespoonfuls 2 inches apart onto cookie sheets.

3) Bake 7 to 10 minutes or until edges are set and tops appear dry. Cool 2 minutes; remove from cookie sheets.

Nutrition Information Per Serving:

Calories:	160	From Fat:	70
Total Fat			8g
Saturated Fat			2.5g
Trans Fat			0g
Cholesterol			20mg
Sodium			170mg
Total Carbohydrate			19g
Dietary Fiber			1g
Sugars			13g
Protein			4g

Triple Chocolate-Cherry Cookies

PREP TIME: 1 HOUR (READY IN 1 HOUR)
SERVINGS: 4 DOZEN COOKIES

1 cup butter or margarine, softened

3/4 cup granulated sugar

1/2 cup packed brown sugar

2 oz bittersweet baking chocolate, melted

1 teaspoon vanilla

2 eggs

2 1/4 cups all-purpose flour

1/4 cup unsweetened baking cocoa

1 teaspoon baking soda

1 1/3 cups white vanilla baking chips (from 12-oz package)

3/4 cup maraschino cherries without stems, coarsely chopped, well drained

1 teaspoon oil

24 maraschino cherries, drained, each cut in half

1) Heat oven to 350°F. Lightly grease cookie sheets. In large bowl, beat butter, granulated sugar and brown sugar with electric mixer on medium speed 1 to 2 minutes or until light and fluffy. Beat in melted chocolate, vanilla and eggs.

2) On low speed, beat in flour, cocoa and baking soda until mixed. Fold in 1 cup of the vanilla baking chips and the cherries. Drop by rounded teaspoonfuls 2 inches apart on cookie sheets.

3) Bake 9 to 11 minutes or until set. Do not overbake. Cool 2 minutes. Remove from cookie sheets to cooling racks. Cool completely, about 15 minutes.

4) Meanwhile, in small microwavable bowl, place remaining vanilla baking chips and oil. Microwave on High 30 seconds; stir. If necessary, microwave in 10-second increments, stirring after each time, until melted and smooth. Spoon drop of mixture in center of each cookie; top each with cherry half. Drizzle remaining mixture over cookies.

HIGH ALTITUDE (3500-6500 FT.): No change.

Nutrition Information Per Serving:

Calories:	130	From Fat:	60
Total Fat			7g
Saturated Fat			4.5g
Trans Fat			0g
Cholesterol			20mg
Sodium			70mg
Total Carbohydrate			17g
Dietary Fiber			0g
Sugars			11g
Protein			2g

White Chocolate Layer Bars

PREP TIME: 10 MINUTES (READY IN 1 HOUR 10 MINUTES)
SERVINGS: 3 DOZEN BARS

e EASY

½ cup butter or margarine

1½ cups chocolate wafer cookie crumbs

1 cup chopped cashews

1 cup white vanilla baking chips

1½ cups coconut

1 can (14 oz) sweetened condensed milk

½ cup chopped red candied cherries

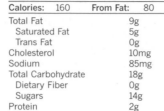

For Christmastime flair without a lot of extra work, just replace some of the red cherries with chopped, green candied cherries.

Nutrition Information Per Serving:

Calories: 160	From Fat:	80
Total Fat		9g
Saturated Fat		5g
Trans Fat		0g
Cholesterol		10mg
Sodium		85mg
Total Carbohydrate		18g
Dietary Fiber		0g
Sugars		14g
Protein		2g

1) Heat oven to 350°F. In 13x9-inch pan, melt butter while oven is heating.

2) Remove pan from oven. Stir cookie crumbs into butter; press evenly in bottom of pan. Sprinkle with cashews, baking chips, coconut and cherries. Pour condensed milk evenly over mixture.

3) Bake 20 to 30 minutes or until light golden brown. Cool completely, about 30 minutes. Cut into 6 rows by 6 rows.

HIGH ALTITUDE (3500-6500 FT.): Bake 25 to 35 minutes.

Peppermint–Chocolate Brownies

PREP TIME: 30 MINUTES (READY IN 2 HOURS 45 MINUTES)
SERVINGS: 4 DOZEN BROWNIES

4 oz unsweetened baking chocolate

1 cup butter or margarine

2 packages (8 oz each) cream cheese, softened

2½ cups sugar

5 eggs

½ teaspoon peppermint extract

1½ cups all-purpose flour

½ teaspoon salt

2 cups créme de menthe baking chips (from two 10-oz bags)

Nutrition Information Per Serving:

Calories: 180	From Fat:	100
Total Fat		11g
Saturated Fat		7g
Trans Fat		0g
Cholesterol		45mg
Sodium		90mg
Total Carbohydrate		19g
Dietary Fiber		0g
Sugars		14g
Protein		2g

1) Heat oven to 350°F. Grease bottom and sides of 13x9-inch pan with shortening or cooking spray (do not use dark pan). In 3-quart saucepan, heat baking chocolate and butter over low heat, stirring frequently, until melted and smooth. Cool 5 minutes.

2) Meanwhile, in medium bowl, beat cream cheese, ½ cup of the sugar and 1 of the eggs with electric mixer on medium speed until smooth. Set aside.

3) Into chocolate mixture, stir remaining 2 cups sugar, remaining 4 eggs and the peppermint extract. Stir in flour and salt until well mixed. Spread half of chocolate batter in pan. Drop cream cheese filling by teaspoonfuls over batter. Carefully spoon and spread remaining batter over filling.

4) Bake 40 to 45 minutes or until toothpick inserted in center comes out clean. Sprinkle evenly with baking chips. Cool completely, about 1 hour 30 minutes. Cut into 8 rows by 6 rows. Store in refrigerator.

HIGH ALTITUDE (3500-6500 FT.): In Step 1, heat baking chocolate and butter over medium-low heat.

No-Bake After-Dinner Mint Bars

PREP TIME: 30 MINUTES (READY IN 45 MINUTES)
SERVINGS: 25 BARS

1/2 cup butter

1 bag (10 oz) mint-flavored semisweet chocolate chips (1 2/3 cups)

2 cups chocolate wafer cookie crumbs

1/4 cup butter, softened

1 tablespoon milk

1/2 teaspoon peppermint extract

1/2 teaspoon vanilla

1 drop green food color

2 cups powdered sugar

1/3 cup butter

1) Lightly grease 9-inch square pan with shortening or nonstick cooking spray. In 2-quart saucepan, melt 1/2 cup butter and 1/4 cup of the chocolate chips over low heat, stirring constantly. Remove from heat. Stir in cookie crumbs until well mixed; press evenly in pan. Refrigerate until firm, about 10 minutes.

2) Meanwhile, in small bowl, beat 1/4 cup butter, the milk, peppermint extract, vanilla and food color with electric mixer on medium speed until well mixed. On low speed, gradually beat in powdered sugar until smooth.

3) Spread peppermint mixture evenly over crumb mixture. In 1-quart saucepan, melt remaining chocolate chips and 1/3 cup butter over low heat, stirring constantly; spread evenly over peppermint mixture. Refrigerate until chocolate is set, 10 to 15 minutes. Cut into 5 rows by 5 rows.

HIGH ALTITUDE (3500-6500 FT.): No change.

Nutrition Information Per Serving:		
Calories: 210	From Fat:	110
Total Fat		13g
Saturated Fat		7g
Trans Fat		1g
Cholesterol		20mg
Sodium		110mg
Total Carbohydrate		23g
Dietary Fiber		0g
Sugars		18g
Protein		1g

Crème de Menthe Truffles

PREP TIME: 2 HOURS 15 MINUTES (READY IN 3 HOURS 55 MINUTES)
SERVINGS: 3 DOZEN TRUFFLES

½ cup whipping cream

1 bag (10 oz) crème de menthe baking chips

1 cup semisweet chocolate chips (6 oz)

10 oz vanilla-flavored candy coating (almond bark)

2 drops green food color

Mini foil candy cups (1½ inch), if desired

Nutrition Information Per Serving:

Calories:	120	From Fat:	70
Total Fat			7g
Saturated Fat			4.5g
Trans Fat			0g
Cholesterol			0mg
Sodium			10mg
Total Carbohydrate			13g
Dietary Fiber			0g
Sugars			12g
Protein			1g

1) In 2-quart saucepan, heat whipping cream over low heat 2 to 3 minutes or until cream is warm. Remove from heat. Add baking chips and chocolate chips; stir until melted and smooth. Cover; refrigerate 1 hour or until firm.

2) Line cookie sheets with waxed paper. Shape mixture into 1-inch balls, dusting hands with powdered sugar or cocoa, if necessary; place 2 inches apart on cookie sheets. Refrigerate 30 minutes.

3) Meanwhile, in deep 1-quart saucepan, melt candy coating over low heat, stirring frequently, until smooth. Remove for heat; cool 10 minutes. In small resealable freezer plastic bag, place ¼ cup melted coating and the green food color; seal bag. Squeeze bag to mix until uniform color; set bag aside.

4) Using fork, dip 1 truffle at a time into white candy coating to coat. Return to waxed paper-lined cookie sheets. Cut off tiny corner of bag containing green coating. Squeeze bag to drizzle coating over each truffle (if necessary, reheat green coating in microwave on High a few seconds to make coating drizzle). Let truffles stand until coating is set, about 10 minutes, before placing in foil candy cups. Store in refrigerator.

HIGH ALTITUDE (3500-6500 FT.): No change.

Sugar and Spice Nuts

PREP TIME: 15 MINUTES (READY IN 1 HOUR 30 MINUTES)
SERVINGS: 21 (1/4 CUP EACH)

 EASY

¾ cup sugar

1 teaspoon salt

2 tablespoons ground cinnamon

1 teaspoon ground ginger

½ teaspoon ground cloves

½ teaspoon ground nutmeg

1 tablespoon water

1 egg white

1 cup pecan halves

1 cup whole cashews

1 cup walnut halves

1 cup red and green candy-coated chocolate candies

1) Heat oven to 300°F. Spray 15x10x1-inch pan with cooking spray. In large bowl, beat sugar, salt, cinnamon, ginger, cloves, nutmeg, water and egg white with electric mixer on high speed 1 to 2 minutes or until mixture is frothy. With rubber spatula, fold in nuts until evenly coated. Spread mixture evenly in pan.

2) Bake 45 to 50 minutes, stirring occasionally, until nuts are fragrant and toasted. Cool completely in pan, about 30 minutes. Stir in chocolate candies. Store in tightly covered container.

HIGH ALTITUDE (3500-6500 FT.): No change.

Nutrition Information Per Serving:

Calories:	190	From Fat:	100
Total Fat			12g
Saturated Fat			2.5g
Trans Fat			0g
Cholesterol			0mg
Sodium			120mg
Total Carbohydrate			18g
Dietary Fiber			2g
Sugars			14g
Protein			3g

Chocolate-Eggnog Cheesecake Squares

PREP TIME: 20 MINUTES (READY IN 4 HOURS)
SERVINGS: 4 DOZEN SQUARES

 EASY

CRUST

2 cups chocolate cookie crumbs (from 15-oz box)

½ cup butter or margarine, melted

FILLING

2 packages (8 oz each) cream cheese, softened

½ cup sugar

1 tablespoon all-purpose flour

½ cup dairy eggnog

2 eggs

½ cup miniature semisweet chocolate chips

¼ teaspoon ground nutmeg

1) Heat oven to 300°F. Line 13x9-inch pan with 18x18-inch square of heavy-duty foil so foil extends over long sides of pan. Spray foil with cooking spray. In small bowl, mix cookie crumbs and butter. Press in bottom of pan.

2) In large bowl, beat cream cheese and sugar with electric mixer on medium speed 1 to 2 minutes or until smooth. Beat in flour, eggnog and eggs on medium speed until smooth, scraping sides of bowl if necessary. With rubber spatula, fold in chocolate chips. Pour filling evenly over the crust.

3) Bake 35 to 40 minutes or until edges are set. Center will be soft but will set when cool. Cool 1 hour. Refrigerate at least 2 hours. Sprinkle evenly with nutmeg. For squares, cut into 8 rows by 6 rows. Remove from foil. Store squares in refrigerator.

HIGH ALTITUDE (3500-6500 FT.): Heat oven to 325°F.

Nutrition Information Per Serving:

Calories:	100	From Fat:	60
Total Fat			7g
Saturated Fat			4g
Trans Fat			0g
Cholesterol			25mg
Sodium			75mg
Total Carbohydrate			7g
Dietary Fiber			0g
Sugars			5g
Protein			2g

Crescent Layer Bars

PREP TIME: 25 MINUTES (READY IN 2 HOURS 20 MINUTES)
SERVINGS: 3 DOZEN BARS

1 can (8 oz) Pillsbury® refrigerated crescent dinner rolls

1 cup white vanilla baking chips

1 cup semisweet chocolate chips

1 cup slivered almonds

1 cup cashew halves and pieces

1 can (14 oz) sweetened condensed milk (not evaporated)

1) Heat oven to 375°F (350°F for dark or nonstick pan). Grease bottom and sides of 13x9-inch pan with shortening or nonstick cooking spray. Unroll dough into 2 long rectangles. Place in pan; press over bottom and ½ inch up sides to form crust. Bake 5 minutes.

2) Remove partially baked crust from oven. Sprinkle vanilla baking chips, chocolate chips, almonds and cashews evenly over crust. Pour sweetened condensed milk evenly over top.

3) Bake 20 to 25 minutes longer or until golden brown. Cool 10 minutes. Run knife around sides of pan to loosen. Cool 1 hour. Refrigerate 30 minutes or until chocolate is set. Cut into 6 rows by 6 rows.

HIGH ALTITUDE (3500-6500 FT.): No change.

Nutrition Information Per Serving:

Calories:	165	From Fat:	80
Total Fat			9g
Saturated Fat			4g
Cholesterol			5mg
Sodium			120mg
Total Carbohydrate			18g
Dietary Fiber			0g
Sugars			14g
Protein			3g

Bars like these that contain sweetened condensed milk can be stored at room temperature.

Soft and Chewy Chocolate Chip Cookies

PREP TIME: 55 MINUTES (READY IN 55 MINUTES)
SERVINGS: 6 DOZEN COOKIES

1¼ cups granulated sugar

1¼ cups packed brown sugar

1½ cups butter or margarine, softened

2 teaspoons vanilla

3 eggs

4¼ cups all-purpose flour

2 teaspoons baking soda

½ teaspoon salt

1 to 2 bags (12 oz each) semisweet chocolate chips (2 to 4 cups)

1) Heat oven to 375°F. In large bowl with electric mixer, beat granulated sugar, brown sugar and butter until light and fluffy. Beat in vanilla and eggs until well blended. Beat in flour, baking soda and salt. Stir in chocolate chips.

2) On ungreased cookie sheets, drop dough by rounded tablespoonfuls 2 inches apart.

3) Bake 8 to 10 minutes or until light golden brown. Cool 1 minute; remove from cookie sheets to cooling racks.

HIGH ALTITUDE (3500-6500 FT.): Bake 9-11 min.

Nutrition Information Per Serving:	
Calories: 120	From Fat: 50
Total Fat	6g
Saturated Fat	3.5g
Trans Fat	0g
Cholesterol	20mg
Sodium	85mg
Total Carbohydrate	16g
Dietary Fiber	0g
Sugars	10g
Protein	1g

Candy Bar Fudge Jumbles

PREP TIME: 25 MINUTES (READY IN 3 HOURS 5 MINUTES)
SERVINGS. 3 DOZEN BARS

1¼ cups packed brown sugar

¾ cup butter or margarine, softened

½ teaspoon vanilla

1 egg

1½ cups quick-cooking oats

1½ cups all-purpose flour

½ teaspoon baking soda

¼ teaspoon salt

1½ cups semisweet chocolate chips (9 oz)

1 can (14 oz) sweetened condensed milk (not evaporated)

5 bars (2.07 oz each) milk chocolate-covered peanut, caramel and nougat candy, chopped (about 2 cups)

1) Heat oven to 350°F. In large bowl, beat brown sugar and butter with electric mixer on medium speed until blended. Beat in vanilla and egg. On low speed, beat in oats, flour, baking soda and salt until well blended. Reserve ¾ cup mixture for topping. Press remaining mixture in bottom of ungreased 13x9-inch pan.

2) In 2-quart saucepan, heat chocolate chips and condensed milk over medium heat for about 5 minutes, stirring frequently, until chips are melted and mixture is smooth. Pour over crust.

3) Sprinkle chopped candy bars evenly over chocolate mixture. Crumble reserved oat mixture over candy.

4) Bake 32 to 37 minutes or until golden brown and set. Cool on cooling rack at least 2 hours. For bars, cut into 6 rows by 6 rows.

HIGH ALTITUDE (3500-6500 FT.): No change.

Nutrition Information Per Serving:	
Calories: 210	From Fat: 80
Total Fat	9g
Saturated Fat	5g
Trans Fat	0g
Cholesterol	20mg
Sodium	100mg
Total Carbohydrate	29g
Dietary Fiber	1g
Sugars	22g
Protein	3g

Peanut-Marshmallow-Chocolate Chip Bars

PREP TIME: 10 MINUTES (READY IN 1 HOUR 5 MINUTES)
SERVINGS: 2 DOZEN BARS

EASY

1 roll (18 oz) Pillsbury® refrigerated chocolate chip cookies

1 cup crisp rice cereal

1 cup miniature marshmallows

½ cup peanut butter chips

½ cup coarsely chopped salted peanuts

Nutrition Information Per Serving:

Calories:	150	From Fat:	70
Total Fat		8g	
Saturated Fat		2g	
Trans Fat		1g	
Cholesterol		0mg	
Sodium		115mg	
Total Carbohydrate		18g	
Dietary Fiber		0g	
Sugars		10g	
Protein		2g	

1) Heat oven to 350°F. In ungreased 13x9-inch pan, break up cookie dough. With floured fingers, press dough evenly in bottom of pan to form crust.

2) Sprinkle with remaining ingredients; lightly press into dough.

3) Bake 16 to 25 minutes or until golden brown. Cool completely on wire rack, about 30 minutes. Cut into 6 rows by 4 rows.

HIGH ALTITUDE (3500-6500 FT.):
Bake 19 to 24 minutes.

Confetti Rocky Road Bars

PREP TIME: 20 MINUTES (READY IN 2 HOURS 20 MINUTES)
SERVINGS: 3 DOZEN BARS

EASY

1 roll (18 oz) Pillsbury® refrigerated sugar cookies

3 cups miniature marshmallows

1½ cups miniature creme-filled chocolate sandwich cookies, halved or coarsely broken

1 cup semisweet chocolate chips (6 oz)

¾ cup salted peanuts

⅓ cup miniature candy-coated chocolate pieces

Nutrition Information Per Serving:

Calories:	150	From Fat:	60
Total Fat		7g	
Saturated Fat		2.5g	
Trans Fat		1g	
Cholesterol		0mg	
Sodium		85mg	
Total Carbohydrate		20g	
Dietary Fiber		0g	
Sugars		12g	
Protein		2g	

1) Heat oven to 350°F. In ungreased 13x9-inch pan, break up cookie dough. With floured fingers, press dough evenly in pan.

2) Bake 13 to 16 minutes or until light golden brown.

3) Immediately sprinkle marshmallows evenly over crust. Sprinkle with half of the cookies. Sprinkle with all of the chocolate chips, peanuts and candy-coated chocolate pieces. Sprinkle with remaining cookies; press lightly into marshmallows.

4) Bake 4 to 5 minutes longer or until marshmallows begin to puff. Cool completely on wire rack, about 2 hours. Cut into 6 rows by 6 rows.

HIGH ALTITUDE (3500-6500 FT.): Knead 2 tablespoons flour into cookie dough before pressing in pan. In Step 2, bake 15 to 18 minutes.

Almond Tree Cookies

PREP TIME: 1 HOUR 30 MINUTES (READY IN 1 HOUR 30 MINUTES)
SERVINGS: 4 DOZEN COOKIES

COOKIES

1 cup butter or margarine, softened

1/2 cup granulated sugar

1/2 teaspoon almond extract

2 cups all-purpose flour

FROSTING

1 cup powdered sugar

2 tablespoons butter or margarine, softened

1 to 2 tablespoons milk

8 or 10 drops green food color

1) Heat oven to 350°F. In medium bowl, beat 1 cup butter, the granulated sugar and almond extract with electric mixer on medium speed until smooth. On low speed, beat in flour.

2) Shape the dough into 1-inch balls; place 2 inches apart on an ungreased cookie sheets.

3) Bake 12 to 15 minutes or until firm to the touch. Cool 1 minute; remove from cookie sheets to cooling racks. Cool completely, about 30 minutes.

4) In small bowl, beat powdered sugar, 2 tablespoons butter and the milk on medium speed until smooth and spreadable. Stir in green food color until uniform color.

5) Spoon frosting into resealable food-storage plastic bag. Seal bag; cut off tiny corner of bag. Squeeze bag to make tree shape in a zigzag pattern on each cookie with frosting.

HIGH ALTITUDE (3500-6500 FT.): No change.

Nutrition Information Per Serving:		
Calories: 80	From Fat:	40
Total Fat		4.5g
Saturated Fat		3g
Trans Fat		0g
Cholesterol		10mg
Sodium		30mg
Total Carbohydrate		9g
Dietary Fiber		0g
Sugars		5g
Protein		0g

Cherry-Almond Fudge

PREP TIME: 30 MINUTES (READY IN 2 HOURS)
SERVINGS: 120 SQUARES

4$\frac{1}{2}$ cups sugar

$\frac{1}{2}$ cup butter

1 can (12 oz) evaporated milk (1$\frac{1}{2}$ cups)

4$\frac{1}{2}$ cups miniature marshmallows

1 bag (12 oz) semisweet chocolate chips

12 oz sweet baking chocolate, cut into pieces

2 oz unsweetened chocolate, cut into pieces

2 teaspoons vanilla

$\frac{1}{4}$ teaspoon almond extract

1$\frac{1}{2}$ cups dried sweetened cherries

$\frac{1}{2}$ cup slivered almonds

$\frac{1}{2}$ cup chopped almonds

1) Line 15x10x1-inch pan with foil, extending foil over sides of pan; grease foil. In 5- to 6-quart saucepan, cook sugar, butter and evaporated milk over medium heat, stirring constantly, until sugar is dissolved. Heat to full boil, stirring constantly. Boil uncovered over medium heat without stirring 5 minutes.

2) Remove saucepan from heat. Add marshmallows; stir until melted. Add chocolate chips, sweet chocolate and unsweetened chocolate, stirring constantly until all chocolate is melted and mixture is smooth. Stir in vanilla, almond extract, cherries and slivered almonds. Quickly spread mixture in greased foil-lined pan. Sprinkle with chopped almonds; press almonds gently into fudge. Cool completely, about 1$\frac{1}{2}$ hours.

3) Remove fudge from pan by lifting foil; remove foil from sides of fudge. With long knife, cut fudge into squares.

HIGH ALTITUDE (3500-6500 FT.): No change.

Peanut Butter Fudge

PREP TIME: 30 MINUTES (READY IN 2 HOURS)
SERVINGS: 120 SQUARES

4$\frac{1}{2}$ cups sugar

$\frac{1}{2}$ cup butter

1 can (12 oz) evaporated milk (1$\frac{1}{2}$ cups)

4$\frac{1}{2}$ cups miniature marshmallows

1 bag (12 oz) semisweet chocolate chips

12 oz sweet baking chocolate, cut into pieces

2 oz unsweetened chocolate, cut into pieces

2 teaspoons vanilla

1 cup candy-coated peanut butter pieces

1 cup chopped peanuts

1) Line 15x10x1-inch pan with foil, extending foil over sides of pan; grease foil. In 5- to 6-quart saucepan, cook sugar, butter and evaporated milk over medium heat, stirring constantly, until sugar is dissolved. Heat to full boil, stirring constantly. Boil uncovered over medium heat without stirring 5 minutes.

2) Remove saucepan from heat. Add marshmallows; stir until melted. Add chocolate chips, sweet chocolate and unsweetened chocolate, stirring constantly until all chocolate is melted and mixture is smooth. Stir in vanilla, candy-coated peanut butter pieces and peanuts. Quickly spread mixture in greased foil-lined pan. Sprinkle with colored sugar. Cool completely, about 1$\frac{1}{2}$ hours.

3) Remove fudge from pan by lifting foil; remove foil from sides of fudge. With long knife, cut fudge into squares.

HIGH ALTITUDE (3500-6500 FT.): No change.

Triple Chocolate Fudge

PREP TIME: 30 MINUTES (READY IN 2 HOURS)
SERVINGS: 120 SQUARES

4½ cups sugar

½ cup butter

1 can (12 oz) evaporated milk (1½ cups)

4½ cups miniature marshmallows

1 bag (12 oz) semisweet chocolate chips

12 oz sweet baking chocolate, cut into pieces

2 oz unsweetened chocolate, cut into pieces

2 teaspoons vanilla

¼ teaspoon almond extract

1 cup chopped walnuts or pecans

Colored sugar, if desired

1) Line 15x10x1-inch pan with foil, extending foil over sides of pan; grease foil. In 5- to 6-quart saucepan, cook sugar, butter and evaporated milk over medium heat, stirring constantly, until sugar is dissolved. Heat to full boil, stirring constantly. Boil uncovered over medium heat without stirring 5 minutes.

2) Remove saucepan from heat. Add marshmallows; stir until melted. Add chocolate chips, sweet chocolate and unsweetened chocolate, stirring constantly until all chocolate is melted and mixture is smooth. Stir in vanilla, almond extract and walnuts. Quickly spread mixture in greased foil-lined pan. Sprinkle with colored sugar. Cool completely, about 1½ hours.

3) Remove fudge from pan by lifting foil; remove foil from sides of fudge. With long knife, cut fudge into squares.

HIGH ALTITUDE (3500-6500 FT.): No change.

Nutrition Information Per Serving:

Calories: 90	From Fat: 30
Total Fat	3.5g
Saturated Fat	2g
Trans Fat	0g
Cholesterol	0mg
Sodium	10mg
Total Carbohydrate	13g
Dietary Fiber	0g
Sugars	12g
Protein	0g

Candy Fudge

PREP TIME: 30 MINUTES (READY IN 2 HOURS)
SERVINGS: 120 SQUARES

4½ cups sugar

½ cup butter

1 can (12 oz) evaporated milk (1½ cups)

4½ cups miniature marshmallows

1 bag (12 oz) semisweet chocolate chips

12 oz sweet baking chocolate, cut into pieces

2 oz unsweetened chocolate, cut into pieces

2 teaspoons vanilla

¼ teaspoon almond extract

1½ cups regular or miniature candy-coated chocolate pieces

1) Line 15x10x1-inch pan with foil, extending foil over sides of pan; grease foil. In 5- to 6-quart saucepan, cook sugar, butter and evaporated milk over medium heat, stirring constantly, until sugar is dissolved. Heat to full boil, stirring constantly. Boil uncovered over medium heat without stirring 5 minutes.

2) Remove saucepan from heat. Add marshmallows; stir until melted. Add chocolate chips, sweet chocolate and unsweetened chocolate, stirring constantly until all chocolate is melted and mixture is smooth. Stir in vanilla, almond extract and walnuts. Quickly spread mixture in greased foil-lined pan. Sprinkle with colored sugar. Cool completely, about 1½ hours.

3) Remove fudge from pan by lifting foil; remove foil from sides of fudge. With long knife, cut fudge into squares.

HIGH ALTITUDE (3500-6500 FT.): No change.

Dulce de Leche Bars

PREP TIME: 20 MINUTES (READY IN 1 HOUR 35 MINUTES)
SERVINGS: 32 BARS

 EASY

1½ cups all-purpose flour

1½ cups quick-cooking or old-fashioned oats

1 cup packed brown sugar

¼ teaspoon salt

1 cup butter or margarine, softened

1 can (13.4 oz) dulce de leche

1 cup toffee bits

1) Heat oven to 350°F. In large bowl, mix flour, oats, brown sugar and salt. With pastry blender or fork, cut in butter until mixture is crumbly. Press ¾ of mixture in ungreased 13x9-inch pan.

2) Bake 10 minutes. Meanwhile, in 1-quart saucepan, heat dulce de leche over low heat 2 to 4 minutes, stirring frequently, until slightly softened.

3) Spread dulce de leche over partially baked crust. Sprinkle evenly with toffee bits and remaining crumb mixture. Bake 20 to 25 minutes or until golden brown. Cool 15 minutes.

4) Run knife around sides of pan to loosen bars. Cool completely, about 30 minutes. Cut into 8 rows by 4 rows.

HIGH ALTITUDE (3500-6500 FT.): Decrease butter to 1/2 cup. In Step 2, heat dulce de leche over medium-low heat 4 to 6 minutes.

Nutrition Information Per Serving:

Calories: 210	From Fat: 90
Total Fat	10g
Saturated Fat	6g
Trans Fat	0g
Cholesterol	25mg
Sodium	90mg
Total Carbohydrate	27g
Dietary Fiber	0g
Sugars	19g
Protein	2g

Spooky Spider Web Cookie

PREP TIME: 40 MINUTES (READY IN 1 HOUR 20 MINUTES)
SERVINGS: 16

1 roll (16.5 oz) Pillsbury® Create 'n Bake™ refrigerated chocolate chip cookies

⅓ cup unsweetened baking cocoa

½ cup vanilla creamy ready-to-spread frosting (from 1-lb container)

5 drops red food color

9 drops yellow food color

7 large black gumdrops

1) Heat oven to 350°F. Line 12-inch pizza pan with foil; grease foil. In large bowl, break up cookie dough. Stir or knead in cocoa until well blended. With floured fingers, press dough in pan to form crust. Bake 11 to 13 minutes or until edges are set. Cool completely, about 30 minutes.

2) In 1-quart saucepan over low heat, melt frosting, stirring constantly. Stir in 5 drops red and 9 drops yellow food color to make orange color.

3) Place frosting in small resealable food storage plastic bag; partially seal bag. Cut small hole in bottom corner of bag. Squeeze bag in spiral pattern, starting from center of cookie. Starting at center, quickly pull edge of knife outward through frosting at 1-inch intervals to make web design. Let stand 15 minutes or until set.

4) Meanwhile, on generously sugared surface, press 4 gumdrops into 2-inch rounds. Slice each thinly into 6 pieces; roll and shape to resemble spider legs. Place remaining 3 gumdrops on spider web to resemble spiders; arrange 8 legs around each spider.

HIGH ALTITUDE (3500-6500 FT.): No change.

Nutrition Information Per Serving:

Calories: 220	From Fat: 90
Total Fat	10g
Saturated Fat	3g
Trans Fat	2g
Cholesterol	0mg
Sodium	125mg
Total Carbohydrate	30g
Dietary Fiber	1g
Sugars	19g
Protein	1g

Lemon Mardi Gras Squares

MRS. JOSEPH NEGROTTO | NEW ORLEANS, LOUISIANA

BAKE-OFF® CONTEST 04,1952

PREP TIME: 40 MINUTES (READY IN 2 HOURS 15 MINUTES)
SERVINGS: 2 DOZEN BARS

BARS

1½ cups all-purpose flour

½ teaspoon salt

¼ teaspoon baking powder

1 cup powdered sugar

1 cup granulated sugar

½ cup butter or margarine, softened

3 eggs

⅓ cup lemon juice

2 tablespoons grated lemon peel

½ cup chopped pecans

FROSTING

1 cup powdered sugar

2 tablespoons butter or margarine, softened

1 tablespoon half-and-half or milk

GARNISH

¼ cup chopped pecans

Lemon slices, if desired

1) Heat oven to 400°F. Generously grease 13x9-inch pan with shortening, lightly flour; or spray with nonstick cooking spray. In small bowl, stir together flour, salt and baking powder; set aside.

2) In large bowl, beat powdered sugar, granulated sugar and butter with electric mixer on medium speed, scraping bowl occasionally, until blended. Beat in 1 egg at a time until blended. Beat 1 minute longer. On low speed, beat in flour mixture alternately with lemon juice, beginning and ending with flour mixture, until well blended. Stir in lemon peel and ½ cup pecans. Pour into pan.

3) Bake 22 to 27 minutes or until golden brown. Meanwhile, in small bowl, beat frosting ingredients on low speed until smooth and spreadable.

4) Spread frosting over warm bars. Sprinkle with ¼ cup pecans. Cool completely in pan on cooling rack, about 1 hour. Cut into 6 rows by 4 rows. Garnish with lemon slices.

HIGH ALTITUDE (3500-6500 FT.): No change.

Nutrition Information Per Serving:		
Calories: 180	From Fat:	70
Total Fat		8g
Saturated Fat		3.5g
Trans Fat		0g
Cholesterol		40mg
Sodium		95mg
Total Carbohydrate		25g
Dietary Fiber		0g
Sugars		18g
Protein		2g

Hoot Owl Cookies

PREP TIME: 1 HOUR (READY IN 2 HOURS)
SERVINGS: 3-1/2 TO 4 DOZEN COOKIES

COOKIES

1 cup packed brown sugar

¾ cup butter or margarine, softened

1 teaspoon vanilla

1 egg

2¼ cups all-purpose flour

2 teaspoons baking powder

½ teaspoon salt

1½ oz unsweetened baking chocolate, melted

¼ teaspoon baking soda

GARNISH

96 semisweet chocolate chips (about ⅓ cup)

48 whole cashews (about ⅔ cup)

1) In large bowl, beat brown sugar and butter with electric mixer on medium speed 1 to 2 minutes or until light and fluffy. Beat in vanilla and egg until well blended. Beat in flour, baking powder and salt until well blended. Place 1 cup of dough in small bowl; blend in melted chocolate and baking soda.

2) On 12x8-inch sheet of plastic wrap, press half of light dough to form 10x4-inch strip. Shape half of chocolate dough into roll 10 inches long; place on strip of light dough. Mold sides of light dough around chocolate dough; wrap in plastic wrap. Repeat with remaining dough. Refrigerate 1 hour for easier handling.

3) Heat oven to 350°F. Cut dough into ⅛- to ¼-inch slices; place 2 slices, sides touching, on ungreased cookie sheets to resemble owl faces. Pinch corner of each slice to form ears. Place chocolate chip in center of each slice for eyes; press whole cashew between slices for beak.

4) Bake 8 to 10 minutes or until edges are light golden brown. Immediately remove from cookie sheets to cooling racks. Cool completely, about 15 minutes.

HIGH ALTITUDE (3500-6500 FT.): Decrease brown sugar to 3/4 cup; increase flour to 2-1/2 cups.

Nutrition Information Per Serving:		
Calories: 100	From Fat: 50	
Total Fat		5g
Saturated Fat		3g
Trans Fat		0g
Cholesterol		15mg
Sodium		90mg
Total Carbohydrate		12g
Dietary Fiber		0g
Sugars		6g
Protein		1g

Cowardly Lion Cookies

PREP TIME: 1 HOUR 10 MINUTES (READY IN 1 HOUR 10 MINUTES)
SERVINGS: 32 COOKIES

1 roll (16.5 oz) Pillsbury® Create 'n Bake™ refrigerated peanut butter cookies

1/4 cup sugar

2 tablespoons miniature candy-coated chocolate baking bits

1 cup chow mein noodles

Brown decorating gel

Nutrition Information Per Serving:	
Calories: 100	From Fat: 30
Total Fat	3.5g
Saturated Fat	1g
Trans Fat	0.5g
Cholesterol	0mg
Sodium	80mg
Total Carbohydrate	15g
Dietary Fiber	0g
Sugars	10g
Protein	1g

1) Heat oven to 350°F. Shape teaspoons of dough into 32 (1-inch) balls; roll in sugar. Place 1 inch apart on ungreased cookie sheets. Press with the bottom of glass to flatten.

2) Arrange baking bits to resemble eyes and nose. Arrange chow mein noodles around top edge of each cookie to resemble mane and a few to resemble whiskers.

3) Bake 9 to 13 minutes or until edges are light golden brown. Cool 1 minute; remove from cookie sheets. Cool completely, about 15 minutes. Pipe decorating gel on each cookie to resemble mouth.

HIGH ALTITUDE (3500-6500 FT.): Bake 7 to 9 minutes.

Rolled Sugar Cookies

PREP TIME: 1 HOUR 25 MINUTES (READY IN 2 HOURS 40 MINUTES)
SERVINGS: 6 DOZEN   LOW FAT

COOKIES

1 cup sugar

1 cup butter or margarine, softened

3 tablespoons milk

1 teaspoon vanilla

1 egg

3 cups all-purpose flour

1 1/2 teaspoons baking powder

1/2 teaspoon salt

Granulated or colored sugar, if desired

GLAZE, IF DESIRED

1 1/2 cups powdered sugar

3 to 3 1/2 tablespoons milk

1) In large bowl, mix 1 cup granulated sugar, the butter, milk, vanilla and egg until well blended. Stir in flour, baking powder and salt until mixed. Cover with plastic wrap; refrigerate 1 hour for easier handling.

2) Heat oven to 400°F. On lightly floured surface, roll out 1/3 of dough at a time to 1/8-inch thickness. Keep remaining dough refrigerated. Cut with floured 2-inch cookie cutter. Place 1 inch apart on ungreased cookie sheets. If not using glaze, sprinkle with sugar.

3) Bake 5 to 9 minutes or until edges are light golden brown. Immediately remove from cookie sheets to cooling racks. Cool completely, about 15 minutes.

4) In small bowl, mix powdered sugar and enough milk with spoon until smooth and spreadable. Spread glaze over cookies. Sprinkle with colored sugar.

Nutrition Information Per Serving:	
Calories: 50	From Fat: 25
Total Fat	2.5g
Saturated Fat	1.5g
Trans Fat	0g
Cholesterol	10mg
Sodium	45mg
Total Carbohydrate	7g
Dietary Fiber	0g
Sugars	3g
Protein	0g

HIGH ALTITUDE (3500-6500 FT.): No change.

Rocky Road Fudge Bars

MARY WILSON | LEESBURG, GEORGIA

Pillsbury **Bake-Off®**

BAKE-OFF® CONTEST 23, 1972 | PRIZE WINNER

PREP TIME: 30 MINUTES (READY IN 1 HOUR 10 MINUTES
SERVINGS: 4 DOZEN BARS

BASE

½ cup margarine or butter

1 oz unsweetened chocolate, cut up

1 cup all-purpose flour

1 cup sugar

1 teaspoon baking powder

1 teaspoon vanilla

2 eggs

¾ cup chopped nuts

FILLING

1 package (8 oz) cream cheese, softened, reserving 2 oz for frosting

¼ cup margarine or butter, softened

½ cup sugar

2 tablespoons all-purpose flour

½ teaspoon vanilla

1 egg

¼ cup chopped nuts

1 package (6 oz) semisweet chocolate chips (1 cup)

FROSTING

2 cups miniature marshmallows

¼ cup margarine or butter

¼ cup milk

1 oz unsweetened chocolate, cut up

2 oz reserved cream cheese

3 cups powdered sugar, sifted

1 teaspoon vanilla

1) Heat oven to 350°F. Grease and flour 13x9-inch pan. In large saucepan, melt ½ cup margarine and 1 oz. unsweetened chocolate over low heat, stirring until smooth. Stir in 1 cup flour and remaining base ingredients; mix well. Spread into greased and floured pan.

2) In small bowl, combine all filling ingredients except ¼ cup nuts and chocolate chips. Beat 1 minute at medium speed until smooth and fluffy; stir in nuts. Spread over chocolate mixture; sprinkle evenly with chocolate chips.

3) Bake for 25 to 35 minutes or until toothpick inserted in center comes out clean. Immediately sprinkle marshmallows over top. Bake for an additional 2 minutes.

4) Meanwhile, in large saucepan over low heat, combine ¼ cup margarine, milk, 1 oz. unsweetened chocolate and reserved 2 oz. cream cheese; stir until well blended. Remove from heat; stir in powdered sugar and 1 teaspoon vanilla until smooth. Immediately pour frosting over marshmallows and lightly swirl with knife to marble. Refrigerate until firm; cut into bars. Store in refrigerator.

HIGH ALTITUDE (3500-6500 FT.): No change.

These fudgy bars can be placed in foil baking cups if desired for a hostess gift or a fun presentation on a cookie tray.

White Chocolate-Cashew-Pretzel Bars

PREP TIME: 25 MINUTES (READY IN 1 HOUR 40 MINUTES)
SERVINGS: 3 DOZEN BARS

- 1 roll (18 oz) Pillsbury® refrigerated sugar cookies
- 1 bag (12 oz) white chocolate chunks or white vanilla baking chips
- 1 cup coarsely chopped pretzel sticks or twists
- 1½ cups semisweet chocolate chips (9 oz)
- ¼ cup peanut butter
- 1 cup chopped cashews

Nutrition Information Per Serving:

Calories:	190	From Fat:	90
Total Fat			11g
Saturated Fat			4.5g
Trans Fat			0.5g
Cholesterol			0mg
Sodium			95mg
Total Carbohydrate			21g
Dietary Fiber			0g
Sugars			15g
Protein			3g

1) Heat oven to 350°F. Spray 13x9-inch pan with nonstick cooking spray. Break up cookie dough into pan. With floured fingers, press dough evenly in bottom of pan to form crust. Sprinkle 1 cup of the white chocolate chunks and the pretzels over dough; lightly press into dough.

2) Bake 16 to 20 minutes or until light golden brown. Cool completely on wire rack, about 30 minutes.

3) In small microwavable bowl, place ¼ cup of the white chocolate chunks; set aside. In large microwavable bowl, microwave remaining white chocolate chunks and the chocolate chips on High 2 minutes, stirring every 30 seconds, until melted and smooth. If necessary, microwave 30 seconds longer. Stir in peanut butter and cashews. Spread mixture evenly over cooled baked crust. Refrigerate until chocolate is set, about 15 minutes.

4) Microwave reserved ¼ cup white chocolate chunks on High 30 seconds; stir until melted and smooth. If necessary, microwave 10 seconds longer. Drizzle over bars. Let stand until set, about 10 minutes. Cut into 6 rows by 6 rows.

HIGH ALTITUDE (3500-6500 FT.): No change.

Pistachio Brittle

PREP TIME: 45 MINUTES (READY IN 1 HOUR 45 MINUTES)
SERVINGS: 64 PIECES

- 2 cups sugar
- 1 cup light corn syrup
- ½ cup water
- 1 cup butter
- 2 cups salted shelled pistachios
- 1 teaspoon baking soda

Nutrition Information Per Serving:

Calories:	90	From Fat:	40
Total Fat			4.5g
Saturated Fat			2g
Trans Fat			0g
Cholesterol			10mg
Sodium			45mg
Total Carbohydrate			11g
Dietary Fiber			0g
Sugars			8g
Protein			0g

1) Heat oven to 200°F. Grease 2 cookie sheets. In heavy 5- to 6-quart saucepan, place sugar, corn syrup and water. Heat to boiling over medium heat, stirring frequently. Stir in butter.

2) Cook over medium heat, stirring occasionally for about 10 minutes until candy thermometer reaches 240°F. Meanwhile, place cookie sheets in oven. (Warm cookie sheets allow the candy to spread easily before it sets up.)

3) Stir pistachios into sugar mixture; continue cooking, stirring frequently, until candy thermometer reaches 300°F. Remove from heat; stir in baking soda (mixture will be light and foamy).

4) Remove cookie sheets from oven; pour candy onto cookie sheets. With buttered spatula, spread until candy is about ¼-inch thick. Cool completely, about 1 hour. Break into pieces. Store in tightly covered container.

HIGH ALTITUDE (3500-6500 FT.): In Step 3, cook until thermometer reaches 290°F.

Ice Cream Sandwich Bars

PREP TIME: 15 MINUTES (READY IN 12 HOURS 15 MINUTES)
SERVINGS: 9

EASY

1 roll (18 oz) Pillsbury® refrigerated chocolate chip cookies

1 quart (4 cups) strawberry ice cream or favorite flavor, slightly softened

Nutrition Information Per Serving:

Calories:	400	From Fat:	190
Total Fat			21g
Saturated Fat			8g
Trans Fat			2.5g
Cholesterol			35mg
Sodium			230mg
Total Carbohydrate			49g
Dietary Fiber			2g
Sugars			31g
Protein			4g

1) Heat oven to 350°F. Line two 8-inch square pans with foil, so foil extends over sides of pans. Cut cookie dough into slices; place half of slices in bottom of each pan. Press dough evenly in pans.

2) Bake 10 to 12 minutes or until light golden brown. Cool in pans on wire racks 15 minutes. Remove cookie layers from pans by lifting foil. Cool completely, about 30 minutes.

3) Remove foil from one cookie layer; place top side down in one of the pans. Spoon ice cream evenly over cookie layer; smooth top with metal spatula.

4) Remove foil from second cookie layer; score top into 9 squares, without cutting all the way through. Place top side up over ice cream; firmly press onto ice cream. Cover pan tightly with foil; freeze until firm, about 3 hours.

5) Cut into 9 sandwich bars using scored lines as guide. Remove from pan; wrap individually in plastic wrap. Freeze at least 8 hours before serving or up to 3 weeks.

HIGH ALTITUDE (3500-6500 FT.): In Step 1, divide dough in half. Add 2 tablespoons all-purpose flour to one half and knead into dough. Repeat with second half of dough. Bake 12 to 14 minutes.

Lemon-Go-Lightly Cookies

MARGARET CONWAY | OCEANO, CALIFORNIA

Pillsbury Bake-Off

BAKE-OFF® CONTEST 27,1976 | PRIZE WINNER

PREP TIME: 20 MINUTES (READY IN 1 HOUR)
SERVINGS: 6 DOZEN COOKIES

EASY

2 cups all-purpose flour

2 cups mashed potato flakes

1 cup sugar

1 cup firmly packed brown sugar

1/2 to 3/4 cup finely chopped nuts

1 teaspoon baking soda

3/4 cup margarine or butter, melted

1 teaspoon grated lemon peel

2 eggs

1/4 cup sugar

1) Heat oven to 350°F. In large bowl, combine all ingredients except 1/4 cup sugar; blend well. (Mixture will be crumbly.) Firmly press into 1-inch balls; roll in 1/4 cup sugar. Place 2 inches apart on ungreased cookie sheets.

2) Bake for 9 to 12 minutes or until golden brown. Cool 1 minute; remove from cookie sheets.

HIGH ALTITUDE (3500-6500 FT.): No change.

Fudgy-Caramel Cashew Brownies

PREP TIME: 25 MINUTES (READY IN 2 HOURS 25 MINUTES)
SERVINGS: 3 DOZEN BROWNIES

3 oz bittersweet baking chocolate, chopped

1 cup butter

1 bag (12 oz) semisweet chocolate chips

4 eggs

1½ cups sugar

2 teaspoons vanilla

1 cup all-purpose flour

1 teaspoon baking powder

½ teaspoon salt

20 creme-filled chocolate sandwich cookies, crushed

40 round chewy caramels in milk chocolate (packaged in gold foil), unwrapped, each cut in half

¾ cup coarsely chopped roasted cashews

1) Heat oven to 350°F (325°F for dark pan). Grease and flour 13x9-inch pan. In 1-quart microwavable bowl, place bittersweet chocolate, butter and 1 cup of the chocolate chips. Microwave on High 1½ to 2 minutes, stirring twice, until melted and smooth. Cool slightly, about 5 minutes.

2) In large bowl with electric mixer, beat eggs, sugar and vanilla on medium speed until smooth. Add cooled chocolate mixture. Beat until well blended. Add flour, baking powder and salt. Beat on low speed until blended. By hand, stir in cookies and remaining chocolate chips. Pour into pan.

3) Bake 35 to 40 minutes or until edges begin to pull away from sides and center is set. Do not overbake. Immediately sprinkle candy on top of hot brownies. Let stand 10 minutes or until completely softened. Pull tip of toothpick through softened candy to spread and swirl. (It won't completely cover top.) Sprinkle with cashews. Cool until set, about 1 hour. Cut into 6 rows by 6 rows.

HIGH ALTITUDE (3500-6500 FT.): Decrease butter to 3/4 cup, sugar to 1-1/4 cups and baking powder to 1/2 teaspoon. Bake 40 to 45 minutes.

Nutrition Information Per Serving:	
Calories: 240	From Fat: 120
Total Fat	14g
Saturated Fat	7g
Trans Fat	0.5g
Cholesterol	40mg
Sodium	150mg
Total Carbohydrate	27g
Dietary Fiber	2g
Sugars	20g
Protein	3g

Halloween Party Pops

PREP TIME: 1 HOUR 15 MINUTES (READY IN 2 HOURS 15 MINUTES)
SERVINGS: 16 COOKIE POPS

COOKIES

1 roll (16.5 oz) Pillsbury® Create 'n Bake™ refrigerated sugar cookies

16 flat wooden sticks with rounded ends

WHITE FROSTING

1 cup powdered sugar

1 tablespoon milk

1 tablespoon butter or margarine, softened

CHOCOLATE FROSTING

1 cup powdered sugar

2 tablespoons unsweetened baking cocoa

1 to 2 tablespoons milk

1 tablespoon butter or margarine, softened

Assorted candies (gumdrops, candy sprinkles, etc.)

1) Freeze cookie dough for 1 hour.

2) Heat oven to 350°F. Cut frozen dough into 16 (½-inch) slices; roll each into ball. Arrange in circle on ungreased cookie sheets, 3 inches apart and 2 inches from edges. Securely insert a wooden stick into each ball with end pointing toward center of cookie sheet.

3) Bake 10 to 14 minutes or until golden brown. Cool 2 minutes; remove from cookie sheet to cooling rack. Cool completely, about 15 minutes.

4) In small bowl, mix all white frosting ingredients until smooth. If necessary, add additional milk 1 drop at a time for desired consistency.

5) In another small bowl, mix all chocolate frosting ingredients except assorted candies until smooth. If necessary, add additional milk 1 drop at a time for desired consistency.

6) Frost half of cookies with white frosting; frost remaining cookies with chocolate frosting. Arrange candies on frosted cookies to create jack-o'-lanterns, owls or ghosts.

HIGH ALTITUDE (3500-6500 FT.): Bake 14 to 18 minutes.

Nutrition Information Per Serving:		
Calories: 250	From Fat:	60
Total Fat		7g
Saturated Fat		2.5g
Trans Fat		1.5g
Cholesterol		15mg
Sodium		95mg
Total Carbohydrate		45g
Dietary Fiber		0g
Sugars		31g
Protein		1g

Spider Web Cookies

PREP TIME: 1 HOUR 15 MINUTES (READY IN 2 HOURS 15 MINUTES)
SERVINGS: 16 COOKIE POPS

COOKIES

1 roll (16.5 oz) Pillsbury® Create 'n Bake™ refrigerated sugar cookies

16 flat wooden sticks with rounded ends

WHITE FROSTING

1 cup powdered sugar

1 tablespoon milk

1 tablespoon butter or margarine, softened

CHOCOLATE FROSTING

1 cup powdered sugar

2 tablespoons unsweetened baking cocoa

1 to 2 tablespoons milk

1 tablespoon butter or margarine, softened

1) Freeze cookie dough for 1 hour.

2) Heat oven to 350°F. Cut frozen dough into 16 (½-inch) slices; roll each into ball. Arrange in circle on ungreased cookie sheets, 3 inches apart and 2 inches from edges. Securely insert a wooden stick into each ball with end pointing toward center of cookie sheet.

3) Bake 10 to 14 minutes or until golden brown. Cool 2 minutes; remove from cookie sheet to cooling rack. Cool completely, about 15 minutes.

4) In small bowl, mix all white frosting ingredients until smooth. If necessary, add additional milk 1 drop at a time for desired consistency.

5) In another small bowl, mix all chocolate frosting ingredients except assorted candies until smooth. If necessary, add additional milk 1 drop at a time for desired consistency.

6) Frost cookies with chocolate frosting. Spoon white frosting in small resealable food-storage plastic bag. Seal bag and cut tiny hole in bottom corner. Over each cookie, squeeze bag to draw coil of white frosting over the chocolate frosting. Drag toothpick through coil from center out for web.

HIGH ALTITUDE (3500-6500 FT.): Bake 14 to 18 minutes.

Black Cat Cookie Pops

PREP TIME: 1 HOUR 15 MINUTES (READY IN 2 HOURS 15 MINUTES)
SERVINGS: 16 COOKIE POPS

COOKIES

1 roll (16.5 oz) Pillsbury® Create 'n Bake™ refrigerated sugar cookies

16 flat wooden sticks with rounded ends

ORANGE FROSTING

1 cup powdered sugar

1 tablespoon milk

1 tablespoon butter or margarine, softened

2 drops yellow food color

1 drop red food color

16 large black gumdrops

1) Freeze cookie dough for 1 hour.

2) Heat oven to 350°F. Cut frozen dough into 16 (½-inch) slices; roll each into ball. Arrange in circle on ungreased cookie sheets, 3 inches apart and 2 inches from edges. Securely insert a wooden stick into each ball with end pointing toward center of cookie sheet.

3) Bake 10 to 14 minutes or until golden brown. Cool 2 minutes; remove from cookie sheet to cooling rack. Cool completely, about 15 minutes.

4) In small bowl, mix all frosting ingredients until smooth. If necessary, add additional milk 1 drop at a time for desired consistency.

5) For each cookie, slice a gumdrop into 3 round pieces. Use small end for head; use large piece for body. Cut ears and tail from third piece.

6) Arrange gumdrop pieces on frosted cookie to form cat.

HIGH ALTITUDE (3500-6500 FT.): Bake 14 to 18 minutes.

Easy Cookie Mix

| PREP TIME: | 10 MINUTES (READY IN 10 MINUTES) |
| SERVINGS: | 12 CUPS |

e EASY   **f** LOW FAT

7¾ cups all-purpose flour

2½ cups granulated sugar

2 cups powdered sugar

4 teaspoons baking powder

1 teaspoon salt

1) In 4-quart bowl, mix 3¾ cups of the flour and the remaining ingredients. Stir in remaining 4 cups flour.

2) Store in tightly covered container up to 3 months.

3) Use mix to make Glazed Peanut Butter Cups (below) and Old-World Jam Rounds (at right).

HIGH ALTITUDE (3500-6500 FT.): No change.

tip Make and bake your cookies with this mix before the holiday season starts. Freeze undecorated cookies for up to 2 months. Decorate before serving or giving as gifts.

Glazed Peanut Butter Cups

| PREP TIME: | 1 HOUR 30 MINUTES (READY IN 2 HOURS 15 MINUTES) |
| SERVINGS: | 4 DOZEN COOKIES |

COOKIES

2 cups Easy Cookie Mix (recipe above)

½ cup creamy peanut butter

⅓ cup butter, softened

1 egg

1 to 2 tablespoons milk, if needed

48 miniature milk chocolate-covered peanut butter cups, unwrapped

GLAZE

½ cup semisweet chocolate chips

2 teaspoons shortening

1) Heat oven to 350°F. Grease 48 mini muffin cups with shortening or nonstick cooking spray. Stir cookie mix before measuring. In large bowl, beat cookie mix, peanut butter, butter and egg with electric mixer on medium speed, scraping bowl occasionally, until dough forms; if needed, add 1 to 2 tablespoons milk.

2) Shape dough into 1-inch balls; place in muffin cups. Press 1 peanut butter cup into each ball.

3) Bake 13 to 18 minutes or until dough is set and golden brown around edges of candy. Cool 5 minutes; remove from pan. Cool completely, about 30 minutes.

4) In small microwavable bowl, microwave glaze ingredients on High 45 to 60 seconds, stirring once halfway through microwaving, until melted. If necessary, continue to microwave on High in 15-second increments, stirring until smooth. Drizzle glaze evenly over cooled cookies.

HIGH ALTITUDE (3500-6500 FT.): No change.

Nutrition Information Per Serving:		
Calories: 90	From Fat:	45
Total Fat		5g
Saturated Fat		2g
Trans Fat		0g
Cholesterol		10mg
Sodium		55mg
Total Carbohydrate		10g
Dietary Fiber		0g
Sugars		6g
Protein		2g

Old-World Jam Rounds

PREP TIME: 1 HOUR 35 MINUTES (READY IN 1 HOUR 35 MINUTES)
SERVINGS: 4 DOZEN COOKIES

COOKIES

- 3 cups Easy Cookie Mix (recipe at top left)
- 1 cup butter, softened
- 1 teaspoon vanilla
- 1 to 2 tablespoons milk, if needed
- 1/4 cup sugar
- 1/2 cup seedless raspberry jam

GLAZE

- 3 oz white chocolate baking bars (from 6-oz box)
- 3 to 4 teaspoons half-and-half or milk

1) Heat oven to 375°F. Stir cookie mix before measuring. In large bowl, beat cookie mix, butter and vanilla with electric mixer on medium speed about 1 minute, scraping bowl occasionally, until dough forms; if needed, add 1 to 2 tablespoons milk.

2) Shape dough into 1-inch balls and roll in sugar; place 2 inches apart on ungreased cookie sheets. With bottom of glass, flatten each until 1½ inches in diameter and about ¼ inch thick (if needed, dip bottom of glass into sugar before flattening).

3) Bake 8 to 11 minutes or until bottoms are lightly browned. Immediately spread about ½ teaspoon jam evenly onto each hot cookie. Remove from cookie sheets; place on wire racks. Cool completely, about 15 minutes.

4) In small microwavable bowl, microwave white chocolate and 2 teaspoons of the half-and-half on High 1 minute, stirring once halfway through microwaving, until white chocolate is melted. If necessary, continue to microwave on High in 15-second increments, stirring until smooth. If needed, stir in additional half-and-half until thin enough to drizzle. Drizzle glaze on cookies.

HIGH ALTITUDE (3500-6500 FT.): No change.

Nutrition Information Per Serving:

Calories: 90	From Fat:	40
Total Fat		4.5g
Saturated Fat		3g
Trans Fat		0g
Cholesterol		10mg
Sodium		55mg
Total Carbohydrate		12g
Dietary Fiber		0g
Sugars		8g
Protein		0g

FROZEN KEY LIME TORTE
PG. 330

After-Dinner Delights

There's always room for dessert, and these recipes make it easy to whip up a winner!

CARAMEL APPLE AND PEAR CRISP
PG. 337

CHOCOLATE CANDY CUPCAKES
PG. 341

TURTLE BROWNIE ICE CREAM
DESSERT
PG. 318

Coconut-Lemon Cream Tartlets

PREP TIME: 1 HOUR (READY IN 1 HOUR)
SERVINGS: 8

$^2/_3$ cup flaked coconut

1 box (15 oz) Pillsbury® refrigerated pie crusts, softened as directed on box

8 ($4^1/_2$x$1^1/_4$-inch) individual foil tart pans

2 teaspoons sugar

$1^1/_2$ cups whipping cream

1 jar (10 oz) lemon curd (1 cup)

$^1/_2$ cup fresh raspberries, if desired

tip

Look for lemon curd in jars next to the jams and jellies at your local supermarket. Before making whipped cream, chill the beaters and bowl in the freezer for about 15 minutes.

1) Heat oven to 350°F. On ungreased cookie sheet, spread coconut evenly. Bake 5 to 7 minutes, stirring occasionally, until light golden brown. Increase oven temperature to 450°F.

2) Remove pie crusts from pouches. Unroll crusts on work surface. With rolling pin, roll each crust lightly to form 12-inch round. Using an upside-down foil tart pan as a guide, cut four 5-inch rounds from each crust.

3) Reserve 2 tablespoons toasted coconut for topping. Sprinkle each crust round with about 1 tablespoon of the remaining coconut and ¼ teaspoon sugar; roll in lightly with rolling pin. Press each round, coconut side up, in bottom and up side of tart pan. Prick bottoms and sides with fork. Place pans on large cookie sheet.

4) Bake at 450°F for 7 to 9 minutes or until edges are light golden brown. Cool completely, about 15 minutes.

5) In large bowl, beat whipping cream with electric mixer on high speed until stiff peaks form. Place 2 cups of the whipped cream in medium bowl; fold in lemon curd until well combined. Spoon into cooled baked tart shells. Top each with dollop of remaining whipped cream. Garnish with fresh raspberries and reserved coconut. To serve, gently slide tarts out of pans; place on individual dessert plates. Store in refrigerator.

HIGH ALTITUDE (3500-6500 FT.): No change.

Nutrition Information Per Serving:

Calories:	450	From Fat:	280
Total Fat			31g
Saturated Fat			17g
Cholesterol			80mg
Sodium			310mg
Total Carbohydrate			40g
Dietary Fiber			0g
Sugars			15g
Protein			3g

Raspberry Fudge Torte

PREP TIME: 45 MINUTES (READY IN 3 HOURS 30 MINUTES)
SERVINGS: 12

CAKE

1 box (1 lb 2.25 oz) chocolate fudge cake mix with pudding

1 container (8 oz) sour cream

¾ cup water

⅓ cup oil

1 teaspoon vanilla

3 eggs

1 cup miniature semisweet chocolate chips

RASPBERRY CREAM

1 package (10 oz) frozen raspberries in syrup, thawed

2 tablespoons sugar

4 teaspoons cornstarch

½ cup whipping cream, whipped

FROSTING AND GARNISH

¾ cup chocolate creamy ready-to-spread frosting

½ pint (1 cup) fresh raspberries

1) Heat oven to 350°F (if using dark or nonstick pans, heat oven to 325°F). Grease and flour two 9-inch round cake pans. In large bowl, beat all cake ingredients except chocolate chips with electric mixer on low speed 30 seconds. Beat 2 minutes on medium speed. Stir in chocolate chips. Pour batter into pans.

2) Bake 30 to 40 minutes or until toothpick inserted in center comes out clean. Cool 15 minutes. Remove from pans; place on cooling racks. Cool completely, about 1 hour. (Wrap and freeze 1 cake layer for a later use.)

3) Meanwhile, to remove seeds from raspberries, place strainer over small saucepan; pour raspberries into strainer. Press raspberries through strainer with back of spoon to remove seeds; discard seeds. Stir sugar and cornstarch into raspberries until smooth. Cook over low heat until mixture is bubbly and thickened, stirring constantly. Boil 1 minute. Place waxed paper or plastic wrap over surface of mixture; refrigerate 30 minutes or until cold. Fold in whipped cream.

4) To assemble torte, place cake layer, top side down, on serving plate. Spread with thin layer of frosting. Top with raspberry cream, spreading to within ½ inch of edge. Frost sides of torte with remaining frosting. Refrigerate at least 1 hour before serving.

5) Just before serving, arrange raspberries around top edge of torte. If desired, garnish with additional fresh raspberries and mint sprigs. Store torte in refrigerator.

HIGH ALTITUDE (3500-6500 FT.): No change.

Nutrition Information Per Serving:	
Calories: 500	From Fat: 220
Total Fat	25g
Saturated Fat	10g
Trans Fat	2g
Cholesterol	75mg
Sodium	120mg
Total Carbohydrate	64g
Dietary Fiber	4g
Sugars	45g
Protein	5g

Three-Berry Cheesecake

PREP TIME: 45 MINUTES (READY IN 4 HOURS 35 MINUTES)
SERVINGS: 12

1 box (15 oz) Pillsbury® refrigerated pie crusts, softened as directed on box

2 tablespoons water

2 tablespoons coarse sugar

2 packages (8 oz each) cream cheese, softened

1¼ cups granulated sugar

1 tablespoon lemon juice

1 teaspoon vanilla

1 container (8 oz) frozen whipped topping, thawed

¼ cup seedless raspberry preserves

1 can (21 oz) cherry pie filling

3 cups fresh strawberries, each quartered

1 cup fresh raspberries

1) Heat oven to 450°F. Remove 1 crust from pouch. Make pie crust as directed on box for One-Crust Baked Shell using 10-inch glass pie plate. Bake 9 to 11 minutes or until golden brown. Cool completely, about 30 minutes.

2) Meanwhile, to make cheesecake decorations, grease cookie sheet with shortening or cooking spray, or line with parchment paper. Remove remaining crust from pouch; unroll onto cookie sheet. Cut crust into large holly leaves using cookie cutter. Cut small circles for holly berries. Place on cookie sheet; sprinkle with coarse sugar.

3) Bake decorations 8 to 10 minutes or until light golden brown. Carefully remove from cookie sheet to cooling rack. Cool completely, about 15 minutes.

4) In large bowl, beat cream cheese, granulated sugar, the lemon juice and vanilla with electric mixer on medium speed until fluffy. Fold in whipped topping until well blended. Spread 2 cups cream cheese mixture in cooled baked shell. Gently spoon and spread preserves over mixture. Spread with remaining cream cheese mixture.

5) In medium bowl, mix pie filling, 2½ cups of the strawberries and ½ cup of the raspberries. Spoon over cream cheese mixture. Sprinkle with remaining strawberries and raspberries. Refrigerate at least 4 hours or until set. Just before serving, arrange some of the holly leaves and the berries on the cheesecake. Serve individual slices with additional holly leaves and berries. Store in refrigerator.

HIGH ALTITUDE (3500-6500 FT.): No change.

Nutrition Information Per Serving:		
Calories: 520	From Fat:	240
Total Fat		26g
Saturated Fat		15g
Trans Fat		0g
Cholesterol		45mg
Sodium		270mg
Total Carbohydrate		67g
Dietary Fiber		3g
Sugars		42g
Protein		4g

Caramel Apple Biscuits

PREP TIME: 25 MINUTES (READY IN 50 MINUTES)
SERVINGS: 3

- 4 teaspoons butter or margarine, softened
- 1/3 cup packed brown sugar
- 3 (1/2-inch-thick) apple rings (from 1 large apple), peeled, cored
- 1 tablespoon sweetened dried cranberries
- 2 tablespoons granulated sugar
- 1 tablespoon frozen apple juice concentrate, thawed
- 3 Pillsbury® Oven Baked frozen Southern-style biscuits (from 25-oz package)

  Ice cream, if desired

1) Heat oven to 375°F. Grease bottoms and sides of three 10-oz custard cups or individual foil tart pans with 1 teaspoon of the butter. Spread 1 teaspoon remaining butter in bottom of each cup. Sprinkle brown sugar evenly over butter in cups. Place apple ring in each cup. Fill centers with cranberries. Place cups on cookie sheet with sides.

2) Bake 8 to 10 minutes or until brown sugar bubbles. Meanwhile, place granulated sugar and apple juice concentrate in separate small bowls.

3) Remove cookie sheet from oven. Dip all sides of each frozen biscuit in juice concentrate; roll in sugar to coat. Place biscuit on top of each apple ring. Sprinkle any remaining sugar over biscuits.

4) Bake 20 to 25 minutes longer or until biscuits are golden brown. Serve in custard cups with ice cream, or turn upside down into dessert bowls.

HIGH ALTITUDE (3500-6500 FT.): After placing biscuits on top of apple rings and sprinkling with any remaining sugar, bake 25 to 30 minutes longer.

Nutrition Information Per Serving:

Calories:	400	From Fat:	125
Total Fat			14g
Saturated Fat			6g
Cholesterol			15mg
Sodium			630mg
Total Carbohydrate			64g
Dietary Fiber			1g
Sugars			43g
Protein			4g

Orange-Cream Angel Cake

PREP TIME: 10 MINUTES (READY IN 10 MINUTES)
SERVINGS: 12

 EASY

1 round angel food cake (10 inch)

2 containers (6 oz each) Yoplait® Original 99% Fat-Free orange crème yogurt

½ cup whipping (heavy) cream

2 teaspoons powdered sugar

2 tablespoons frozen orange juice concentrate

Nutrition Information Per Serving:		
Calories: 200	From Fat:	35
Total Fat		4g
Saturated Fat		2.5g
Trans Fat		0g
Cholesterol		15mg
Sodium		380mg
Total Carbohydrate		36g
Dietary Fiber		0g
Sugars		29g
Protein		4g

1) Cut cake in half horizontally; separate layers. Place bottom cake layer, cut side up, on serving plate. Spread yogurt over cut surface. Place top cake layer on bottom layer, cut side down.

2) In medium bowl, beat whipping cream and powdered sugar with electric mixer on high speed until stiff peaks form. On low speed, beat in orange juice concentrate just until blended. Serve whipped cream with cake. If desired, garnish with orange peel curls. Store in refrigerator.

HIGH ALTITUDE (3500-6500 FT.): No change.

Chocolate-Hazelnut-Pear Turnovers

PREP TIME: 20 MINUTES (READY IN 35 MINUTES)
SERVINGS: 8

 EASY

1 can (8 oz) Pillsbury® refrigerated crescent dinner rolls

¼ cup hazelnut spread with cocoa (from 13-oz jar)

2 tablespoons chopped hazelnuts (filberts)

½ ripe medium pear, peeled, chopped

1 teaspoon powdered sugar

Nutrition Information Per Serving:		
Calories: 170	From Fat:	70
Total Fat		8g
Saturated Fat		1g
Cholesterol		0mg
Sodium		350mg
Total Carbohydrate		21g
Dietary Fiber		1g
Sugars		11g
Protein		3g

1) Heat oven to 375°F. Do not unroll dough; separate long roll into 2 shorter rolls at center perforations. Refrigerate 1 roll. Unroll other roll, separating into 2 rectangles. Press each to form 8x4-inch rectangle, pressing perforations to seal. Cut each rectangle into two 4-inch squares.

2) Spoon about ½ tablespoon hazelnut spread onto center of each square; spread to within ½ inch of edges. In small bowl, gently mix hazelnuts and chopped pear. Spoon ⅛ of pear mixture over hazelnut spread on each square. Fold corners over filling, forming triangles; press edges with fork to seal. Place on ungreased cookie sheet. Prick tops of each with fork. Repeat with remaining roll of dough, hazelnut spread and pear mixture.

3) Bake 12 to 15 minutes or until golden brown. Sprinkle powdered sugar over warm turnovers. Serve warm or cool completely before serving.

HIGH ALTITUDE (3500-6500 FT.): No change.

Hazelnut spread with cocoa originated in Europe. Rich and sweet, it's used in much the same way we use peanut butter. Look for it near the peanut butter at your grocery store.

Irish Cream Chocolate Tart

PREP TIME:	15 MINUTES (READY IN 4 HOURS 5 MINUTES)
SERVINGS:	12

e EASY

TART

1 Pillsbury® refrigerated pie crust (from 15-oz box), softened as directed on box

1½ cups semisweet chocolate chips

1 can (14 oz) sweetened condensed milk

⅓ cup Irish cream liqueur or whipping cream

2 eggs

TOPPING

½ cup powdered sugar

⅓ cup unsweetened baking cocoa

Dash salt

1½ cups whipping cream

1 teaspoon vanilla

Additional unsweetened baking cocoa, if desired

White chocolate curls, if desired

1) Heat oven to 425°F. Remove crust from pouch; press in bottom and 1½ inches up side of 9-inch springform pan. Bake 9 to 11 minutes or until golden brown.

2) Place chocolate chips in medium microwavable bowl. Microwave on High 40 seconds. Stir; microwave 5 to 15 seconds longer or until chocolate is melted and smooth. Cool 3 minutes.

3) In large bowl, beat condensed milk, liqueur, eggs and melted chocolate with electric mixer on medium speed until smooth. Pour into cooled baked shell.

4) Bake 15 minutes. Reduce oven temperature to 350°F; bake 20 to 30 minutes longer or until center is set. Cool completely on cooling rack, about 1 hour. Refrigerate 2 hours.

5) In medium bowl, beat all topping ingredients except additional cocoa and chocolate curls with electric mixer on high speed until stiff peaks form. Spread topping over tart; sprinkle with additional cocoa and garnish with chocolate curls. Store in refrigerator.

HIGH ALTITUDE (3500-6500 FT.): Place pan of water on oven rack below the rack tart will be baked on. In Step 3, add ¼ cup all-purpose flour to ingredients in bowl. In Step 4, increase second bake time at 350°F to 25 to 35 minutes.

Nutrition Information Per Serving:	
Calories: 440	From Fat: 220
Total Fat	25g
Saturated Fat	14g
Trans Fat	0g
Cholesterol	85mg
Sodium	150mg
Total Carbohydrate	48g
Dietary Fiber	2g
Sugars	36g
Protein	6g

Lemon Bavarian Cream with Raspberry Sauce

PREP TIME: 20 MINUTES (READY IN 1 HOUR 20 MINUTES)
SERVINGS: 6

e EASY

1 box (3 oz) lemon-flavored gelatin

¾ cup boiling water

2 cups ice cubes

2 teaspoons grated lemon peel

2 tablespoons lemon juice

2 cups frozen (thawed) reduced-fat whipped topping

1 package (10 oz) frozen raspberries in syrup, thawed

1 tablespoon powdered sugar

Fresh raspberries, if desired

Fresh mint leaves, if desired

1) In medium bowl, dissolve gelatin in boiling water. Add ice cubes; stir about 2 minutes or until gelatin begins to thicken. With slotted spoon, remove any unmelted ice. Stir in lemon peel and lemon juice.

2) With wire whisk or electric mixer at low speed, thoroughly blend whipped topping into gelatin. Refrigerate until set, about 1 hour.

3) Meanwhile, in blender or food processor, place raspberries and powdered sugar. Cover; blend until smooth. Place strainer over small bowl; pour berry mixture into strainer. Press mixture with back of spoon through strainer to remove seeds; discard seeds.

4) Into each of 4 dessert dishes, spoon about ½ cup lemon mixture. Top each with 2 to 3 tablespoons sauce. Garnish with fresh berries and mint.

HIGH ALTITUDE (3500-6500 FT.): No change.

tip

The sauce for this refreshing dessert can be made up to one day in advance. Just be sure to cover and refrigerate it until serving time.

Nutrition Information Per Serving:

Calories:	170	From Fat:	30
Total Fat			3.5g
Saturated Fat			3g
Trans Fat			0g
Cholesterol			0mg
Sodium			85mg
Total Carbohydrate			33g
Dietary Fiber			2g
Sugars			29g
Protein			2g

Lemon-Pineapple Dessert Squares

PREP TIME: 15 MINUTES (READY IN 2 HOURS)
SERVINGS: 18

e EASY

2 boxes (4-serving size each) lemon-flavored gelatin

1¹/₂ cups boiling water

1 can (20 oz) crushed pineapple in juice, well drained, liquid reserved

1 container (12 oz) frozen whipped topping, thawed

1 round angel food cake (9 or 10 inch)

2 cups sliced fresh strawberries

1) In large bowl, mix gelatin and boiling water until gelatin is completely dissolved. In 2-cup measuring cup, mix reserved pineapple liquid and enough cold water to make 2 cups. Stir into gelatin mixture. Refrigerate until thickened but not set, about 45 minutes.

2) Stir pineapple into thickened gelatin mixture. With rubber spatula, fold in 3 cups of the whipped topping.

3) Tear angel food cake into 1-inch pieces, placing half of the pieces in ungreased 13x9-inch (3-quart) glass baking dish. Spoon half of gelatin mixture evenly over cake pieces. Repeat layers. Cover tightly with plastic wrap; refrigerate until set, about 1 hour.

4) Cut dessert into serving pieces; place on dessert plates. Top each with about 2 tablespoons strawberries and about 1 tablespoon remaining whipped topping.

HIGH ALTITUDE (3500-6500 FT.): No change.

Nutrition Information Per Serving:	
Calories: 190	From Fat: 35
Total Fat	3.5g
Saturated Fat	3g
Trans Fat	0g
Cholesterol	0mg
Sodium	250mg
Total Carbohydrate	37g
Dietary Fiber	1g
Sugars	31g
Protein	3g

Brownie-Cherry-Ice Cream Dessert

PREP TIME: 30 MINUTES (READY IN 2 HOURS 45 MINUTES)
SERVINGS: 16

1 box (1 lb 3.8 oz) fudge brownie mix

½ cup vegetable oil

¼ cup water

1 teaspoon almond extract

2 eggs

4 cups vanilla ice cream, slightly softened

1 bag (12 oz) frozen dark sweet cherries, halved

⅓ cup chocolate-flavor syrup

1) Heat oven to 350°F. Grease 13x9-inch pan with shortening. In large bowl, stir brownie mix, oil, water, almond extract and eggs with spoon until well blended. Pour batter into pan.

2) Bake 22 to 25 minutes or until toothpick inserted in center comes out clean. Cool completely, about 1 hour.

3) In another large bowl, mix ice cream and cherries. Place heaping spoonfuls of ice cream mixture over brownies; lightly press with back of spoon to smooth. Freeze at least 1 hour before serving.

4) If too firm to cut, let stand at room temperature 10 minutes. Drizzle individual servings with syrup. Garnish with a mint leaf and a maraschino cherry, if desired.

HIGH ALTITUDE (3500-6500 FT.): Make and bake brownies following High Altitude Directions on box for 13x9-inch pan.

Nutrition Information Per Serving:	
Calories: 320	From Fat: 120
Total Fat	13g
Saturated Fat	4.5g
Trans Fat	1g
Cholesterol	40mg
Sodium	170mg
Total Carbohydrate	47g
Dietary Fiber	2g
Sugars	35g
Protein	4g

Raspberry-Mango Shortcakes

NANCY FLESCH | KENT, OHIO

Pillsbury Bake-Off®   BAKE-OFF® CONTEST 37,1996

PREP TIME: 50 MINUTES (READY IN 50 MINUTES)
SERVINGS: 8

SHORTCAKES
- $1/2$ cup flaked or shredded coconut
- $1/4$ cup granulated sugar
- $1/2$ teaspoon ground ginger
- 1 can (16.3 oz) Pillsbury® Grands!® Homestyle refrigerated biscuits
- 2 tablespoons butter or margarine, melted

FRUIT
- 2 cups fresh or frozen (partially thawed) raspberries
- $1 1/2$ cups chopped peeled fresh mangoes or 1 jar or can (16 oz) mangoes or peaches, drained, chopped
- 2 tablespoons granulated sugar

TOPPING
- 1 cup whipping cream
- 2 tablespoons packed brown sugar
- $1/4$ teaspoon ground ginger

1) Heat oven to 375°F. In small bowl, mix coconut, $1/4$ cup sugar and $1/2$ teaspoon ginger.

2) Separate dough into 8 biscuits. Dip top and sides of each biscuit in melted butter; dip top and sides in coconut mixture. Place biscuits, coconut side up, 2 inches apart on ungreased cookie sheet. Sprinkle any remaining coconut mixture over tops of biscuits.

3) Bake 14 to 18 minutes or until biscuits and coconut are light golden brown. Cool 5 minutes.

4) Meanwhile, in medium bowl, gently stir fruit ingredients to mix. In small bowl with electric mixer, beat topping ingredients on high speed until stiff peaks form.

5) To serve, split warm biscuits; place bottom halves on individual dessert plates. Spoon generous $1/3$ cup fruit mixture over each biscuit half; top each with $1/4$ cup topping and biscuit top. Store fruit and topping in refrigerator.

HIGH ALTITUDE (3500-6500 FT.): No change.

Nutrition Information Per Serving:		
Calories: 430	From Fat:	220
Total Fat		25g
Saturated Fat		13g
Cholesterol		50mg
Sodium		650mg
Total Carbohydrate		49g
Dietary Fiber		3g
Sugars		26g
Protein		5g

Key Lime Cheesecake with Raspberry Sauce

PREP TIME: 30 MINUTES (READY IN 8 HOURS 15 MINUTES)
SERVINGS: 16

CRUST

1 cup shortbread cookie crumbs (15 cookies) or vanilla wafer crumbs (25 wafers)

2 tablespoons butter or margarine, melted

FILLING

3 packages (8 oz each) cream cheese, softened

1 cup sugar

3 eggs

1 tablespoon grated lime peel (about 2 limes)

¼ cup Key lime juice

RASPBERRY SAUCE

1 box (10 oz) frozen raspberries in light syrup, thawed

1 tablespoon cornstarch

⅓ cup red currant jelly

1) Heat oven to 325°F. In medium bowl, mix crust ingredients. Press in bottom of ungreased 9-inch springform pan. Refrigerate.

2) In large bowl, beat cream cheese until smooth. Gradually beat in sugar. At low speed of electric mixer, beat in eggs 1 at a time, blending just until smooth. Add remaining filling ingredients; beat until smooth. Pour into crust-lined pan.

3) Bake 55 to 65 minutes or until set. (To minimize cracking, place shallow pan half full of hot water on lower oven rack during baking.) Turn oven off; let cheesecake stand in oven 30 minutes with door open at least 4 inches. Remove from oven; let stand 10 minutes. Remove side of pan; cool to room temperature on cooling rack. Cover cheesecake and refrigerate overnight or up to 2 days.

4) To make sauce, drain raspberries, reserving syrup. Add water to syrup to make ¾ cup. In 1-quart saucepan, mix syrup mixture and cornstarch. Add jelly; cook and stir over medium heat until thickened and clear. Stir in raspberries. Refrigerate until cold. Serve cheesecake with sauce. Cover and refrigerate any remaining cheesecake and sauce.

HIGH ALTITUDE (3500-6500 FT.): No change.

Nutrition Information Per Serving:	
Calories: 320	From Fat: 180
Total Fat	20g
Saturated Fat	11g
Trans Fat	1g
Cholesterol	95mg
Sodium	200mg
Total Carbohydrate	30g
Dietary Fiber	1g
Sugars	24g
Protein	5g

tip

For special occasions, you can decorate the top of this no-fuss cheesecake with raspberries and edible flowers.

Fresh Strawberry and Rhubarb Sauce Parfaits

PREP TIME: 25 MINUTES (READY IN 1 HOUR 25 MINUTES)
SERVINGS: 8

2 cups chopped fresh rhubarb

1 cup granulated sugar

1/4 cup cranberry-apple drink

3 cups sliced fresh strawberries

1 cup whipping cream

1 tablespoon powdered sugar

1 teaspoon vanilla

1 package (16 oz) frozen pound cake loaf, thawed, cubed

Nutrition Information Per Serving:	
Calories: 490	From Fat: 230
Total Fat	25g
Saturated Fat	13g
Trans Fat	2g
Cholesterol	100mg
Sodium	60mg
Total Carbohydrate	61g
Dietary Fiber	2g
Sugars	45g
Protein	5g

Angel food cake or sponge cake cups can be used instead of pound cake in this recipe.

1) In 2-quart saucepan, cook rhubarb, granulated sugar and drink over medium heat 10 to 15 minutes, stirring occasionally, until rhubarb is tender and mixture is syrupy.

2) Add 1 cup of the strawberries; cook and stir 1 to 2 minutes, mashing slightly. Remove from heat. Stir in remaining strawberries. Cool slightly. Refrigerate at least 1 hour until chilled.

3) Just before serving, in medium bowl, beat whipping cream, powdered sugar and vanilla until stiff peaks form. In each of 8 parfait glasses, layer sauce, cake cubes and whipped cream; repeat layers. Serve immediately. If desired, garnish each serving with fresh strawberry slice.

HIGH ALTITUDE (3500-6500 FT.): No change.

Mini Cherry Cheesecakes

PREP TIME: 20 MINUTES (READY IN 2 HOURS 15 MINUTES)
SERVINGS: 24

24 vanilla wafer cookies

2 packages (8 oz each) cream cheese, softened

3/4 cup sugar

2 eggs

1 teaspoon almond or vanilla extract

1 can (21 oz) cherry pie filling

1/2 cup toasted, sliced almonds

Nutrition Information Per Serving:	
Calories: 150	From Fat: 80
Total Fat	9g
Saturated Fat	4.5g
Trans Fat	0g
Cholesterol	40mg
Sodium	75mg
Total Carbohydrate	16g
Dietary Fiber	0g
Sugars	13g
Protein	3g

1) Heat oven to 375°F. Line 24 regular-size muffin cups with paper liners. Place 1 vanilla wafer cookie in bottom of each cup.

2) In large bowl, beat cream cheese, sugar, eggs and almond extract with electric mixer on medium-high speed 1 to 2 minutes or until mixture is light and fluffy. Spoon evenly into muffin cups (about 2/3 full).

3) Bake 20 to 25 minutes or until toothpick inserted in center comes out clean. Remove from muffin cups to cooling rack. Cool completely, about 30 minutes. Refrigerate at least 1 hour or up to 24 hours before serving.

4) Just before serving, top each cheesecake with generous tablespoon pie filling; sprinkle with almonds.

HIGH ALTITUDE (3500-6500 FT.): Bake 22 to 25 minutes.

Peppermint-Fudge Pie

PREP TIME: 25 MINUTES (READY IN 2 HOURS 10 MINUTES)
SERVINGS: 8

1 Pillsbury® refrigerated pie crust (from 15-oz box), softened as directed on box

2 cups milk

1 box (4-serving size) chocolate pudding and pie filling mix (not instant)

½ cup semisweet chocolate chips

1 package (8 oz) cream cheese, softened

½ cup powdered sugar

1 teaspoon peppermint extract

2 drops red or green food color

2 cups frozen (thawed) whipped topping

Shaved chocolate, if desired

1) Heat oven to 450°F. Make pie crust as directed on box for One-Crust Baked Shell using 9-inch glass pie plate. Bake 9 to 11 minutes or until light golden brown. Cool completely, about 30 minutes.

2) Meanwhile, in 2-quart saucepan, heat milk and pudding mix to a full boil over medium heat, stirring constantly. Remove from heat. Stir in chocolate chips until melted. Place plastic wrap directly over the surface of the pudding. Refrigerate the pudding for 45 minutes or just until cooled.

3) In small bowl, beat cream cheese, powdered sugar, peppermint extract and food color with electric mixer on medium speed until smooth. On low speed, gradually beat in 1 cup of the whipped topping until combined. Spread in cooled baked shell.

4) Stir cooled pudding mixture; spread over cream cheese layer. Carefully spread remaining 1 cup whipped topping over pudding layer. Garnish with chocolate shavings. Refrigerate 1 hour or until chilled before serving. Store in refrigerator.

HIGH ALTITUDE (3500-6500 FT.): No change.

Nutrition Information Per Serving:

Calories:	430	From Fat:	225
Total Fat			25g
Saturated Fat			13g
Cholesterol			40mg
Sodium			280mg
Total Carbohydrate			45g
Dietary Fiber			1g
Sugars			27g
Protein			6g

Cherry-Berry Cobbler

PREP TIME: 25 MINUTES (READY IN 1 HOUR 15 MINUTES)
SERVINGS: 9

1 bag (10 to 12 oz) frozen pitted sweet cherries

1 bag (10 to 12 oz) frozen mixed berries

¾ cup sugar

2 tablespoons cornstarch

2 tablespoons water

1 egg white

2 teaspoons ground cinnamon

1 can (12 oz) Pillsbury® Golden Layers® refrigerated biscuits

¼ cup sliced almonds

Whipped cream, if desired

1) Heat oven to 375°F. Spray 8-inch square (2-quart) glass baking dish with cooking spray. In 3-quart saucepan, mix cherries, mixed berries, ½ cup of the sugar, the cornstarch and water. Cook over medium-high heat, stirring frequently, until mixture boils and thickens. Pour into baking dish.

2) In medium bowl, beat egg white with wire whisk until frothy. In another medium bowl, mix remaining ¼ cup sugar and the cinnamon.

3) Separate dough into 10 biscuits. Cut each into quarters. Dip dough pieces in egg white, then toss in sugar mixture to coat. Arrange on hot fruit mixture. Sprinkle almonds over top.

4) Bake 25 to 30 minutes or until biscuits are deep golden brown and no longer doughy in center. Let stand 20 minutes before serving. Serve warm cobbler with whipped cream.

HIGH ALTITUDE (3500-6500 FT.): No change.

Nutrition Information Per Serving:

Calories:	250	From Fat:	60
Total Fat			6g
Saturated Fat			1g
Trans Fat			1.5g
Cholesterol			0mg
Sodium			410mg
Total Carbohydrate			45g
Dietary Fiber			2g
Sugars			27g
Protein			4g

Turtle Brownie Ice Cream Dessert

PREP TIME: 20 MINUTES (READY IN 4 HOURS 30 MINUTES)
SERVINGS: 20

e EASY

BROWNIES

- 1 box (1 lb 3.8 oz) fudge brownie mix
- ½ cup vegetable oil
- ¼ cup water
- 2 eggs
- ½ cup chopped pecans

FILLING

- 2 quarts (8 cups) dulce de leche ice cream, slightly softened
- ½ cup hot fudge topping, heated until warm
- ½ cup chopped pecans
- 1 cup frozen (thawed) whipped topping, if desired

1) Heat oven to 350°F. Spray bottom only of 15x10x1-inch pan with cooking spray. In large bowl, beat brownie mix, oil, water and eggs 50 strokes with spoon. Stir in ½ cup pecans. Spread batter in pan.

2) Bake 16 to 22 minutes or until center is set. Do not overbake. Cool completely on wire rack, about 45 minutes.

3) Spoon ice cream evenly over brownies; smooth with back of spoon or rubber spatula. Freeze uncovered until firm, about 3 hours.

4) To serve, drizzle hot fudge topping over dessert with fork using quick strokes. Sprinkle with ½ cup pecans. Let stand at room temperature about 5 minutes before cutting. Serve topped with whipped topping.

HIGH ALTITUDE (3500-6500 FT.): Add 1/2 cup all-purpose flour to dry brownie mix. Decrease oil to 1/3 cup; increase water to 1/3 cup.

Nutrition Information Per Serving:		
Calories: 450	From Fat: 230	
Total Fat		26g
Saturated Fat		11g
Trans Fat		1g
Cholesterol		100mg
Sodium		180mg
Total Carbohydrate		48g
Dietary Fiber		0g
Sugars		36g
Protein		5g

Lemon Supreme Cheesecake

PREP TIME: 20 MINUTES (READY IN 5 HOURS 50 MINUTES)
SERVINGS: 16

🄴 EASY

CRUST

1½ cups vanilla wafer crumbs
(40 cookies)

2 tablespoons sugar

½ teaspoon grated lemon peel

¼ cup butter, melted

FILLING

3 packages (8 oz each) cream cheese, softened

¾ cup sugar

3 eggs

1 cup whipping (heavy) cream

1 tablespoon grated lemon peel

3 tablespoons fresh lemon juice

¼ teaspoon salt

TOPPING

1 jar (10 or 11¼ oz) lemon curd
(about 1 cup)

½ cup whipping (heavy) cream

1 tablespoon sugar

1) Heat oven to 325°F. In medium bowl, mix crust ingredients. In ungreased 9-inch springform pan, press crumb mixture in bottom and 1 inch up side. (For best results, do not use dark pan.)

2) In large bowl, beat cream cheese with electric mixer on medium speed until fluffy. Gradually beat in ¾ cup sugar until smooth. Add eggs, one at a time, beating well after each addition. On low speed, beat in 1 cup of the whipping cream, the lemon peel, lemon juice and salt until smooth. Pour mixture into crust-lined pan.

3) Bake 55 to 60 minutes or until set but still slightly jiggly in center. Cool in pan on wire rack 20 minutes. Carefully run knife around side of pan to loosen, but do not remove side of pan. Cool 1 hour 30 minutes.

4) In small bowl, stir lemon curd to soften mixture; spread evenly over top of cheesecake to within ½ inch of edge. Refrigerate at least 3 hours or overnight.

5) Just before serving, remove side of pan. In small bowl, beat ½ cup whipping cream and 1 tablespoon sugar with electric mixer on high speed until stiff peaks form. Spoon or pipe whipped cream around edge of cheesecake. If desired, garnish with lemon peel. Store in refrigerator.

HIGH ALTITUDE (3500-6500 FT.): In Step 3, place pan of hot water on oven rack below cheesecake; bake 1 hour 15 minutes.

Nutrition Information Per Serving:	
Calories: 410	From Fat: 250
Total Fat	28g
Saturated Fat	16g
Trans Fat	1g
Cholesterol	135mg
Sodium	250mg
Total Carbohydrate	33g
Dietary Fiber	0g
Sugars	28g
Protein	5g

Fruit and Cream Cake

PREP TIME: 20 MINUTES (READY IN 1 HOUR 50 MINUTES)
SERVINGS: 16

 EASY

CAKE

- 1 round angel food cake (8 or 9 inch)
- 1 cup raspberry sherbet, slightly softened
- 1 cup lime sherbet, slightly softened
- 1 cup orange sherbet, slightly softened

FROSTING

- 1 pint (2 cups) whipping cream
- ½ cup powdered sugar
- 1 teaspoon vanilla

Nutrition Information Per Serving:		
Calories: 230	From Fat:	90
Total Fat		10g
Saturated Fat		6g
Trans Fat		0g
Cholesterol		35mg
Sodium		260mg
Total Carbohydrate		33g
Dietary Fiber		1g
Sugars		27g
Protein		3g

1) Slice cake horizontally into 4 equal layers. Place bottom cake layer on freezer-safe serving plate; spread with raspberry sherbet. Top with second cake layer; spread with lime sherbet. Top with third cake layer; spread with orange sherbet. Place fourth cake layer on top. Freeze until sherbet is firm, about 1 hour.

2) In large bowl, beat all frosting ingredients with electric mixer on low speed until soft peaks form. Beat on high speed until stiff peaks form, scraping side of bowl occasionally. Frost side and top of cake. Freeze until firm before serving, at least 30 minutes.

HIGH ALTITUDE (3500-6500 FT.): No change.

Pomegranate Tartlets

PREP TIME: 45 MINUTES (READY IN 1 HOUR 45 MINUTES)
SERVINGS: 36 TARTLETS

- 3 Pillsbury® refrigerated pie crusts (from two 15-oz boxes), softened as directed on box
- 1 pomegranate
- 1 box (4-serving size) vanilla pudding and pie filling mix (not instant)
- 1¾ cups whipping cream
- 2 tablespoons dark rum or ½ teaspoon rum extract
- 1 teaspoon powdered sugar

Nutrition Information Per Serving:		
Calories: 90	From Fat:	60
Total Fat		6g
Saturated Fat		3g
Trans Fat		0g
Cholesterol		15mg
Sodium		60mg
Total Carbohydrate		8g
Dietary Fiber		0g
Sugars		3g
Protein		0g

1) Heat oven to 450°F. Remove crusts from pouches; place on work surface. With 2½-inch round cutter, cut crusts into 36 rounds. Press each round into ungreased mini muffin cup.

2) Bake 7 to 9 minutes or until light golden brown. Remove tartlet shells from muffin cups; place on cooling racks. Cool 10 minutes.

3) Meanwhile, cut pomegranate in half; remove seeds. Set aside.

4) In medium saucepan, stir pudding mix and whipping cream with wire whisk until blended. Cook over medium heat for about 5 minutes or until mixture comes to a boil, stirring constantly. Remove from heat; stir in rum.

5) Immediately spoon about 2 rounded teaspoons filling into each tartlet shell. Top each with about 1 teaspoon pomegranate seeds. Cover loosely; refrigerate at least 1 hour or until serving time.

6) Just before serving, sprinkle tartlets with powdered sugar.

HIGH ALTITUDE (3500-6500 FT.): No change.

Caramel Cashew Cheesecake

PREP TIME: 25 MINUTES (READY IN 9 HOURS)
SERVINGS: 16

1½ cups finely crushed cinnamon graham cracker crumbs (16 squares)

¼ cup butter, melted

4 packages (8 oz each) cream cheese, softened

1¼ cups packed brown sugar

¼ cup whipping cream

2 teaspoons vanilla

1 cup caramel topping (from 12-oz jar)

4 eggs

1 cup miniature chocolate chips

1 cup whipping cream

½ cup cashew halves

1) Heat oven to 325°F. Wrap outside of 9-inch springform pan with foil. In small bowl, mix graham cracker crumbs and butter with fork until well blended. Press firmly against bottom and up sides of pan. Bake 8 to 10 minutes or until set. Reduce oven temperature to 300°F.

2) In large bowl, beat cream cheese with electric mixer on medium speed until smooth. Gradually beat in brown sugar, beating until light and fluffy. On low speed, beat in ¼ cup whipping cream, the vanilla and ¼ cup of the caramel topping. Add eggs, one at a time, beating well after each addition. Fold in chocolate chips. Pour over crust in pan.

3) Bake 1 hour 25 minutes to 1 hour 35 minutes or until cheesecake is set 2 inches from edge and center is slightly jiggly. Turn oven off; open oven door at least 4 inches. Let cheesecake remain in oven 30 minutes. Remove cheesecake from oven. Run knife around edge of pan to loosen; cool 30 minutes at room temperature. Cover; refrigerate at least 6 hours or overnight.

4) In small bowl, beat 1 cup whipping cream with electric mixer until stiff peaks form. Remove side of pan. Top individual servings with whipped cream; drizzle with remaining caramel topping. Sprinkle with cashews.

HIGH ALTITUDE (3500-6500 FT.): Place pan of water on oven rack below cheesecake.

Nutrition Information Per Serving:		
Calories: 540	From Fat: 320	
Total Fat		36g
Saturated Fat		21g
Trans Fat		1g
Cholesterol		145mg
Sodium		330mg
Total Carbohydrate		46g
Dietary Fiber		1g
Sugars		38g
Protein		8g

Pear and Cranberry Pie

PREP TIME: 20 MINUTES (READY IN 1 HOUR 35 MINUTES)
SERVINGS: 8

 EASY

CRUST AND FILLING

- 1 Pillsbury® refrigerated pie crust (from 15-oz box), softened as directed on box
- 2 medium ripe pears, peeled, cut into 1/4-inch slices
- 1 cup fresh cranberries
- 1/2 cup sugar
- 1/4 teaspoon nutmeg
- 1/2 cup sour cream
- 3 eggs

SAUCE

- 1 teaspoon cornstarch
- 1 cup dairy eggnog
- 1 tablespoon light rum or 1/2 teaspoon rum extract

1) Heat oven to 425°F. Make pie crust as directed on box for One-Crust Baked Shell as directed on box using 9-inch glass pie plate. Prick crust generously with fork.

2) Bake 9 to 11 minutes or until golden brown. Reduce oven temperature to 350°F. Cool 5 minutes. Layer pear slices and cranberries in baked crust.

3) In medium bowl, with wire whisk, beat sugar, nutmeg, sour cream and eggs until smooth and well blended. Pour evenly over fruit.

4) Bake 15 minutes. Cover edge of crust with strips of foil to prevent excessive browning. Bake 40 to 45 minutes longer or until custard is just set and pears are fork-tender. Cool completely, about 1 hour.

5) In small saucepan, mix cornstarch with 1 tablespoon of the eggnog until mixture is smooth. With wire whisk, beat in remaining eggnog; cook over medium heat 6 to 8 minutes, stirring constantly, until mixture just begins to boil. Remove from heat; stir in rum. Serve warm sauce over pie. Store pie and sauce in refrigerator.

HIGH ALTITUDE (3500-6500 FT.): No change.

Nutrition Information Per Serving:	
Calories: 280	From Fat: 120
Total Fat	13g
Saturated Fat	5g
Trans Fat	0g
Cholesterol	115mg
Sodium	160mg
Total Carbohydrate	36g
Dietary Fiber	2g
Sugars	20g
Protein	4g

Snowball Cupcakes

PREP TIME: 40 MINUTES (READY IN 1 HOUR 30 MINUTES)
SERVINGS: 24 CUPCAKES

CUPCAKES

- 1 box (18.25 oz) Devil's food cake mix with pudding
- ½ cup water
- ⅓ cup vegetable oil
- ½ cup sour cream
- 2 eggs
- 1 package (3 oz) cream cheese, cut into 24 cubes

FROSTING

- ½ cup sugar
- 2 tablespoons water
- 2 egg whites
- 1 jar (7 oz) marshmallow creme
- 1 teaspoon vanilla
- 2 cups coconut

Nutrition Information Per Serving:		
Calories: 220	From Fat:	80
Total Fat		9g
Saturated Fat		4.5g
Trans Fat		0g
Cholesterol		25mg
Sodium		220mg
Total Carbohydrate		32g
Dietary Fiber		0g
Sugars		23g
Protein		2g

1) Heat oven to 350°F. Line 24 regular-size muffin cups with paper baking cups. In large bowl, beat cake mix, water, oil, sour cream and eggs with electric mixer on low speed 30 seconds, scraping bowl occasionally. Beat on medium speed 1 minute.

2) Spoon batter into muffin cups. Place 1 cube cream cheese in center of each cupcake; press down into batter almost to center (top of cream cheese will still show).

3) Bake 18 to 24 minutes or until toothpick inserted near center of cupcake comes out clean (test between cream cheese and edge). Remove cupcakes from pan to cooling racks. Cool completely, about 30 minutes.

4) In 2-quart stainless steel or other non-coated saucepan, mix sugar, water and egg whites. Cook over low heat, beating continuously with electric hand mixer at high speed until soft peaks form, about 4 minutes. Add marshmallow creme; beat until stiff peaks form. Remove saucepan from heat. Beat in vanilla.

5) Spread frosting evenly over cupcakes; sprinkle each with generous tablespoon coconut. Store cupcakes in refrigerator.

HIGH ALTITUDE (3500-6500 FT.): No change.

Coffee-Pecan Tarts

PREP TIME: 25 MINUTES (READY IN 1 HOUR 15 MINUTES)
SERVINGS: 4 TARTS

1 Pillsbury® refrigerated pie crust (from 15-oz box), softened as directed on box

4 foil tart pans (4½ to 5 inch)

   Coarse sugar or granulated sugar

1 egg

¼ cup granulated sugar

¼ cup light corn syrup

2 tablespoons coffee-flavored liqueur or coffee

   Dash salt

½ teaspoon vanilla

½ cup pecan halves

½ cup whipped cream or whipped topping, if desired

1) Heat oven to 375°F. Remove crust from pouch; place on lightly floured surface. With 4½-inch round cookie cutter or top of 4½-inch diameter bowl as pattern, cut 4 rounds from crust. Fit rounds in bottom and ½ inch up sides of foil tart pans. With fork, prick bottoms and sides generously. Place pans on ungreased cookie sheet.

2) If desired, cut small star shapes from remaining pie crust; place on same cookie sheet with tart pans. Prick stars with fork; sprinkle lightly with coarse sugar.

3) Bake tart shells and stars 6 to 8 minutes or just until shells are dry and stars are golden brown.

4) Meanwhile, in medium bowl, beat egg with wire whisk. Beat in ¼ cup granulated sugar, the corn syrup, liqueur, salt and vanilla.

5) Remove partially baked tart shells and baked stars from oven. Remove stars from cookie sheet. Arrange pecans evenly in tart shells. Pour egg mixture evenly over pecans.

6) Return tarts to oven; bake 16 to 20 minutes longer or until crusts are golden brown and center is set. Cool 30 minutes. Remove tarts from pans. Top each with whipped cream; garnish with baked pie crust stars.

HIGH ALTITUDE (3500-6500 FT.): In Step 3, bake tart shells and stars 8 to 10 minutes. Add 1 tablespoon all-purpose flour to egg mixture. In Step 6, bake tarts 16 to 18 minutes.

Nutrition Information Per Serving:		
Calories: 480	From Fat: 220	
Total Fat		24g
Saturated Fat		6g
Trans Fat		0g
Cholesterol		60mg
Sodium		300mg
Total Carbohydrate		61g
Dietary Fiber		1g
Sugars		25g
Protein		3g

Chocolate Tiramisu Cake

PREP TIME: 25 MINUTES (READY IN 1 HOUR 35 MINUTES)
SERVINGS: 8

CAKE

1 box (1 lb 2.25 oz) German chocolate cake mix with pudding

Water, oil and eggs called for on cake mix box

SOAKING SYRUP

¼ cup granulated sugar

1 teaspoon instant coffee granules or crystals

¼ cup water

¼ cup coffee-flavored liqueur

FILLING

1 cup whipping cream

1 container (8 oz) mascarpone cheese or 1 package (8 oz) cream cheese, softened

2 tablespoons powdered sugar

2 teaspoons vanilla

GARNISH

1 teaspoon unsweetened baking cocoa

1) Heat oven to 350°F (325°F for dark or nonstick pans). Grease bottoms and sides of 2 (9-inch) round cake pans with shortening or cooking spray. Make and bake cake as directed on box, using water, oil and eggs. Cool 10 minutes. Remove from pans to cooling racks. Cool completely, about 25 minutes.

2) Meanwhile, in 1-quart saucepan, mix granulated sugar, instant coffee and water. Heat to boiling over medium heat. Boil and stir 1 minute. Remove from heat. Stir in coffee liqueur. Cool completely, about 30 minutes.

3) Brush flat side of each cake layer with soaking syrup until absorbed. Place cakes in freezer for 5 minutes.

4) In chilled 1-quart bowl, beat whipping cream with electric mixer on high speed until stiff peaks form. (Do not overbeat.) In another small bowl, beat mascarpone cheese, powdered sugar and vanilla with electric mixer on low speed until blended. Fold whipped cream into mascarpone mixture until smooth and creamy.

5) Place 1 cake layer rounded side down on serving plate. Top with half of mascarpone mixture. Place second layer rounded side down on top. Top with remaining mascarpone mixture. Cut cake into wedges; place on individual dessert plates. Place cocoa in fine strainer; sprinkle plates and cake with cocoa. Store cake in refrigerator.

HIGH ALTITUDE (3500-6500 FT.): Follow High Altitude directions on cake mix box for 2 (9-inch) round cake pans.

Nutrition Information Per Serving:		
Calories: 640	From Fat: 340	
Total Fat		38g
Saturated Fat		16g
Trans Fat		1g
Cholesterol		135mg
Sodium		540mg
Total Carbohydrate		67g
Dietary Fiber		2g
Sugars		42g
Protein		7g

Bananas Foster Pie

PREP TIME:	20 MINUTES (READY IN 3 HOURS)		
SERVINGS:	8	**e** EASY	

SAUCE

- ¾ cup caramel topping
- 1 tablespoon dark rum or 1 teaspoon rum extract
- ¼ teaspoon ground cinnamon

FILLING

- 1 Pillsbury® refrigerated pie crust (from 15-oz box), softened as directed on box
- 2 medium bananas, cut into ⅛-inch slices
- 1¼ cups milk
- 1 box (4 serving size) banana instant pudding and pie filling mix
- 1 cup whipping cream

  Banana slices, if desired

1) Heat oven to 450°F. In small bowl, mix all sauce ingredients until well blended; set aside.

2) Make pie crust as directed on box for One-Crust Baked Shell using 9-inch glass pie plate. Bake 9 to 11 minutes or until golden brown. Cool completely, about 30 minutes.

3) In medium bowl, toss banana slices with 3 tablespoons of the sauce until coated. Layer bananas in bottom of cooled baked shell.

4) In large bowl, beat milk and pudding mix with wire whisk 2 minutes or until thickened. In small bowl, beat whipping cream with electric mixer on high until stiff peaks form. Fold into pudding until well combined. Spread evenly over bananas. Refrigerate 2 to 4 hours or until firm.

5) Top individual servings of pie with additional banana slices and sauce. Store in refrigerator.

HIGH ALTITUDE (3500-6500 FT.): No change.

Nutrition Information Per Serving:	
Calories: 390	From Fat: 150
Total Fat	17g
Saturated Fat	9g
Trans Fat	0g
Cholesterol	40mg
Sodium	420mg
Total Carbohydrate	54g
Dietary Fiber	1g
Sugars	31g
Protein	3g

tip You'll want to use firm bananas for this recipe. And for extra speedy preparation, use thawed whipped topping to fold into the pudding.

Caramel Apple Cheesecake

PREP TIME: 15 MINUTES (READY IN 3 HOURS 10 MINUTES)
SERVINGS: 12

⊜ EASY

1½ cups graham cracker crumbs

2 tablespoons sugar

¼ cup butter, melted

2 packages (8 oz each) cream cheese, softened

½ cup sugar

2 eggs

1 cup chopped unpeeled apple

¾ cup caramel topping

Frozen whipped topping, thawed

1 medium apple, sliced, if desired

1) Heat oven to 350°F. In medium bowl, mix crumbs, 2 tablespoons sugar and the butter. Press in bottom and 1 inch up sides of ungreased 9-inch springform pan.

2) In large bowl, beat cream cheese and ½ cup sugar with electric mixer on medium speed until smooth. Add eggs, one at a time, beating until smooth after each addition. With spoon, fold in apples. Pour into crust-lined pan.

3) Bake 30 to 40 minutes or until set. Cool 15 minutes. Run knife around edge of cheesecake; remove side of pan. Cool completely, about 1 hour. Refrigerate 1 hour or until chilled. Top individual servings with caramel topping, whipped topping and apple slice.

HIGH ALTITUDE (3500-6500 FT.): No change.

Nutrition Information Per Serving:

Calories:	350	From Fat:	190
Total Fat			21g
Saturated Fat			13g
Trans Fat			1g
Cholesterol			85mg
Sodium			280mg
Total Carbohydrate			37g
Dietary Fiber			0g
Sugars			28g
Protein			5g

Strawberries in Chocolate with Pastry Snowflakes

PREP TIME: 45 MINUTES (READY IN 55 MINUTES)
SERVINGS: 6

SAUCE

¼ cup packed brown sugar

¼ cup unsweetened baking cocoa

¼ cup orange juice

¼ cup light corn syrup

½ teaspoon vanilla

PASTRY SNOWFLAKES

1 Pillsbury® refrigerated pie crust (from 15-oz box), softened as directed on box

2 teaspoons coarse sugar

STRAWBERRIES

3 cups (1½ pints) fresh strawberries, sliced

1) In 1-quart saucepan, heat brown sugar, cocoa, orange juice and corn syrup to boiling over medium heat, stirring constantly. Remove from heat; stir in vanilla. Cover; refrigerate.

2) Heat oven to 450°F. Remove crust from pouch; unroll on work surface. With floured cutter, cut 12 snowflakes from crust. On ungreased cookie sheet, place snowflakes 1 inch apart. Sprinkle coarse sugar over snowflakes. Bake 5 to 8 minutes or until light golden brown.

3) To serve, spoon about 2 tablespoons sauce onto each dessert plate. Top each with ½ cup strawberries and 2 pastry snowflakes.

HIGH ALTITUDE (3500-6500 FT.): No change.

Nutrition Information Per Serving:

Calories:	290	From Fat:	90
Total Fat			10g
Saturated Fat			3.5g
Trans Fat			0g
Cholesterol			0mg
Sodium			160mg
Total Carbohydrate			47g
Dietary Fiber			3g
Sugars			20g
Protein			1g

Peppermint Candy Tarts

PREP TIME: 1 HOUR 30 MINUTES (READY IN 1 HOUR 30 MINUTES)
SERVINGS: 32 TARTS

TART SHELLS

- 1/2 cup granulated sugar
- 1/2 cup butter or margarine, softened
- 1/2 teaspoon peppermint extract
- 1 egg
- 1 1/2 cups all-purpose flour
- 1/4 teaspoon baking soda
- 1/4 teaspoon salt

FILLING AND GARNISH

- 2 cups powdered sugar
- 3 tablespoons butter or margarine, softened
- 2 or 3 drops red food color
- 2 to 3 tablespoons milk
- 1/2 cup crushed hard peppermint candies (about 18 candies)

1) Heat oven to 350°F. Grease bottoms only of 32 mini muffin cups with shortening or nonstick cooking spray. In large bowl, beat granulated sugar and 1/2 cup butter with electric mixer on medium speed until fluffy. Beat in peppermint extract and egg until blended. On low speed, beat in flour, baking soda and salt.

2) Shape dough into 1 1/2-inch balls. Press each ball in bottom and up side of muffin cup.

3) Bake 9 to 12 minutes until set and edges are light golden brown. Cool 1 minute; remove from muffin cups to cooling racks. Cool completely, about 15 minutes.

4) In small bowl, beat filling ingredients except crushed candies with electric mixture on medium speed until smooth and creamy. Stir in 1/4 cup of the candies. Spoon or pipe 1 rounded measuring teaspoon filling into center of each tart shell. Sprinkle with remaining crushed candies.

HIGH ALTITUDE (3500-6500 FT.): No change.

Nutrition Information Per Serving:		
Calories: 130	From Fat:	40
Total Fat		4g
Saturated Fat		2.5g
Trans Fat		0g
Cholesterol		15mg
Sodium		60mg
Total Carbohydrate		21g
Dietary Fiber		0g
Sugars		16g
Protein		0g

Tiramisu Ice Cream Squares

PREP TIME: 30 MINUTES (READY IN 5 HOURS 30 MINUTES)
SERVINGS: 18

- 1 quart (4 cups) coffee ice cream
- 22 creme-filled chocolate sandwich cookies, crushed (2 cups)
- 1/4 cup butter, melted
- 1 quart (4 cups) cherry ice cream
- 1 container (8 oz) mascarpone cheese
- 1/4 cup light rum or 1 teaspoon rum extract
- 2 cups frozen whipped topping, thawed

1) Place coffee ice cream in refrigerator for 15 to 20 minutes to soften slightly. In ungreased 13x9-inch pan, place cookie crumbs and butter. With fork, stir to mix and press evenly in bottom of pan.

2) Remove coffee ice cream from container into large bowl and stir with wooden spoon until softened. Spoon and carefully spread over cookie crumbs in pan. Freeze until firm, about 1 hour.

3) Place cherry ice cream in refrigerator for 15 to 20 minutes to soften slightly. Remove ice cream from container into large bowl and stir with wooden spoon until softened. Spoon and spread over coffee ice cream. Use back of spoon to smooth surface. Freeze until firm, about 1 hour.

4) In medium bowl, beat mascarpone cheese with electric mixer on medium speed 1 to 2 minutes or until light and fluffy. Beat in rum on low speed until well blended. With rubber spatula, fold in whipped topping. Spread evenly over ice cream. Cover and freeze at least 3 hours or up to 1 week.

HIGH ALTITUDE (3500-6500 FT.): No change.

Nutrition Information Per Serving:

Calories:	290	From Fat:	160
Total Fat			17g
Saturated Fat			10g
Trans Fat			1g
Cholesterol			40mg
Sodium			160mg
Total Carbohydrate			29g
Dietary Fiber			1g
Sugars			18g
Protein			4g

Frozen Key Lime Torte

PREP TIME: 15 MINUTES (READY IN 4 HOURS 30 MINUTES)
SERVINGS: 10

e EASY

1 pint (2 cups) lime sherbet

1 pint (2 cups) lemon sorbet

1 pint (2 cups) vanilla frozen yogurt

1¼ cups graham cracker crumbs

2 tablespoons sugar

¼ cup butter or margarine, melted

1 tablespoon Key lime juice

¼ cup coconut, toasted

1) Place sherbet, sorbet and frozen yogurt in refrigerator to soften while preparing the crust.

2) In small bowl, mix graham cracker crumbs, sugar and butter. Press mixture in bottom of 9-inch springform pan. Freeze 15 minutes.

3) Spoon or scoop softened sherbet, sorbet and frozen yogurt into large bowl. Add lime juice; stir gently to mix. Spoon mixture over crust in pan, spreading evenly. Sprinkle with coconut; lightly press into sherbet mixture. Freeze until firm before serving, at least 4 hours.

4) To serve, let stand at room temperature for 15 minutes. Cut into wedges.

Note: To toast coconut, spread on cookie sheet; bake at 350°F 7 to 8 minutes, stirring occasionally, until light golden brown.

HIGH ALTITUDE (3500-6500 FT.): No change.

Nutrition Information Per Serving:		
Calories: 260	From Fat:	70
Total Fat		8g
Saturated Fat		4.5g
Trans Fat		0.5g
Cholesterol		15mg
Sodium		150mg
Total Carbohydrate		44g
Dietary Fiber		1g
Sugars		35g
Protein		3g

Applesauce Spice Cake

PREP TIME: 30 MINUTES (READY IN 1 HOUR 10 MINUTES)
SERVINGS: 15

CAKE

- 2¼ cups all-purpose flour
- 1½ cups granulated sugar
- 2 teaspoons ground cinnamon
- 1 teaspoon baking powder
- 1 teaspoon baking soda
- 1 teaspoon salt
- 1⅓ cups applesauce
- ⅓ cup oil
- 2 eggs
- ¾ cup chopped peeled apple (1 medium)
- ½ cup raisins, if desired

FROSTING

- ¼ cup butter (do not substitute margarine)
- 4 cups powdered sugar
- ¼ teaspoon ground cinnamon
- 1 teaspoon vanilla
- 6 to 8 tablespoons apple juice or milk

1) Heat oven to 350°F. Grease and flour 13x9-inch pan. In large bowl, mix flour, granulated sugar, 2 teaspoons cinnamon, the baking powder, baking soda and salt. Add applesauce, oil and eggs; beat on low speed of electric mixer until moistened. Beat 2 minutes on high speed. With spoon, fold in apple and raisins; pour into pan.

2) Bake 28 to 38 minutes or until toothpick inserted in center comes out clean. Cool completely, about 1 hour.

3) Heat butter in medium saucepan over medium heat until light golden brown, stirring frequently. Remove from heat; cool 2 to 3 minutes. Beat in powdered sugar, ¼ teaspoon cinnamon, the vanilla and enough apple juice for desired spreading consistency. Immediately spread over top of cooled cake. (Frosting sets up quickly.)

HIGH ALTITUDE (3500-6500 FT.):
Decrease granulated sugar in cake to 1-1/4 cups.

Nutrition Information Per Serving:

Calories:	380	From Fat:	80
Total Fat			9g
Saturated Fat			3g
Trans Fat			0g
Cholesterol			35mg
Sodium			310mg
Total Carbohydrate			73g
Dietary Fiber			1g
Sugars			56g
Protein			3g

Be sure to use butter for the frosting. Browning the butter gives the frosting a toasty flavor, and margarine does not brown like butter does.

Orange-Cranberry Pound Cake

PREP TIME: 20 MINUTES (READY IN 3 HOURS)
SERVINGS: 16 SLICES

e EASY

3/4 cup butter, softened

3/4 cup granulated sugar

3 eggs

2 tablespoons orange juice

1 teaspoon vanilla

1 1/2 cups all-purpose flour

1 teaspoon baking powder

1/4 teaspoon salt

3/4 cup sweetened dried cranberries

1 tablespoon grated orange peel

2 tablespoons coarse or granulated sugar

1) Heat oven to 350°F. Grease and flour 9x5-inch loaf pan. In large bowl, beat butter and 3/4 cup granulated sugar with electric mixer on medium speed 3 minutes until light and fluffy. Add eggs, one at a time, beating well after each addition. Add orange juice and vanilla; beat 30 seconds or until well blended.

2) Add flour, baking powder and salt; beat on low speed 30 seconds or just until blended. With spoon, fold in cranberries and orange peel. Spoon batter into pan. Sprinkle with coarse sugar.

3) Bake 50 to 55 minutes or until toothpick inserted in center comes out clean. Cool 15 minutes. Remove from pan to cooling rack. Cool completely, about 1 hour 30 minutes.

HIGH ALTITUDE (3500-6500 FT.): No change.

Nutrition Information Per Serving:

Calories: 200	From Fat: 90
Total Fat	10g
Saturated Fat	6g
Trans Fat	0.5g
Cholesterol	65mg
Sodium	140mg
Total Carbohydrate	25g
Dietary Fiber	0g
Sugars	15g
Protein	3g

Cream Cheese Jewel Tart

PREP TIME: 15 MINUTES (READY IN 2 HOURS 45 MINUTES)
SERVINGS: 8

e EASY

CRUST

1 Pillsbury® refrigerated pie crust (from 15-oz box), softened as directed on box

FILLING

1 package (8 oz) cream cheese, softened

1/3 cup sugar

1 tablespoon orange-flavored liqueur or orange juice

4 cups assorted fresh whole berries (such as small strawberries, blueberries, raspberries, and/or blackberries)

1/3 cup red currant jelly, melted

1) Heat oven to 450°F. Make pie crust as directed on box for One-Crust Baked Shell using 9-inch tart pan with removable bottom. Bake 9 to 11 minutes or until lightly browned. Cool completely, about 30 minutes.

2) In small bowl, beat cream cheese, sugar and liqueur with electric mixer on medium speed until well blended and smooth. Spread evenly in cooled baked shell.

3) Top tart with berries; brush berries with melted jelly to glaze. Refrigerate at least 2 hours before serving. Store in refrigerator.

HIGH ALTITUDE (3500-6500 FT.): No change.

Nutrition Information Per Serving:

Calories: 330	From Fat: 150
Total Fat	17g
Saturated Fat	9g
Trans Fat	0g
Cholesterol	35mg
Sodium	200mg
Total Carbohydrate	40g
Dietary Fiber	3g
Sugars	21g
Protein	3g

Cherry-Topped Brownie Dessert Squares

PREP TIME:	15 MINUTES (READY IN 3 HOURS 15 MINUTES)	
SERVINGS:	16	**e** EASY

BROWNIES

- 1 box (1 lb 2.3 oz) fudge brownie mix
- 2/3 cup oil
- 1/4 cup water
- 2 eggs

FILLING

- 2 packages (8 oz each) cream cheese, softened
- 1 container (1 lb) vanilla ready-to-spread frosting
- 1 teaspoon almond extract

TOPPING

- 1 can (21 oz) cherry pie filling, chilled

1) Heat oven to 350°F. Grease bottom only of 13x9-inch pan with shortening. In large bowl, stir brownie ingredients until well blended with spoon. Spread in pan.

2) Bake 24 to 26 minutes or until toothpick inserted 2 inches from side of pan comes out almost clean. Cool completely, about 30 minutes.

3) In large bowl, beat filling ingredients until smooth. Spread over cooled brownies. Cover; refrigerate at least 2 hours or until set.

4) To serve, spoon pie filling over top. Cut into squares.

HIGH ALTITUDE (3500-6500 FT.): Bake brownies following High Altitude directions on box for 13x9-inch pan.

Nutrition Information Per Serving:

Calories:	480	From Fat:	240
Total Fat			27g
Saturated Fat			9g
Trans Fat			2.5g
Cholesterol			60mg
Sodium			270mg
Total Carbohydrate			55g
Dietary Fiber			2g
Sugars			44g
Protein			4g

tip The brownie base of this dessert can be baked, cooled and frozen in the pan. Up to a day before serving it, fill and top the brownies as directed in the recipe. Refrigerate the dessert until serving time.

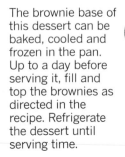

Tropical Pineapple–Cream Cheese Tart

PREP TIME: 25 MINUTES (READY IN 1 HOUR 50 MINUTES)
SERVINGS: 10

CRUST

1 Pillsbury® refrigerated pie crust (from 15-oz box), softened as directed on box

1 teaspoon sugar

FILLING

1 package (8 oz) cream cheese, softened

¼ cup sugar

1 teaspoon coconut extract

1 egg

TOPPING

1 can (20 oz) crushed pineapple in syrup, well drained, ¼ cup liquid reserved

2 teaspoons cornstarch

Nutrition Information Per Serving:

Calories:	260	From Fat:	125
Total Fat			14g
Saturated Fat			8g
Cholesterol			50mg
Sodium			160mg
Total Carbohydrate			31g
Dietary Fiber			0g
Sugars			23g
Protein			3g

1) Heat oven to 450°F. Remove pie crust from pouch; unroll crust on work surface. Sprinkle with 1 teaspoon sugar; roll in lightly with rolling pin. Press crust, sugar side up, in bottom and up side of 10- or 9-inch tart pan with removable bottom. Trim edges if necessary.

2) Bake 7 to 9 minutes or until light golden brown. Cool partially baked shell while preparing filling. Reduce oven temperature to 400°F.

3) In small bowl, beat cream cheese with electric mixer on medium speed until light and fluffy. Add ¼ cup sugar, the coconut extract and egg; beat until well blended. Pour into partially baked shell. Carefully spoon pineapple over cream cheese mixture. (Pineapple will not completely cover cream cheese.)

4) Bake at 400°F for 20 to 25 minutes or until filling is puffed around edges and set.

5) Meanwhile, in 1-quart saucepan, mix reserved ¼ cup pineapple liquid and the cornstarch until smooth. Cook over medium heat, stirring frequently, until glaze boils and thickens.

6) Spoon pineapple glaze over pineapple. Cool completely, about 1 hour, before serving. Store in refrigerator.

HIGH ALTITUDE (3500-6500 FT.): For pineapple topping, reserve 1/3 cup pineapple liquid. After adding cream cheese filling and pineapple to partially baked shell, bake at 400°F for 25 to 30 minutes.

Cinnamon Streusel Sweet Potato Pie

PREP TIME: 25 MINUTES (READY IN 3 HOURS 50 MINUTES)
SERVINGS: 8

CRUST AND FILLING

- 1 Pillsbury® refrigerated pie crust (from 15-oz box), softened as directed on box
- 1 1/2 cups mashed cooked dark orange sweet potatoes (about 1 lb uncooked)
- 1/2 cup packed brown sugar
- 2 tablespoons corn syrup
- 1 cup evaporated milk
- 3 eggs
- 1 teaspoon ground cinnamon
- 1/2 teaspoon ground nutmeg
- 1/8 teaspoon ground cloves
- 1/8 teaspoon ground ginger

STREUSEL

- 1/4 cup packed brown sugar
- 2 tablespoons all-purpose flour
- 1/4 teaspoon ground cinnamon
- 1/4 cup chopped pecans
- 1/4 cup chopped walnuts
- 2 tablespoons butter or margarine

TOPPING

- 1 cup sweetened whipped cream, if desired

1) Place cookie sheet on middle oven rack. Heat oven to 425°F. Make pie crust as directed on box for One-Crust Filled Pie using 9-inch glass pie plate.

2) Place sweet potatoes in food processor; cover and process until smooth. In large bowl, mix sweet potatoes and all remaining filling ingredients with wire whisk until smooth; pour into crust.

3) Place pie on cookie sheet in oven; bake 15 minutes. Reduce oven temperature to 350°F; bake 20 minutes longer.

4) Meanwhile, in small bowl, mix all streusel ingredients. Remove pie from oven; carefully sprinkle streusel over filling.

5) Return pie to oven; bake 10 to 15 minutes longer or until knife inserted in center comes out clean and streusel is golden brown. Cool completely, about 3 hours.

6) Serve pie with sweetened whipped cream. Store in refrigerator.

HIGH ALTITUDE (3500-6500 FT.): In Step 5, bake pie 20 to 25 minutes longer.

Nutrition Information Per Serving:

Calories:	410	From Fat:	160
Total Fat			18g
Saturated Fat			6g
Trans Fat			0g
Cholesterol			95mg
Sodium			220mg
Total Carbohydrate			54g
Dietary Fiber			3g
Sugars			30g
Protein			7g

Chocolate Chip Peanut Butter Torte

PREP TIME: 30 MINUTES (READY IN 4 HOURS 30 MINUTES)
SERVINGS: 12

1 roll (16.5 oz) Pillsbury® Create 'n Bake™ refrigerated chocolate chip cookies

1 package (8 oz) cream cheese, softened

¼ cup sugar

1 egg

1 cup miniature semisweet chocolate chips

1 cup chopped honey-roasted peanuts

1 cup butterscotch chips

¼ cup peanut butter

¼ cup chocolate-flavored syrup

1) Heat oven to 350°F. Break up cookie dough into ungreased 10- or 9-inch springform pan. Press in bottom to form crust. Bake 15 to 18 minutes or until light golden brown. Cool 10 minutes.

2) Meanwhile, in medium bowl, beat cream cheese with electric mixer on medium speed until light and fluffy. Add sugar and egg; beat until well blended. Stir in ½ cup of the chocolate chips and ½ cup of the peanuts. Pour over cooled crust; spread evenly.

3) In medium microwavable bowl, microwave butterscotch chips on High 1 minute, stirring twice, until melted and smooth. Stir in peanut butter until smooth. Drizzle over cream cheese mixture. Sprinkle with remaining chocolate chips and peanuts.

4) Bake 30 to 40 minutes longer or until edges are set but center is still slightly jiggly. Cool on cooling rack 10 minutes. Run knife around side of pan to loosen; carefully remove side of pan. Cool 1 hour. Refrigerate about 2 hours or until completely cooled.

5) To serve, cut torte into wedges. Drizzle 1 teaspoon chocolate syrup onto each dessert plate. Place wedges over syrup. Store in refrigerator.

HIGH ALTITUDE (3500-6500 FT.): No change.

Nutrition Information Per Serving:	
Calories: 540	From Fat: 280
Total Fat	31g
Saturated Fat	14g
Trans Fat	1.5g
Cholesterol	45mg
Sodium	270mg
Total Carbohydrate	56g
Dietary Fiber	2g
Sugars	42g
Protein	9g

Using miniature chocolate chips makes it easier to distribute the chips evenly, and makes the dessert easier to cut.

Caramel Apple and Pear Crisp

PREP TIME: 25 MINUTES (READY IN 1 HOUR 15 MINUTES)
SERVINGS: 8

FRUIT MIXTURE

- 2 medium apples, peeled, sliced (2½ cups)
- 2 medium pears, peeled, sliced (2½ cups)
- 2 tablespoons granulated sugar
- ¼ teaspoon ground allspice
- ⅓ cup caramel topping

TOPPING AND GARNISH

- ½ cup packed brown sugar
- ½ cup quick-cooking oats
- ½ cup chopped walnuts
- ¼ cup all-purpose flour
- ¼ cup butter or margarine
-   Whipped cream
-   Caramel topping

1) Heat oven to 375°F. Spray 8-inch square (2-quart) glass baking dish with nonstick cooking spray. In baking dish, mix apples, pears, granulated sugar and allspice. Drizzle evenly with ⅓ cup caramel topping.

2) In medium bowl, mix brown sugar, oats, walnuts and flour. With pastry blender or fork, cut in butter until mixture resembles coarse crumbs. Sprinkle evenly over fruit mixture; press lightly.

3) Bake 30 to 35 minutes or until fruit is tender and topping is crisp. Cool at least 15 minutes before serving.

4) To serve, spoon liquid from baking dish over fruit. Top with whipped cream and caramel topping. Store in refrigerator.

HIGH ALTITUDE (3500-6500 FT.): No change.

Nutrition Information Per Serving:

Calories: 370	From Fat: 110
Total Fat	13g
Saturated Fat	5g
Trans Fat	0g
Cholesterol	20mg
Sodium	180mg
Total Carbohydrate	60g
Dietary Fiber	4g
Sugars	43g
Protein	3g

Peppermint Truffle Pie

PREP TIME: 20 MINUTES (READY IN 8 HOURS 30 MINUTES)
SERVINGS: 12

e EASY

1 bag (12 oz) semisweet chocolate chips

1 cup half-and-half

¼ cup butter, cut into pieces

1½ teaspoons peppermint extract

1 Pillsbury® refrigerated pie crust (from 15-oz box), softened as directed on box

1 cup white chocolate chunks or white vanilla baking chips

1½ cups whipping cream

12 hard peppermint candies, crushed

Nutrition Information Per Serving:

Calories:	530	From Fat: 320
Total Fat		36g
Saturated Fat		21g
Trans Fat		0.5g
Cholesterol		55mg
Sodium		140mg
Total Carbohydrate		47g
Dietary Fiber		2g
Sugars		37g
Protein		4g

1) Heat oven to 450°F. In medium microwavable bowl, place chocolate chips, half and half, and butter. Microwave on High 2 minutes to 2 minutes 30 seconds or until melted, stirring once or twice. Stir in peppermint extract. Beat with electric mixer or wire whisk until well blended. Refrigerate 45 to 60 minutes or until thickened.

2) Meanwhile, make pie crust as directed on box for One-Crust Baked Shell using 9-inch glass pie plate. Bake 9 to 11 minutes or until golden brown. Cool completely, about 30 minutes.

3) In small microwavable bowl, place white chocolate chunks and whipping cream. Microwave on High 1 minute 30 seconds or until smooth, stirring once or twice. Cover and refrigerate 2 hours or until chilled.

4) Pour semisweet chocolate mixture into cooled baked shell. Reserve 3 peppermint candies. Crush remaining candies and sprinkle over top. Refrigerate 2 hours or until firm.

5) In medium bowl, beat white chocolate mixture with electric mixer on high speed until light and fluffy. Do not overbeat. Carefully spoon and spread over chocolate. Refrigerate at least 4 hours or until firm. Just before serving, garnish with peppermint candies or fresh mint. Store in refrigerator.

HIGH ALTITUDE (3500-6500 FT.): No change.

tip

This refreshing pie can be made and stored in the refrigerator up to 24 hours before you are ready to serve it. That's just one of the reasons why it makes a great addition to your holiday menus.

Peanut Butter Cups

PREP TIME: 20 MINUTES (READY IN 55 MINUTES)
SERVINGS: 24

e EASY

1¾ cups all-purpose flour

1¼ cups packed brown sugar

3 teaspoons baking powder

1 teaspoon salt

1 cup milk

⅓ cup shortening

⅓ cup peanut butter

1 teaspoon vanilla

2 eggs

24 miniature chocolate-covered peanut butter cup candies, unwrapped

Nutrition Information Per Serving:

Calories:	170	From Fat:	60
Total Fat			7g
Saturated Fat			2g
Trans Fat			0.5g
Cholesterol			20mg
Sodium			210mg
Total Carbohydrate			23g
Dietary Fiber			0g
Sugars			15g
Protein			3g

1) Heat oven to 350°F. Place paper baking cups in each of 24 regular-size muffin cups. In large bowl, beat all ingredients except peanut butter cups with electric mixer on low speed until moistened, scraping bowl occasionally. Beat on medium speed 2 minutes, scraping bowl occasionally.

2) Divide batter evenly among muffin cups, filling each ⅔ full. Press 1 peanut butter cup into batter in each cup until top edge of candy is even with batter.

3) Bake 18 to 28 minutes or until tops spring back when touched near center. Cool 5 minutes; remove from muffin cups. Serve warm or cool.

HIGH ALTITUDE (3500-6500 FT.): Decrease baking powder to 2 teaspoons. Bake 23 to 28 minutes.

Strawberry-Kiwi Tart

PREP TIME: 20 MINUTES (READY IN 1 HOUR 50 MINUTES)
SERVINGS: 8

e EASY

CRUST

1 Pillsbury® refrigerated pie crust (from 15-oz box), softened as directed on box

FILLING

1½ cups vanilla low-fat yogurt

1 container (8 oz) reduced-fat sour cream

1 box (4-serving size) vanilla instant pudding and pie filling mix

2 tablespoons orange marmalade

TOPPING

1 cup halved fresh strawberries

2 kiwifruit, peeled, thinly sliced

2 tablespoons orange marmalade

1) Heat oven to 450°F. Make pie crust as directed on box for One-Crust Baked Shell using 9-inch tart pan with removable bottom or 9-inch glass pie plate. Bake 9 to 11 minutes or until light golden brown. Cool completely, about 30 minutes.

2) In medium bowl, mix all filling ingredients with wire whisk until well blended. Pour into cooled baked shell. Arrange strawberries and kiwifruit on filling.

3) In small microwavable bowl, microwave marmalade on High 5 to 10 seconds or until melted. Brush over fruit. Refrigerate 1 hour or until set before serving. Store in refrigerator.

HIGH ALTITUDE (3500-6500 FT.): No change.

Nutrition Information Per Serving:

Calories:	300	From Fat:	190
Total Fat			10g
Saturated Fat			4g
Cholesterol			15mg
Sodium			340mg
Total Carbohydrate			48g
Dietary Fiber			1g
Sugars			29g
Protein			5g

Chocolate Cranberry Bread Pudding

PREP TIME: 30 MINUTES (READY IN 1 HOUR 30 MINUTES)
SERVINGS: 12

BREAD PUDDING

- 8 oz day-old French bread, cut into ½-inch cubes (5 to 6 cups)
- 1 cup sweetened dried cranberries
- 4 eggs
- 1¼ cups packed brown sugar
- ½ cup unsweetened baking cocoa
- 3 cups half-and-half

SAUCE

- ½ cup granulated sugar
- 2 tablespoons butter
- 1 cup white vanilla baking chips
- 1 cup whipping cream
- 2 tablespoons bourbon or 1 teaspoon vanilla extract

1) Heat oven to 350°F. Spray 12x8-inch (2-quart) glass baking dish with nonstick cooking spray. Place bread and cranberries in baking dish; toss to mix.

2) In large bowl, with wire whisk, beat eggs, brown sugar, cocoa and half-and-half until well blended. Pour over bread mixture. Stir mixture gently with large spoon to coat bread with liquid. Let stand 10 minutes. Stir mixture.

3) Bake uncovered 45 to 50 minutes or until knife inserted in center comes out clean.

4) In 1-quart saucepan, mix granulated sugar, butter, baking chips and whipping cream. Cook over medium heat 3 to 4 minutes, stirring frequently, until slightly thickened and smooth. Remove from heat; stir in bourbon (sauce will be thin). Serve sauce over warm bread pudding.

HIGH ALTITUDE (3500-6500 FT.): No change.

Nutrition Information Per Serving:	
Calories: 510	From Fat: 210
Total Fat	23g
Saturated Fat	14g
Trans Fat	0.5g
Cholesterol	120mg
Sodium	230mg
Total Carbohydrate	66g
Dietary Fiber	2g
Sugars	53g
Protein	8g

Chocolate Candy Cupcakes

PREP TIME: 25 MINUTES (READY IN 1 HOUR 40 MINUTES)
SERVINGS: 18

CUPCAKES

- 2 packages (3 oz each) cream cheese, softened
- 2 tablespoons powdered sugar
- 1 egg
- 2 chocolate-covered nougat, caramel and peanut candy bars (2.07 oz each), unwrapped, finely chopped
- 1½ cups all-purpose flour
- 1 cup granulated sugar
- ⅓ cup unsweetened baking cocoa
- 1 teaspoon baking soda
- ½ teaspoon salt
- 1 cup buttermilk
- ⅓ cup vegetable oil
- 1 teaspoon vanilla

FROSTING

- ⅓ cup packed brown sugar
- ⅓ cup butter or margarine
- 3 tablespoons milk
- 1½ cups powdered sugar
- 1 chocolate-covered nougat, caramel and peanut candy bar (2.07 oz), unwrapped, finely chopped, if desired

Nutrition Information Per Serving:

Calories:	290	From Fat:	120
Total Fat			13g
Saturated Fat			6g
Trans Fat			0g
Cholesterol			35mg
Sodium			220mg
Total Carbohydrate			40g
Dietary Fiber			1g
Sugars			30g
Protein			4g

1) Heat oven to 350°F. Place paper baking cups in each of 18 regular-size muffin cups. In small bowl, beat cream cheese, 2 tablespoons powdered sugar and the egg with electric mixer on medium speed until smooth. With spoon, stir in 2 chopped candy bars; set aside.

2) In large bowl, mix flour, granulated sugar, cocoa, baking soda and salt. Add buttermilk, oil and vanilla; beat 2 minutes with mixer on medium speed. Divide batter evenly among muffin cups, filling each half full. Spoon 1 tablespoon cream cheese mixture in center of batter in each cup.

3) Bake 23 to 30 minutes or until cream cheese mixture is light golden brown. Cool in pans 15 minutes. (Cupcakes will sink slightly in center.) Remove cupcakes from muffin cups. Cool completely, about 30 minutes.

4) Meanwhile, in 1½-quart saucepan, cook brown sugar and butter over medium heat just until mixture boils, stirring frequently. Remove from heat. Stir in milk. Cool 30 minutes. With spoon, beat 1½ cups powdered sugar into brown sugar mixture until spreading consistency, adding 1 tablespoon additional powdered sugar at a time if necessary.

5) Frost cooled cupcakes. Sprinkle with chopped candy bar.

HIGH ALTITUDE (3500-6500 FT.): Heat oven to 375°F. Bake 16 to 23 minutes.

Noel Napoleons

PREP TIME: 20 MINUTES (READY IN 1 HOUR)
SERVINGS: 12

e EASY

1 sheet frozen puff pastry (from 17$\frac{1}{4}$-oz package)

1 box (4-serving size) cheesecake instant pudding and pie filling mix

1$\frac{1}{2}$ cups milk

2 tablespoons almond-flavored liqueur or 1 teaspoon almond extract

1 can (21 oz) raspberry pie filling

1$\frac{1}{2}$ cups frozen cranberry raspberry juice concentrate, thawed

1 tablespoon powdered sugar

$\frac{1}{4}$ cup toasted sliced almonds

1) Heat oven to 400°F. Let puff pastry stand at room temperature 20 minutes to thaw.

2) Unfold pastry; cut into 3 strips along fold lines. Cut each strip crosswise into 4 equal pieces; place on ungreased cookie sheet. Bake 12 to 15 minutes or until golden brown. Remove from cookie sheet to cooling racks.

3) In medium bowl, with wire whisk, beat pudding mix and milk 2 minutes. Stir in liqueur. Cover and refrigerate.

4) In medium bowl, mix raspberry pie filling and juice concentrate until well blended. Cover and refrigerate.

5) Just before serving, cut each pastry horizontally in half to make 2 layers. Place bottom half of each pastry on dessert plate. Spoon 2 tablespoons pudding evenly over pastry; cover with top half of pastry. Sprinkle each with powdered sugar and 1 teaspoon toasted almonds. Spoon 3 tablespoons raspberry sauce onto plate around each pastry.

HIGH ALTITUDE (3500-6500 FT.): No change.

Nutrition Information Per Serving:		
Calories: 290	From Fat:	70
Total Fat		8g
Saturated Fat		3g
Trans Fat		0.5g
Cholesterol		25mg
Sodium		180mg
Total Carbohydrate		49g
Dietary Fiber		1g
Sugars		36g
Protein		3g

tip

The pastries, filling and sauce can be made a day ahead of time and then simply assembled in minutes just before serving.

Café Latte Crème Brûlée

PREP TIME: 30 MINUTES (READY IN 4 HOURS 35 MINUTES)
SERVINGS: 6

3 cups whipping cream

2 teaspoons instant coffee granules or crystals

5 egg yolks

2 whole eggs

½ cup granulated sugar

1 teaspoon vanilla

6 tablespoons packed brown sugar

Nutrition Information Per Serving:	
Calories: 530	From Fat: 370
Total Fat	41g
Saturated Fat	24g
Trans Fat	1g
Cholesterol	305mg
Sodium	70mg
Total Carbohydrate	34g
Dietary Fiber	0g
Sugars	33g
Protein	6g

1) Heat oven to 325°F. In 15x10x1-inch pan, place 6 (6-oz) round or oval ceramic ramekins. In 2-quart saucepan, mix whipping cream and coffee granules. Heat just to a simmer, stirring occasionally. Remove from heat.

2) In medium bowl, beat egg yolks and whole eggs with wire whisk until well blended. Stir in granulated sugar until combined. With wire whisk, gradually stir hot cream mixture into egg mixture until well blended. Stir in vanilla. Pour mixture evenly into ramekins.

3) Place pan with ramekins in oven. Carefully pour hot water into pan until ½ to ¾ inch up sides of ramekins. Bake 30 to 35 minutes or until centers of custards are soft set.

4) Carefully remove pan from oven. Remove ramekins from water bath and place on cooling rack. Pour water from pan. Cool custards 30 minutes.

5) Transfer ramekins to same pan. Refrigerate at least 3 hours or overnight.

6) Before serving, set oven control to broil. Top each custard with 1 tablespoon brown sugar. Watching carefully, broil with tops 4 to 6 inches from heat 1 to 2 minutes or until sugar is melted. Or melt brown sugar with kitchen torch. Garnish with fresh cranberries and mint leaves, if desired. Store in refrigerator.

HIGH ALTITUDE (3500-6500 FT.): Bake 45 to 50 minutes.

Alphabetical Index

General Recipe Index

This handy index lists every recipe by food category, major ingredient and/or cooking method, so you can easily locate recipes to suit your needs.

GENERAL RECIPE INDEX **351**